A CENTURY
OF
INNOVATION

LESLEY UNIVERSITY

CYNTHIA FARR BROWN AND
MICHELE FORINASH, EDITORS

PublishAmerica
Baltimore

First printing

PublishAmerica has allowed this work to remain exactly as the author intended, verbatim, without editorial input.

Hardcover 978-1-4626-2323-5
Softcover 978-1-4626-2324-2
PUBLISHED BY PUBLISHAMERICA, LLLP
www.publishamerica.com
Baltimore

Printed in the United States of America

TABLE OF CONTENTS

EDITOR'S NOTE

The Centennial: 1909 2009

MICHELE FORINASH, DA, MT-BC, LMHC

In the spring of 2008, Cynthia Farr Brown suggested the creation of a centennial publication to celebrate the founding of the Lesley School, where 12 kindergarten students enrolled in the fall of 1909, and its growth into a university with an attendance of 6,000 in 2009. I agreed with enthusiasm to sign on as primary editor, and we submitted a call for papers. We are very grateful to the educators, authors, artists, arts therapists, and administrators in the greater Lesley community whose essays form this collection, and whose gifts and experience have sustained and evolved Lesley's mission and programs. Our conversations with them, and our exchanges via e-mail and post, were more than informative; they inspired and taught us. In their generosity, our contributors have illuminated what President Joseph Moore calls "our most precious inheritance": "Edith Lesley's purposeful integration of theory and practice, her intentional connection between the academy and the community, and her relentless focus on each student's imagination and capacity for action."

Page four of the 1928 Lesleyan Yearbook, featuring a portrait of founder Edith Lesley Wolfard wearing a white fox stole with her signature below the photograph. Donated by Dorene Lengyel from her mother Irene Johnson, class of 1929. 1928. Photograph courtesy of The Lesley University Archives.

Photograph of female Lesley College graduate student teaching elementary school; featuring several students with yearbook annotations attached to the front and copyright holder's information on the back. 1984. Photograph courtesy of The Lesley University Archives.

Sixteen students working on art projects. 1958. Photograph courtesy of The Lesley University Archives.

PROLOGUE

Lesley University

Joseph B. Moore

This collection of essays by Lesley University faculty in recognition of Lesley's centennial offers a historic perspective, not just about Lesley but about American higher education over these past 100 years. When Edith Lesley began to train kindergarten teachers, she could not have envisioned the growth of her school from the initial 12 students in the fall of 1909 to the 6,000 enrolled in the fall of 2009. She also could not have predicted the various influences that would change American higher education—and Lesley—over the 20th century.

In reading these essays you will recognize some of the major changes in American education over these 100 years: the growing influence of the state and federal government in funding and regulating K-12 education and higher education; the expanding role of women in education; the efforts to make education more inclusive through the expansion of compulsory attendance policies; the influence of the Civil Rights Movement; the passage of state and national special education legislation; and the growth in the number of adult learners. You will also see how various historical events and eras, from World War II to Sputnik, the Vietnam War, and the conservatism of the Reagan years, influenced education programs and institutions.

These essays, however, are more than historical reflections. Higher education is highly regarded and often criticized for its preoccupation with language, verbal and written. From admissions materials to course readings, from course syllabi to degree requirements, from faculty scholarship to student publications, from institutional policies to accreditation reports, and from lectures to commencement speakers, higher education is an enterprise driven by words. But these essays are different from standard higher education documentation.

They are different because the authors had an unusual freedom to describe how programs at Lesley were developed, drawing on the historical context, but also identifying and describing the real people who inhabited, influenced, and made history. In these essays we read about those faculty, administrators, and students who acted to create something new, to connect the institutional mission with a social trend or challenge. Some might call it an entrepreneurial spirit, but it's more than that at Lesley. Today we call it "making a difference"— coordinating the academic resources of a private institution to yield a public benefit.

In addition to capturing some of the history of American higher education and the development of Lesley University, the authors describe key themes and tensions that some might think are new issues. Most are not. In these essays we witness the tension between a method that teaches the "whole student" and a pedagogy that focuses on the transmission of skills and facts, whether the recipient is a kindergarten student or a graduate student. We read Edith Lesley's own words reflecting her concerns about the bureaucratization of Lesley when it officially became a college, introducing anxiety about institutional size and personal relationships. We read in numerous essays about the positive and negative influence of state and federal policies on teaching and learning, from the federal funding that followed Sputnik to the Massachusetts Education Reform Act of 1993 to No Child Left Behind.

We also witness through these program descriptions vivid accounts about the importance of the imagination, student-centered learning, the arts and creativity, and free play. This particular influence, beginning with Edith Lesley and Friedrich Froebel, remains a driving and unifying force at Lesley. The notion of student engagement, of a pedagogy that places each student at the center of the learning experience, is a challenge addressed in each of these essays, whether it is about the liberal arts at Lesley College, the curriculum at the Art Institute of Boston, or the goals of the Threshold Program. It is clear that the faculty not only talk about student engagement, but that they plan it, expect it, and stimulate it. It is our legacy.

You will also find in these essays many references to the implicit and explicit goals of higher education. You will learn about faculty scholarship and about contributions of faculty members to their particular academic fields; public service initiatives and events that extend Lesley's reach into various parts of local, regional, national, and international communities; and the history of Lesley as a sequence of new program developments.

All of these activities serve our primary mission: the engagement of our students and the success of Lesley graduates. In the current preoccupation with a perverse form of accountability that reduces educational impact to standardized test scores, we can easily forget the more complex, comprehensive, and humane aspirations that drew most of us into education. It is these aspirations that are captured in the following essays by the frequent use of the word "holistic," and by descriptions of thoughtful student-centered program designs, the development of meaningful "field placements," and continuing reflection about the most appropriate teacher-student relationship. The Lesley student remains at the center of any discussion about program planning, resource allocation, or facility improvements.

This focus on student learning began with Edith Lesley's concern about a five-year-old using her imagination, playing, pretending, making art, hearing and telling stories, and learning to interact with other five-year-olds. These children needed teachers who could put the young child at the center of the teacher's thoughts, plans, and energies. In these faculty essays, that same focus on the learner is revealed time and time again. Our primary commitment is always to the student. It is a legacy that we will sustain, especially when particular political trends and administrations frown upon it.

There is one final principle that these essays record: generosity. The authors identify faculty and administrators, and occasionally students and people beyond Lesley, who were instrumental in developing a program. In almost every case there are leaders, but one of the attributes of Lesley is a belief in the creativity of the collective, and these essays reflect that. An effective education in general, and at Lesley in particular, is always a cooperative venture.

PART I: 1909–1960

Introduction

JOSEPH B. MOORE

Going to college was unusual in the early 1900s. American higher education at the turn of the 20th century comprised 500 or so institutions enrolling about 240,000 students. Less than 5% of the population between the ages of 18 and 22 was enrolled in college (Cole, 2009).

However, conditions were being set for significant growth in the number of institutions and students in the next few decades. Industrial expansion was generating new wealth and ushering in a new era and scale of philanthropy, and higher education institutions were among its primary beneficiaries. States were enacting more regulations requiring school attendance, and employment was less tied to the agricultural calendar. Various technologies were leading industrial growth, from manufacturing to transportation to utilities. Rural school districts were consolidating, and urban districts were engaged in efforts to systematize schooling based on the factory efficiency model of mass production.

As more immigrants arrived, local schools were increasingly viewed as the logical locations for teaching democratic values. Religion and religious leaders as a dominant force on social norms were being usurped by business and industry leaders and, in some regions, by high-profile university presidents. While this secular leadership was associated with rational thought—as opposed to spiritual thought— many of these secular leaders retained a religious perspective. Their language was less overtly spiritual, but not their perspective.

The three essays in this section provide context for the life and work of Edith Lesley; document the development of early childhood programs from the founding of Lesley University to the present day; and trace the role of faculty and their teaching from those early days. The connections are revealing.

As Cynthia Brown notes, Edith Lesley was able to start a school to train kindergarten teachers because the market was changing. Local school boards were voting to install kindergartens in their districts, and there were few programs to train kindergarten teachers. Miss Lesley knew that there was about to be a significant demand and that there was little supply.

Edith Lesley also personified many of the themes that continue to influence Lesley University today:

- *Theory.* She was familiar with the work of Friedrich Froebel, including the concept of gifts ("play items") and occupations ("domestically oriented activities such as sewing...").
- *Experience.* She had studied independently, with others, and during her travels to Germany. But her major experience was actually teaching kindergarten. She understood both the setting and the context for which she was preparing future kindergarten teachers.
- *Community.* Miss Lesley visited her kindergarten students' homes to meet their parents; visited the settlement houses that served new immigrants in Cambridge; and developed a rich network of academics and nonacademics to support the initiation and continuation of her school.

Early childhood education has been the touchstone of the Lesley University curriculum for 100 years. In this publication, Lawton, Mindess, Fiore, Mardell, and Szamreta describe the history of early childhood education at Lesley, and highlight external events that have influenced the school's academic programs. Whether it was World War II, Sputnik, the Civil Rights Movement, the Women's Movement, special education, new fears about immigration, or mandated

standardized testing, each influence can be identified through curriculum changes, state regulations, and even programmatic outcomes and student internships. There are now other programs at Lesley with larger enrollments and their own histories, but it seems fair to say that all Lesley programs emanate from that original student focus to engage and train kindergarten teachers in the early decades of the past century.

This focus on student engagement requires a talented faculty. If we aspire to maintain our commitment to the centrality of the student learning experience, we must engage in critical dialogue about effective pedagogy. Powerful alumni narratives include vivid descriptions of effective faculty, but also make specific references to what the students needed to do, to write, and to experience. Byers, Hirshberg, and Sanville describe the respect felt by students for faculty who involved them as fellow learners, as people who could improve the condition of the world not just through righteousness, but also through study, experience, collaboration, and commitment.

For just over 100 years Lesley University has added new programs and schools, served more students, and delivered programs in new locations, many of them well beyond Cambridge. There is ample evidence in these essays and in the work of our faculty that Edith Lesley's purposeful integration of theory and practice, her intentional connection between the academy and the community, and her relentless focus on each student's imagination and capacity for action remain our most precious inheritance.

REFERENCE

Cole, J. (2009). *The great American university: Its rise to preeminence, its indispensable national role, and why it must be protected.* New York, NY: PublicAffairs.

CHAPTER ONE

Edith Lesley Wolfard: Founder of Lesley University

Cynthia Farr Brown, PhD

Edith Lesley Wolfard founded the Lesley School, now Lesley University, in 1909. She has never been the subject of a stand-alone biography, nor included in standard biographical references. On the face of it, other than the founding of Lesley, her contributions to American education, thought, and leadership do not appear significant. Attention to her life story and to the parallel early history of the Lesley School, however, reveals a woman entrepreneur, activist, and educator whose life is emblematic of the experience of a number of women and men of her era. Her story suggests how new vocations and gateway educational institutions created economic and social opportunities for hundreds of thousands of women and men in the 20th century. Understanding these opportunities is critical to understanding how and why American society evolved in this period as it did.

Consider Edith Lesley's statement on the "purpose of the school" in the original Lesley Normal School circular:

> The Normal Course for Kindergartners, herewith announced, aims to give to young women a thorough preparation for kindergarten work, together with certain opportunities for general culture, and for the attainment of a clear view of the larger issues of education.

23

By linking the experiences and public activities of Edith Lesley, until the time when she began her school, to the three broad purposes she articulated in this initial announcement, we can begin to assess the significance of Edith Lesley Wolfard.

FAMILIES

Of her origins Edith Lesley Wolfard later said that her parents' families represented "two phases of Maine life of the period the rugged and thrifty farm life, and life on the sea" (Buxton, 1938). While there was some truth to this representation, the facts of her parents' lives create a more complex portrait.

"I had perished had I not persisted" was the family motto of the Leslies, minor Scottish nobility. For a time it was also the motto of the Lesley School. Whether or not the Lesleys descended from Scottish nobility, as she apparently believed, Edith Lesley was right to cite the idea of persistence as a core value in her family story and in the story of her school.

Alonzo Lesley was born in about 1823 in Sidney, Maine.[1] The Lesley family ended up in Carmel, Maine, where they struggled financially; family land was sold at auction to satisfy debts in 1841 (*Bangor Whig and Courier*, 1841). Alonzo moved to Bangor, 16 miles east of Carmel, in the mid-1840s. He probably trained there as a shoemaker. By 1849 he was a partner in Crowell & Leslie, makers of boots and shoes. His sister Amanda married Charles Hayward, who would build a substantial grocer's business and serve a term as mayor of Bangor. The business, political, and social connections Charles and Amanda Hayward could provide probably served the Lesleys well.[2]

---

1 U.S. Census records: 1820, 1830, 1840, 1850. The spelling of the family name in most early records is "Leslie." The consistent spelling of "Lesley" appears only in Cambridge and Lesley school records, but it is adopted here for earlier generations of the family because it is the spelling Edith Lesley used. While no vital record has been located that definitively names Alonzo as a son of Amasa, deed activity and the execution of a power of attorney in 1850 clearly link the two. Also, Joseph Leslie, certainly a son of Amasa, named one of his own sons Alonzo.

2 Quotations without attribution are from the *Bangor Daily News* or its successor, the *Bangor Daily Whig and Courier*, or both.

Alonzo Lesley joined the California gold rush in 1850, apparently staying there for more than a decade. By 1864 he was living in Panama, then called New Grenada, where he worked for the Panama Railroad. In the summer of 1866 the company sent him back to Bangor to recruit employees.

It was probably on this trip that Alonzo proposed marriage to Rebecca Cousens; whether they were already acquainted is not known. They married on Feb. 20, 1867, at Christ Church in Aspinwall, New Grenada (now Colon, Panama).

Rebecca Wilson Cousens was born in 1832, probably in Trenton, on the Maine coast. Her father was a mariner who worked his way up to ship's captain. In about 1851 the family relocated to Belfast. It is likely the family enjoyed some material advantages. Rebecca probably attended school for more than the usual five or six years. Possibly she received private tutoring or even attended a private school. Rebecca Lesley would write the "Lesley Hymn" for her daughter's school, indicating artistic interests and possibly formal arts instruction. These interests would be echoed in Edith Lesley's concerns with culture and cultivation in her life and that of her school. The Cousens family were also ardent Unitarians, and Edith Lesley embraced both the Unitarian faith and concomitant liberal social causes throughout her adult life.

Following the deaths of her parents, by the late 1850s Rebecca Cousens was the head of the family, taking care of her younger siblings. In 1860 they were living in a Belfast widow's household, and Rebecca listed her occupation as "domestic," indicating the family's economic straits. By 1866, with her sisters settled and her brother home from the Civil War, she may have felt free to strike out on her own.

Alonzo and Rebecca Lesley had been married almost five years when their first child, Edith Leah, was born on Jan. 27, 1872, probably in the village of San Pablo, a station along the Panama Railroad. Rebecca Lesley was 39; Alonzo was about 48. New Grenada was largely the creation of the Panama Railroad, which existed primarily to take erstwhile Californian gold miners from the eastern port to the western port of the isthmus (McCullough, 1977). Alonzo's work for the Panama Railroad may have been as an engineer or surveying for the line. The family probably lived in railroad-constructed housing, with supplies coming from Aspinwall. Doctors had not unlocked the secrets of illnesses such as yellow fever, typhoid, and malaria, while the tropical environment wreaked havoc with European and American technology, clothing, and food. An American family would have found it difficult to maintain a familiar style of living (McCullough, 1977).

Years later Edith Lesley Wolfard said of this period,

> During the time my father was in Panama he had many interesting experiences. Among them was a visit from Louis Agassiz, the great naturalist and some of his associates. My father collected many specimens for him, and this collection is now in the Agassiz Museum at [Harvard University,] Cambridge. (Buxton, 1938)

This story refers to the so-called Hassler Expedition that Professor Agassiz made in 1872. This is the first known connection of the Lesleys to Harvard, with which both Edith Lesley and the Lesley School later had important associations.

The family emigrated to Bangor in 1874 or 1875, consistent with the startup of Alonzo Lesley's shoe and boot business in Bangor in September 1875. Edith Lesley later reported that her parents were advised to relocate because of the dangers of bringing up a child in the tropics.

The Lesleys' second child, Olive, was born in December 1875. The family moved to 7 Adams St., and by 1880 Rebecca Lesley was operating that residence as a boardinghouse. Evidence suggests she operated boardinghouses more or less continuously for at least the next 20 years.

It is fair to inquire whether Edith or Olive Lesley attended kindergarten, or whether Rebecca Lesley was affected by kindergarten ideas. The kindergarten as named and invented by Friedrich Froebel was transplanted to the United States beginning in the 1860s. Froebel believed kindergarten complemented the care given by mothers through structured nurture offered by trained teachers. He created "a new culture of child nurture and education in which older child-rearing methods were renovated and put to modern uses" (Allen, 1988 p. 25; Beatty, 1995; Shapiro, 1983). Froebel believed that man is the physical embodiment of God's reason. The material world is only an expression of inner divinity. The evolution of natural forms corresponds to the stages of child growth, and the best education leads the child to the consciousness of unity and how to reach it.

At the core of the Froebelian kindergarten were the "gifts and occupations." Gifts were 20 play items, and with them teachers and children were to perform activities meant to develop innate understandings and knowledge of the forms and actions they embodied. The occupations included domestically oriented activities such as sewing, drawing, weaving, clay modeling, and paperwork. Songs and games gave an avenue for self-expression and taught the individual that she contributed to the whole (Ross, 1909).

Froebel believed all women possessed a maternal nature, and called upon those who were also sensible, intellectually active, and single to apply their maternalism in working in kindergartens. Indeed, his system called for regular home visits by kindergartners to demonstrate these methods to mothers. Froebel's spiritual beliefs were grounded in a generalized conception of unity. Liberal Protestants and others could embrace the kindergarten movement and could use the democratic, cooperative spirit of the kindergarten as a model of tolerance regarding cultural, religious, and ethnic differences (Allen, 1988).

At the time of his death in 1852, Froebel had wanted to transplant his ideas to America. Elizabeth Peabody, American teacher and woman of letters, was inspired by reading about his methods and opened Boston's first kindergarten the nation's second in 1860. In 1867 she went to Germany and met several prominent Froebelian educators, and realized she knew relatively little about Froebel's actual system. Miss Peabody returned to Boston, renounced her former practice, and resolved to educate the lay public about the true kindergarten.

During the 1870s the opening of kindergartens, and general interest in the movement, began to accelerate (Baylor, 1965). Boston was the site of key events and institutions during kindergarten's early days. In 1874, for example, Elizabeth Peabody founded *The Kindergarten Messenger*. She used this publication not only to spread the word about kindergartening, but also to endorse legitimate Froebel training classes and their graduates (Harvey, 1928).

Among Miss Peabody's receptive listeners was philanthropist Pauline Agassiz Shaw. The public kindergarten that Elizabeth Peabody had opened in Boston in 1870 had closed when appropriations were not sufficient. Mrs. Shaw reopened the closed school and gradually underwrote an extensive network of kindergartens, eventually supporting 31 of them in Boston, Cambridge, and other nearby towns (Baylor, 1965).

One of the movement's most important training sites, the Garland Training School, was also located in Boston. Its graduates included Caroline Aborn and Lailah Pingree, who would both become kindergarten supervisors in the Boston schools, and Anne L. Page, who would train the Lesley sisters as kindergartners.

The permanent establishment of the kindergarten idea in Bangor dates from 1875, just as the Lesley family would have arrived back from Panama. In July of that year the local paper reported interest by "prominent Bangor ladies" in the system and *The Kindergarten Messenger*. In that same fall Annie Arnold opened a kindergarten in the city. In 1877 an advertisement in the local newspaper announced the opening of another kindergarten by "the Misses EP and AF Hammatt," who were trained in Boston and Philadelphia. By 1879 three more private kindergartens were operating in Bangor, all run by women entrepreneurs.

Thus in answer to the question, could the Lesley sisters have attended kindergarten? it is clear that they could have, and that Rebecca Lesley could have been one of the "ladies of Bangor" who interested themselves in kindergartens, mothers' classes, and the like. Whether further research will settle this point remains to be seen.

The Lesley home in Bangor served as a center of young women's comings and goings, beginning with family members and encircling others over time. Rebecca Lesley was also involved in the lives of her nieces Emily and Maud Alden and nephew Carlos Alden, the children of her sister Adelaide, who had died in 1875. It appears their widowed father shared their care with his sister-in-law. Emily in particular appears to have lived more or less full-time with the Lesleys until her marriage in 1890. Thus Rebecca Lesley reprised her role as caretaker for younger family members, this time with the children of her deceased sister.

In about 1883 the Lesleys moved to No. 1 Broadway, a gracious brick home at the foot of a wide avenue. Built by lumber merchant Samuel Veazie, this imposing structure became the family's next boardinghouse venture. By chance or by design, it also became a nexus of female educators whose ideas and characters must have influenced Edith Lesley.

The previous tenant of No. 1 Broadway, Mrs. Eben Blunt, had let rooms to Anna M. Warner, a graduate of the Garland Training School, to open a kindergarten in 1882. In 1884 Anna Warner moved her successful enterprise into a new facility, at 35 Columbia St. A private elementary school was also opened there by Bertha M. Howe, a graduate of the Framingham, MA, state normal school. A newspaper story explained how the success of the kindergarten led to the establishment of the school, and that Miss Howe was assisted by "Miss Emily Alden, of this city." Anna Warner and Bertha Howe boarded with the Lesleys in 1885 and 1886; Emily Alden, Edith and Olive's cousin, also lived at No. 1 Broadway. Maud Alden would go on to become a kindergarten teacher in Brooklyn, suggesting all four cousins were heavily influenced by these kindergarten enterprises and the women behind them.

Edith Lesley graduated from elementary school in June 1887. For the next two years she studied with Helen I. Newman of Bangor, who later ran a private school in Bangor for nearly 30 years. Her obituary would state:

> Scholarly in her own tastes and acquirements, exact in her knowledge in a surprising number of fields, a lover of art

> and all things beautiful, rigid in her standards as an educator, she put into the life of her school the spirit of refinement and aspiration which were native to her.

The emphasis on refinement and culture would be important to Edith Lesley in her own school design.

By the time she left Maine, Edith Lesley had spent her teenage years acquainted with and watching at work at least three women who ran their own schools; one of these schools had operated in her own family's home. Several teachers boarded with the Lesleys, including her cousin. Their planning, meetings, receiving of prospective students, and preparations would have gone on in the Lesley boardinghouse, and the adults living there would have discussed all kinds of matters related to these endeavors. It is difficult to escape the idea that these experiences influenced Edith and generated, or continued, her interest in schooling and in becoming a teacher; even led, as she expressed later, to her wanting "a school of my own."

The Lesley family's tenure at No. 1 Broadway ended with its sale to a boardinghouse operator. The Lesleys moved to 112 State St., where Rebecca Lesley's attempts to fill rented rooms produced the only advertising found in connection to her various ventures. This may indicate that the family was struggling to reestablish its business. In the spring of 1890, the Lesley family moved to Boston.

Why the family relocated is not entirely clear. Alonzo Lesley would have been familiar with Boston through his business. Boston's progressive environment featured many educational and cultural options for women, suggesting multiple paths to vocations as well as for volunteering; fewer options were available in Maine. Subsequent events suggest the primary motivation was economic: Rebecca Lesley's ability to succeed as a boardinghouse operator was probably imperative in maintaining the full family income. Boston, with its more varied clientele and its high boarding and lodging rates, may have appeared a better opportunity. Soon after their move, however, the family abandoned this enterprise:

Mr. Alonzo Leslie, who went from this city to Boston a short time ago with the intention of conducting a boarding house in that city, has found the outlook not as he expected, and has given up the place which he had decided upon.

The family remained in Boston until the following year, while Alonzo plied his shoemaking trade. The most arresting fact that has emerged from this period is in the form of a brief newspaper story from early December 1891:

The announcement of the engagement of Mr. Owen G. Davis of Middlesborough, Ky., and Miss Edith Lesley, of Boston, has just been made. Both formerly resided in this city and they will receive the congratulations of many friends here and elsewhere.

Owen G. Davis was the son of Owen Warren Davis, who owned the Katahdin Charcoal Iron Company and later founded a railroad. In about 1888 the family moved to Kentucky, where Owen W. pursued coal mining and coke making. Though we know that the younger Owen both wrote and performed in Bangor's amateur theatricals, it is not clear where or how his early schooling took place. He entered Harvard College in 1890, attended for two years, then studied geology at the Lawrence Scientific School for a year. He did not finish a degree, and by the summer of 1893 he was working as a mining engineer in Kentucky. How long Edith and Owen were acquainted before Owen proposed is not known.

The family's Boston interlude, including Edith Lesley's engagement, is nowhere referenced by Edith, though she remained closely connected to Boston affairs for the rest of her life. Sometime during 1891, the family relocated to the Agassiz neighborhood of Cambridge, and Alonzo Lesley again set up a shoemaking business. It can be assumed, however, that the family was once again looking for a boardinghouse opportunity.

The neighborhood north of Harvard Yard, east of Massachusetts

Avenue (then called North Avenue) and west of Harvard's Agassiz Museum and Divinity Hall grounds was largely residential. To the south, Harvard had acquired the majority of the so-called Jarvis estate, and for many years the college's main athletic fields, Jarvis and Holmes, occupied much of the area. In 1890 the college moved its team play to Soldier's Field, presaging new building in the area. Industries in East Cambridge and along the river attracted workers, and residential housing sprang up in the surrounding neighborhoods (Emmet, 1978). Whereas once the smaller villages of Cambridge were separated and surrounded by open fields, orchards and woods, rapid building characterized the city at the turn of the 20th century.

Reconstructing Edith Lesley's life until 1897, when she began to work as a kindergartner in the public schools, requires extensive interpretation of limited sources. We know that she never completed high school. Whether Rebecca Lesley ran a boardinghouse at 11 Everett St., where the family resided from 1892 until 1898, is not known, but the evidence points that way. In October 1896, Alonzo Lesley was hit by a drover's team while he was crossing a street in Harvard Square. A local paper reported, "It is thought he was seriously injured." As he died five years later after a protracted illness, including paralysis, it may be that this accident disabled him.

Edith Lesley did not marry Owen G. Davis, so sometime in this period their engagement ended. Neither mentions the other in any records that have survived. Perhaps his dropping out of Harvard in 1893 precipitated the breakup, or perhaps the broken engagement led him to drop out. Perhaps his lack of respectable vocational direction dismayed Edith, or her parents. At this point, thoughts of a life of service or the taking up of a profession may have taken center stage for her.

CHARITY AND COMMUNITY

The themes of culture and of larger views of education, two of the goals of the early Lesley School, are reflected in Edith Lesley's sustained interest in and support of the Cambridge Neighborhood House, East End Mission, and Margaret Fuller House settlements in Cambridge, as well as her involvement with Boston's Elizabeth Peabody House during the 1910s and 1920s. Her later connections may indicate volunteer work at one or more of these settlements beginning earlier. Throughout the urban United States, settlement houses were organized to promote better relationships between the classes, and to bring culture, education, and refuge to the immigrant neighborhoods of major American cities. Those founded in Cambridge were no exception.

Cambridge Neighborhood House, opened in 1879 as a day nursery and kindergarten and incorporated by Pauline Agassiz Shaw in 1910, focused on programs to benefit mothers and children. The girls' trade school that was run by the organization, with courses in dressmaking, designing and cooking, was eventually absorbed into the city's schools. The Margaret Fuller House, founded in 1902 by the YWCA, served young girls living in the heavily immigrant-settled East End of Cambridge (Woods and Kennedy, 1911).

Edith Lesley's ties to the Elizabeth Peabody House were perhaps the most important in discerning influences on her as well as the sphere of her subsequent activities, because it was founded as a kindergarten-focused settlement for Boston's immigrant-populated West End. For many years the house hosted meetings of local kindergarten groups, and for a time the alumnae association of each local kindergarten training school furnished and supported a room in the house and stocked an educational library. It is possible that Edith Lesley volunteered at the Peabody House, before or after becoming a kindergarten teacher; her connection and that of the Lesley School to its activities is documented as early as 1913.

Based on later connections and donations, we can also surmise that Edith Lesley and the rest of the family were closely tied to the First Parish Church (Unitarian) in Harvard Square. Its minister would perform her marriage, for example. She gave money to the First Parish Church and various Unitarian charitable funds all throughout the period for which there are records of her giving. Many early ceremonies of the Lesley School were held in the church itself, ranging from convocation to baccalaureate sermons. While further work may reveal more focused activity on committee service at the church, it is certainly clear that the connections between the First Parish and the Lesley School were multilayered and ongoing throughout Edith Lesley Wolfard's active tenure as head of the school.

EDUCATION AND VOCATION

Edith Lesley Wolfard self-reported studying in Freiburg, Germany, after the period of her education in Maine and before her kindergarten training, suggesting that this was the order of her educational experiences (Sargent, 1930). Probably after this trip, Edith Lesley completed her kindergarten training at the Page Kindergarten Normal School in Boston.

The Page School was operated by a distinguished local kindergartner. Anne Lemist Page was born to a wealthy Danvers family in 1828. She was able to pursue academic interests in botany and other subjects. Her education was eclectic. When the Danvers public high school opened, for example, she was 20 years old; nonetheless she enrolled in and graduated from it. After that she remodeled a barn on the family property and kept a school for young children. Anne chose to learn about the kindergarten in her late 40s, completing the Garland Training School's program in 1879. She taught kindergarten for a time in an immigrant Boston neighborhood, at the Cushman School; later she taught in Danvers. She wrote a biography of Froebel that formed a chapter of the popular book *The Kindergarten and the School* (Page, 1886). In addition to her educational activities, she helped found or fund the free kindergarten in Danvers, the Danvers Historical Society and the Danvers Women's Association, and publicly supported women's suffrage.

"Manifestly spiritual," she believed it was "her supreme duty as a religious woman to train as many children as possible, and later to train as many young women as possible, in the higher and more spiritual ideals of education." Miss Page founded her training school in 1885. Her local influence was considerable; when Wellesley College built its child study center in 1913, the funding came from one of her students, at whose request the building was named in Miss Page's honor.

Anne Page's interests would echo some major themes of Edith Lesley's life, and this path, as well as Miss Page's very public spiritualism, may have been factors in Edith Lesley's choice of the Page School. In addition to providing training, Anne Page was yet another entrepreneurial woman founding a kindergarten training school in her own name, adding to the several examples Edith Lesley had already witnessed.

The public school teaching career of Edith Lesley began in November 1897, when she was appointed assistant kindergartner at the Riverside School on Putnam Avenue in Cambridgeport, at a salary of $400 a year. In March 1899, she was promoted to head kindergartner and her sister Olive, who had also trained with Miss Page, was appointed her assistant an arrangement that continued for several years.

That the Lesley sisters embarked on teaching in urban public kindergartens is probably no surprise given their interest in addressing the needs of immigrant and poor people. Boston was at the forefront of the burgeoning municipal kindergarten movement, and due to its proximity to Boston as well as the influence of Harvard leaders, Cambridge was not far behind. Pauline Shaw underwrote three free kindergartens in Cambridge beginning in 1878. In 1888 some 1,600 citizens petitioned the Cambridge School Committee that these kindergartens should be incorporated into the public schools. The School Committee voted in 1890 to establish public kindergartens. In a few years there were eight kindergartens employing 16 teachers and serving more than 400 students (Gilman, 1896).

The growth of immigrant neighborhoods such as Cambridgeport, where the Riverside kindergarten was located, meant rapid increases in the schools' class sizes. By 1903 there were two graded classrooms there, averaging 68 students each; while the kindergarten class size is not stated, one can assume it was equally large. In the Lesleys' own neighborhood, parents petitioned the committee to put kindergarten in the Agassiz School. The committee denied this petition, based on lack of space. The success of Cambridge's public kindergartens was manifest, but the city struggled to provide enough resources for them.

The inclusion of kindergartens in public school systems was an important development. The public kindergarten movement balanced idealism about the purposes of education with assumptions about the ability of poorer and immigrant parents to assimilate themselves and their children into American society. In Massachusetts, 12 of the 20 largest cities and towns had public kindergartens by 1914, including several contiguous with or within commuting distance of Cambridge, such as Somerville, Newton, and Salem. Smaller communities such as Brookline also adopted the kindergarten in this period, which meant that opportunities for trained teachers were expanding.

Proponents of "new" or "progressive" education were influenced by many kindergarten ideas, including the child-centered approach, the significance of play, and the idea of classroom as community. John Dewey adapted the term *occupations* from Froebel to describe some of his own pedagogic activities, while G. Stanley Hall lauded Froebel's idea of racial recapitulation. The kindergartners were also embracing some of the new ideas in psychology and physiology as they impacted teaching and learning. Lucy Wheelock, for example, urged her students to update their teaching with the best of new educational techniques and theories. More kindergartners experimented with materials and free play, and even with fixed curriculum.

Edith Lesley worked the classic kindergarten split schedule: mornings in the classroom with the children and afternoons visiting homes, counseling mothers, and promulgating the latest child-raising ideas. This was one of Froebel's core ideas, and faithful followers held fast to it. Merl Ruskin Wolfard, husband of Edith Lesley Wolfard, later stated that Edith Lesley was one of these committed disciples, "and endeavored to teach through 'doing' as far as is practicable." She was what we might call today a situational educator, who thought education meant "disciplining the mind so as to be able to take in something of the total situation in which both teacher and pupils must function in any particular environment" (Wolfard, n.d.).

Throughout her career in Cambridge schools, Edith Lesley would have had contact with many teachers, families, school board members, Harvard faculty, and others who would later play roles in the founding and building of the Lesley School. This network would prove important in establishing the Lesley School. It also reaffirmed her progressive interests and may have introduced her to another cause: the playground movement.

The establishment and funding of public free playgrounds was a social-reform effort contemporaneous with the settlement movement, with which it shared many features. The playground movement emphasized the links among organized play, personal health, character-building, safety, and democracy. The first supervised public playground, the Sand Gardens, was opened in Boston in 1886. The movement spread rapidly to other cities, and in 1906 the Playground Association of America (PAA) was established. Boston reformer and Harvard alumnus Joseph Lee, an early supporter, became an internationally known playground champion; he served as president of the PAA and wrote extensively about the playground. The city of Boston as well as private organizations and area settlement houses soon included playground work as a staple of their offerings (Anderson, 2006). In 1910 Lee Hamner declared,

> The playground of today is the republic of tomorrow. If you want twenty years hence a nation of strong, efficient men and women, a nation in which there shall be justice and square dealing, work it out today with the boys and girls on the playground (1910).

In addition to promoting certain virtues, the playground inoculated against less desirable contagions: "Recreation is stronger than vice and recreation alone can stifle the lust for vice," according to Jane Addams. The supervised games and activities were not just promoting the natural playfulness and need for physical exercise of children; they also built character and promoted republican values.

Like so many of the progressive impulses of the day, the playground movement married sincere wishes for reform and opportunity with concerns that without intervention, disorder and disharmony would build within an increasingly heterogeneous society.

The Idea of a School

In 1900 the Lesleys moved, for what proved to be the last time, to 29 Everett St. This move may have been made to allow Rebecca Lesley to again operate a boarding establishment. Perhaps Edith and Olive influenced this choice, because their new home already had a history as a multiple family house and private school. If even then Edith Lesley was planning to open her own school, there were few sites better suited for it.

In about 1875 Sarah H. Page (no relation to Anne L. Page) had opened her "select school" for young children out of the family home at 29 Everett St. She was born in 1821 in Newburyport, and was living in Cambridge as early as 1859, when she worked as an assistant teacher at the Washington School. By 1863 she is listed as boarding at "T. A. Carew's, 29 Everett." Thomas A. Carew had married her sister Mary Page in 1848. They had two daughters, Mary and Abby.

The Carew family did not own the property; Sarah had purchased it together with another sister, Abby. The house was both home to the extended family and their place of business. Several of the teachers Sarah Page employed boarded with her sister Mary; one business fed the other. By the late 1880s, niece Mary Carew was one of these teachers. All may not have been well in the Carew household; in the 1880 U.S. Census, Mary Carew listed herself as head of house, even though Thomas Carew was alive. A separation and attendant economic hardship may explain why Mary Carew took boarders. It is striking how closely the early Lesley School would follow this pattern: its intimate size, the combination of boarding with a school, and the involvement of family members.

During the 1890s the Carew daughters married and moved away, and Thomas and Mary Crew both died. In late 1899, Sarah and Abby Page moved to Lowell to live with their widowed niece. The Lesley family was living and taking boarders at 29 Everett St. by 1900, probably paying rent to the Page family. A year later, Alonzo Lesley died.

What finally impelled Edith Lesley to plan her school? Was it, as she implied in a statement many years later, a wish of hers over many years? Was she tiring of the routines of public schools, or the low pay, or both? Had she always planned to retire from active teaching when she turned 40? Did she perceive opportunities in training for young women that she wished to pursue? Having worked so closely with Olive, did she and her sister decide to start the business together?

Gertrude Malloch, an early faculty member and later principal of the school, suggested that the founding was linked to the donation of a million dollars by Joseph Lee to Harvard's then Division of Education to encourage kindergarten education. She also recalled that a committee of Cambridge women trying to open more kindergartens in the city met in the "annex" (probably Sarah Page's schoolroom) behind 29 Everett, and that their work together with heightened interest in kindergarten may have impelled Edith Lesley to make her plans (Malloch, 1959). There was also legislative activity regarding kindergartens: a bill to require all communities of 10,000 residents or more to open kindergartens was filed in the Massachusetts legislature in 1909, perhaps raising Edith Lesley's hopes and those of other committed kindergartners that larger enrollments, and thus greater demand for trained teachers, were around the corner.

Edith Lesley's public comments on why she was establishing a school dovetail with the first statement of the school's purpose, pointing to larger aims:

> I plan not merely to set up another training school; I plan for us to be different; to consider the individual of basic importance; to inculcate the ideal of gracious living; and to foster the tradition of American democracy.

Promoting individual development, the importance of culture, and an interest in engendering citizenship and democratic principles would continue to be themes during the next three decades of the school's history.

Merl Wolfard later explained Edith Lesley's belief that "education consisted in disciplining the mind so as to be able to take in something of the total situation in which both teacher and pupils must function in any particular environment" (Wolfard, n.d.). Her own statement about her approach to education as a community function complements this analysis:

> It has always been my opinion that whatever extremists may say about education one fact remains: education should be a preparation for life…life in this world necessitates cooperation with others. Communities, families and professions are not just a collection of individuals; they are made up of human beings who are dependent upon each other for success.

There is an underlying intellectual framework implied in her statements about kindergarten being embedded in a larger set of educational issues. In this phrasing we can glimpse Edith Lesley as a thinker, and we can see the influence of her deliberate and selective college studies.

From 1904 to 1908, Edith Lesley enrolled as a Special Student at Radcliffe College. She took courses such as General Introduction to Philosophy, Metaphysics, and The Kantian Philosophy taught by Josiah Royce; a yearlong seminary, Mind and Body, given by Hugo Munsterberg; and George Palmer's Ethical Seminary. The focus on philosophy may indicate she was striving to broaden her formal education, contemplating an avocation beyond the kindergarten classroom. She participated in at least one social organization at Radcliffe, the Deutscher Verein, which organized German cultural events and lectures every other Friday. She took similar coursework at the Harvard Summer School. Taken together these studies and activities suggest Edith Lesley constructed a deliberate plan of self-improvement and expansion of her knowledge.

As Edith Lesley began to organize her ideas for a kindergarten training school, she would have surveyed existing local programs. While municipal kindergartens were supported in both Cambridge and neighboring Somerville, two of the 10 largest cities in Massachusetts, there was no kindergarten teacher training in either city. In Boston, the Boston Normal School included a kindergarten training program and was free to city residents. In the spring of 1909 the Garland Training School ceased to offer kindergarten training, ostensibly because its leaders found young women could not mature sufficiently as teachers in a two-year course of study. Miss Wheelock's Kindergarten Training School offered Froebelian kindergarten training and supplemental work in the primary grades and social welfare. Annie Coolidge Rust operated a training school that included playground courses (added perhaps a few years afterward) and a mothers' course. The Perry Kindergarten Normal School and the Training School for Kindergarten were also options. At each the tuition was $100 a year, which is precisely what Edith Lesley would charge (Lazaerson, 1971).

Another influence would have been the division in the profession about what the content of kindergarten, and, by extension, of teacher training for kindergarten, ought to be. By the first decade of the 20th century, the movement's rapid growth and the impact of American progressive education had led to dissensions among kindergartners. The International Kindergarten Union (IKU) attempted to sort out claims and concerns during a nine-year process (1903 1912) of trying to agree on a comprehensive statement of Froebelian principles. The so-called Committee of Nineteen could not agree, however, and ended up writing a report in three parts. The "Uniform Program" of strict Froebelian orthodoxy was championed by St. Louis educator and writer Susan E. Blow; Patty Smith Hill of Teachers College, New York, focused on flexibility and modernization; and Elizabeth Harrison of Chicago took a moderate position, maintaining some classic kindergarten methods while inviting innovation.

We can gain some insight into where Edith Lesley and thus the Lesley School fell within this continuum from the list of core texts in the school's 1913-1914 catalogue. Two of the eight recommended books were by Susan E. Blow, two were by Elizabeth Harrison, and one was by Anne L. Page. Judging from these texts, Edith Lesley Wolfard was a moderate to conservative disciple of Froebel. The major influence of modern educational thought, perhaps a result of her Radcliffe experiences, was the inclusion of a required psychology course, and later psychological measurement, in the Lesley School's core curriculum.

THE NEW SCHOOL

The school's circular, "A New School for Kindergarteners," was published in the first half of 1909. An advertisement appeared three times in the *Cambridge Chronicle*. These publications, together with word of mouth, were how Edith Lesley promoted her new school. She was now lead kindergartner at the Houghton School, built in 1904 to replace the Riverside School a few blocks east on Putnam Street. While she did collaborate with others to teach the courses, including her sister Olive, it seems that the planning of the new school was closely held. This is consistent with Gertrude Malloch's later observation that in general Edith Lesley Wolfard "seldom discussed a new plan, she just announced it" (Malloch, 1959).

Edith Lesley's first idea for where to hold her school was probably to use space at the Houghton. The Cambridge School Committee minutes of April 1909 state that her request "to use the kindergarten room in certain afternoons, was referred to the acting superintendent." She ended up renting three classrooms from the Cambridge School for Girls, at 36 Concord Ave. Classes were held in the Concord Avenue school for several years before moving onto what became the Everett Street campus. The school also used Brattle Hall (now the Brattle Theater) near Harvard Square for actives games, socials, and formal dances.

The Lesley School opened on Sept. 17, 1909, probably with seven students. Classes were added semester by semester to create the first curriculum for the students. Their training was dominated by classic kindergarten methods. A member of the first class, Anna Savolainen, recalled a classroom project:

> Making paper designs which were pasted in a large book with black covers. The books were used in kindergarten instruction. In them we copied music of kindergarten songs, made original programs for the school year, etc. All these were marked for neatness and originality. I still have my black book.

The re-creation of the occupations and presenting the examples in bound books is a classic Froebelian instructional technique, practiced in most American kindergarten training classes of this period. Evidence suggests that Lesley students continued to produce these books well into the 1920s, as long as the Froebelian philosophy dominated the curriculum of the school.

The first circular of the Lesley School provides a valuable window into the thinking and planning of Edith Lesley for her school. Miss Lesley arranged the original courses into three groups: Kindergarten Theory and Practice; Education; and Supplementary Courses. She separated kindergarten from (other) education, and included in the "supplementary" coursework physical education and primary education methods. In her thinking the purely kindergarten training course comprised one compartment; formal theories of education another; and methods outside of kindergarten were yet another way or mode of thinking about education.

Attention to the arts signals the importance of the arts and culture in Edith Lesley's philosophy. There is agreement that kindergarten education "contributed heavily to changing the primary school program" in art education, changing it from a practical and vocational skill "to a more aesthetic and expressive activity for the child." Imagination, not imitation, was the primary goal of this approach (Anderson, 2006). One can see in this focus the seeds of Lesley University's ongoing attention to the arts and a consistent connection to expression and creativity.

In addition to kindergarten training, the first circular proposed "A Course for Work in the Playground." In 1909 the PPA published "A Normal Course in Play" that included subjects such as child development, play theory, eugenics, games and activities, handicraft, and nature study, consistent with subjects studied by kindergartners. The proliferation of playgrounds requiring trained supervisors may have spurred Edith Lesley to add this emergent vocational field to her offerings.

The seven original faculty represented the significant strands of Edith Lesley's professional and intellectual development up to this time. In addition to herself and her sister, they were Elsie Aldrich Burrage, Boston kindergartner; Ernst Hermann, director of physical education for the city of Quincy; Harvard education faculty Henry W. Holmes; Martin Mower, Harvard instructor in fine arts; and Josiah Royce, who, as we have seen, was Edith Lesley's teacher at Radcliffe. Anna Savolainen remembered Edith Lesley teaching "philosophy of life," child study, and the theory and methods of Friedrich Froebel. She also recalled Olive Lesley teaching folk dancing, games, and storytelling. Ernst Hermann was a distinguished playground educator, while the influence of Harvard and the centrality of its network in Miss Lesley's plans are evident.

The Froebelian philosophy included the idea that individuals are all important and unique; Miss Lesley took time to know each student, and indeed "even after the school had developed to the point where she had many teachers in her faculty, she insisted on teaching one or two classes herself in order to keep a personal contact with the student's individuality." Edith Lesley Wolfard could also be strict; her husband recounted an instance in which a student tried to justify her misconduct by saying, "'I did the best I could,'" and was told, "'Perhaps your best is not good enough.'" Likewise, she advised others to hold Lesley students to high expectations, telling a later president and dean, "'The girls at Lesley will give their best when the best is expected from them. Insist on these standards. Demand the top, not the second-rate.'"

As the focus of the school was on teaching and learning, there was little organized social life at first. Occasionally Miss Lesley would hold a tea at her home for the students. In December of 1911 she organized the school's first Candlelight Service, a time to tell Christmas stories and sing traditional songs and carols, which continued for decades. The first students also gave public recitals or demonstrations of what they were learning, from at least 1913 on, as was the custom with all kindergarten schools in Boston.

None of the students in either the first or second entering class boarded there; all lived at home. The second extant catalogue, and those for several years afterward, specifically reference the access to Lesley afforded by "the new subway." During the third or fourth year of the school's history, a few young women desiring boarding were placed in the neighborhood.

Edith Lesley worked in the Cambridge public schools until September f 1911, a few months after the first class graduated; she would marry the following February. Olive left teaching at about the same time. Edith and Olive Lesley would have worked mornings in their kindergarten classroom, and taught at the new school in the afternoons; one wonders how they also kept up a schedule of home visits, the typical afternoon work of kindergartners, unless they divided those duties.

The fact is that the early school was one among several commitments for the Lesley sisters. Olive Lesley, for example, organized "a regular summer school" kindergarten for Dr. Wilfred Grenfell at his Labrador mission between 1910 and 1912. She also spoke about kindergarten methods and demonstrated folk dancing in area schools, opening a School of Dance at the Lesley School in 1914, though this effort does not seem to have lasted long (Grenfell, 1919). The sisters maintained a network of connections to the kindergarten movement within and beyond the Boston-Cambridge area. In 1913, for example, Olive addressed the IKU annual meeting in Washington, D.C. The sisters also participated in the early stages of the U.S. Girl Scout movement. Edith Lesley Wolfard was elected president of the Boston council of scouting in 1914, and in 1916, Olive Lesley was lecturing on scouting in Fitchburg.

The school was notably enmeshed in progressive movements of the day. Lesley students volunteered or were placed in settlement house venues to apply their skills. Several early graduates were employed in local summer playgrounds, and it may be that further research will reveal an ongoing connection to playground supervision.

Not later than 1913, the Lesley School expanded its offerings to include training for elementary teachers, focused on the early elementary grades (first through third, later expanded to grade 4). This is consonant with the movement to influence primary education and to ensure that kindergarten and primary teachers knew each other's work. Primary teachers were increasingly organizing their classrooms to be cooperative, use more games and songs, and embrace the idea of education enhancing individual development. The connections to kindergarten ideas were organic, and the appeal of an elementary school curriculum is equally clear; the school would appeal to many more potential students were elementary education offered.

By 1913 there were about 43 graduates of the Lesley School, and most of them were teaching. Early research on the origins and subsequent lives of these young women has suggested some interesting commonalities. Many were second-generation Americans, and the first in their families to attend any kind of postsecondary institution. A few were nontraditional students; one was a widow with a young son who went on to a career in kindergarten teaching; another was an orphan living with relatives in a nearby town; Anna Savolainen was older and had completed some kindergarten training in Finland before emigrating. Whether by accident or design and if further research can shed light on this distinction, it would be important to know the Lesley School was a gateway institution for some number of its students, a fact that continues to shape the institution's mission.

CONCLUSION

Explaining Edith Lesley's decision to found her school, as well as its subsequent growth, requires looking at environmental and personal conditions. Christine Ogren has argued that public normal schools served a distinctive student body through the 1900s, which was older, heavily female, and likely to have had previous work experience, with less access to liberal arts colleges. In the north she sees evidence that these schools also served ethnic minority groups. By the turn of the century traditional colleges were becoming more elite, and less attainable because of rising tuition; state normal schools provided an important option for those desiring education and career paths in teaching. We can extend this argument to help explain the proliferation of private normal schools in some areas, such as Greater Boston: A confluence of liberal attitudes toward women's roles and girls' education; employment opportunities; and the lack of a state-sponsored normal school in Boston itself all probably contributed to the founding of so many private teacher training schools, many focused on kindergarten and early primary grades, in the late 19th and early 20th centuries (Ogren, 2005).

As Claudia Goldin has demonstrated, just after the Lesley School opened, enrollments in U.S. high schools began to climb rapidly, particularly enrollment in the so-called English curriculum, not the Greek and Latin preparatory curriculum required at elite liberal arts colleges. This uniquely American phenomenon reflected the emergence of jobs that required more education than common schooling but not four years of college, including kindergarten and elementary school teaching, fields that until the 1940s were dominated by women holding normal school degrees (Goldin, 1998). High school degrees opened the door to occupations with status, and conversely, large numbers of high school graduates who could go into teaching meant that the expansion of public education could continue unabated.

We can posit that these conditions, combined with the entrepreneurial models she witnessed and the sense of mission she developed, linked to her concern with social conditions, led Edith Lesley to open her school. Training in kindergarten had a wide-ranging appeal for young women and their parents—even in those families in which formal education past grade school was not common—and for first- or second-generation Americans. Networked into Harvard

College and local social change movements, Edith Lesley Wolfard gave her students a wide exposure to culture, politics, and vocations. We are accustomed to think of the higher education revolution in the United States—wide access to a college education—as occurring after World War II. If we expand our notion of this revolution to postsecondary education of all kinds, we might see Edith Lesley Wolfard and her peers as contributing to another important social change, one that extends far beyond the boundaries of early childhood education and that continues to have consequences today, and that has the potential to widen and deepen our collective understanding of the choices and opportunities that were open to America's young people in the first half of the 20th century.

REFERENCES

Allen, A. T. (Spring, 1988). "'Let us live with our children': Kindergarten movements in Germany and the United States, 1840 1914." *History of Education Quarterly, 28.*

Anderson, L. M. (2006). "'The playground of today is the republic of tomorrow': Social reform and organized recreation in the USA, 1890 1930's." *The Encyclopedia of Informal Education.*

Baylor, R. M. (1965). *Elizabeth Palmer Peabody: Kindergarten Pioneer.* Philadelphia, PA: University of Pennsylvania Press.

Beatty, B. (1995). *Preschool education in America: The culture of young children from the colonial era to the present.* New Haven, CT: Yale University Press.

Emmet, A. (1978). *Cambridge, Massachusetts: The changing of a landscape.* Cambridge, MA: Harvard College.

Goldin, C. (1998). America's graduation from high school: The evolution and spread of secondary schooling in the twentieth century. *Journal of Economic History, 58*(2).

Grenfell, W. (1919). *A Labrador doctor.* Boston, MA: Houghton and Mifflin.

Hamner, L. (1910). "Health and playgrounds." *Proceedings of the National Conference of Charities and Corrections.*

Harvey, A. K. (1924). *Pioneers of the kindergarten in America.* New York, NY: Century Co.

Lazerson, M. (1971). *Origins of the urban school: Public education in Massachusetts, 1870 1915,* Cambridge, MA: Harvard University Press.

Malloch, G. (1959). "On the Occasion of the Commemorative Convocation celebrating the Semicentennial Anniversary of Lesley College." TS. May 8.

McCullough, D. (1977). *The path between the seas: The creation of the Panama Canal, 1870 1914.* New York, NY: Simon & Schuster.

Ogren, C. (2005). *The American state normal school: "An instrument of great good."* New York, NY: Palgrave Macmillan.

Page, A. L. (1886). *The kindergarten and the school.* Springfield, MA: Milton Bradley & Co.

Ross, W. (1909). *The kindergarten crusade: The establishment of preschool education in the United States.* Athens, OH: Ohio University Press, 1976.

Sargent, P. (1930). *Handbook for private schoolteachers.* Boston, MA: Porter E. Sargent.

Shapiro, M. S. (1983). *Child's garden: The kindergarten movement from Froebel to Dewey.* University Park, PA: Pennsylvania State University Press.

Wolfard, M. R. (n.d.). Untitled biography of Edith Lesley Wolfard. Submitted to the Association of Childhood Education International Archives, Box, p. 2.

Woods, R. A., & Kennedy, A. J. (1911). *Handbook of settlements.* New York, NY: Charities Publication Committee.

CHAPTER TWO

Early Childhood Education at Lesley University: 100 Years

Mary Beth Lawton, EdD
Mary Mindess, EdM
Lisa Fiore, PhD
Ben Mardell, PhD
Joanne Szamreta, PhD

SOCIAL JUSTICE AND PEACE

In May 2008, two early childhood educators who are affiliated with Lesley University were honored by the Urban College of Boston for their outstanding contributions to their field.

Venitte Burke, a Roxbury, MA, Head Start teacher and single parent, was honored for her work with low-income children and families. Burke is a Professional Enrichment in Early Childhood Education (PEECE) Scholar who received her bachelor of science degree at Lesley, along with 16 other Head Start teachers, through a grant-funded scholarship secured by Professor Connie Counts of the Adult Learning Division.

Nancy Carlsson-Paige is a member of Lesley's graduate faculty in early childhood education. She is a pioneer in exploring the effects of violence in children's lives and ways to promote more peaceful childhoods. The Urban College of Boston honored her for her most recent book, *Taking Back Childhood: Helping Your Kids Thrive in a*

Fast-Paced, Media-Saturated, Violence-Filled World (2008).

Almost 100 years earlier, Edith Lesley, a pioneer in early childhood education, founded the Lesley School to educate young women for careers in this field. The first student at Lesley, Anna Tikkonnen, was unable to afford the tuition, and was dedicated to serving young children and their families. Tikkonnen was admitted despite her inability to pay, and Edith Lesley found her a job in a settlement house. In 1934, Edith Lesley articulated her goals for the school:

> A good education for all to develop one's potential and use it to achieve a greater good, a nation at peace and in harmony with the family of nations, a nation in which the good of all shall be the concern of all, a nation in which the enemies...of poverty have been destroyed because their causes have been obliterated. (Edith Lesley papers, 1909)

The values of equity in education, education as a tool for social reform and social justice, and the creation of a peaceful, just society have been enduring philosophical underpinnings of early childhood education at Lesley University since its inception.

CREATIVITY AND THE ARTS

During the 2007–2008 academic year, Lella Gandini, teacher, researcher, and Liaison for the Dissemination of the Reggio Emilia Approach in the United States, joined the Lesley community as a visiting scholar. Through the sponsorship of Provost Martha McKenna and in collaboration with early childhood faculty members Mary Mindess, Ben Mardell, Lisa Fiore, and Joanne Szamreta, Gandini led seminars for faculty in early childhood, art therapy, and expressive arts and taught a graduate course titled Advanced Reflections on the Reggio Emilia Approach.

Reggio Emilia is a small city in northern Italy where, after World War II, parents and the inspired educator Loris Malaguzzi created schools in which children could pursue their interests through exploration and inquiry and construct knowledge in creative, aesthetically appealing, and engaging environments (Edwards, Gandini, & Foreman, 1998). The Reggio Emilia approach has captivated early childhood educators throughout the world, including faculty and students at Lesley University.

Since 1993, under the leadership of Mary Mindess, and since 2004, under the leadership of Joanne Szamreta, Lesley has offered annual conferences and institutes that center on the Reggio Emilia approach. Early childhood faculty Lisa Fiore, Ben Mardell, and Joanne Szamreta participate in a Democracy Inquiry Group to study the Reggio Emilia practice of documenting and "making visible" children's learning. Fiore, current chair of the Graduate Program in Early Childhood Education, recently coedited an edition of *Theory into Practice* on using documentation to transform teaching and learning (Fiore & Suarez, 2010). Ben Mardell's work explores the use of Reggio Emilia inspired sustained group inquiry projects, with children, that emerge from child or adult interests. A video describing one of these ventures, the Boston Marathon Project, was selected by the National Association for the Education of Young Children (NAEYC) for inclusion in its widely read publication *Developmentally Appropriate Practice in Early Childhood Programs* (Mardell, 2008). In *Insights and Inspirations from Reggio Emilia: Stories from Teachers and Children from North America* (Gandini, Etheridge, & Hall, 2008), Professor Mindess (2008) published an article on curriculum inspired by the Reggio Emilia approach. In February 2006, Lesley undergraduate students Leah Valley, Liana Mitman, Katelyn Bull, and Meghan Donahue, along with early childhood professor Mary Beth Lawton, participated in a student-professor study tour to Reggio Emilia in Italy.

One of the core tenets of the Reggio Emilia approach is that creativity is essential to the construction of knowledge. Children learn when they are able to communicate their thinking or understanding in creative ventures, to express and represent their ideas in what Malaguzzi refers to as the "100 languages of children" (Edwards, Gandini, & Forman, 1998).

A central feature of the Reggio Emilia schools is the atelier, a place where children represent their theories and ideas in creative venues. Gandini (2005) describes its essential features: "The atelier is a sort of multiplier of possibilities, of explorations, of knowledge. For the children, this is evident for they continually exercise their creativity, communicating it through objects they produce and through their thought processes" (p. 60). "The atelier makes the relationship between art, emotion, knowledge and creativity more clear." (p. 59)

Joanne Pressman is a Lesley graduate who directs the Community Nursery School—a preschool inspired by the Reggio Emilia approach—in Lexington, MA. She described her deepening understanding of the atelier as a result of Gandini's course:

> We brought to the class a vast array of papers as materials to use for experimentation and creation as we investigated the role of the atelier in the schools of Reggio Emilia. We spent time working with these papers to explore their properties and discover how our interactions might change them. Next, we joined in small groups and were asked to create something collaboratively. Finally, an idea emerged that generated much excitement—[We would create] an atelier! We would construct a model of these special places that hold infinite possibilities for the exploration, sharing, expression, and representation of ideas. [Thus] the idea of the atelier as a metaphor for the Reggio [Emilia] way came to life for me. (Pressman, 2008, pp. 11-13)

The link between creativity and intelligence was clearly recognized by Lesley University founder Edith Lesley. In fact, the early curriculum for prospective kindergarten teachers of the Lesley School was exclusively devoted to the creative arts: Weaving; Clay Modeling; Folk Dance; Art Appreciation; Music; Drawing; Design; Basketry; Nature Studies; and Costume Design for Plays *(Lesley School Catalogues, 1915 1935)*. Merl Wolfard, husband of Edith Lesley Wolfard, wrote in a correspondence to the Association of Childhood International Collection at the University of Maryland,

Mrs. Wolfard was a little saddened when the trend in education drifted toward the requirement of a more academic training for kindergarten and elementary teachers. Nonetheless, Mrs. Wolfard did cooperate diligently with educational accrediting committees and with the requirements of the educational authorities in Massachusetts, which led to the establishment of Lesley College and its wide accreditation as a college devoted to educational activities. (Wolfard, n.d.)

COLLABORATION BETWEEN SCHOOLS AND FAMILIES

In the spring of 2008, Lauren Dodge, an undergraduate senior majoring in early childhood education at Lesley, was completing her senior practicum. As a requirement for the course Dodge was asked to participate in and reflect on parent conferences. She approached her first parent conference with some trepidation, wondering, "What if they do not see me as a teacher?" "What if they do not recognize my role in their children's lives?" "What if they do not value my opinions?" After the first few conferences, she felt at ease. The parents arrived with stories their children had told them of her importance to them and their love for her. Her perspective on parents shifted: She now saw herself as an equal who could enter into collaborative relationships.

For early childhood educators today, one of the greatest challenges is developing collaborative relationships with parents from diverse cultural and linguistic backgrounds; welcoming these parents into the schools is part of the challenge. The research indicates that parent involvement is the primary variable predicting achievement in school (Henderson, 1987). Often, the early childhood educator is the first person to communicate information about the child's development to families, and plays an important role in supporting parents, who in turn can better support their children's efforts to learn. An alumna of Lesley College's class of 1963, Joyce Epstein has been in the forefront of teaching and research on how to build effective partnerships with children and families, and is a leading scholar-practitioner in the area of support for school-family relationships. She directs the National Network of Partnership Schools and the Center on School, Family and Community Partnerships, and is principal research scientist and research professor of sociology at John Hopkins University.

Roopnarine and Johnson (2000) wrote: "The role of the teacher [is becoming] more complex as it expands to include consultation and support for families in ways reminiscent of...the settlement houses associated with the day nurseries of the 19th century" (p. 29). Slattery (1984/1985), recalling the early days of kindergarten education at the Lesley School, noted that in the afternoons, teachers visited children's homes, counseled mothers on child development, and met with mothers' groups that were connected to the settlement house movement. The importance of the connection between teachers and families and the important role of the early childhood teacher as a child development educator have been core values of early childhood education at Lesley University since its inception.

This chapter is divided into two main parts. In Part 1, we review the history of early childhood education at Lesley since its inception in 1909. In Part 2, five faculty members discuss the four goals of Lesley's current approach to early childhood education: (1) defining an image of the child; (2) developing a theory of learning; (3) deepening the role of the teacher in engaging children in the learning process; and (4) exploring the realities and possibilities of classrooms and schools in a democratic society.

PART 1

EARLY CHILDHOOD EDUCATION AT LESLEY FROM 1909–1940: FROEBELIAN INFLUENCES

Edith Lesley founded the Lesley School in 1909 to educate and train kindergarten teachers. At its inception Lesley University, like many other teacher-training institutions, defined itself by its early childhood focus, which underscores "the enormous influence early childhood education has had on the rest of education" (*Lesley College Current*, 1980). Over the next 100 years, the Lesley University program in early childhood education would become internationally known as a leader in the preparation and professional development of teachers of young children.

The early leaders of the kindergarten movement in the United States were inspired by the values and ideals of Friedrich Froebel, founder of the kindergarten, or "children's garden," in Germany. Led by "politically active and socially concerned" liberals, many of them early feminists, the Froebelian Kindergarten Movement aimed to eliminate the evils of poverty and social injustice and to create political-social reform (Ellsworth, 1988, p. 14). Froebelian ideology also embraced the objectives of civil rights, tolerance and harmony among the social classes, and international peace (Ellsworth, 1988).

The authors of the Froebelian Kindergarten Movement believed that the proper education of the young child would result in happiness, fulfillment, and harmony in adults. "Early Froebelians viewed kindergarten as a seedbed to nurture public-minded citizens" (Ellsworth, 1988, p. 8). Their belief was that if a child could be educated as a creative, inventive spirit, in harmony with others and the world, then he or she would become a happy, productive citizen who would contribute to the creation of a just and democratic society.

Froebel, and the ideals and values of the Froebelian Kindergarten Movement, shaped the thinking of the visionary Edith Lesley and her curriculum for kindergarten teachers at the Lesley School. Central to the Froebelian philosophy was a set of core values: the importance of free, joyful, active learning through play; the development of the whole child (physical, cognitive, social, and emotional); learning connected to real life; child-initiated learning; unity between home and school; and the integration of theory and practice (Lascarides & Hinitz, 2000; Nourot, 2000; Wortham, 1992).

Under the tutelage of Edith Lesley, prospective kindergarten teachers at the Lesley School studied curriculum that used free play and the creative arts to support the developmental needs of young children. Students were also trained with Froebel's "gifts and occupations," teacher-directed curriculum materials designed to promote "three forms of knowledge" that Froebel viewed "as the basis of all learning":

> Forms of life such as gardening, care of animals and domestic tasks; forms of mathematics such as geometric forms and their relation to one another...and forms of beauty such as designs with color and shape, or harmonies in music and movement. (Nourot, 2000, p.10)

The curriculum inspired by the Froebelian Kindergarten Movement remained the core course of study at Lesley well into the early 1940s.

1940–1960: The Child Study Movement, Dewey, and the Lesley Lab Schools

By the late 1930s and early 1940s, several significant influences had led to major reforms in early childhood education and to a shift away from aspects of the Froebelian curriculum. The Child Study Movement, which flourished in the mid-1920s and then gained prominence in American universities, constituted a scientific approach to the study of child development. With the growth of the Child Study Movement came a decision by the National Research Council to create a Child Development Committee (McBride & Barbour, 2003, p. 13), signaling the council's recognition of child study "as a distinct research domain." A highly influential event in precipitating the field of child development was the publication in 1883 of *The Content of Children's Minds on Entering School*, by G. Stanley Hall, a lecturer in education at Harvard University. G. Stanley Hall had gone on to conduct numerous child development studies, and their conclusions led to a critique of the Froebelian "gifts and occupations" curriculum:

> It was learned, for example, that large muscle development preceded small muscle development; therefore, Froebelian materials requiring fine motor skills were inappropriate. Larger building blocks, dolls, a playhouse with kitchen utensils and toy animals were recommended... (Wortham, 1992, p. 19)

Another mid-century challenge to aspects of the Froebelian curriculum was the Progressive Movement, fathered by John Dewey. Dewey was highly influenced by Froebel's thinking about the importance of play, active learning with materials, the child's construction of her own ideas, and the connection between home and school. Dewey also believed, like Froebel, that education must be connected to real life; indeed, he viewed this connection as the basis of education. However, he questioned the rigidity of Froebel's notion of gifts and occupations, and favored free play over teacher-directed play (Roopnarine & Johnson, 2000). Make-believe play, constructive play, and thematic learning were highly valued by Dewey. So too was a concern for the physical and social-emotional health of children (Nourot, 2000; Wortham, 1992).

Dewey's educational thought predominated in early childhood curricula from the late 1930s to the 1950s, along with the influence of Freud's thinking. Freud's contributions to early childhood curricula centered on his articulating the importance of attending to the child's emotional needs for warmth, affection, security, and expression (Wortham, 1992).

Around the time that the Child Study Movement was flourishing in the mid-1920s, Dewey established one of the country's first laboratory schools at the University of Chicago. On the relationship of the laboratory school to the university, Dewey said: "The problem is to unify, to organize education, to bring all its various factors together, through putting it as a whole into organic union with everyday life" (Lascarides & Hinitz, 2000, p. 20).

Laboratory schools proliferated on college campuses from the late 1920s through the 1950s, and served the varied purposes of modeling best practice, training teachers, educating parents, and providing opportunities for observation and research. It was in this philosophical and theoretical context—the rise of the Child Study Movement, the influence of Progressivism, and the creation of university lab schools—that Lesley College, beginning in 1948, purchased and operated three schools in Cambridge that became known as the Lesley Lab Schools: the Lesley Ellis School, which served preschoolers and kindergartners; a remedial school that became known as the Lesley-Dearborn School; and the Carroll-Hall School, which served children with special needs (Lesley College Archives).

The Lesley-Ellis School provided the ideal opportunity to integrate theory and practice for prospective early childhood teachers. Lesley College early childhood education students observed child development and early childhood pedagogy. They also had the opportunity to complete their student teaching practica in a model early childhood setting. Lesley College faculty and students conducted child development and early childhood research at the school.

The goal that Dewey described for the University of Chicago Lab School—"A school that could become a cooperative community while developing in individuals their own capacities and satisfying their own needs" (Lascarides & Hinitz, 2000, p. 220)accurately describes the philosophy of the Lesley-Ellis School, according to Barbara Beatty, its director from 1972 to 1978, and Nancy Carlsson-Paige, a former kindergarten teacher at the school (Barbara Beatty, oral history interview, October 23, 2008, & Nancy Carlsson-Paige, personal communication, December 17, 2008). Modeled on Dewey's progressive philosophy, the pedagogy of the Lesley-Ellis School featured hands-on experimental learning in a play-centered, project-based curriculum. The classes were small "to promote the free and meaningful growth of the individual student within a democratic climate" (Lesley University Archives). As an integral part of the school community, families assisted with policy decision making, fundraising, planting gardens, and building classroom furniture (Barbara Beatty, oral history Interview, October 23, 2008, and Nancy Carlsson-Paige, personal communication, November 23, 2008).

1960–1970: Civil Rights, Head Start, the Ecological Model, and the New England Kindergarten Conference

External and internal forces converged in the early 1960s and shaped early childhood education at Lesley for years to come. The Civil Rights Movement achieved full strength in the early 1960s and served as a powerful catalyst for change in early childhood education. *Brown v. Board of Education,* in 1954, had established "the universal right of all children to a decent education" (Ramey & Ramey, 1998, p. 109). Minority groups across the nation demanded social, economic, and educational equality.

A second source of influence was a growing body of research (Bloom 1964; Hunt, 1961) indicating that early experience is critical to the development of intelligence. Hunt (1961) posited that the mothering a child receives, as well as the child's environment, influences intellectual development. Bloom (1964) argued that the IQ of a four-year-old child is predictive of the IQ of that child as an adult. Believing that early experience can increase a child's intelligence, Bloom and Hunt called for early intervention programs.

The work of Urie Bronfenbrenner, professor of human development and psychology at Syracuse University, also played an important role in shaping ideas about child development and early education in the early 1960s. Bronfenbrenner's ecological theory postulated that the numerous contexts, or systems, in which a child participates—family, school, culture—and the connections between them significantly affect a child's development. Of critical importance to child outcomes, including academic success, he said, are family and school (which he termed *microsystems*) and the relationship between them (a *mesosystem*) (Santrock, 2007). Later research by Lesley alumna Joyce Epstein and others (Epstein, 2001; Epstein, Sanders, Salinas, Simon, Jansorn & Van Vooris, 2002; Epstein & Saunders, 2002) supports Bronfenbrenner's conviction that parents and school must be integrally connected, strongly indicating that parent involvement predicts student achievement and healthy development. The launching of Sputnik by the Russians, in 1957, also influenced thinking about early childhood education. This feat created a belief, in many, in the inferiority of the American educational system compared to the Russian system. Thus, the importance of a child's emotional life, advocated for by Freud and Dewey, began to give way to a more primary emphasis on cognitive development and the acquisition of academic skills (Roopnarine & Johnson, 2000).

The convergence of these forces—the Civil Rights Movement; a belief that early experience is important in cognitive development; and the understanding that parents, and the relationship between parents and schools, affect children's educational achievement—led to the creation of Head Start, a national, federally funded program for low-income children, operated by the Office of Economic Opportunity as a key component of the War on Poverty. Like their predecessors in the Froebelian Kindergarten Movement, the creators of Head Start believed that early education is the solution to eliminating poverty and achieving economic prosperity. A key feature in the design of Head Start was parent involvement. Parents participated in policy decisions and in educational curricula; volunteered in the classroom; and were supported in their own educational and economic development.

In 1959, Mary Mindess arrived at Lesley College as a faculty member in early childhood education, and she soon became a dynamic internal force. An inspired innovator, Professor Mindess would shape early childhood education at Lesley for the next 50 years. One of her most enduring legacies is the New England Kindergarten Conference (NEKC), which she founded and coordinated. Professor Mindess put Lesley on the map as an international leader in the field of early childhood teacher training and development.

Lesley University sponsored NEKC for 42 years after its inception. Its motto characterized the visionary drive of its founder: "If you can dream it, Lesley is the place where you can make it happen." For more than four decades, NEKC provided an engaging venue for in-service and preservice professional development for early educators.

The immediate goal of the conference was to engage with the most pressing challenges in early childhood education by bringing the most current research and points of view in the field to the attention of educators in New England and surrounding states. Over the years, Mary Mindess invited the country's leading researchers, educators, psychologists, and practitioners to respond to the critical issues of the time.

In November 1962, Lesley held its first Kindergarten Conference. Professor Mindess, who had no prior experience in organizing conferences, managed to recruit as one of the speakers Jerome Bruner (1960), a renowned Harvard psychologist whose recently published book *The Process of Education* contained the often quoted and somewhat controversial idea that: "any subject can be taught effectively in some intellectually honest form to any child at any stage of development" (p. 33).

At the second NEKC, keynote speaker Alice Keliher had the task of announcing to the attendees that President John F. Kennedy had been shot and killed. Continuing to stand before her stunned audience, she courageously went on to deliver one of the most moving speeches of that year's conference, titled "The Dangerous Vacuums of Today's Programs," referring to the social-emotional domains of a child's development that had been ignored since the launching of Sputnik (Keliher, 1963).

In 1979, a segment of the conference expanded to the Mid-Atlantic states, in Tenafly, NJ. "We are moving toward our goal," said Mary Mindess, "of establishing a comprehensive and pervasive Early Childhood Network throughout the United States for the sharing and dissemination of information and research relating to all aspects of early childhood education" (*Lesley College Current*, 1980, p.6).

With the implementation of Head Start in 1965, there emerged an immediate and dire need for appropriately trained teachers (Osborn, 1991), and the Lesley College Early Childhood Program was poised to participate on numerous fronts. To meet the imminent need for Head Start teacher training, six days' worth of funds were provided, and the trainees became known as "the Six-Day Wonders." Lesley was one of the colleges selected to provide the training, and was assigned a group of 30 teachers from Cape May, NJ. With less than a week's training under their belt, these aspiring Head Start teachers left Lesley imbued with a new understanding of child development, some age-appropriate strategies for working with young children, and a supply of carefully selected materials.

The War on Poverty and the creation of the Head Start Program led to the development of specific models designed to help low-income children "catch up" to their financially advantaged peers. In the 1960s and 1970s, programs with varied models were developed by the federal government to determine which models correlated with school success. Wortham (1992) wrote:

> Never before or since in the history of early childhood education was an era of innovation and change so quickly accomplished and funded. Never before had a variety of philosophies and approaches to early childhood education been developed simultaneously and disseminated so widely. (p. 51)

Three of the best-known early models—Bereiter-Engelmann, High Scope, and Child Study—were based on divergent theoretical assumptions and have remained competing paradigms in early childhood education to this day.

The Bereiter-Engelmann model, grounded in behaviorist or social learning theory, is a teacher-directed program in which children are drilled in specific academic skills (Wortham, 1992). Teachers impart knowledge to children by means of direct instruction, in a didactic manner. The assumptions of the behaviorist philosophy are that learning is affected by three main mechanisms: conditioning through reward, conditioning through punishment, and imitation or observation learning (Salkind, 2004). Thus, the child's on-target, on-task behaviors and responses are rewarded, while off-task behaviors or responses are punished or ignored.

The High Scope (Perry Preschool Project) model is based on the constructivist, cognitive development theory of Jean Piaget, who has had wide influence in early childhood education since the early 1960s. In Piaget's view, children construct knowledge through active, hands-on, experiential learning, using play and direct engagement with materials. The child organizes knowledge into schemes, according to Piaget, and, when presented with new information, either integrates the knowledge into existing schemes or adapts the knowledge to accommodate new ideas. Lev Vygotsky, also a constructivist, believed that social interaction is significant in cognitive development, as is make-believe play (Forman & Landry, 2000; Santrock, 2007; Wortham, 1992). In this model, teachers and children are co-constructors of knowledge, and the curriculum is both child and teacher directed.

In the Child Study model, the child learns through a carefully prepared environment with engaging points of contact that serve as the curriculum, such as blocks, a water table, a make-believe play area, and a literacy corner. This model involves a largely child-initiated pedagogy in which the "child's involvement in planning and implementing instruction is considered important" (Wortham, 1992, p. 51).

In 1973, Mary Mindess invited Bereiter and Engelmann, proponents of a teacher-directed model, and David Weikart of the child-directed High Scope Perry Preschool Project to put forth their competing perspectives at the NEKC. Weikart presented a study of the various models, with important conclusions. For the models to be successful, he said, they must (1) represent a specific model, rather than a mixture of models; (2) attend to staff relationships and interactions; (3) provide ample time for planning; and (4) include a system of training and quality assessment (Weikart, 1973).

The appearance of Bereiter and Engelmann at the conference was highly controversial. Local early childhood educators with a constructivist, Piagetian, play-based philosophy were troubled by Bereiter and Engelmann's narrow focus on academic skills and the use of punishment as a motivator for children. Many opposed their invitation to the conference. However, Mindess believed it was important for teachers of young children to be exposed to diverse points of view, to think critically about them, and then to make reflective judgments about the relative value of these approaches.

Two longitudinal studies compared the three early education models (Schweinhart, Barnes, & Weikart, 1993; Schweinhart & Weikart, 1997) and concluded that preschool leads to positive outcomes in children's lives. Children who participated in the High Scope model were less likely to be arrested as adults, had higher earnings, were more likely to graduate from high school, and had higher literacy scores at age 19 (Schweinhart, Barnes, & Weikart, 1993). In the second longitudinal study (Schweinhart & Weikart, 1997), the three models were compared in terms of their effectiveness. The most significant finding was that the IQ scores of all three groups rose significantly after one year in preschool. However, in regard to the social-emotional well-being of adults who as children had participated in the three types of early education, those who had engaged with the High Scope and Child Study models fared better than their Bereiter-Englemann counterparts. Thus, the direct-instruction model comes at a cost to social-emotional intelligence. Favorable outcomes occur when children can engage in play and initiate their own learning.

1970–1980: Inclusion, the Women's Movement, and Open Education

Born of the educational and social issues of the time, major innovations in special education, day care, and open education occurred in the early childhood education programs at Lesley in the 1970s.

Through the years, major changes have occurred in the provision of educational experience for children with special needs. No aspect of early childhood education has undergone as great a shift. At the New England Kindergarten Conferences in the late 1960s and early 1970s, whenever children with special needs were discussed the focus was on the "deficit model" rather than a model that considered the development of the whole child.

In 1975, the Education for All Handicapped Children Act (PL-94-142) (later renamed the Individuals with Disabilities Education Act) stipulated that children with special needs should be educated along with their peers in "the least restrictive environment." This change occurred as attention was directed toward the benefits that derive from peer modeling when typically developing children interact with children who have special needs.

From the late 1970s to the present, the Lesley College Early Childhood Program has participated actively in preparing teachers to meet the needs of young children with special needs in the least restrictive environment. Program changes made it possible for early childhood education students to meet the requirements of the new Massachusetts certification titled Teacher of Young Children with and without Disabilities, (PreK-2).

In the summers of 1978 and 1979, the Lesley College Early Childhood Program received two Into the Mainstream grants, coordinated by Mary Mindess and adjunct faculty member Paula Elitov (Mindess & Elitov, 1979). About 30 early childhood teachers from the Boston and Cambridge areas received intensive one-week training for educators in the inclusive classroom.

Early childhood education was significantly affected by social changes initiated by the Women's Movement of the 1970s, as "women insisted on becoming contributing members of society" (Lascarides & Hinitz, 2000, p. 366). Women entered or returned to the work force in massive numbers, creating a need for child care programs for young children. Day care services proliferated in a variety of venues and models: in day care centers, in family day care settings, and on sites sponsored by corporations, linked to universities, and situated in hospitals and public schools (Lascarides & Hinitz, 2000).

In the mid-1970s, Lesley undertook a grand experiment that, although short-lived, made important contributions to the early childhood field. Belle Evans, adjunct faculty at Lesley and author of many of the first texts in day care programming and administration, designed a day care center that operated for two years in a renovated house on the Lesley campus, serving Lesley employees and community residents. Caring for approximately 45 infants, toddlers, and preschoolers, the center based its approach on the Lesley Laboratory Schools, and trained graduate and undergraduate students in exemplary early childhood practice. Evans contributed significantly to the day care field, publishing extensively in the area of day care programming, curriculum, and administration (Evans 1973; Evans, Saia, & Evans, 1974).

Day care for infants and toddlers was highly controversial at this time, especially in regard to its effects on their social-emotional development and attachment relationships. Jerome Kagan, professor of psychology at Harvard University, found in a demonstration program of "high-quality care for infants" that there were "no adverse effects of infant care" (Santrock, 2007, p. 262). Of course, the concern was about programs of lower quality.

Kagan also influenced and shaped the "nature-nurture" debate in child psychology and early childhood education: Does one's biological inheritance (nature) or the influence of parents and the environment (nurture) shape personality and temperament? Whereas attachment theorists (summarized in Karen, 1998) believe that early relationships are the most important predictor of a child's social-emotional behaviors, Kagan provided evidence that children are born with temperamental tendencies that influence their relational abilities. He also believed these tendencies could be changed by the environment (Santrock, 2005). In 1980, Mary Mindess brought Kagan to speak at the New England Kindergarten Conference on the topic of responding to the temperamental differences among children. Kagan invited the assembled educators to consider the cognitive style, intellectual competence, and motivation of each child, and how they could accommodate to these sources of variation (Kagan, 1980).

Jay Featherstone (1971) introduced in the United States the ideas of the British Infant Schools and open education. The theoretical underpinnings of the open education philosophy are found in the work of Dewey, Piaget, and educators John Holt and Herbert Kohl. The core principles of open education include child-directed, thematic learning in engaging environments where children are offered "varied and challenging materials" (Lascarides & Hinitz, 2000, p. 585). Proponents of open education strongly valued preserving children's freedom, individuality, independence, and total development while maintaining close connections with their families. Learning environments and centers, set up in hallways and in multiage classrooms, often without walls, enabled children to explore at will. A high value was placed on respecting children through relating to them in "democratic, nonhierarchical relationships" and involving them in decisions that affected them (Lascarides & Hinitz, 2000, p. 585).

In the early 1970s, interest in open education grew among early childhood educators at Lesley, including Cynthia Cole, assistant professor of education and director of the Independent Studies Program from 1971 to 1979. An "innovative educational philosopher" and "progressive spirit," Cole developed one of the first master's programs in open education (Baig, 1984, p. 7). The program was offered to graduate students for five years and was then absorbed into the regular education curriculum. A noteworthy 1976 graduate of the program was Nancy Carlsson-Paige, who went on to become a kindergarten teacher at the Lesley-Ellis Lab School, which operated with the open education philosophy.

1980–2009: Early Intervention, Bilingual Education, Standards-Based Education, and Universal Pre-Kindergarten

Since the 1980s, issues that have captured the attention of early childhood educators include early intervention, bilingual education, standards-based education, and universal pre-kindergarten.

In 1986, the Education of the Handicapped Act was amended to include comprehensive programs of early intervention for infants and toddlers. This legislation created opportunities to serve children from birth to three who were emotionally or developmentally at risk due to premature birth, low birth weight, or diagnosed disabilities, or who experienced relational issues such as abuse or attachment disorders. Over the years, there had been a growing realization that while early intervention is necessary, the venue of preschool is too late, owing to the realities of brain development:

> The mounting evidence about the significance of early experience in brain development, summarized in *Rethinking the brain: New insights in early Development* (Shore, 1997), provides a stronger than ever impetus for systematic efforts to enhance children's learning opportunities and development in the first three years of life. (Ramey & Ramey, 1998, p. 12)

In 1983, Dr. Joanne Szamreta, former director of two early intervention programs, joined the Lesley College early childhood faculty and, along with Samuel Madoono of the Psychology Department, created an early intervention specialization-certification for early childhood education and child and family study majors, one of the first in Massachusetts on the undergraduate level. Szamreta, a passionate public policy advocate for early intervention and the developmental needs of infants and toddlers, served as a Schott Fellow in 2005–2006 and coauthored a position paper titled "Everybody's baby: Early education and care for infants and toddlers" (Ellis, Jones, & Szamreta, 2006).

Mary Beth Lawton, adjunct faculty in the School of Education from 1987 to 2000, joined the Lesley College undergraduate faculty in 2000. In collaboration with the Astra Foundation, Lawton brought a new course to the early intervention curriculum: An Introduction to the DIR (Developmental, Individual, Relationship-based method), or "Floortime" approach, of Dr. Stanley Greenspan, a competing model with the behaviorist, ABA approach to working with developmental disorders.

During this time, educators were also paying increased attention to children's social-emotional development. Mary Mindess and Lesley professor Jerome Shultz, founder of the Learning Lab at Lesley, developed the first online course offered through Lesley: Children with Behavior Problems: Responding to the Challenge. Through the years, this course has attracted early childhood educators not just in the United States but from India, Japan, the Netherlands, Belgium, Germany, and England.

The Bilingual Education Act of 1968 invalidated the previous "English-only" policies in education and led to an effort to achieve educational equity for English language learners. A growing body of evidence recognized the importance of the child's first language as a bridge to the second language and as an important source of identity and self-esteem (Cordasco, 1976).

In November 2000, Lily Wong-Fillmore, professor of graduate education at the University of California, Berkeley, presented at the New England Kindergarten Conference at the request of Mary Mindess. Wong-Fillmore's topic was "The Educator's Role in Supporting Dual Language Development in Children." She encouraged early childhood educators to build on children's cultural and linguistic heritage, and encouraged parents of English language learners to maintain the child's native language in the home (Wong-Fillmore, 2000).

Joanne Szamreta, recognizing the shortage of trained bilingual teachers, applied for and received a five-year federal grant, in partnership with the Boston Public Schools, to train bilingual teachers from 1999 to 2004. Dr. Maria Serpa, graduate faculty in the School of Education, later joined the project. Over the course of the grant, 40 Spanish, Haitian Creole, Portuguese, Chinese, and Vietnamese students were trained in bilingual education. In the third year of the grant, the Massachusetts law changed, eliminating bilingual education, and it became necessary to adapt the grant to the current law.

Characteristic of this period was the emphasis on standards-based education and teacher licensure. The Massachusetts Education Reform Act of 1993 created significant changes in early childhood education at Lesley. New certification regulations, the Massachusetts Teacher Education Licensure Test, and the Massachusetts Comprehensive Assessment System for students resulted in important revisions to the early childhood course of study at Lesley. Early childhood courses were aligned with the Massachusetts Curriculum Frameworks in all areas while at the same time retaining sound early childhood practice.

A major issue in the minds of early childhood educators at Lesley and beyond, in 2009, was universal preschool (UPK), a comprehensive, nationwide system of preschool education for all children. The quest for UPK takes us back to the Froebelian Kindergarten Movement and the forces that shaped Edith Lesley. Beatty (1995) suggests that we can learn from these early education pioneers in our efforts to realize universal preschool. She writes: "The campaign for public kindergarten was a women's issue and one of the most successful examples of the political and social power women held in America in the late nineteenth and early twentieth centuries" (p. 201). She goes on to suggest, while quoting George Stoddard (1933), "that for preschools to be universalized, 'millions of people' will have 'to rise up and demand' that access to preschool education in America be provided for all our children" (p. 207).

In March 2009, under the leadership of President Joe Moore, Provost Martha McKenna, Dean Mario Borunda of the School of Education, and the graduate and undergraduate early childhood faculty at Lesley convened a conference titled "Universal Preschool: Myths, Tensions, and Inspirations." State and local leaders in early childhood education were invited to discuss and inform diverse perspectives on universal pre-kindergarten.

Some of the most pressing questions the conference tackled were as follows: Where should preschools be located, in public schools or in diverse child care venues? Should the goal of UPK be school readiness or development of the whole child? Should the focus of UPK be "skilling and drilling" or should it be play-oriented, best practice in early childhood education? It is interesting that many of the tensions that face UPK have existed since the 1870s, when the primary question was whether kindergartens should be located in public schools (Lascarides & Hinitz, 2000). The "inspirations" of the conference were presentations by Lella Gandini and by Amelia

Gambetti, Reggio Children International Network Coordinator and Liaison for Consultancy in Schools, on the Reggio Emilia approach to early education, and by Jennifer Marino Rojas on the work and research of Marian Wright-Edelman.

One of the panelists and state leaders at the UPK conference was Hanna Gebretensae, now division chair of Early Childhood Programs at Urban College in Boston. A freedom fighter and an early childhood education leader in the nation of Eritrea, Gebretensae created an underground infrastructure to support early childhood education in her country in a period of war. Connections with an Eritrean Head Start director in Boston led her to pursue her education in the United States and to a meet with Mary Mindess, Joanne Szamreta, and Nancy Heims, International Relations Program director at Lesley. Impressed by the promise of this young woman, Mindess, Szamreta, and Heims approached then president Margaret McKenna, who granted Gebretensae a full four-year scholarship. Like her predecessor Edith Lesley, McKenna "walked the talk" in providing financial support for promising, culturally diverse international students who would have otherwise been unable to access a Lesley education.

Gebretensae recalls: "I remember Nancy Heims calling me to say that I had been granted a scholarship and could come to Lesley. I was speechless! I couldn't talk!" (H. Gebretensae personal communication, May 7, 2009). The promise that the early childhood faculty and President McKenna saw in Hanna Gebretensae was more than fulfilled. After graduating with a B.S. from Lesley, Gebretensae received a master's in educational policy from Harvard; became director of Acorn Child Care in Chinatown; and served as a consultant in diversity and cultural competence training, as adjunct faculty in Lesley's Bilingual Education Program, and as a training and technical assistance consultant for Head Start Quality Initiatives before assuming her current position at Urban College. Her contribution to early care and education in Massachusetts has been extensive, and her work is in part a tribute to her Lesley College early childhood education.

PART 2
FOUR ASPECTS OF EARLY CHILDHOOD EDUCATION AT LESLEY

Over the past 100 years, despite changes in economic, political, and social climates, four themes have predominated in efforts to sustain innovative content and delivery in Early Childhood Education Programs at Lesley University. These key elements are best described as (1) defining an image of the child; (2) developing a theory of learning; (3) deepening the role of the teacher; and (4) exploring the realities and possibilities of schools.

1. DEFINING AN IMAGE OF THE CHILD

Fundamental to good teaching is a deep understanding of children. The path to establishing a foundational image of the child begins with an awareness of young children's cultural contexts, competencies, development, and emotional milestones. Teachers know that from birth, children are capable of making social connections, expressing emotions, and building mental models of how the world works. Young children operate as poets, philosophers, scientists, mathematicians, artists, and actors, as they question, investigate, explore, and make sense of their world. As active participants in their own learning, children bring their unique perspectives and backgrounds to bear on educational experiences.

The notion of the "image of the child" has been evolving for early childhood faculty members at Lesley, particularly as they have become increasingly immersed in the Reggio Emilia approach to early childhood education. The importance of the teacher's image of the child is expressed in the words of Carla Rinaldi, executive consultant for Reggio Children and a professor at the University of Modena and Reggio:

In substance, the child is defined by our way of looking at and seeing him. But since we see what we know, the image of the child is what we know and accept about children. This image will determine our way of relating with children, our way of forming our expectations for them and the world that we are able to build for them. (Rinaldi, 2006, p.91)

The first eight years of life is a time of tremendous growth, in which cognitive, linguistic, physical, social, and emotional milestones create a context for how children should be taught. Three-year-olds often have similar ways of relating to peers, parents, and materials. Certain materials, songs, games, and subject matter capture the interest of many five-year-olds. There are typical seven-year-old approaches to academic challenges. At the same time, gender, culture, family constellation, and personality influence each child's approach to learning. These are the understandings that a Lesley early childhood education student must develop.

Children have an innate desire to make sense of their world, and to communicate their understandings to others. To do this, they use multiple strategies, or "languages," such as facial expressions, words, acting, dancing, drawing, singing, storytelling, and writing. Children also learn a great deal from observing. Teachers are champions of all these endeavors, extending and enhancing the learning of each student as an individual and as a member of a group.

2. Developing a Theory of Learning

Piaget (1969), Dewey (1916), Vygotsky (1978), and others have written about the importance of engaging children actively and socially in the learning process and, through this activity, helping children to build knowledge that has personal meaning for them. One may ask whether children will learn critical skills such as literacy and numeracy in first grade if teachers aren't telling them exactly what they need to learn and what they need to do. Those who favor the key aspects of constructivism—active dialogue, questioning, and critical thinking—respond that this approach to teaching does prepare children in the first grade to move on with their education. They believe that it teaches children how to collaborate, to engage in debate and dialogue with others over disagreements, and to question and become thoughtful about the ambiguities of life. By developing a direction that has significant interest for children, and then creating activities that meet the standards within that direction, teachers can help children build learning that has lasting meaning for them *and* that meets the standards. Because of this meaning making, chances are that the children will remember what they've learned far longer than any memorized information required for a test.

Piaget (1969) and Vygotsky (1978) write about the critical nature of direct experience in learning, especially for young children. Piaget describes the notion of schema, or patterns of learning and behavior, that are developed through these direct experiences and that help facilitate children's understanding of the world. Vygotsky has added the idea of the Zone of Proximal Development, or the place of learning opportunity for a child, in which a more experienced learner, often the teacher but possibly more experienced peers, can build on the child's existing knowledge and support him in acquiring new skills, new knowledge, and new understandings through relationships.

Dewey's work (1916) focused on relationships in the context of the school community, which he believed should provide children with the opportunity to develop democratic principles within the group experiences of classroom life and the school as a whole. Children need to learn to question and to find out how to answer these questions. They need to learn to contribute to the larger society through asking questions and contributing what they know and can do for that society. For Dewey, school was not a holding place for children where teachers transmit knowledge to passive learners for the sake of getting right answers on tests. Rather, it was a dynamic community in which all the joys, tensions, issues, and concerns of the individuals who form the community were addressed mainly through dialogue and discussion. In Dewey's ideal school, children learned and contributed actively, with the support of teachers, in their own classroom and in the larger school.

Erikson (1963) described the early childhood years as an important time for developing autonomy, initiative, and trust. Earlier, Piaget (1951) had written about the inseparability of cognitive and affective development in learning. Gardner (1993) discusses the many intelligences with which we are born, and explains that these develop over time if given the opportunity to do so.

In the early childhood program at Lesley, we strive to support students in examining their own educational experience. We encourage students to consider the influence of this experience on their ideas about teaching, and to discover the inquiring minds of the children they encounter in their prepracticum and practicum placements. We help students understand that curiosity, questioning, and inquiry are essential to the teaching and learning process. We hope that, in turn, our students will support their own students in these ways, and that they will see the importance of continuing to learn alongside them. Everyone has a fund of knowledge to share.

3. DEEPENING THE ROLE OF THE TEACHER

The Lesley University early childhood education mission statement reflects the influence of the Reggio Emilia approach to early childhood education. Two passages in particular stand as examples:

> Teachers have multiple roles and responsibilities in early childhood classrooms. They support children's efforts to make meaning, foster connections to classmates and content, help individuals develop their potential, and see learning possibilities in ordinary moments.

> Based on careful observation and assessment of their students, along with knowledge of child development and content, teachers organize curricula (creative and prescribed)

that engage children in ongoing investigations. Teachers embody the memory of the group in their acts and the artifacts they encourage their students to create, helping students learn about learning.

The notion of intellectual vibrancy is central in the Reggio Emilia approach and in Lesley's vision of engaging children in the learning process. Key to this vision is the teacher's interest in the material at hand. Only when the teacher feels excited about learning can she involve children in a similar process. When the teacher's excitement about learning joins with the child's natural curiosity, the co-construction of knowledge takes place in the early childhood classroom. In collaborating to identify problems and conduct investigations, teachers and children bring the learning process to life.

The teacher's role is indeed complex, and very demanding. Besides being enthusiastic and skilled collaborators, successful teachers are exceptional listeners and observers. They cultivate the group setting as a means for developing individual potential, and they perceive the learning potential in ordinary moments.

4. EXPLORING THE REALITIES AND POSSIBILITIES OF SCHOOLS

The Early Childhood Education Program at Lesley espouses the belief that schools should promote peaceful communities and prepare children to participate in a democracy. We want our graduates to help students respect diversity, create equity and social justice, and develop the social and emotional skills that are required to work harmoniously and cooperatively with others. We believe it is essential for new teachers to know that many children arrive at school with essential needs unmet, and bearing the effects of families stressed by poverty.

Multiculturalism. The philosophy of multiculturalism emerged in the 1960s when women, gays, lesbians, and underrepresented racial, ethnic, and cultural minorities asserted claims to fairness, justice, equity, and equality (Grant, 1994).

In classrooms that support multiculturalism, children construct a positive identity and self-concept as individuals and as members of a group. Erik Erikson (1968) provides theoretical support for the importance of developing a positive identity. Referring to his work, Beverly Tatum (1997) writes that a child's identity is based on "who the world says I am...Am I represented in the cultural images around me? Or, am I missing from the picture altogether" (p. 18)? When children see their race, ethnicity, language, gender, abilities, and family composition represented in the school curriculum, their identities are validated and affirmed.

In a multicultural classroom, children learn to be socially conscious, critically thinking citizens; to take a stand against injustice; and to work toward equality. Grant (1994) describes the multicultural school:

> It demands a school staff that is multiracial and multiculturally literate, and that includes staff members who are fluent in more than one language. It demands a curriculum that organizes concepts and content around the contributions, perspectives and experiences of the myriad of groups that are a part of the United States society. It confronts and seeks to bring about change of current social issues involving race, ethnicity, socio-economic class, gender and disability. (p. 191)

Early childhood education courses at Lesley foster an appreciation of bilingualism. They teach students that a child's first language is a bridge to her second language, and that it positively affects the acquisition of her second language. Equally important is the inclusion of children's native languages in the curriculum.

Miller-Endo (2004) acknowledged the high stress of English language learners, along with the importance of reducing their anxiety and increasing their motivation and self-esteem.

The social-emotional lives of children in schools: education for participation in a democracy. Children bring their emotional selves to the classroom. Their chances for academic success, and the climate of the classroom, are affected by the range of their feelings. When they bring with them the stress and trauma of coping with violence, alcoholism, emotional abandonment, neglect, or loss, there is a significant negative impact. Helfat (1973) writes:

> When we try to learn more about the children who cause problems in our classrooms, we find that they are for the most part youngsters who are expressing a great deal of anger and hurt feelings. These are the children who are so preoccupied with psychic needs, who have so many emotional battles to fight, that it is almost impossible for them to devote themselves to learning. (p. 31)

The Early Childhood Education Program at Lesley has long recognized the critical importance of tending to the emotional lives of schoolchildren, and to their emotional traumas, near and far. Sondra Langer, chair of the graduate program in early childhood education from 1979 to 2006, developed a course to help teachers support children in coping with emotional issues. In the wake of the tragedies of September 11, 2001, Professor Mary Mindess invited early childhood educators Nancy Carlsson-Paige, Mary Beth Lawton, and others to the New England Kindergarten Conference, where they exchanged ideas with teachers and generated strategies for helping children cope. Professor Lisa Fiore, current chair of the graduate program in early childhood education, coauthored the book *Your Anxious Child: How Parents and Teachers Can Relieve Anxiety in Children* (Dacey & Fiore, 2000). Dacey and Fiore's work helps adults cope with children's anxiety and stress through teaching children self-comforting strategies, breathing techniques, meditation, and problem-solving strategies. In "The Case of Miss D," in his book *From Basketball to the Beatles: In Search of Compelling Early Childhood Curriculum,* Lesley professor Ben Mardell encourages teachers to meet the emotional and relational (attachment) needs of children with problematic behaviors instead of resorting to rewards and punishment (Mardell, 1999).

In the early 1980s, a rise in poverty, a diminution of family and neighborhood supports, and a high divorce rate caused concerns about the impact of these trends on children and families (Krasnow, Seigle, & Kelly, 1994). Recognizing that many children were entering schools without the ability to emotionally communicate and relate to others, the National Institute of Mental Health encouraged schools to develop social-emotional curricula to address problematic behavior in the classroom. Through affective (social-emotional) curricula, children learn how to participate in a group; develop codes of conduct for group and classroom participation; develop respect for similarities and differences; learn democratic principles such as cooperation, problem solving, and cooperation; and learn specific social-emotional skills such as how to listen and how to express anger in appropriate ways (NAEYC, 2001).

A growing body of research indicates that social competency skills are linked to social and academic success and to success in life (Seigle, Lange, & Macklem, 1997). Academic success is more likely when children feel they are accepted and welcome in the classroom community (Goleman, 1995; Goleman, 1998; Hennessey, 2007; Krasnow, et al., 1994).

In 1991, in response to teachers' concerns about children's social-emotional skills and the rise of violence in schools, Lesley faculty members Nancy Carlsson-Paige and Linda Brion-Meisels created the Center for Peaceable Schools. Their articulated goal for the center was "a vision…of peaceable schools, places where the ideals of democracy and diversity would be put into practice in the curriculum, social life and governance of schools" (Center for Peaceable Schools website). Over the years, the center, "rooted in the values of equity and social justice," has supported educators and community leaders through professional development, consultation, and research. In 1993, Lesley offered the First Annual Summer Institute of Peaceable Schools. That same year, Nancy Carlsson-Paige, in partnership with Educators for Social Responsibility, cofounded the nation's first master of education in conflict resolution and peaceable schools.

CONCLUSION

Lesley early childhood students, responding to the needs of immigrant English language learners and supporting children in creating peaceful, respectful communities in which the "good of all is the concern of all" and in which they can realize their potential, bring us back full circle to the dream of Edith Lesley. Much has changed in early childhood education since Edith Lesley's time, owing to the influence of major thinkers and sociopolitical movements. Unquestionably, however, many of the values of Edith Lesley—education as a tool for social justice; the centrality of creativity, the arts, and play; and the importance of collaboration between schools and families—have remained constant at Lesley University over the past 100 years, and the best of forces from outside the school have been integrated with these core ideals.

REFERENCES

"'A vocation from on high': The birth of early childhood education." *Lesley College Current*. Vol. VII, No.1.

Baig, B. (Winter 1984; Spring 1985). *Lesley College Current*, 1 6. Lesley University Archives.

Baig, B. (1984). Lesley College Graduate School: The first thirty years. Lesley University Archives. Lesley University, Cambridge, MA.

Beatty, B. (1995). Preschool education in America. New Haven, CT: Yale University Press.

Beatty, B. (October 2003). Oral History: Cynthia Brown and Alyssa Pacy Interview. Lesley University Oral History Archive, University Archives. Cambridge, MA.

Bloom, B. (1964). Stability and change in human characteristics. New York, NY: John Wiley.

Bruner, J. (1960). The process of education. Cambridge, MA: Harvard University Press.

Carlsson-Paige, N. (2008). Taking back childhood: Helping your kids thrive in a fast-paced, media-saturated, violence-filled world. New York, NY: Hudson Street Press.

"Conference expands to Mid-Atlantic states." (Winter 1980). *Lesley College Current.* Vol. VII, No.1.

Cordasco, F. (1976). Bilingual schooling in the United States. New York, NY: McGraw Hill.

Dacey, J., & Fiore, L. (2000). Your anxious child: How parents and teachers can relieve anxiety in children. New York, NY: Jossey Bass.

Dewey, J. (1916). Democracy and education: An introduction to the philosophy of education. New York, NY: Macmillan.

Edwards, C., Gandini, L., & Forman, G. (1998). The hundred languages of children: The Reggio-Emilia approach—advanced reflections. Greenwich, CT: Ablex Publishing Corp.

Ellis, L. A., Jones, K., & Szamreta, J. (2006). Everybody's baby: Early education and care for infants and toddlers. Schott Foundation. Unpublished position paper.

Ellsworth, E. (1988). The Froebelian kindergarten movement 1850 1880: An international crusade for political and social progress. Boston, MA: Wheelock College.

Epstein, J. L. (2001). School, family and community partnerships. Boulder, CO: Westview Press.

Epstein, J. L., & Sanders, M. G. (2002). Family, school and community partnerships. In M. H. Bornstein (Ed.), Handbook of parenting (2nd ed.). Malwah, NJ: Erlbaum.

Epstein, J. L., Sanders, M. G., Salinas, K. C., Simon, B.S, Jansorn, N. R., & Van Voorhis, F. L. (2002). School, family and community partnerships. (2nd ed.). Thousand Oaks, CA: Corwin Press.

Erikson, E. H. (1963). Childhood and society. New York, NY: W. W. Norton.

Erikson, E. H. (1968). Identity, youth and crisis. New York, NY: W.W. Norton.

Evans, E. B. (1973). Day care: How to plan, develop and operate a day care center. Boston, MA: Beacon Press.

Evans, E. B., Saia, G., & Evans, E. E. (1974). Designing a day care center: How to select, design and develop a day care center. Boston, MA: Beacon Press.

Featherstone, J. (1971). Schools where children learn. New York, NY: Liveright Publishing Corporation.

Fiore, L. B., & Suarez, S. C. (Eds.). (2010). Observation, documentation and reflection to create a culture of inquiry. *Theory into Practice, 49*(1).

Forman, G., & Landry, C. (2000). The constructivist perspective on early education: Application to children's museums. In J. L. Roopnarine & J. E. Johnson (Eds.),Approaches to early childhood education. Upper Saddle River, NJ: Prentice Hall.

Gandini, L., Caldwell, L., & Schwall, C. (Eds.). (2005). In the spirit of the studio: Learning from the atelier of Reggio Emilia. New York, NY: Teachers College Press.

Gardner, H. (1993). Multiple intelligences. New York, NY: Basic Books.

Goleman, D. (1995). Emotional intelligence: Why it can matter more than IQ. New York, NY: Bantam Books

Goleman, D. (1998). Working with emotional intelligence. New York, NY: Bantam Books.

Grant, C. A. (Winter, 1994). Challenging the myths about multicultural education. *Multicultural Education, 2*(2).

Helfat, L. (October, 1973). The gut level needs of kids. *Learning: The magazine for creative teaching,* 31 34.

Henderson, A. T. (1987). The evidence continues to grow: Parent involvement improves student achievement. National Committee for Citizens in Education: Columbia, MD.

Hennessey, B. (June, 2007). Promoting social competence in school-age children: The effects of the Open Circle Program. *Journal of Social Psychology, 45*(3), 349 360.

Hunt, J. M. (1961) Intelligence and experience. New York, NY: Ronald Press.

Kagan, J. (1980). Responding to individual differences: Proceedings of the 1980 New England Kindergarten Conference. Lesley College. Cambridge, MA.

Karen, R. (1998). Becoming attached: First relationships and how they shape our capacity to love. New York, NY: Oxford Press.

Keliher, A. (1963). New Directions in Kindergarten Programs: Proceedings of the 1963 New England Kindergarten Conference. Lesley College, Cambridge, MA.

Krasnow, J. H., Seigle, P. J., & Kelly, R. (1994). Social Competency Program: Reach Out to Schools Project. Retrieved April 10, 2009, from http: //www.eric.ed.gov/Eric web portal/record detail/ 361830-30K

Lascarides, V. C., & Hinitz, B. F. (2000). The history of early childhood education. New York, NY: Falmer Press.

Lesley, Edith. Biographical data. Lesley University Archives. Lesley University, Cambridge, MA.

Lesley, Edith. Papers. Lesley University Archives. Lesley University, Cambridge, MA.

Lesley University Archives. Lesley University, Cambridge, MA.

Lesley University Catalogues. 1909 2009. Lesley University Archives. Lesley University, Cambridge, MA.

Lesley University Center for Peaceable Schools Website. Retrieved March 22, 2009, from http://www.lesley.edu/academic_centers/peace/institute.html

Mardell, B. (1997). From basketball to the Beatles: In search of compelling early childhood curriculum. Portsmouth, NH: Heinemann.

Mardell, B. (2008). An example of developmentally appropriate curriculum study: The Boston Marathon curriculum. In C. Copple & S. Bredekamp (Eds.), Developmentally appropriate practice in early childhood programs serving children birth to age 8. (3rd ed.). Washington, D.C.: NAEYC.

McBride, B., & Barbour, N. (Eds.). (2003). Bridging the gap between theory, research and practice: The role of child development laboratory programs in early childhood education. *Advances in early education and day care, 12*. Boston, MA: Elsevier JAI.

Miller, P., & Endo, H. (June 2004). Understanding and meeting the needs of ESL students. Phi Delta Kappan.

Mindess, M. (2008). When two cultures meet. In L. Gandini, S.

Etheredge, & L. Hall (Eds.), Insights and inspirations from Reggio Emilia: Stories from teachers and children from North America. Worcester, MA: Davis.

Mindess, M., & Elitov, P. (1979). Creating educational opportunities in the least restrictive environment for young children with special needs: A training manual. Supported by a grant from the Massachusetts Department of Education.

National Association for the Education of Young Children Initial Licensure Standards. (July 2001).

Nourot, P. M. (2000). Historical perspectives on early childhood education. In J. L. Roopnarine & J. E. Johnson (Eds.), Approaches to early childhood Education. Upper Saddle River, NJ: Prentice Hall.

Osborn, D. K. (1991). Early childhood education in historical perspective. Athens, GA: Educational Associates.

Piaget, J. (1951). The child's conception of the world. Savage, MD: Littlefield Adams.

Piaget, J., & Inhelder, B. (1969). The psychology of the child. (H. Weaver, Trans.) New York, NY: Basic Books.

Pressman, J. (2008). Advanced reflections on the Reggio-Emilia approach: Investing in listening. Unpublished paper.

Ramey, C. T., & Ramey, S. L. (February 1998). Early intervention and early experience. *American Psychologist. 53*(2), 109 120.

Rinaldi, C. (2006). In dialogue with Reggio-Emilia: Listening, responding and learning. New York, NY: Routledge.

Salkind, N. (2004). An introduction to theories of development. Thousand Oaks, CA: Sage Publications.

Santrock, J. W. (2007). Children. (9th ed.). Boston, MA: McGraw Hill.

Schweinhart, L. J., Barnes, H. V., & Weikart, D. P. (1973). Significant Benefits: The High Scope Perry Preschool Study through age 27. Monographs of the High/Scope Educational Research Foundation, No. 10. Ypsilanti, MI: High Scope Press.

Schweinhart, L. J., & Weikart, D. B. (1997). Lasting differences: The High Scope preschool curriculum comparison study through age 23. Ypsilanti, MI: High Scope Press.

Schweinhart, L. J., Weikart, D. B., & Larner, M. B. (1986). Consequences of three preschool models through age 16. *Early Childhood Research Quarterly, 1,* 15 45.

Seigle, P., Lange, L., & Macklem, G. (1997). Open Circle Curriculum, Reach out to Schools Social Competency Program, The Stone Center, Wellesley College, Wellesley, MA.

Shore, R. (1997). Rethinking the brain: New insights in early development. New York, NY: Families and Work Institute.

Slattery, J. (Winter, 1984; Spring, 1985). A brief birthday speech for Lesley College. *The Lesley College Current,* Vol. XI, No. 2.

Stoddard, G. (1933). Proceedings of the National Association of Nursery Education. (Fifth Conference). New York, NY: NANE, 1993.

Tatum, B. (1997). The complexity of identity: Who am I? Why are all the black kids sitting together in the cafeteria and other conversations about race. New York, NY: Basic Books.

Vygotsky, L. (1978). The mind in society: The development of higher psychological process. Cambridge, MA: Harvard University Press.

Weikart, D. (1973). Quality Education Makes a Difference: Proceedings of the 1973 New England Kindergarten Conference. Lesley College, Cambridge, MA.

Wolfard, M. (1953). ACEI Collections. University of Maryland, Lesley University Archives. Lesley University, Cambridge, MA.

Wong-Fillmore, L. (2000). Making a Difference: Proceedings of the 2000 New England Kindergarten Conference. Lesley College, Cambridge, MA.

Wortham, S. C. (1992). Childhood: 1892 1992. Wheaton, MD: Association for Childhood International.

CHAPTER THREE

Froebel and the Firefly: Legacies of Excellence in Teaching

Julia Byers, EdD, ATR-BC, LMHC
Matthew Hirshberg, PhD
Priscilla Sanville, PhD

Excellence in teaching is a complex process that is not easily measured quantitatively. In 2008, as a result of a Graduate School of Arts and Social Sciences (GSASS) grant, six Lesley University professors, including the three authors of this chapter, met to explore that topic. In the spirit of the Lesley mission and in light of the Lesley centennial, we not only shared narratives of teachable moments as exemplars of unexpected instances in which our interactions with students led to special insight and learning, but also investigated our historical roots. Alyssa Pacy, centennial archivist at Lesley University, helped us discover the first documented cases of some extraordinary graduates, and Celia Morris, a Lesley colleague, helped us craft our narrative. To our profound surprise, we "found" a living legacy, one of the first degree recipients in Lesley College, Lois Zimmerman, or, as she is known when she tells stories, Firefly. This chapter provides a brief summary of the six interview sessions conducted by the authors with Lois in May and June of 2009, along with quotations from those interviews. Personal narratives from the grant participants were transcribed during the grant period. We focused on excellence in teaching and the development of social competency through the themes of empowerment, growth, conflict, active discovery, and the student-centered approach.

We will start with some background on Lois Zimmerman. Twenty-three young women graduated in the Lesley College class of 1945. Thirteen received diplomas in teaching and five in home economics. But the real stars of the June 10, 1945, Commencement were the five women who had accomplished something new—they earned bachelor of science degrees in education, the first ever awarded by Lesley College.

Of those five trailblazers, Lois Zimmerman was the most noticeable. She told us that whispers were audible as she walked down the aisle to receive her diploma, in a cap and gown, visibly pregnant. Those were still the days when aspiring young teachers were expected to remain unmarried and certainly childless. Lois, born "Loie" Milton, had "willfully" married Donald Zimmerman in December of her senior year, but, as she put it, "I had not expected such quick results."

Such behavior was not always tolerated at Lesley. As Lois explained:

> The dean and the powers that be had to meet to decide whether they would allow a pregnant student to be at Lesley, because she might teach the other girls things they shouldn't know. Well, little did they know what some of these girls knew!

The decision was made in the affirmative, and thus it was that Lois Zimmerman completed her degree and marched with her class, perhaps making her doubly a pioneer on that June day.

"I HAD PERISHED HAD I NOT PERSISTED"

The education that Lois Zimmerman and the other four trailblazing graduates in the class of 1945 received was grounded in Lesley University's traditional emphasis on experiential learning, which stemmed from the school's roots in the work of German pedagogue and kindergarten pioneer Friedrich Froebel. As we learned from our research, preserving that tradition has not always been easy.[3] Edith Lesley's husband, Merl Wolfard, reported that the motto on the original Lesley School coat of arms was "perissem ni perstissem," which means "I had perished had I not persisted." Lesley indeed persisted. As teaching became an increasingly academic profession, the school continued to develop itself and its mission, while remaining true to its philosophical roots.

During Lesley's first 100 years, trends toward structured, academic teaching have sometimes conflicted with the original emphasis on spontaneous, experiential learning. Over those years, the growing importance of obtaining academic degrees certified by accreditations and assessments has required educators, both at the college level and in the schools, to spend more time teaching to achieve academic goals and less time cultivating students' holistic growth and creativity.

Even so, while Lesley has developed into a strong academic university with a broad array of scholarly and professional courses, experiential learning has remained at the heart of its pedagogy. At Lesley, faculty members typically allow time for flowing spontaneity in their courses, and professor-facilitated activities provide opportunities for student-driven learning. We concluded that excellent teachers let go of habits and take risks, opening their classrooms to possibilities for creative group experiences that transcend the presentation of academic material.

Generations of graduates have emerged from Lesley well versed in their academic fields and aware of the educational importance of play and experiential learning. Those graduates, including Lois Zimmerman, have glided out like fireflies, enlightening each successive generation with their neo-Froebelian luminescence.

---

3 After Edith Lesley's death, Merl Ruskin Wolfard, her husband, provided extensive reminiscences about her tenure at Lesley in a long letter. Much of our understanding of her thoughts comes from that secondhand document and from letters written by Edith Lesley as well as from perusal of the college catalogues, meeting minutes, and articles in the school newspaper (*The Lantern*) and yearbook (*The Lesleyan*), all of which can be found in the Lesley Archives.

LESLEY COLLEGE IN THE 1940S

During the early 20th century, Lesley followed many other teacher preparation schools by adding first a three-year and then a four-year program option to its foundational two-year program. The school's 1940–1941 catalogue noted a trend in teacher education toward "full academic training," and claimed that the proposed Lesley four-year program was "designed to meet the requirements of states where a four year Teacher-training course is required, but not necessarily a degree." The four-year bachelor of science in education degree was finally authorized by the state in time to award the first degrees in 1945.

In 1945, *The Lesleyan* reported that Lois Zimmerman was named the "most sophisticated" member of her graduating class. By the time she reconnected with Lesley in 2009, after 64 years filled with parenting, teaching, and professional clowning, Lois was well past sophistication. The words of folksinger Bob Dylan (1964) come to mind: "Ah, but I was so much older then; I'm younger than that now."

Bright, energetic, and in her 80s, Lois beamed herself from her home in Ann Arbor, Michigan, onto our computer screen via Skype. We were eager to learn from one of Lesley's very first four-year degree recipients. She was more than happy to comply. "I don't know how I ended up at Lesley," she said with a grin, "but I'm glad I did."

Lois told us that she had always wanted to be a teacher, and when her parents sent her to a liberal arts college in Connecticut, she intentionally failed a course in order to be allowed to transfer to a teacher's college. She remembers that her parents were initially interested in a school founded by Miss Wheelock, but they eventually decided to send her to Lesley in 1942, leaving her well placed to take advantage of the new four-year degree program.

At Lesley, Lois's favorite teacher was the popular professor Mark Crockett. A retrospective, published in the May 31, 1961, edition of the Lesley school newspaper, *The Lantern*, reported that during his 23-year tenure, Crockett was legendary for his lively lectures, charismatic personality, and penetrating blue eyes. Lois remembered that Dr.

Crockett, a social studies professor, made history come alive and brought politics into the classroom. She recalled that in 1944 she brought her first absentee ballot with her to her Government and United States History class, and Crockett focused the discussion on voting and the candidates on her ballot. Lois proudly stood at the grand piano that sat in the front of the classroom, and marked her ballot right there. She felt doubly special, as the star of her beloved professor's "show" and as a valued voting citizen of her country. Lois has cherished that moment (and has voted) ever since. This demonstrates the sense of empowerment and growth that the expertise of an excellent Lesley professor helped her obtain.

Lois was on the 1945 yearbook staff, and that year's Lesleyan was dedicated to Mark Crockett. The inscription reads, "His greatness lies in the manner in which he meets life." Dr. Crockett was a key player in the transformation of Lesley School into Lesley College. On December 13, 1941, minutes report that he was elected first president of the board of trustees and first chairman of the newly formed Corporation of the College (the two bodies had mostly overlapping membership at their inceptions). As board president he was an ex officio member of all its committees, and he undoubtedly played a major role in Lesley's transition to a degree-granting academic college. According to the May 31, 1961, edition of *The Lantern*, Dr. Crockett chaired the original Curriculum Committee and was involved in the development of the new college curriculum. On January 18, 1943, the minutes indicate that he was unanimously reelected to the board of trustees, as president, and to a four-person executive committee that included founder Edith Lesley Wolfard and school principal Gertrude Malloch. As the year progressed, conflict plagued Lesley's governing bodies, though the details are not clear. The date of Dr. Crockett's last appearance in Corporation minutes is June 22, 1943. When the Corporation elected a new board of trustees on July 7 of that year, Crockett's name was not on the list.

Dr. Walter Dearborn, elected to replace Dr. Crockett as president, received a letter from Edith Lesley Wolfard, dated October 16, 1943, that evoked a sense of the tensions of the times at Lesley: "I have of course been very troubled of late years about the future status of the school and particularly its change to a college." The exact nature of her concerns remains unknown. We might speculate that while she and others realized that the survival and relevance of Lesley depended on its becoming a full college, there may have lingered a sense of unease about how this change would affect the ideals of the kindergarten-focused mission that had informed the school from its founding.

CHANGING GOALS, ENDURING VALUES

What exactly was Lesley's first mission? The Lesley Normal School originally focused on kindergarten training, and the teachings of Friedrich Froebel dominated the curriculum, including his emphasis on play. Once trained in this pedagogy, a teacher could use Froebel's methods to guide children through playful processes of active discovery, and to channel their play into organic experiences of self-expression, empowerment, and growth (Baader, 2004). To this day Lesley's enduring emphasis on student-centered experiential learning has its philosophical roots deeply grounded in Froebel's ideas.

By the time Lois Zimmerman arrived at Lesley in 1942, the school's course catalogue included offerings in English, social studies, psychology, and music, as well as a variety of approaches to education. But the Froebelian tradition still lay at the heart of Lesley's pedagogy. Lois and her classmates learned about the educational importance of play and physical activity (kinesthetic learning) and had plenty of opportunity to try out the new songs and games, and they also learned—so Lois remembers—with the children as their teachers.

After graduating, Lois had four children of her own, and it was 1966 when she started her career as a kindergarten teacher. Still, she never forgot what she had learned at Lesley. "I put it to good use when I had the chance," she told us. In her years as a kindergarten teacher, Lois was partial to the noncompetitive circle games that give each child a turn to shine most brightly. In one of her favorites, one child (we'll call her Shana) would begin in the center of the circle. The game would begin with the circle singing, "What can you do, Shana, Shana?

What can you do, Shana, today?" Shana would wave her hands and jump up and down, or otherwise strut her stuff. Her classmates would sing, "We can do it too!" They would join her in movement and then sing, "Who do you choose?" Shana would choose the next star, and around they would go.

Of course, Lois played too. "During my turn," she explained, "I would choose the less popular children, who might otherwise be ignored by their classmates." Every child ended up feeling included and special, and they all learned to take turns leading and following. In the process, they developed motor skills and blew off some steam. And it was fun for all, especially for Lois Zimmerman.

About her teaching career, Lois said, "I used to think I shouldn't really be paid for doing something I enjoyed so much." But she is also keenly aware of her impact on her students. "Kindergarten was their first experience in education," she said. "It could color their feelings about school for the rest of their lives." And apparently her students felt that way as well. She was deeply honored when a group of graduating high school students, years later, remembered their kindergarten teacher, Lois Zimmerman, and presented her with a teaching excellence award.

After 16 years of teaching kindergarten, Lois began teaching "readiness first grade," a class for kindergarten graduates deemed not yet mature enough to succeed in first grade. She was aware that these children, having been held back from first grade, might be demoralized by feelings of inferiority and inadequacy. To teach reading, she used a program called Super Kids, developed by Pleasant Rowland for Addison-Wesley. This provided Lois with an effective way to bolster and maintain the children's collective self-esteem. "We just became the Super Kids," she recalled. "The kids in the story in the program formed a Super-Kids Club, so our classroom became our own Super-Kids Club. We were a very special group of people. I was a Super Kid too, of course."

After a few years, Lois's Super-Kids Club received new recruits when Indianapolis's court-ordered desegregation program bused underprivileged inner-city African American children to her school in Wayne Township, Indiana. Lois remembers vividly one of those new students, a little girl named Patty. Lois loved to watch the children come in the door in the morning "with big smiles on their faces, just saying, 'What exciting thing is going to happen today?'" Sometimes Patty came in like that—excited and ready for action. Sometimes she just waited outside the door to be invited in. Sometimes she would mix right in with the other children. Sometimes she would come in, sit down, and cry. Lois always found ways to bridge Patty's involvement in the class, and even today thinks lovingly of her.

Before desegregation, Lois's readiness first grade class consisted of children who had benefited from an excellent kindergarten but still had needed a year to mature enough to do well in first grade. With desegregation, she found that the buses brought children who were mature but who were inadequately prepared for first grade. The two groups needed entirely different types of teaching, and her frustrated attempts to serve both at the same time ended up serving neither. "I still feel bad," she said, "that I couldn't help either group adequately." After her requests to have the class split up were turned down, she decided that she was not willing to teach under such conditions.

LEARNING FROM KINDERGARTENS

Lois took early retirement in 1985 but did not leave the field of teaching. She spent 16 years—two days a week—helping her daughter teach readiness first grade for language-delayed children, and she still tutors kindergartners. She is the epitome of a Lesley-educated lifelong learner.

"Edith Lesley Wolfard," said Lois, "would be very unhappy to see kindergartens today, because they're so structured, so academic. There's very little play and very little spontaneity." Lois blames this trend on the influence of the federal No Child Left Behind legislation, which she feels squeezes out spontaneity and play, depriving kindergartners of crucial opportunities to use and develop their imaginations. A number of educators believe the standardized exams now pervasive in the country have squeezed out play in curricula; the emphasis on academics has even led to the elimination of recess in some states (Jeynes, 2006). "By emphasizing standardized testing and rigorous academics, pre-first grade in the United States acts merely as an extension of subsequent elementary years, which Froebel never intended" (Jeynes, 2006, p. 1953).

The problem is an old one; standardized tests of educational success are used to hold educators accountable and to make sure that education dollars are spent in ways that yield measurable results. The tests measure academic attainment, but they do not tap the sorts of things that children develop particularly well in classic kindergarten environments, such as imagination, creativity, efficacy, enthusiasm, and self-discipline. Schools and their teachers today are saddled with the practical task of preparing students for tests first, life second. This motivates early childhood educators to spend less time on stories, songs, and play and more time on reading, writing, and arithmetic.

Froebel believed that the three Rs do not belong in kindergarten; rather time is better spent on the whole child's "spiritual and character development," through guided play activities with a "well-trained and motherly teacher" (Dombkowski, 2001, p. 528). Once students are developmentally ready to learn to read, they will do so in elementary school, Froebel believed. "We notice," he wrote, "that if children are not given the care which takes their stage of human development into consideration, they will lack the foundation for the task ahead in school and for their later lives in general" (http://www.friedrichfroebel.com).

In Lesley's early days, kindergartens were on the fringe of American education—only about one in 10 U.S. schools had kindergartens in 1920. As the country progressed toward almost universal kindergarten by the 1980s, the nonacademic, play-centered methods of Froebelian kindergartens were subjected to increased scrutiny (Dombkowski, 2001). Why waste time and money on kids playing around, when kindergartners could get an early start on the academic learning they would continue in elementary school? "Time and again," writes Kristin Dombkowski, "the nonacademic emphasis of the kindergarten has come under attack. Time and again, the kindergarten has struggled

95

to define itself in relationship to the public primary school" (p. 528).

Pressure to "beef up" kindergarten has been particularly strong when it has seemed that the United States was losing its economic or technological dominance in the world. Yet, as Mitchel Resnick, director of the Lifelong Kindergarten group at the MIT Media Lab, suggests, creative thinking skills are key to success in a competitive world. He argues that kindergartens in the Froebelian tradition develop creative thinking by empowering children to imagine, create, play, share, reflect, and imagine some more. When academically oriented worksheets and flashcards invade kindergartens, students are deprived of crucial creativity-building experiences. "Instead of making kindergarten like the rest of school," he writes, "we need to make the rest of school (indeed, the rest of life) more like kindergarten" (Resnick, 2007, p.1).

This tension between experiential and academic pedagogy exists at all educational levels—even in universities. While some room may still be preserved in early childhood education for playful, spontaneous learning experiences guided by nurturing teachers in homey classrooms, as children progress up the grades they are met with increasingly structured academic lessons delivered by authoritative teachers or professors in sterile, regimented settings. The transition from kindergarten through the school grades eases future workers out of their childhood homes and into the workplace. Almost invariably, highly structured, academic education is the norm by high school, and few universities leave much room for experiential learning and educational play.

At Lesley this tension has played out in a unique way. Historically, Lesley has survived by expanding its offerings and adjusting its pedagogy to fit changing social, political, legal, technical, and economic realities. In the process, Lesley has moved strongly, if incrementally, in the academic direction. The degree requirements and standardized tests that aspiring teachers must pass to be certified to teach have affected teacher training at Lesley.

But not everyone has welcomed these developments, and there has been strong counterpressure. The road has not always been easy. Even Edith Lesley Wolfard apparently had very mixed feelings as she helped the institution she founded as a Froebelian school for kindergarten teachers to transform itself into a liberal arts college. In the reminiscence Merl Wolfard wrote after Edith's death, he spoke of her divided sentiments:

> Mrs. Wolfard was a disciple of Froebel and endeavored to teach through "doing" as far as is practicable… Mrs. Wolfard's spirit was a little saddened when…the trend in education drifted toward the requirement of a more academic training for kindergarten and elementary teachers. Nonetheless, Mrs. Wolfard did cooperate diligently with educational accrediting committees and with the requirements of the educational authorities in Massachusetts, which led up to the establishment of Lesley College and its wide accreditation as a college devoted to educational activities. (Wolfard, n.d.)

EXCELLENCE IN TEACHING

In its first 100 years Lesley University has distinguished itself as an academic institution with a strong emphasis on experiential learning, derived in large measure from Froebelian influences; and that emphasis has been revisited and reviewed in recent years. For undergraduates and many graduate students, experiential courses are required, along with internships or student teaching. Class size is kept small to encourage student participation. Student-driven discussions and group exercises, rather than formal lectures, are the instructional norm. Lesley's conscious effort to combine academic and experiential learning is part of what makes it a very special place. Continuing with this legacy and the centrality of "experience" at Lesley University today, we now turn to the discussions with professors that took place as part of a GSASS initiative.

In the spring of 2008, six Lesley professors began meeting to discuss the nature of excellent teaching and to identify the attributes and methods of Lesley's most excellent teachers. The group included the three authors of this chapter, with Julia Byers as chair, along with Alexandra Johnson, Amy Morrison, and Donna Newman Bluestein. We examined the kind of teaching that developed and continues to develop students such as Lois Zimmerman. The six participants represented a variety of fields, including social science, human services, creative writing, expressive therapies, and creative arts and learning. The group included undergraduate and graduate teachers, core and adjunct faculty, old hands and relative newcomers to Lesley. The diversity of the group yielded rich discussions through which we identified common themes and principles of teaching excellence that transcend the boundaries of disciplines. The discussion that follows flowed from the interviews with Lois Zimmerman; the brainstorming sessions that formed the impetus for this chapter; and continued reflection on the relevance of the Lesley University mission to the subjects discussed here.

The university's website proclaims the school's clearly articulated mission:

> Lesley University is committed to active learning, scholarly research, critical inquiry, and diverse forms of artistic practice through close mentoring relationships among students, faculty, and practitioners in the field. Lesley prepares graduates with the knowledge, skill, understanding, and ethical judgment to be catalysts who shape a more just, humane, and sustainable world. (http://www.lesley.edu/about/mission-and-values.html)

Guided by this mission, our six-member panel reasoned that excellence in teaching is displayed to the extent that teachers empower their students to make life better for themselves and others. Many themes emerged from our discussions on the topic of excellence in teaching.

We concluded that part of the Lesley professor's job is indeed to facilitate the attainment of academic skills and knowledge. Lesley graduates, who gain professional skills, specialized knowledge, and the ability to demonstrate academic achievement, are empowered to make a difference. But to make a significant, positive difference, graduates must also possess inquiring minds, creativity, wisdom, compassion, ethics, enthusiasm, and practical experience. Excellent Lesley professors manage to foster all these attributes in their students. Excellent professors approach their teaching holistically, with the higher goal of preparing their students for the many demands of a life of service. But they never forget that teaching advanced skills and knowledge is a fundamental part of their job.

EMPOWERMENT AND GROWTH THROUGH CREATIVE CONFLICT

In our discussions about excellence in teaching, we discovered that for all of us, teaching well has required negotiating the tension between careful pedagogical planning of academically grounded lessons and flexible openness to the organic flow of an engaged classroom. We agreed that although it is tempting to play it safe and strictly structure our teaching, it is crucial to risk allowing room for those unpredictable moments when the deepest learning can take place. In taking that risk, however, it is important not to use precious class time to indulge in unfocused diversions of tangential value.

Donna Newman Bluestein emphasized the importance of not letting students derail the classroom learning, and described her way of dealing with it. Creatively she names the disagreement with a topic or circumstance and then moves forward with the curriculum goals of the day. She remembers a time when a student who misunderstood a curriculum task was acting out and purposely not agreeing with the direction of the class. The student's response was clearly triggered by something in her prior experience. Newman Bluestein chose to explore the behavior with her student after class, reflecting on the meaning of the resistance and of her own response so that both parties could learn from the experience. She was very tempted to have this discussion in the class but realized that the content was too subjective.

An excellent teacher is able to plan classroom processes that allow relevant learning to unfold from spontaneous interactions. Another effective method is to elicit conflict, or cognitive dissonance, by challenging strongly held beliefs, presenting perplexing dilemmas, or initiating discussion on controversial topics. As students work through conflicting perspectives in the classroom and in their individual minds, and later reflect on them, they can be guided to process material deeply and exercise their reasoning muscles, building empowerment and growth.

There was a time when Prilly Sanville was teaching in a Lesley off-campus program, in a graduate course on drama and critical literacy. One day, during a discussion of class and race, two students became very angry with each other. She described what happened next:

> It was a moment of cognitive dissonance for all in the class. This occurred right before lunch, so I let the students go to lunch. I sat and thought, What do I do now? This has to be addressed, but how? And then I knew I had to trust who I was and not what I knew. When the students came back I acknowledged the incident and then asked, "Are we agreed we are all professionals here, and we are here to make the world better for the children we teach?" Then I proceeded to do an experiential learning through drama teaching, using Augusto Boal's Theater of the Oppressed tools. The students chose a common social situation which they all could relate to. Then I facilitated their work in groups, role playing from different human perspectives within the chosen situation. It was an eye-opening moment. The class atmosphere changed and the playing field was leveled. The group came together and crossed racial and class divides not only in the drama work but also in their reflective discussion. I had taken a risk in bringing the conflict into the class curriculum, but in the process gained a sense of awe in trusting the students' outcome. I witnessed educators coming forward to support each other in a way that I had not been sure was possible in this particular class.

The teacher's role is to allow the learning process to develop organically while keeping it on track. Doing this well requires a sharp focus and a light but strong and precise touch. It is only after years of preparation and practice that the teaching professional can walk into a classroom with the confidence and experience necessary to lead and follow the flow of collective learning.

Thus, expecting the unexpected is another skill that excellent teachers must have as their practice. Prilly Sanville told of another formative experience in her teaching career:

> A moment in teaching that goes back many years and that has deeply informed my teaching is a time I was teaching middle school students in an after-school program designed to keep youth off the streets. This was an urban setting in New England. This experience informed my teaching at an early stage of my career and has been part of my foundation in working with teachers at Lesley.
>
> I was teaching a drama class with a mixed group of Latino and Hispanic, African American, and European American students, mostly from working class families. We were very engaged in drama. One afternoon, two unannounced high school students walked into the classroom. The tallest, and clearly the leader, pulled out a knife. Immediately all the students hid behind me. It was a frozen moment. In one split second, I humored myself, thinking that the children thought I was their shield and that I could protect them as the young man towered over me pointing the knife. I looked this young man dead straight in the eye. I saw that he wanted to say something. His face did not appear threatening, but he actually looked afraid. I asked him to please put down the knife as he was scaring all of us. He seemed to forget he had the threatening knife in his hand but now knew he had our attention. He said he needed to talk with me. I said I couldn't talk to him if he had a knife. Again he looked perplexed that he actually had a knife, but proceeded to close it and give it to me. Subsequently,

he said, "It isn't fair that the middle school kids have drama and the high school kids don't have a drama class." He was here because he wanted a drama class! I suddenly realized that this young man only knew power through the threat of a weapon, not by using words or organizing. I knew this was a crucial moment in learning. It was not okay that he had pulled a knife, but there was also an opportunity to learn in the classroom about the role of advocacy. I could teach him and his friends to do things differently at least in this setting. I told him I agreed with his comment and that later, after the class was dismissed, I would assist him in organizing a group to present a proposal to the director for drama for the high school students. (I also let him know he needed to face consequences for using the knife most inappropriately in the building and scaring us. The director of the program was responsible to follow up with remediation, since I did not press official charges.) The high school youth did finally receive a drama program. But this was only after the director and I negotiated and used a process that taught the youth another way of relating to the school rules, policies, and behaviors. This experience of on-the-job training early in my career taught me how to look at power and about the importance of understanding the underlying dynamics of power in assisting teachers and students. To this day, teaching about power is a cornerstone of my teaching. This frightened young man was my teacher that day.

At Lesley, both at the undergraduate and postgraduate levels, tensions between experiential and academic learning have surfaced in a discourse about the issue of rigor. Some ambitious students have felt that various courses have not been intellectually challenging enough and have not contributed sufficiently to their academic advancement. At the same time, some faculty members have been concerned with the general academic achievement levels of their students. This has led us into creative conflict as we discuss how standards of academic rigor can be raised and maintained. As Lesley University moves into its second century, we find ourselves grappling in particular with how best to use new technologies to enhance our pedagogical practices while maintaining Lesley's enduring Froebelian emphasis on active learning through experience. This topic is increasingly important as we experiment with various formats for distributed learning. Siemens and Matheos (2010) contend that there are benefits we have yet to realize:

> Emerging technologies offer faculty additional opportunities to increase engagement with colleagues and learners (Siemens & Tittengerger, 2009). A spectrum of online, blended, and physically based learning centres [sic], each advocating a participatory approach to pedagogy, can serve the needs of all learners (from highly motivated and self-directed to those who prefer greater structure and guidance). (A model of future universities, para. 8)

Just as Professor Mark Crockett encouraged Lois Zimmerman years ago, we must continue to prepare our students, and allow ourselves, to be open to new learning. Sixty years after graduating from Lesley, Lois Zimmerman, in true Lesley tradition and still eager to learn, taught herself to use Skype in order to dialogue "in person" with us.

ACTIVE DISCOVERY

One goal of excellent teachers is to facilitate inspired, creative academic learning through lessons that challenge the intellect and encourage student involvement and playful flow. As our colleague Alex Johnson pointed out in a conversation with the authors of this chapter, a great example of this sort of excellence was demonstrated repeatedly by her mentor, MIT physics professor Walter Lewin:

> Professor Lewin understood the equation between learning and play. He once used his 6-foot-2 frame as a pendulum,

swinging across the stage to show how pendulums are independent of mass. He mockingly beat a student with cat fur to explain electrostatics. He fired a canon with a golf ball at a monkey in a bullet-proof vest to demonstrate the trajectories of objects in free fall. "Physics works!" he shouted after such spirited in-class demonstrations. It might be said the physics of his creative teaching is what works.

Like her mentor, in her creative writing class, Alex is always looking for ways to give her students new prompts to inspire their learning. Professor Lewin taught her that the value of experiential learning can occur across any discipline. The value of students feeling engaged and alive is crucial to the retention of knowledge.

Excellence in teaching also requires sensitivity to the different capabilities, backgrounds, personalities, and needs of individual students and to the socio-emotional context in which their collective learning takes place. Such sensitivity allows teachers to foster healthy classroom communities and to effectively tailor their teaching to each of their students. Without it, students may feel alienated, invalidated, or unmotivated in one-size-fits-all classrooms that do not serve their needs. The way Lois Zimmerman tailored learning to different needs, as with her student Patty, provides a good example of this.

Lois's sensitivity was a cornerstone of her pedagogy. She gave each student in her class the opportunity to be honored as "child of the week"—to be the center of attention and to lead for one week. Lois got to know each of her students better this way; they learned more about each other; and inclusive classroom bonds were reinforced. This strategy also helped Lois remain sensitive to the needs of each student while fostering a healthy socio-emotional environment in the classroom.

At the graduate level, Julia Byers frequently uses warm-up activities to engage higher-education students in facilitating community awareness of deeply embedded assumptions and biases that often occur in the learning setting. She described one such experience in this way:

One day, I brought in approximately 20 large fieldstones and hid inspiring quotations under different rocks for students to spontaneously choose. After students had the opportunity to share how they related to the quotations, such as "Common sense is the knack of seeing things as they are and doing things as they ought to be done" (C. E. Stowe), or "Courage is rightly esteemed the first of human qualities because it is the quality which guarantees all others" (Winston Churchill), or "Actions speak louder than words" (proverb), I asked for volunteers to engage in a fish bowl experience. The students selected if they wanted to take on a female role or male role, thus to investigate assumptions behind stereotypical roles, or be an observer of the process. The directive of the activity was to construct a tower of balancing rocks to make the highest structure possible. The metaphor was used to explore the dynamics of negotiation and meaning in achieving tasks such as graduate school assignments. The enjoyment of watching the trial and error of balancing rocks produced a humorous and yet serious atmosphere. After 15 minutes of exploring the tension of power dynamics, mediating roles, and other characteristics in the solving of the task, one group figured out that they could hold or put the rocks on chairs or tables to elevate the height of their sculpture. We witnessed and were amazed by the classmates' initial choice to stick with what they traditionally knew or what they thought was expected of them. Then they realized that new ideas were honored and in fact encouraged. Rather than compete, the two groups decided to work as a whole team to complete the task. One student commented that they didn't need to read the book *Communities of Practice* by Etienne Wenger (1998), since they had witnessed all the issues of negotiation, reification, and change within the observational activity. We then proceeded to deconstruct the process of how the group had worked together and finally achieved the outcome that they felt was the best response to the task. Both teachers and therapists in the interdisciplinary class came away from the experience remembering the symbolic meaning of the rocks and far beyond. This warm-up activity created an example of active discovery rather than using textbooks to define operational definitions, emphasizing constructivist knowledge.

STUDENT-CENTERED APPROACH: THE MAGICIAN AND THE FIREFLY

In her days as a student at Lesley, storytelling was Lois Zimmerman's favorite class. Since taking that course, she has nurtured the imaginations of thousands of children as a storyteller herself, perfecting her skills inside and outside the classroom. Her advice: Sit down at the children's level, make plenty of eye contact, speak with enthusiasm, and, for the little ones, use plenty of repetition. Lois says that a good Winnie the Pooh story really gets kids' imaginations flowing and, for her, that is one of the most important things a teacher can do.

Lois also enjoys painting her face and transforming herself into a magical clown named Firefly. Firefly and her longtime sidekick, a clown doll named Friendly Freddy, have been entertaining and enlightening children for many years. Lois begins her magic shows with a lesson on fireflies and a discussion on the difference between "real" and "pretend." Then Firefly tells the children a story. Later, she flashes her light and asks the children, "Would you like to see my magic tricks now?"

Just because children "grow up" doesn't mean that they must lose their playfulness. Adult demands and stresses often burden both students and faculty in their quest for learning. It is hard to maintain a sense of freshness, innovation, and original critical thinking when society surrounds today's students with overwhelmingly convergent, not divergent, ways of processing information. While Lesley honors the balance between academic rigor and creative opportunities, the emphasis is on helping students find their own balance between a sense of individual and collective needs in education. Lois, as a pioneer in early education, still serves to remind us of the inherent simple attributes of relating to others in meaningful ways that bring out their best qualities.

Teaching well at Lesley University, according to the six professors involved in these discussions, requires balancing meticulous preparation with a willingness to indulge in student-driven feasts of learning. Practicing a balanced art of teaching has been one of Lesley's most precious traditions. Whether through acting in the moment in response to adverse circumstances, or building innovative, surprise learning environments within the science and art of teaching, or engaging students in direct individual and collective awareness for social competence, collaboratively we celebrate all the firefly educators who strive to reach excellence in teaching. To our own legendary torchbearer, Edith Lesley Wolfard, we are grateful for her enterprise, vision, and, ultimately, openness to change. And we thank Lois, one of thousands of Lesley-educated teachers, a magical firefly who has enlightened, entertained, and enriched the lives of countless children through excellence in teaching.

We would like to dedicate this chapter to Janet Kendrick, 1942–2008, a lifelong learner, community leader, and student whose last days were spent in joyful learning in the classroom at Lesley University.

REFERENCES

Baader, M. (2004). Froebel and the rise of educational theory in the United States. *Studies in Philosophy & Education, 23*(5/6), 427 444.

Dombkowski, K. (2001). Will the real kindergarten please stand up?: Defining and redefining the twentieth-century U.S. kindergarten. *History of Education, 30*(6), 527 545. DOI: 10.1080 /0046760011006476 2

Dylan, B. (1964/1992). My back pages. On *Another side of Bob Dylan* [record]. New York, NY: Columbia.

Froebel, F. (1844). The education of children (J. Liebschner, Trans.) Retrieved from http://www.friedrichfroebel.com

Jeynes, W. (2006). Standardized tests and Froebel's original kindergarten model. *Teachers College Record,108*(10), 2006, 1937 1959.

Siemens, G., & Tittenberger, P. (2009). *Handbook of emerging technologies for learning.* Retrieved on April 30, 2009, from http://umanitoba.ca/learning_technologies/cetl/HETL.pdf

Siemens, G., & Matheos, K. (May 2010). Systemic changes in higher education. *In education, 16*(1). Retrieved from http://ineducation.ca/article/systemic-changes-higher-education

Wenger, E. (1998). *Communities of practice: Learning, meaning, and identity.* Cambridge, MA: Cambridge University Press.

PART II: 1960–1980

Introduction

JOSEPH B. MOORE

At least three key events set up the conditions for higher education in the 1960s. First, President Franklin Delano Roosevelt signed the GI Bill in June 1944, which subsequently enabled eight million veterans to attend college (Cole, 2009). Beyond the sheer numbers of veterans who enrolled, this legislation gave recognition to higher education as the country experienced sharp economic and demographic growth following the war. It was the federal government's seal of approval for higher education, making explicit the expectation that college enrollment was good for the individual and for the country.

The second key event was the 1957 launch of Sputnik by the Soviet Union. This was not only a technological victory for the cold-war nemesis of the United States, but a shattering recognition that the American school system might not be the best in the world. This awareness in turn raised economic and security questions, and led to a more intense federal involvement in higher education funding, especially in science, but also in K-12 educational policy.

And then, in 1960, Clark Kerr released the Master Plan of 1960 for Higher Education in California (Cole, 2009). Despite increasing federal involvement in education, states retained dominant control and responsibility for all education. This effort by Kerr was the most comprehensive plan to design a three-tiered system (community colleges, comprehensive colleges, research universities) that could enhance access for a wide variety of students and aspire to the highest levels of academic quality, especially at the research institutions. In fact, Kerr's plan moved California to become one of the strongest state postsecondary systems in the country for almost five decades. It also provided a high profile for the role of community colleges— institutions that grew in number, and in number of students served, through the 1960s and 1970s.

The four essays in this section build from these three events that set up the context for higher education between 1960 and 1980. Shaun McNiff's essay about the first arts-based graduate program could not have been written without the changes that took place in higher education in the late 1960s. The antiwar demonstrations of that period led to antiauthority protests, especially at colleges and universities. Degree requirements and common core requirements were challenged. Styles of teaching (especially lectures) were associated with power structures and the passivity of students. Critiques of traditional education were widespread, from Paolo Friere's (1973) *Pedagogy of the Oppressed* to Postman and Weingartner's (1969) *Teaching as a Subversive Activity*. Many educators were rereading John Dewey. New institutions were started with new philosophies and new curricula that sought to engage students more fully in their education, and in decisions about their degree plans. New institutions were started to craft learning opportunities for adults who were working and raising families. It was a period of criticism and creativity.

Each of these four essays is a post-sixties essay. McNiff's phrase "how the arts can liberate human expression and understanding" and his comment about "my lifelong commitment to self-designed learning" were actually made possible by the changes in higher education in the sixties. Marcow Speiser and Samuel Schwartz's description of the Expressive Therapies Program in Israel shows how that program came about through various historical realities and circumstances, particularly in relation to Marcow Speiser's immigration from South Africa to Israel and the Yom Kippur War; her meeting Shaun McNiff and enrolling in the Expressive Therapies Program; and her eventual return to Israel to initiate the program there. Wauhkonen, Fink, and Pluto provide background about the curriculum expansion at Lesley

College, specifically the liberal arts, but argue convincingly that this is an evolution of the college from its narrower, professional curriculum and that it retains the Lesley commitment to theory and practice, the classroom, and the community. Finally, Kossak provides a detailed description of the origins and growth of the Expressive Therapies Program, citing its academic origins and the tensions within the division as it grew and had the opportunity to specialize, in part in response to state regulations.

Essays such as these would have been rare in the 1950s or early 1960s. They show how individual faculty engaged in program developments that drew upon their academic background, their colleagues, and their worldview. The faculty also reveal a propensity to act, to shape not just programs, but their own futures. They sought to identify audiences who might benefit from programs that they could design and deliver, whether those potential students were in state hospitals, elementary schools, or communities traumatized by violence. These faculty have been able to craft new disciplines, or modify existing ones, to create programs and curricula that speak to new realities.

Moving beyond the radical literature of the sixties and beyond the rhetoric of power and oppression, these examples show the application of theory to higher education program design, and the integration of academic theory with field-based practice in response to genuine community needs and opportunities.

REFERENCES

Cole, J. (2009). *The great American university: Its rise to preeminence, its indispensable national role, and why it must be protected.* New York, NY: PublicAffairs.

Friere, P. (1973). *Pedagogy of the oppressed.* New York, NY: Seabury Press.

Postman, N., & Weingartner, C. (1969). *Teaching as a subversive activity.* New York, NY: Dell.

CHAPTER FOUR

A Vision of Arts Integration and Knowing: The Creation of Lesley's First Arts-Based Graduate Programs

Shaun McNiff

The spirit and methods of arts-based knowing and academic integration permeated everything we did when establishing the Institute for the Arts and Human Development at Lesley University in early 1974. Programs were informed by a philosophy that embraced the whole of expression, the intelligence of creative imagination, and the interplay between artistic and psychological inquiry. Although these ideas were not new, Lesley was the first institution to thoroughly join all of the arts in graduate training programs focused on therapy, education, and cultural institutions within an overall context where these domains were thoroughly integrated with one another.

I will briefly describe the environment of the early 1970s that led to the creation of the Institute for the Arts and Human Development, and will then focus on the foundations for integrated arts in education programs at Lesley and their close ties to the arts in therapy.

ARTS IN THE SERVICE OF OTHERS: THE FORMATIVE CONTEXT OF 1970–1973

As many have emphasized, the growth of Lesley University over the past four decades can be attributed largely to how the institution gave people opportunities to initiate programs that could not be developed within other colleges and universities. My start was arguably the most irregular of Lesley initiatives. Bill Perry, the dean and vice president of graduate studies at Lesley, says that he found me selling newspapers in Harvard Square and I asked if I could engage the school in the arts; that he took me to lunch at the Harvard Faculty Club, which he did often do, and gave me a job (McNiff, 1981, p. 2). In his clever fiction Bill described the unlikely way we began.

Having left law school in 1969 to commit myself to art and social service, I found myself four years later teaching and starting graduate programs at Lesley. Between the time I left law school and began at Lesley, I had received the support of Rudolf Arnheim, professor of the psychology of art at Harvard; Christopher Cook, director of the Addison Gallery of American Art at Phillips Academy in Andover; William Goldman, MD, commissioner of the Massachusetts Department of Mental Health;[4] and others for the work that I was doing in establishing expressive arts therapy in the Commonwealth via the program I had initiated at Danvers State Hospital. I was working closely with the Goddard graduate program, where I discovered my lifelong commitment to self-designed learning, first as a student and then as a field faculty member, and where I became aware of a great interest in how the arts could be used to serve others.

It was a remarkable time, an era of progressive experimentation when barriers of every kind were questioned, when values of revolutionary transformation and turning the tables on ingrained attitudes were pervasive. Through Arnheim and Christopher Cook, a

---

4 I was a member of Dr. Goldman's advisory committee, which tied all new training funds to multidisciplinary practice. Goldman, a national leader in community mental health from Northern California, was appointed by Governor Francis Sargent (1969-1975). A Republican, Sargent made appointments in Corrections, Youth Services, and Mental Health that were designed to bring major, arguably radical, change to these chronically institutionalized systems. Goldman questioned professional silos and encouraged psychiatrists to work seamlessly in teams with psychologists, nurses, social workers, and what he called "expressive therapy," which included all of the arts therapies. As one of the few arts therapists who had ever worked within the Department of Mental Health, I represented this "potential profession" in a committee together with deans and faculty from the Heller School at Brandeis, Harvard Medical School, the Boston University School of Nursing, and others. Lesley became a partner in the Greater Lawrence Mental Health Training Consortium, funded by the Department of Mental Health to offer a multidisciplinary education for psychologists, social workers, and practitioners of expressive therapy. Joan Klagsbrun, who later became a Lesley faculty member, was hired as the coordinator.

conceptual artist who had just spent a year directing the Institute of Contemporary Art in Boston as a work of art, I became involved with John Hagerty, who founded the Massachusetts Prison Art Project as a Harvard student. I served on the board of the prison project and collaborated with a group of former MCI inmates in the Goddard master's program. I was mentored by both Arnheim and Truman Nelson, the historical novelist and friend of Malcolm X who wrote many books dealing with abolitionist and revolutionary themes (Schafer, 1989).

I focused from the start of my Danvers State Hospital experience on how the arts can liberate human expression and understanding. Oriented to the whole person and human dignity in an era of institutionalization, we demonstrated how withdrawn and incapacitated people could express themselves with depth and intelligence in various forms of artistic expression.

Through my collaboration with Karen Gallas, a 1972 graduate of Lesley's Open Education master's program, directed by Cynthia Cole, I began to apply the same principles to children with learning difficulties. I was introduced to Lesley through Gallas, and in 1973 offered the first art therapy course in the experimental January program. The class was oversubscribed, and I was invited to continue teaching courses on art therapy and learning disabilities—offerings that drew large numbers from Lesley's new Special Education graduate program, directed by Jill Hamilton.[5] The lack of preexisting arts departments in the graduate school allowed us to freely integrate the arts with one another and with other disciplines (McNiff, 1981).

It was Peter Von Mertons, the youthful assistant dean of Lesley's graduate school, who in 1973 encouraged me to "think bigger" than my original idea of linking expressive arts therapy and special education. He said, "You should create an arts center" at Lesley. Peter envisioned more of a crafts and studio facility that would serve as an educational resource center, but his "anything can happen here" attitude challenged the imagination. My exhibition "Art Therapy at

---

5 Graduate studies in Special Education at Lesley burgeoned in response to the Commonwealth's now historic passage of Chapter 766, and were a primary growth engine for other graduate programs as well.

Danvers" was traveling to the Carpenter Center for the Visual Arts at Harvard, and Peter took Bill Perry to see it. Deeply moved when viewing the patients' art, and himself the parent of a child with special needs, Bill was receptive.

When given the opportunity to establish a center for the arts, my inclination was to link creative expression to the Lesley educational mission and the evolving area of therapy. My experiences at Danvers, the Addison Gallery, the collaborative work with Gallas in public schools, studies with Arnheim, and interactions with a progressive community of colleagues in the early 1970s had thoroughly reinforced the necessity of bringing something new and radically different into the world.

ESTABLISHING THE INSTITUTE FOR THE ARTS AND HUMAN DEVELOPMENT

The entrepreneurial atmosphere of Lesley's graduate school, together with its tradition of field-based professional training, offered a unique opportunity to develop the experimental work I had done at Goddard into more formal courses and programs. Lesley was also oriented to children, and I felt that an expressive arts therapy program would require a solid basis in child psychology.

The Institute for the Arts and Human Development was established at Lesley University in March of 1974, and it quickly became known as the Arts Institute. I was starting alone with an administrative assistant before hiring core faculty, and my original scheme was to focus on creating two separate but interrelated graduate programs, one committed to the assimilation of the arts in therapy, and the other to integrating the arts in education, special education, and cultural institutions. If I was to establish a "community" of artists, the institute would have to be inclusive—open to a variety of art forms and disciplines. At the end of two years we had enrolled 70 full-time graduate students, and the programs were just beginning to grow.

While other graduate programs in the creative arts therapies and education developed prescribed and relatively uniform courses of study for students, we took a more liberal approach, offering common core courses in both education and therapy but then encouraging students to individualize their curricula. Both programs required courses in more than one artistic discipline, and I was especially impressed by how artists with an MFA in visual art might focus on dance and vice versa, or how a poet explored all of the arts. I believed that every person integrates experience in unique ways and needs the freedom to combine areas of interest. In contrast to smaller programs that were functioning as cohorts following a single course of study, which were the norm in the creative arts therapies, we became a college within the college, offering a rich variety of courses. Our philosophy was in sync with Lesley's orientation to growth.

In the first years of the Arts Institute, the therapy and education programs were thoroughly integrated. It was a time when people thought much more about commonalities than about differences. Of course we celebrated variety and the uniqueness of every person and expression, but this emphasis took us to a transcendent sense of humanity. In keeping with our art-based[6] methods, differences were embraced as elements that contributed to a common pulse, to an understanding of universal needs, and to cross-cultural elements of creation, healing, and learning (McNiff, 1979; 1984, 2009b).

At first the Integrated Arts in Education Program attracted artists who were involved more with community arts and cultural institutions than with schools.[7] However, my personal vision, kindled by the collaboration with Karen Gallas, was always concerned with classrooms, and I kept saying, "That's where the children are." The silos of professions and regulations, inside and outside Lesley, made it difficult to realize the true integration of the arts in education.

We asked: How might the visual arts and storytelling further reading, writing, and mathematics learning for young children?

6 My definition of "art" and art-based methods includes all arts disciplines and artists.

7 This orientation was influenced by our relationship with Christopher Cook at the Addison Gallery. Cook and I were also involved with The Art Museum as Educator project (Newsome & Silver, 1978), coordinated by the Council on Museums and Education in the Visual Arts.

What core experimental practices can characterize both science and the arts? How might a fuller appreciation of the body and its movement enhance self-confidence and motivation to learn? Can musical improvisation help children listen more sensitively and focus attention in all areas of school experience? How might elements from all of the arts be similarly related to educational outcomes across the whole school experience?

As with the continuities of progressive education, we examined the problem or issue at hand, utilizing whatever disciplines and modes of inquiry informed learning. We also believed that the creative imagination is an essential intelligence that is most effectively cultivated through the use of the full spectrum of a person's and community's resources (Cobb, 1992).

In the early 1970s, when I was formulating a vision and methods of arts integration, before coming to Lesley, Karen Gallas was my primary partner. As I mentioned earlier, she was studying in Lesley's Open Education graduate program while I was setting up the Danvers expressive arts therapy program. She introduced me to the work of Sylvia Ashton-Warner (1963) and Elwyn Richardson (1964), which pioneered the comprehensive integration of the arts in the early childhood classroom. Gallas and I emphasized the similarities between what I was doing with adults and her work with young children, the interplay between therapy and education, and the need to approach learning with psychological understanding.

I visited Gallas's K-3 classrooms, and we explored how to integrate the expressive arts therapies into school settings (McNiff & McNiff [Gallas], 1976). I covered the more artistic and therapeutic aspects of the work—arts media and the psychology of art—and Gallas became expert in the practice of integrating the arts with math, science, reading, writing, and other school subjects (Gallas, 1991; 1994; 2003).

Prior to my arrival at Lesley, Arnheim was the major contributor to the shaping of my image of art-based knowing. Beginning in 1971 he affirmed my tendency to see the arts as primary modes of original, unique psychological inquiry rather than just objects to be analyzed from the perspective of preestablished, finite criteria. Cynthia Cole and others at Lesley during the 1970s were immersed in the writings of

Jean Piaget and especially the idea that learning is informed by actions in the material world. Although I supported these developmental and cognitive studies, I felt that the arts were also tied to depth psychology, Gestalt psychology, and their own distinct ways of knowing. No one theoretical tract can hold the whole, and our programs reflected this openness.

I kept returning to the formative experience of creative expression as the source for the various applications of the arts to be made by educators and therapists. Arnheim would always say that we had practical experiences with the arts that he did not have, and this acknowledgement of practice stayed with me. I realized that every person needs to work from what I later called "the authority of experience" (1993). This immersion in the "art-basis" of the work has always been the key to its transformative power, clinical application, and adaptation to educational outcomes.

When discussing with her my plans for the Institute for the Arts and Human Development, Karen Gallas said to me, "You have to go after Norma Canner," whom she had recently met in an institute run by the Eliot-Pearson Department of Child Development at Tufts. Canner started at Lesley as an adjunct instructor, and she was the first core faculty member whom I hired during the second year of the graduate program. Ultimately, the entire Tufts team followed—Paolo Knill, Iris Fanger, Mariagnese Cattaneo, and Elizabeth McKim.

In suggesting that my first priority should be recruiting Canner, Karen Gallas instinctively knew that the work I was attempting to do had to be based on the best possible experience of the creative process. As a young, philosophically inclined visual artist who was closely associated with the Boston conceptual art community, I needed a senior partner who could provide a complementary mastery of creative improvisation in the performing arts. Norma Canner was skilled in working with large groups, and she played a vital role in establishing the spirit of creative community that permeated the Lesley Arts Institute. Paolo Knill, and his unique way of making music with wind instruments and spontaneous sounds, became the third lead contributor to our collective expression. Quality art experiences provided the basis for psychological reflection, learning, research, and applications to the broad spectrum of situations in which people work with others.

All of the Arts Institute faculty members supported one another and their students in embracing uncertainty, and the discomfort it often generates, as fundamental qualities of creative discovery. New advances tend to emerge from a crucible that dissolves ingrained and habitual ways of acting, and in which uncertainty is supported as a rite of passage on the path to revelation.

We strove, as Gallas later wrote, to move imagination from the periphery to "the center of the educational process" (2003, p. 11). Her books on art-based classroom methods, including Languages of Learning (1994) and Imagination and Literacy (2003), fulfilled the early educational strivings of the Arts Institute. In the 1991 symposium on Arts as Education, published by the Harvard Educational Review, Gallas describes how the arts help children to "transcend the limitations" they encounter and "regardless of their differences, to participate fully in the experience of education" (p. 50). She exhorts teachers to "expand" rather than continuously "narrow" educational narratives (1994, p. xvi), to see how "children do not naturally limit the forms that their expressions take" (p. xv), to appreciate how meaning is always "built into" the expressions of children (p. xiv), and to sustain these innate intelligences that are too often overlooked by adult ideologies and systems of communication.

This expansion of expression and learning was at the heart of the original Arts Institute mission. We constantly emphasized working with everything we have, opening all sensory channels of understanding, and approaching the arts as essential ways of knowing that need not be reduced to the prevailing orthodoxies of education-related research.[8]

---

8 As I review the first things that I wrote about the Arts Institute programs, I am taken aback by how early articulations of our purpose have been upheld over the years. In a 1975 guest editorial for New Ways, the newsletter of the Educational Arts Association, I encouraged support for "all of a person's expressive powers" if art is to open itself to the fullness of experience (p. 15). I also spoke of how concerns for individualized learning require the integration of educational and therapeutic ways of using the arts. It was in these early exchanges with Gallas, Arnheim (1954, 1971, 1972), and Paolo Knill, my theoretical partner within the Arts Institute, that I began to formulate the principles of art-based inquiry and knowing that ultimately led to the coining of the term "art-based research" and my 1998 book on this subject. The receptivity to and growth of interest in arts-based research has been one of the most surprising and pleasing outcomes of our experimentation at Lesley.

Children, Adults, and the Full Range of Human Experience

One of the institutional tensions during my early years at Lesley was the gap between the college's almost exclusive focus on childhood, which I viewed as an asset for the school as a whole, and the way I envisioned the Arts Institute dealing with all people. In calling our center the Institute for the Arts and Human Development rather than Child Development, I subtly tried to suggest that every stage of life is essential. Still, in creating the first brochure for the Arts Institute, I pointedly made images that were adapted from the art of young children.

Image courtesy of Shaun McNiff.

The early faculty members whom I recruited for the education program and the larger therapy program—Canner, Knill, Fanger, Cattaneo, McKim, Peter Rowan, and Jared Kass—were involved almost totally with the arts and child development. John Langstaff was one of many prominent adjuncts who offered child-related arts courses. I was the only one of our group who had been involved in the full-time practice of expressive arts therapy within a psychiatric context for a number of years and with adults. On the Expressive Therapies side of the Arts Institute we hired Shep Ginandes, a psychiatrist who ran an arts-based therapeutic center for adolescents in Concord, MA, called The School We Have (1973). Together with Peter Rowan, Ginandes gave our faculty more clinical balance, and his center, which moved to Lesley's Cambridge campus, reinforced ties between clinical contexts and Lesley's focus on education.

I was consciously trying to build a faculty that would signal to the larger Lesley community that we were immersed in the arts as they related to child development in a comprehensive sense. A number of years after I came to Lesley, the institution prominently developed a new mission logo emphasizing programs that served "the world of children." In addition to my caution about triggering a mission conflict,[9] we wanted to address the child-oriented interests of many students at Lesley.

To the extent to which the Lesley mission now embraces all age groups, these early under-the-radar experiences with adults were a significant part of moving from a Graduate School of Education to what later became the Graduate School, including education and other fields. My strategy was that as long as we were prominently involved with programs serving children, we would be just fine within the institution. Our inclusiveness was not a difficult choice for me and the faculty, since we were all committed to the full range of human experience. As our courses engaged adults in experientially based learning, the Arts Institute quietly but forcefully became a center that

---

9 Even with progressives like Cole, Hamilton, Perry, and Lenore Parker, the head of Elementary Education who became a close colleague on the Graduate Council, there was a general understanding at the time that Lesley was an institution focused on childhood studies and professions.

engaged the arts as vehicles of transformation for all ages and sectors of society.

THE GROWTH OF INTEGRATED ARTS IN EDUCATION STUDIES

Iris Fanger was the first coordinator of the Integrated Arts in Education master's program. As a child drama teacher and dance critic, Iris reinforced the early focus of the program on community arts. She taught both expressive therapy and education students, and made many contributions to the Arts Institute's overall mission of integrating therapy and education.

In an effort to engage classroom teachers in the Integrated Arts in Education Program, I developed Lesley's first off-campus master's degree program in cooperation with the Attleboro, MA, public schools in 1976, before many of the early faculty were hired.[10] I did this because we were not attracting teachers in Cambridge. It was challenging to operate the off-campus cohort program without organizational structures and staff, and after the first group was graduated, the model could not be sustained.

Still trying to do more with classrooms and curriculum, we hired Nancy Langstaff in the early 1980s. An expert in the area of arts integration, Langstaff had supervised Gallas's student teaching at the Cambridge Friends School. She understood the cognitive dimensions of the arts and their application to learning, and helped realize the goal of excellent teacher training on the Cambridge campus.[11] However, the program stayed small, especially in comparison to the rapidly expanding expressive arts therapy domain.

The most intense burst in growth for arts in education at Lesley

10 Attleboro had established a national reputation for its art education and sensory learning programs led by Don Brigham, whose work was championed by Rudolf Arnheim. The assistant superintendent of schools in Attleboro, Bart O'Connor, who taught curriculum and drama for Lesley, was Brigham's partner in delivering this experimental program, which undertook a comprehensive integration of the arts into every aspect of the school experience. The program realized many ideal methods of arts integration.

11 A teacher licensure tract was also offered in cooperation with the Education Division of the graduate school.

occurred in the late 1980s, when Vivien Marcow Speiser returned from Israel and became assistant dean of the Institute for the Arts and Human Development. Marcow Speiser was responsible for the first major expansion of Arts Institute programs in 1979 via our affiliate in Israel, and this success was followed with similar programs in Scandinavia (Phillip Speiser) and Switzerland and Germany (Paolo Knill). Even though Speiser's Scandinavian institute promulgated integrated arts in education, the affiliate students who came to Lesley to study all focused on expressive arts therapies.

At the time of Marcow Speiser's return to Cambridge, the Integrated Arts in Education master's degree had just been approved for delivery via Lesley's National Outreach Program, developed by Dean Richard Wylie, who had come to Lesley from the University of Colorado at Denver to head the graduate school. In contrast to our experience with the Attleboro pilot group, the new national programs and the infrastructure established by Wylie's office provided systems for supporting large numbers of students and the ensuing programmatic multiplication.

Fortuitously, this new sphere of programming was given to Marcow Speiser as part of her new role. Adept at program development, she brought the skills she honed in Israel to the arts in education program. Rather than replicate the approaches we took in Attleboro and Cambridge, she infused the off-campus cohorts, then primarily in Colorado, with expressive arts therapy faculty and methods for furthering creative expression and placed primary emphasis on students' direct experimentation with the arts.[12] The dramatic growth of arts education studies, now taking place in 23 U.S. states, emerged directly from this orientation to teaching.

When teachers were invited to engage the creative process in various media within a supportive environment, enrollments soared. This program realized my personal vision for arts integration with a wide variety of professional disciplines more than any other that we initiated at Lesley (2009a). In spite of its considerable international

---

12 Marcow Speiser also began a partnership with Fritz Bell and his Creative Classrooms program at Walnut Hill in Raymond, New Hampshire, and this collaboration led to the provision of off-campus Lesley programs in the wider New England region.

success and influence, the expressive arts therapy program has not yet achieved this kind of cross-disciplinary participation.

When I moved onto the faculty in 1989, I focused part of my teaching schedule on the off-campus arts in education program because it was so personally rewarding to help administrators, counselors, teachers from all grade levels and subjects, and other educators discover their creative potential. I was privileged to receive startling feedback in working with art, history, and foreign language teachers from the high school that I attended. When the teachers encountered their fears, resistances, uncertainties, and vulnerabilities in regard to artistic expression, they consistently said, "Now I understand how the students feel."

Because teachers are so conditioned to plan everything at the start, they resisted artistic activities where the end cannot be known at the beginning. We discovered that the force of the resistance tended to generate a proportionate sense of liberation when participants were able to stay with the work and let it carry them to new understanding about themselves and teaching. These experiences inspired my book *Trust the Process: An Artist's Guide to Letting Go* (1998).

I concluded that the dramatic growth of the off-campus program resulted from giving learners firsthand knowledge of the creative process, and then supporting them in making their own connections to classrooms and other work settings. Since this was not an initial licensure program, all of the students tended to be experienced professionals with varied areas of expertise, and we could avoid many of the restraints that exist within entry-level professional training, including expressive arts therapy.

Robert Coles was a frequent Arts Institute guest in the mid-1970s, and a supporter of our work.[13] He said at the time, "Too little attention is paid to the drive for self-expression and affirmation of one's artistic sensibility" (McNiff, 1976, p. 2). We helped each person experiment with the creative process within an affirming group environment. People realized that they could take risks, encounter their fears and

13 Coles, a child psychiatrist, had won the 1973 Pulitzer Prize for his Children of Crisis series of books, and later received a MacArthur Award, the Presidential Medal of Freedom, the National Humanities Medal, and a Lesley honorary doctorate.

resistances to expression, and emerge not only intact, but thoroughly transformed. They learned the ways of creative expression and brought the benefits to others.

SUSTAINED ADVOCACY

In the early years of the Arts Institute, we did everything possible to combine the arts and therapy with special education. I served with the original National Committee of the Arts for the Handicapped at the Kennedy Center in Washington, and was the committee's first Massachusetts state chair in 1976–1977. We brought the Very Special Arts Festival to the Commonwealth, which was coordinated by Maida Abrams, a Lesley graduate and art teacher in Newton.[14]

I persist in encouraging close collaboration between the arts therapies and special education (1997). But the specialized interests of both areas and the regulations they establish hinder the potential that helped establish arts programs at Lesley. The Expressive Therapies and Creative Arts and Learning Programs that emerged from the original vision of integration have grown exponentially and have had a significant social impact, but they are ironically, to this date, distinct entities, and both are separate from Lesley's programs in special education.

Where I originally saw expressive arts therapy, as established at Lesley, integrating all of the creative arts therapies, the different arts specializations have established separate status, and expressive arts therapy has paradoxically become a successful and expanding "discipline" (McNiff, 2009a). This is an outcome that I neither predicted nor supported, but I accept it with a smile, and what may be the necessary role of disciplinary silos, which I nevertheless continue to challenge.

I can also report that the Institute for the Arts and Human Development came to an end in the early 1990s as part of an effort to consolidate Expressive Therapies with Counseling Psychology, and Creative Arts and Learning with Education. I supported both

14 Abrams founded Very Special Arts Massachusetts in 1980 and served for many years as its president.

consolidations, in keeping with principles of integration that could benefit students and the people we serve, even if it meant the end of the Arts Institute that I founded. The programs continue to be separated many years after these changes were made. Creative Arts and Learning, now called Integrated Teaching through the Arts, has recently moved to the School of Education to once again explore cooperation with other spheres of teacher training.

Even though the Arts Institute no longer exists, all of its original programs continue to prosper as separate domains, and perhaps with less tension, since professional specializations owe their constancy not necessarily to the creativity I advocate, but to strong forces of self-preservation that I respect.

I have not yet realized my beginning goal of integrating the arts therapies with special education, but I remain hopeful, since this is so clearly in the interest of Lesley graduates seeking socially significant careers, and of course it will benefit children, adolescents, adults, families, schools, communities, and professions.

The most essential and original principle of all Arts Institute programs—the idea that the arts are primary ways of knowing, which has been verified throughout human history—has flourished. Within the inevitable strictures of professional disciplines, the philosophy and methods of art-based inquiry, understanding, and healing are being appreciated and independently discovered today in all sectors of education, social science, health, and the arts themselves.

The unrealized goals and setbacks encountered since the inception of the Arts Institute have been more than offset by unexpected expansions. Lesley doctoral students in both Educational Studies and Expressive Therapies are advancing arts-based epistemologies and research, and their work deepens the studies that were initiated at the master's level. I am especially encouraged by the many traditional-age and adult undergraduate students at Lesley College who are pursuing degrees in areas pioneered by the Institute for the Arts and Human Development. We now have a community of learners from the bachelor's degree through the doctorate who are preparing to serve others and further human understanding through the arts. It appears that the end of the original Institute for the Arts and Human Development as a center of creation has enabled other sectors inside and outside Lesley to adopt its vision as their own.

REFERENCES

Arnheim, R. (1954). Art and visual perception: A psychology of the creative eye. Berkeley and Los Angeles, CA: University of California Press.

Arnheim, R. (1971). Visual thinking. Berkeley and Los Angeles, CA: University of California Press.

Arnheim, R. (1972). *Toward a psychology of art: Collected essays.* Berkeley and Los Angeles, CA: University of California Press.

Ashton-Warner, S. (1963). Teacher. New York, NY: Simon & Schuster.

Cobb, E. (1992). The ecology of imagination in childhood. Dallas, TX: Spring Publications.

Gallas, K. (1991). Arts as epistemology: Enabling children to know what they know. Harvard Educational Review, *61*(1), 40 50.

Gallas, K. (1994). The languages of learning: How children talk, write, dance, draw, and sing their understanding of the world. New York, NY: Teachers College Press.

Gallas, K. (2003). Imagination and literacy: A teacher's search for the heart of learning. New York, NY: Teachers College Press.

Ginandes, S. (1973). How troubled, fed-up adolescents get together with creative adults at The School We Have. New York, NY: Delacorte Press.

McNiff, S. (1975). Strategies for unification. New Ways, *1*(4), 2 & 15.

McNiff, S. (1975). New careers in the arts. The Current-Lesley College, *3*(12), 6 7.

McNiff, S. and McNiff [Gallas], K. (1976). Art therapy in the classroom. Art Teacher, *6*(2), 10 12.

McNiff, S. (1976). The emergence of an Arts Institute. The Lesley College Graduate School Newspaper, *1*(1), 2.

McNiff, S. (1979). From shamanism to art therapy. *Art Psychotherapy*, *6*(3), 155 161.

McNiff, S. (1981). How it all began. The Current Lesley College, *8*(2), 2 5.

McNiff, S. (1984). Cross-cultural psychotherapy and art. *Art Therapy: Journal of the American Art Therapy Association*, *1*(3), 125 131.

McNiff, S. (1993). The authority of experience. The Arts in Psychotherapy, *20*(1), 3 9.

McNiff, S. (1997). Art therapy: A spectrum of partnerships. The Arts in Psychotherapy, *24*(1), 37 44.

McNiff, S. (1998). Trust the process: An artist's guide to letting go. Boston, MA: Shambhala.

McNiff, S. (1998). *Art-based research*. London, England: Jessica Kingsley.

McNiff, S. (2009a). Integrating the arts in therapy: History, theory, and practice. Springfield, IL: Charles C. Thomas.

McNiff, S. (2009b).Cross-cultural psychotherapy and art. *Art Therapy: Journal of the American Art Therapy Association*. 26(3), 100 106.

Newsome, B., & Silver, A. (Eds.). (1978). The Addison Gallery of American Art: Video for special audiences. In The art museum as educator: A collection of studies as guides to practice and policy, prepared by the Council on Museums and Education in the Visual Arts, pp. 170 176. Berkeley and Los Angeles, CA: University of California Press.

Richardson, E. (1964). In the early world. New York, NY: Pantheon.

Schafer, W. J. (Ed.). (1989). *The Truman Nelson reader*. Amherst, MA: University of Massachusetts Press.

ACKNOWLEDGMENTS

Thanks to Phillip Speiser, Karen Gallas, and Vivien Marcow Speiser for reading the manuscript to confirm historical facts.

CHAPTER FIVE

Reflections on the Development of Lesley University's Extension in Israel

VIVIEN MARCOW SPEISER, PHD, BC-DMT, LMHC, REAT
SAMUEL SCHWARTZ, MPP

In the span of 30 years, Lesley University's programs in Israel have succeeded in influencing generations of therapists, educators, and activists. Lesley's presence in Israel has significantly affected the Cambridge campus by offering complex and engaging teaching experiences, human interactions, and research opportunities to its Cambridge-based faculty, researchers, and administrators.

Lesley's programs in Israel began in 1979, when a group of Lesley alumni, including Yaacov Naor, Toby Zaitchik, and Vivien Marcow Speiser, returned to Israel and found a strong interest for expressive therapies studies that was not being met by Israeli academic institutions. Founding director Marcow Speiser created a nonprofit organization for the purpose of teaching expressive therapies, and established an affiliation relationship with Lesley in which students would train in Israel and then travel to Cambridge to complete their degree. This relationship changed in 1997 when the Israel program became a full-fledged extension of Lesley University. Today, at Lesley University's extension in Israel, in Netanya, about 300 students study in five master's degree programs. Graduates of these programs have gone on to assume top positions in Israel's therapeutic and educational communities. The extension in Israel has become synonymous with quality arts-based education, and the name Lesley, with creative learning approaches that integrate the arts.

Lesley's success in Israel has emerged from the synergy between the goals and values of the parent university and the needs of the country. Professor Speiser noted in her 2008 graduation address that "Lesley has been operating in Israel for half of the state's existence." Indeed, the history of Lesley's extension has been bound to the history of the state of Israel.

We begin by presenting the history of Lesley's operations in Israel, from the first class in 1979 until the present. In addition to describing the development of Lesley's programs of study in Israel, the chapter highlights special extracurricular projects and conferences that Lesley has organized, which put it at the vanguard of applying the arts to therapeutic and educational issues. After surveying the history, we discuss the impact that Lesley has had on Israel and the effects of the Israel extension on the parent university. We conclude by considering the reasons for the success of this partnership.

A HISTORY OF LESLEY IN ISRAEL

Until the early 1980s, the field of expressive therapies was relatively unknown in Israel. Few academics or practitioners were working on integrating the arts into therapeutic and educational programs. Those who understood the power of the arts and wanted to learn how to harness them had to travel abroad to acquire an academic education.

One such student was Vivien Marcow Speiser. She immigrated to Israel from South Africa in the early 1970s and soon after her arrival, experienced the trauma of the Yom Kippur War. In a surprise attack on Judaism's holiest day, the armies of two neighboring countries nearly succeeded in taking over the country. As a young mother to an infant, she experienced, along with her neighbors, the existential fear of extermination. In the aftermath of the war, she observed the extensive and continuing national and personal trauma all around her. She volunteered at a rehabilitation center and saw firsthand the powerful impact of injury and posttraumatic stress disorder (PTSD).

The country's psychological services were not equipped to deal with the war's emotional consequences. With her background and belief in the arts, she thought that a new therapeutic paradigm would be necessary to treat an entire country suffering from severe PTSD. She realized that she needed to acquire skills that were not taught in Israel. To this end, she traveled to the United States to study in the Expressive Therapies Program at Lesley College.

In Cambridge, she met Shaun McNiff, dean of the Expressive Therapies Program that he had founded in 1974. The program attracted a community of artists and activists from around the world who created a new way of working therapeutically with all of the arts, and a new way of engaging the imagination and the creative process. In the heady days of the mid-1970s, anything and everything seemed possible.

On returning to Israel, Professor Marcow Speiser found a country in need of an innovative approach to working therapeutically with the arts. Together with Lesley alumni Yaacov Naor and Toby Zaitchik, she discovered that there was much interest in Lesley's expressive therapies approach. She didn't have a guidebook or mentor in Israel, but she knew that she needed to teach this powerful healing method, and she became the founding director of Lesley's inchoate program.

The first formal Lesley event in Israel took place in December 1979 at the Dance Library in Tel Aviv, when Norma Canner, now a Lesley professor emeritus, offered a dance movement therapy workshop. Following her presentation, Canner engaged in a vehement debate with some of the country's established dance therapists about the merits of a multimodal therapeutic approach and a single modality approach.

Israel is the kind of country where word travels by mouth, and following this workshop, there was a deluge of inquiries about training. Canner consulted with Dean McNiff, and, together with Naor and Zaitchik and with the addition of Dorit Amir, began offering Lesley courses in a basement in a fashionable Tel Aviv suburb.

One day, Canner got a surprise call from a representative of Israel's Council of Higher Education, the country's accrediting body. She remembers the amusing interaction, in which she was told, "It is not possible to offer Lesley courses in Israel—what you would need to do is to create an Israeli nonprofit organization which could affiliate with Lesley." Wanting to comply with local laws, Marcow Speiser created a nonprofit organization in Israel for the purpose of teaching expressive therapies, called the Arts Institute Project in Israel (AIPI). The program was moved to the Ramat Aviv Hotel, and teaching space was rented from the neighboring Seminar HaKibbutzim College.

In those years, students took AIPI training courses in Israel and, at a certain point in their studies, traveled to the United States to complete their master's degree. In 1981, the first class of Israeli students graduated from Lesley. The Cambridge expressive therapies summer school, consisting predominantly of Israeli students but including other internationally affiliated students, contributed in no small measure to the growth and vibrancy of the Expressive Therapies Program from the early 1980s till the mid-1990s.

In 1982, Marcow Speiser cochaired the First International Conference in Expressive Therapies at Kibbutz Shefayim. This professional gathering brought world authorities in the field to Israel for the first time and raised the profile of expressive therapies in the country. Marcow Speiser noted,

> The reason this conference was so important was that it was a pivotal moment in the history of the country. Israel was fighting in Lebanon and many of the conference participants were in uniform. The late Professor Peter Rowan mounted a psychodrama with a protagonist soldier that was one of the most powerful pieces of work I have ever witnessed. (2009, p. 11)

In 1985, following the first war in Lebanon, with the Lesley-affiliated Israel program on its feet, Marcow Speiser returned to Boston, where she became the assistant dean of Lesley's Institute for the Arts and Human Development. While she always maintained her connection to the program in Israel, Baruch Zadik, Talila Mor, and Dalia Ben

Shoshan have since then directed the local nonprofit partner, AIPI.

The program continued to grow, and dozens of Israeli expressive therapies students arrived each summer in Cambridge to train on campus with Lesley faculty. Faculty fondly recall their days of teaching these challenging yet endearing students. Like the native Israeli sabra prickly pear plant, these students might have been prickly on the outside yet were soft and surprising inside.

The next big change in the program occurred in 1994, when Lesley moved to its current location in Netanya's then new industrial park. By knocking down walls and using creative design techniques, Lesley transformed a drab commercial building into a thriving educational communal structure with the arts at its core.

In 1995, Lesley introduced its master of arts in education degree in the Creative Arts in Learning Division. This program's focus on integrating the arts complemented the ongoing expressive therapies studies. It met an academic need at that time, when it attracted hundreds of educators from the entire length of Israel. Teachers from the Golan Heights in the north to Eilat in the south flew in to participate in the program, which they completed in summer intensives in the United States.

Lesley was one of the first foreign universities to operate in Israel, but in the intervening years, many other institutions have established campuses. The Israeli government tried to supervise the foreign programs, and its parliament, the Knesset, passed a law requiring all such institutions to seek a license of operation by 1998. Lesley understood the direction in which the government was moving and, in 1997, the Lesley extension program in Israel applied for and received a license to operate as an official extension from Israel's Council of Higher Education.

In 1998, Samuel Schwartz took over as the extension's associate director. He had worked as the spokesperson for Israel's Consulate General to New England, where he first was introduced to Lesley. After serving as the director of Academic Affairs for Israel's Los Angeles Consulate, he and Marcow Speiser, who had been promoted to the position of director of International and Collaborative Programs, took over the work at the extension. One of their first jobs was preparing for the introduction of new programs of study. Schwartz noted:

> For decades Lesley had been associated with expressive arts therapy. However, students in other disciplines were also intrigued by Lesley's unique approach to learning. There were many related subjects that the mainstream universities were not teaching, and we hoped to pioneer the academic studies of these. (2001, p. 3)

In Schwartz's first year, Lesley opened its third program of study, a master of arts degree in interdisciplinary studies with a focus in women's studies and the arts. This marked the first time that a master's level women's studies program had opened in Israel. In 1999, Lesley followed up with two new interdisciplinary studies foci, holistic health and the arts and group leadership and the arts. The holistic health program was the first academic program of its type in the country, and continues to be the only one. In 2003, Lesley's extension in Israel submitted three more foci to the country's Council of Higher Education, in elder studies, creative leadership, and creative mediation. The council was impressed with these programs and approved them the following year. Lesley College still known as such nearly a decade after it achieved university status has instant name recognition internationally to nearly anyone interested in the integration of therapy, education, and the arts.

SOCIAL ACTION PROJECTS IN ISRAEL ALONGSIDE THE PROGRAMS OF STUDY

Throughout its years in Israel, Lesley has maintained its commitment to social activism and has operated numerous extracurricular programs targeted to the wider community alongside its degree programs. For many years, Lesley maintained a subsidized low-cost treatment clinic for at-risk youth in the Netanya area. For a nominal fee, local-area children were able to receive treatment from some of Lesley's top expressive arts therapists.

Every March for the past decade, Lesley has sponsored a public seminar on International Women's Day, focusing on a specific aspect of women's experiences in Israel. These events feature a combination of scholarly inquiry, reports from the field, and experiential, arts-based participatory workshops, in the best Lesley tradition.

A particularly exciting and moving event took place in 2004, when the extension invited members of the Hebrew Israelite community of Dimona to visit the Netanya campus. The visit took place in the context of the Traditions and Cultures course that is part of the master of arts program in interdisciplinary studies with a focus on women's studies and the arts. The Hebrew Israelite community was founded in 1967 by Ben Ammi Ben Israel. He led several hundred African Americans in "returning home" to Israel in 1968, founding a community in the southern Israeli city of Dimona, near the Negev desert. Today, the community numbers about 3,000 people. During the visit, Lesley students engaged in fascinating interchanges with the Hebrew Israelite women about their unique culture, which in many ways diverges from and challenges the Western norm. The visit concluded with a performance by the community's Spirit of David Dance Theater, which featured the community's distinct clothing, music, and artwork.

In recent years, the extension has been involved in three intensive extracurricular undertakings. In April 2006, to mark Lesley's 25th anniversary in Israel, the university sponsored an international conference titled "Imagine: Expression in the Service of Humanity— Creative Approaches to Working with Conflict in Groups." Marcow Speiser explained that the vision of the conference emerged at a particularly wrenching time:

> The second Intifada was in full swing, suicide bombings in the areas were on the rise, and the cycle of violence, occupation, and retaliation was intensified. We felt we needed to do "something" to help professionals working with the

pain and the trauma of both the Israeli and the Palestinian populations and to show support for creative action in the face of uncontrollable political events. (Serlin & Marcow Speiser, 2007, p. 280)

Almost immediately, the idea of the conference caught on. All the major universities in Israel, as well as a few in Palestine and numerous international psychological organizations, became cosponsors. The conference attracted 350 participants, including a group of 60 Palestinians. Most participants came from the fields of counseling, including psychologists, expressive arts therapists, group psychoanalysts, social workers, and healers, while educators, artists, and grassroots activists represented large minorities of conference attendees. Marcow Speiser remembered that throughout the lectures, seminars, panels, and artistic presentations, there were "deep, difficult, and always meaningful dialogs" (Serlin & Marcow Speiser, 2007, p. 282). For the most part, political slogans were put aside and participants engaged in direct, personal communication, sharing their insights about ways of healing traumatized populations. Marcow Speiser (2009) recalled that "While many of the underlying tensions came to the surface it was a great opportunity to also talk, sing, dance and create together" (p. 13).

The camaraderie among conference participants was intense, and professional collaboration continued in the months that followed. Israeli and Palestinian scholars who met at the conference went on to engage in cooperative research projects and published joint academic articles (Joubran & Schwartz, 2007). At Al-Quds University in Abu Dis, Lesley sponsored a series of additional workshops on using the arts to heal trauma.

Also in 2006, Lesley University began a community organization project in cooperation with the Israeli municipality Nes Ziona in order to improve the quality of life of the city's Ethiopian immigrant population. Schwartz (2009) noted that previous programs that aimed to integrate Ethiopian immigrants were only partially successful, owing to cultural, economic, linguistic, religious, and technological gaps between the Ethiopian and Israeli societies. Lesley began by holding numerous fact-finding meetings with various officeholders and employees in the Nes Ziona municipality. Lesley's senior faculty conducted a town meeting with a cross-section of Ethiopian immigrants in order to identify the community's needs. The extension also brought representatives of potential funders to Nes Ziona in order to get a firsthand understanding of the situation.

In 2007, Lesley University sponsored a leadership training seminar for Ethiopian youth after their mandatory military service. This group was identified by the municipality as most at risk for social alienation. Schwartz (2007) noted that participants indicated that the workshop offered them "opportunities for creativity and expression" and that they expressed a "desire to continue" (p. 23). Longtime Lesley faculty member Avi Hadari led the workshop.

The extension followed up in April 1998 by conducting a day-long seminar titled "Imagining the Future: Building Dreams" at a Nes Ziona middle school with a large Ethiopian student population. This event featured performances and workshops by the Peace Train, a social movement founded in 1993 by South African musician Sharon Katz. In order to promote a peaceful transition from apartheid to democracy, Katz had organized a group of 150 musicians who began by traveling South Africa by train, bringing diverse ethnic groups together and using music to dissolve conflicts and violence. Katz now takes the Peace Train to many other conflict points around the globe.

In the spring and summer of 2008, Lesley conducted an art therapy support group for young Ethiopian mothers of small children. Led by Lesley graduate and art therapist Keren Askayo, this workshop served not just to help the participants process their issues through the arts; it also helped bridge the gaps between Ethiopian immigrants and the Israeli establishment.

In parallel, Lesley began working with Ethiopian immigrants and their children at the Hadassah Neurim Youth Village's boarding school, located north of Netanya. The students at this state boarding school come from particularly difficult backgrounds, and Lesley hoped to apply the expertise developed in Nes Ziona to the problems of Ethiopian pupils and other students at Hadassah Neurim. In the spring of 2008, Lesley conducted a smaller version of the "Imagining the Future" workshop on the Neurim campus as well. In the fall of 2008, the extension organized some of the school's Ethiopian young women in a women's empowerment seminar, and made Hadassah Neurim a focus for the practical training of its expressive therapies students.

In 2009, Lesley, together with Israel's union of expressive and creative arts therapists, sponsored an academic conference titled "Creative Arts Therapies Approaches to Working with Conflict and Trauma." The event gathered a multidisciplinary group of about 200 researchers and practitioners from the fields of expressive therapies, psychology, education, group leadership, and the arts. Distinguished scholars from around the world, including some of the founders of the field of expressive therapies, presented workshops and lectures. A highlight was an onstage dialogue between Professors Shaun McNiff and Paolo Knill about the evolution of expressive therapies, from the perspective of their own work over a period of four decades.

In the framework of this conference Lesley organized a reprise of the Peace Train, this time working with Jewish and Arab youth around the subject of music and coexistence. In cooperation with Israel's Ministry of Education and the nonprofit organizations Artsbridge, Jerusalem Heartbeat, and Seeds of Peace, Lesley brought three groups of Jewish and Arab youth to the Netanya campus, where they took part in workshops that culminated in a combined musical performance.

THE IMPACT OF LESLEY AND ITS GRADUATES ON ISRAELI SOCIETY

Since its founding, Lesley University has been one of the largest institutions in Israel, and often the only one, that offers academic courses in its fields of study. Lesley has been Israel's most influential and pioneering educational institution in the field of expressive therapies.

More than 30 years after Norma Canner first passionately espoused the virtues of multimodal expressive therapy, Lesley continues to serve as the standard bearer for this approach in Israel.

Similarly, Lesley has defined and has come to be seen as the definition of experiential learning in Israel. When Israelis speak of "the Lesley way," they refer specifically to the triangular formulation of theoretical studies, practical training, and experiential learning that the extension has exclusively popularized over the last three decades.

For Lesley's students, faculty, and administrators, Lesley has served as an island of peace and tranquility. Professor Mary Clare Powell, former head of the Creative Arts and Learning Division, noted that Israeli students told her, "Lesley is an oasis for us, a normal place; we are glad to be spending a week in this course" (2002, p. 19). During the country's most tumultuous periods, the hours spent at Lesley provide immersion in arts-based training that does not just distract from the painful and ubiquitous personal and national psychic assaults. The time spent at Lesley also heals and enriches those who work and study here, while providing hope for a future that contains less trauma and suffering.

Faculty members at Lesley are gratified that the university has been able to help its students and staff to distance themselves from the most painful parts of their realities in Israel. Yet the goal of learning at Lesley is not to cut one's self off from the events of the wider community, however difficult they are. To the contrary, faculty at Lesley are proud to teach students the skills, and prepare them with the experiences, that are necessary to overcome external hardships, and to help others to do so. This has been one of Lesley's greatest gifts during Israel's troubled times.

Generations of Lesley graduates have spread the learning they acquired at Lesley to every part of Israel. Lesley alumni have risen to serve in top echelons in the country's government, nonprofit organizations, and private initiatives. They are recognized for their contributions in the fields of therapy, education, and community activism. Some of Lesley's graduates have achieved national recognition, and often mention to the public and the media the important influence a Lesley education has had on their careers.

One such graduate is Judith Yovel-Recanati. After completing her studies at Lesley College in 1989, Yovel-Recanati became a licensed art therapist in Israel. She conducted individual and group treatments through art psychotherapy, working with PTSD patients at the Beit Levinstein Hospital, the National Institute for Rehabilitation of Head Injury Patients, and the Neurological Rehabilitation Center at Sheba Medical Center.

Yovel-Recanati's therapeutic work brought her into repeated contact with victims of terror, and with the families of these victims. Many of these individuals have undergone the most extreme of traumas and were in need of rehabilitative services. In this environment, in 1998, Yovel-Recanati cofounded NATAL, the Israel Trauma Center for Victims of Terror and War. In its more than 10 years of operation, NATAL has treated tens of thousands of trauma victims through its individual and group therapy sessions and telephone hotline. For her efforts in founding and running NATAL, Yovel-Recanati was awarded second prize as Israel's Community Innovator of 2005, and in 2007 she received Lesley University's Alumni Community Service Award.

Lesley has made other direct contributions to Israeli society by focusing the knowledge and experience of its instructors, students, and administrators on the most pressing problems that face Israeli society. In the framework of its practicum training, Lesley sends its students to assist populations that include the mentally ill, battered women, the developmentally and physically disabled, at-risk youth, Ethiopian and Russian immigrants, victims of eating disorders, and prison inmates.

THE IMPACT OF THE EXTENSION IN ISRAEL ON THE GREATER LESLEY COMMUNITY

The people and experiences that characterize the Lesley extension have left an indelible impression on faculty and administrators at the parent campus in Cambridge. Instructors from the United States who teach in Israel consistently note that the experience is one of the most challenging of their careers, yet one of the most rewarding. Lesley faculty have established long, meaningful, and enduring friendships with their Israeli students and colleagues. The Israeli milieu has proved to be an extraordinarily fruitful laboratory for research and academic advancement.

For the past 10 years, Schwartz has briefed each new Cambridge-based faculty member before she or he teaches for the first time in Israel. Schwartz noted that these discussions are frequently eye-opening. He said:

> I tell them that on the one hand, they should be prepared for students who will violate all the conventions of the faculty student relationship. Most important, when the students walk into the classroom, they haven't adopted the most basic educational assumption, that the teacher has something to teach them. On the other hand, I tell them that they have probably never taught more open, engaging, challenging or heartwarming students in their careers. After the course, I check with the faculty, and I am usually right on both counts. (S. Schwartz, personal communication, July 14, 2008)

Professor Mary Clare Powell (2002) added, "I always find Israeli students enthusiastic and passionate, opinionated and smart, but I don't remember them being grateful before [this last trip]" (p. 19).

In its years of operation, dozens of Cambridge-based faculty members have taught in Israel, and many of them ask to come back, time after time. Mary Clare Powell (2002) wrote, "Just about every night I was invited out to Sam's home, to Noya's and to Nira's (Lesley's librarian)" (p. 20). Israel has an extremely informal culture, and students and faculty members often form meaningful personal relationships even before their courses are over. Lesley faculty members are frequently overwhelmed by the demonstrations of appreciation they receive from their Israeli students. Professor Julia Byers (2004), also a former director of the Division of Expressive Therapies, remembered that following a particularly dynamic off-campus orientation course, her students gave her an artwork consisting of a matchbox out of which emerged a feed of folded paper bearing miniature images of the students as well as their words of gratitude for teaching them the concept of "letting go." Byers recalled being deeply moved.

Lesley faculty members have frequently conducted important research during their visits to Israel, and have published academic papers about their experiences there. Israel's multiethnic demographic and the rich experiences that are to be had there make it an ideal laboratory for testing theories in the fields of therapy, education, and intercultural study.

On a number of occasions, whole publications have been dedicated to the work at Israel's Lesley extension. The fall 2002 issue of *Lesley Magazine* was titled "Teaching at War," and featured recollections of visits to the extension. The July 2007 special edition of the *Journal of Humanistic Psychology* was dedicated exclusively to Lesley's 2006 Imagine Conference in Israel. The upcoming edition of Lesley's *Journal of Pedagogy, Pluralism, and Practice* will focus on the recollections of faculty members who have taught at the Israel extension.

THE SECRET OF LESLEY'S SUCCESS

Why is Lesley's Israel extension a success? Professor Shaun McNiff sharpened the question by asking, "Why do so many thousands of people in Israel, such a large percentage of the total population, unparalleled by another nation, show such interest in the arts and healing?" (McNiff, May 31, 2009)

The authors would like to point to a synergy that functions both in principle and in practice, between the goals and values of the parent university and the needs of Israel. The extension program in Israel has retained the spirit and philosophy of the Institute for the Arts and Human Development at Lesley, from which it was born.

The nontraditional teaching style pioneered by the extension, and now known in Israel as the Lesley way, speaks to the soul of the people of Israel. Generations of Israeli students have embraced the mix of academic theory, practical applications, and experiential learning. All three elements of the Lesley way are contained in the first line of the university's mission statement (2009), which reads, "Lesley University is committed to active learning, scholarly research, critical inquiry, and diverse forms of artistic practice through close mentoring relationships among students, faculty, and practitioners in the field." The mix of traditional and alternative ways of experiencing the learning process, so beloved by Israeli students, is also directly referenced. Lesley's mission statement continues: "Central to the mission of all its programs is a commitment to excellence, creative instruction, the integration of academic and field-based learning, and responsiveness to the needs of society and the student."

Lesley's mission statement encompasses the institution's belief in and commitment to the arts, which is central to every program of study offered at the Israel extension. The extension has defined itself through the arts as an organizing principle, in the realms of therapy, education, group leadership, women's studies, and holistic health. As a means of overcoming conflict, dealing with trauma, and building hope, the arts have served the Israeli people well.

Lesley's focus on diversity and social justice also resonates with the people of Israel, whose biblical traditions of striving to repair the world (tikkun olam) and providing "a light unto the nations" through demonstrations of social equity fits with Lesley's mission "to provide opportunities for all to participate in the cultural, political, and economic life of the nation and the world." Lesley's slogan "Let's Wake Up the World" appears to be a modern take on the ancient Israelites' biblical injunction. Theater critic Joel Derfner (2009) argues that the arts both bring about, and are a form of, tikkun olam, and quotes D. H. Lawrence's study in 1923 of Walt Whitman:

> The essential function of art is moral. Not aesthetic, not decorative, not pastime and recreation. But moral. The essential function of art is moral. But a passionate, implicit morality, not didactic. A morality which changes the blood, rather than

the mind. Changes the blood first. The mind follows later, in the wake. (D. H. Lawrence, quoted in Derfner, 2009, p. 56)

In just over 60 years, Israel has emerged from the ashes of the European Holocaust to become a world leader in scholarship, science, and the arts. This transformation has created an opportunity for Lesley's programs to thrive there. During these same six decades, Israel has fought seven wars and lost nearly 30,000 of its people to conflict—circumstances in which Lesley's programs of study meet demands for healing and hope. Marcow Speiser (2009) captured some of this complexity as follows:

> There are deep wounds in this society, yet at the same time there is a dynamic at work in this area, which far transcends the boundaries of territoriality, and this is the area I am calling the spiritual domain. This is the area that encompasses all people's hopes and all people's pain. This is the area that contains the cultural continuities and contradictions of the accumulated human experience. Here is where transformation and healing can take place. This then is the ground in which we do our teaching. (p. 65)

Lesley's focus on intercultural and interdisciplinary learning is also well suited to the needs of Israelis. Israel is home to citizens from dramatically different backgrounds, and fissures along religious, national, economic, linguistic, and cultural lines are commonplace. With their missions of inclusion and multicultural education, Lesley's programs help Israelis to flourish in their complex society.

As this chapter has shown, Lesley's contribution to the development of Israel over the past 30 years has been significant. This is largely because of the great extent to which Lesley's values and practical education have been uniquely matched to the needs of the state of Israel. It is also clear that Lesley as an institution, along with its faculty and administrators, have highly benefited from their collective experiences in Israel. Over the past three decades, Lesley has developed an interest in Israel in teaching the concepts, skills, and values that it holds dear, and it has laid a foundation for doing so. Whatever the future holds for Lesley University's extension in Israel, the legacy that Lesley has already established there will endure into the future.

REFERENCES

Byers, J. G., & Forinash, M. (Eds.). (2004). *Educators, therapists, & artists on reflective practice.* New York, NY: P. Lang.

Derfner, J. (March 24, 2009). The Search for Love in Manhattan. *Faustus, M.D.* Retrieved from http://www.joelderfner.com/blog/2009/03/post_407.html

Joubran, N., & Schwartz, S. (July 2007). From Enemies to Friends: Personal Conflict Resolution at Imagine. *Journal of Humanistic Psychology, 47*(3), 340 350.

Lawrence, D. H. (1923). *Studies in classic American literature.* New York, NY: Thomas Seltzer; LesleyUniversity. (2009). Mission and Values Statements. Retrieved from http://www.lesley.edu/about/mission.html

Marcow Speiser, V. (2009). The Lesley University Extension Program in Israel: Teaching in a Troubled Land. *Journal of Pedagogy, Pluralism, and Practice, 13.*

McNiff, S. (May 31, 2009). [Article About Lesley]. Powell, M. C. (Fall 2002). Teaching at War. *Lesley Magazine,* 18 21.

Schwartz, S. (2001). *Lesley's Early Years in Israel.* Arts Institute Project in Israel. Netanya, Israel.

Schwartz, S. (2009). Cross Cultural Observations Emerging from Lesley's Partnership with Israel's Ethiopian Immigrant Community. *Journal of Pedagogy, Pluralism, and Practice 13.*

Schwartz, S. (June 2007). *Feedback on Avi Hadari's Group Leadership Skills Workshop for Ethiopian Army Graduates in Nes Ziona.* Lesley University. Netanya, Israel.

Serlin, I. A., & Marcow Speiser, V. (July 2007). Introduction. *Journal of Humanistic Psychology, 47*(3), 280 287.

CHAPTER SIX

The Liberal Arts at Lesley College: Three Perspectives

ROBERT WAUHKONEN, EdD
ROSALIE FINK, EdD
ANNE PLUTO, PhD

In this chapter, three professors highlight exciting liberal arts traditions at Lesley and fascinating recent innovations that have received wide attention. First, Professor Robert Wauhkonen sets the historical context and discusses the liberal arts from theoretical and practical perspectives. He goes on to explain how, for 100 years, liberal arts traditions at Lesley have been linked with timely innovations, especially with experiential learning.

In the next section, Professor Rosalie Fink describes her unique approach to active experiential learning. Fink merges dance, rhythm, and visual art with the reading of texts to enrich students' understanding of literary and other text forms. In her classes students create and perform their own rap songs, Readers' Theater scripts, poems, and movement sequences. Recently, for example, after reading and analyzing Barack Obama's 1995 memoir *Dreams from My Father: A Story of Race and Inheritance*, students reviewed for a test by creating their own rap songs, including "The Obama Rap," "He Leads the Nation Despite Discrimination," "Private School, It Ain't That Cool," and "He'll Take Our Country Out of Economic Hell."

In the chapter's last section, Professor Anne Pluto shows how she adapts a wide variety of Shakespeare plays to create enthralling Shakespeare productions. In summary, the chapter presents lively vignettes and enlightening examples of Lesley's innovative, hands-on approaches to teaching the liberal arts.

WEDDING TRADITION AND INNOVATION

Ask someone at Lesley College about what defines the college's educational mission, and you're likely to get the same response that faculty and students have been giving for nearly 100 years: to make a difference in the world. From the earliest days of Edith Lesley's normal school, which educated women to be teachers, to today's coeducational college, with numerous programs and majors, Lesley's educational focus has been to send graduates out into the world to improve the lives of others.

This focus on making a difference is reflected in Lesley's programs in education, counseling, art and expressive arts therapy, human services, management, communication and technology, environmental studies, and the liberal arts. Lesley has a long and distinguished tradition of graduating students who have gone on to make a difference in each of these fields. A critical part of Lesley's success in educating students in these areas is its strong commitment to the liberal arts. Traditionally, study in the liberal arts has focused on broadening and enriching students' lives in ways that go beyond their professional education. Liberal arts study at Lesley has long shared this vision. In contrast to many other colleges, however, where study in the liberal arts is viewed as separate from study in the major, Lesley has long sought to integrate the two, creating an unusually rich and meaningful educational experience. In taking such an approach, Lesley has been in the vanguard. The Association of American Colleges and Universities has argued recently that the traditional distinction between liberal and professional education needs to be abandoned (Schneider & Shoenberg, n.d.), and recommends the integration of the two in the way that Lesley has long practiced. Lesley's innovative approach to the liberal arts is also reflected in the way in which faculty teaching liberal arts courses seek to connect study in the liberal arts to real-world issues and concerns.

Nothing speaks more to Lesley's commitment to relating study in the liberal arts to students' professional education than its long-standing commitment to experiential learning. All Lesley students, regardless of major, undertake experiential learning from their first year of study. Common forms of experiential learning include student practica in education; internships in health clinics, hospitals, and businesses; work in clinics and community-based organizations; research in laboratories; and assisting with writing and research. By the time Lesley students graduate, they have undertaken the equivalent of three to four courses in some form of experiential learning.

Whatever the form of experiential learning that students undertake, they get to apply knowledge and skills learned in their liberal arts and professional classes in ways that reinforce one another and strengthen the overall learning experience. Applying theory and knowledge learned in the classroom in experiential learning settings develops understanding in ways beyond what classroom learning alone can provide. Addressing career-related challenges in real-life settings helps students develop critical thinking skills and the capacity for creative problem solving. A recent graduate, commenting on the connection between classroom and experiential learning, noted how her classes had laid the foundation for work she did in her internship, but "it was the internship itself that helped me put the skills into practice."

The capacity for experiential learning to reinforce classroom learning is documented in research done by T. K. Stanton. "Learning activities that require learners to apply knowledge and skills to the solution of problems," Stanton found, "more often develop the higher cognitive skills than do traditional classroom methods" (DiConti, 2004, p. 172). Moreover, the opportunity that experiential learning provides students to apply theory and skills learned in their classes makes learning more meaningful in allowing students to apply knowledge and skills to their career interests.

Experiential learning contributes not only to students' cognitive development, but to growth in social awareness and interpersonal skills as well. Development in each of these areas is central to the goals of liberal education. In interviews with recent Lesley graduates, students said that their participation in internships, community service, teaching practica, and apprenticeships had been key in enhancing their social awareness. Such opportunities, students noted, allowed them to work with people from varying racial, ethnic, and socioeconomic backgrounds, and thus to develop greater comfort with those whose backgrounds differed from their own. Similarly, students noted that experiential learning had strengthened interpersonal skills in the opportunities it afforded for working in real-world settings. Study in liberal arts classes deepened students' understanding of political and social issues and contributed to growth in personal development, but experiential learning, students reported, gave them an opportunity to engage real-world concerns in ways that they found especially meaningful. As with students' cognitive development, the opportunity that experiential learning provided to work in real-world settings added a dimension of learning that classroom learning alone could not provide.

Lesley's emphasis on relating study in the liberal arts to students' lives is also evident in the ways in which faculty connect study in the liberal arts to students' personal lives and the world in which they live. As at most colleges, Lesley students have historically taken a variety of courses in the liberal arts domains of the humanities, social sciences, and sciences. Through courses in literature and the arts, students learn to appreciate different forms of artistic expression and come to understand how works of art have both shaped and reflected the cultures of the world. History courses enable students to see the present as a point of intersection between the past and the future, and provide the understanding and perspective that are critical for informed citizenship. Language courses teach students not only how to speak and write in a different language, but how to appreciate other cultures. Courses in psychology and sociology help students to better understand themselves and the dynamics of group and social behavior. Study in science not only teaches students the methodology by which scientists look at and understand the world, but also helps students to develop the knowledge and understanding that are critical for living in a democracy where more and more public policy issues have a scientific or technological component. As part of Lesley's commitment to graduating students with a strong sense of global awareness, all students pursue studies of non-Western cultures to learn about values, beliefs, and practices that differ from their own.

Taken together, studies in all these areas develop the breadth of vision that defines a liberal arts education. The subject areas in which Lesley students engage are similar to those at most colleges, but what distinguishes liberal arts study at Lesley is the emphasis that faculty place on making such study relevant and meaningful. In composition courses, students write about the environment, homelessness, public art, and other topics that matter to them and society. In their encounter with questions that lie at the heart of what it means to be human, students in literature and art courses learn not only *about* literature and art but *through* them. Students learn math through investigating statistics in sports, matters related to the economy and global warming, and many topics in between. Courses in the social sciences develop perspectives on key issues of race, culture, and gender, and enable students to become agents for social change. Studies in world cultures and religions impart knowledge of different beliefs and values, essential for understanding the global dynamics that shape today's world.

Lesley's success in making study in the liberal arts meaningful is based not only on *what* faculty teach, but *how*. Recognizing the important role that pedagogy plays in learning, Lesley faculty have long sought to engage students as active learners, and to make classroom learning a dynamic, transformative process. Far more than "talking heads," faculty at Lesley work to make the classroom experience interactive. Discussion is strongly emphasized, not only to engage students, but also to promote cross-fertilization of ideas. Peer assignments, group presentations, research projects, and other forms of collaborative learning are common. Whether it be a literature or a math class, faculty work to make learning come alive by engaging students as active participants in the learning process.

Beyond the formal academic curriculum, learning in the liberal arts and related areas is supported through a wide variety of cultural activities and events outside the classroom. Each year, liberal arts programs sponsor an array of lectures, forums, and seminars tied to current social and cultural issues. Speakers include Lesley faculty as well as scholars, artists, and public figures from outside the college. The recent development of Lesley's English and Creative Writing majors has brought about an increase in the number of readings at the college by students, faculty, and established writers. Adding to the richness of cultural events and offerings are the many art shows in galleries in Cambridge and at the Art Institute of Boston campus, as well as lectures and gallery talks by well-known and emerging artists. A new event designed to celebrate the scholarship of students and faculty alike is Annual Scholarship Day, during which students and faculty present research and papers to the larger Lesley academic community.

Students also participate in numerous arts-related activities. Each spring the Oxford Street Players, established in 1991, stages a Shakespeare play or a play from that era. Recently, dramatic productions have increased to include a contemporary play or a musical each fall. Students participate in all parts of the production, from acting to set design to musical accompaniment. Lesley's Concert Choir and Gospel Choir present several performances each year, as does a recently formed a capella group. Each year, Lesley's English Department publishes *Commonthought*, a student-run literary and arts magazine in which students and faculty showcase their work. Students also run a number of film series throughout the year.

In recent years, a growing number of Lesley students have been taking advantage of another source of liberal arts exploration—the various study abroad programs that Lesley has developed. Students commonly take courses in a foreign language, in literature, and in other aspects of liberal arts through these programs. As many students have noted, studying a foreign language and culture in a native environment is an especially meaningful learning experience.

Indeed, the cultural immersion that comes with studying and living abroad is deeply educational in itself, and for this reason, the college is encouraging more and more students to take advantage of study abroad options.

An important development at Lesley in the last decade has been the development of stand-alone liberal arts majors. For much of Lesley's history, the liberal arts existed primarily to provide service courses to the professional majors. Over the last 10 years, liberal arts majors have been developed in art history, English, history, history and literature, and mathematics. Certification requirements in education provided the first impetus for the development of the majors, but members of Lesley's liberal arts faculty spearheaded the transformation. Lesley now highlights its liberal arts majors in admissions materials, presenting the college as a place where students can do innovative and challenging work in the liberal arts with the benefit of an experiential learning component. Currently, more than 20% of incoming students cite their intention to pursue a liberal arts major rather than a professional major.[15] This change has entailed a transformation in the liberal arts faculty and its view of the liberal arts at Lesley. No longer solely providers of service courses, liberal arts faculty are at the heart of a changing university, teaching a deeper curriculum that offers more junior- and senior-level courses.

Over the past 100 years, the scope of liberal arts study at Lesley has grown tremendously, from the range of courses offered to the establishment of liberal arts majors. So, too, has the variety of cultural activities and events related to the liberal arts. What has remained constant is Lesley's commitment to connecting study in the liberal arts to students' personal and professional development through experientially based learning and engaged, dynamic teaching. One hundred years ago, Lesley students had a more narrow exposure to the liberal arts, but they were very familiar with the college's commitment to making such study a transformative experience.

---

15 This information was provided by Dr. Christine Evans, professor of comparative literature at Lesley College.

Inspiring Interest and Motivation in College Readers and Writers

The No Child Left Behind Act of 2001, which was intended to improve American education in the 21st century, created enormous controversy and had profound effects on education across the United States. In Massachusetts it led to a series of high-stakes tests called the Massachusetts Comprehensive Assessment System (MCAS), which every student must pass in order to graduate from high school. With the advent of MCAS, a perception developed at Lesley that more students arrive on campus better prepared in basic, traditional reading and writing skills, and better prepared to deal with complex college texts.

Notwithstanding the preparation that now accompanies freshmen to campus, most books used at Lesley and other universities face stiff competition from the click of a mouse on the Internet, iPods, Facebook, and Twitter. These enticing forms of dynamic communication are fabulous, because they provide access to information worldwide and engage students in almost instantaneous communication with voices that speak to them in 21st-century tones. We know that students relate easily to these tones, but research shows that these new forms of literacy, while exciting and valuable, are not sufficient to enable students to develop deep understandings of issues and strong motivation and desire to read further, investigate deeply, and integrate what they have read. What else is needed, besides these forms of online literacy? What is our challenge at Lesley University going forward?

Lesley's Challenge in the 21st Century

Our challenge in the 21st century is to connect students to great literature through their own vernacular, such as rap songs, and through activities that resonate with relevant themes in students' lives (such as MCAS tests, personal relationships, career choices, and the cost of a college education). How can we accomplish this? How can we inspire our students to be captivated by texts, and to read them closely and reflectively? What can we do to attract students to the delights of literacy so that once they are out in the world and on their own, they choose to read avidly and become critical readers, writers, and thinkers, engaged in the dynamic social questions of our time? These questions challenge me each semester as I begin teaching anew.

For me, answers came in part from my research at Harvard on students who had had severe difficulties with reading yet overcame their challenges. I interviewed men and women from across the United States to find out how those who had struggled with reading ultimately became highly successful readers and writers in fields that demand high levels of literacy (such as medicine, law, business, psychology, education, and the arts and sciences). My sample included a Nobel laureate and many who were movers and shakers in their fields. Conducting this research encouraged me to write two books about reading and writing in the 21ˢᵗ century: *Why Jane and John Couldn't Read—And How They Learned: A New Look at Striving Readers* (Fink, 2006) and *Inspiring Reading Success: Interest and Motivation in an Age of High-Stakes Testing* (Fink & Samuels, 2008).

One of the most compelling findings from my research was that the fascinating people whom I studied had overcome their learning difficulties and had learned to read extremely well. How? By reading avidly on a topic of passionate personal interest (Fink, 2006). Whether the topic was science, history, literature, biography, or auto mechanics, the key to their success was their overwhelming interest, which spurred them into the habit of sustained reading.

This observation led me to develop the Interest-Based Model of Reading, which helps me address an important 21ˢᵗ-century Lesley goal: to help *all* kinds of students, from diverse backgrounds, achieve the highest levels of literacy—students who are gifted and talented, who are "average," who struggle on account of poverty, and who have learning disabilities and emotional differences, as well as students for whom English is not the home language. The Interest-Based Model of Reading that I developed is central to my teaching and is pivotal to both of my books. The model has five key components, each of which I incorporate into my courses.

Five Components of the Interest-Based Model

1. Personal choice of texts based on the student's passionate, personal interest
2. Avid, sustained, topic-specific reading and writing
3. Deep background information and knowledge
4. Contextual reading strategies
5. A supportive mentor (such as a Lesley professor!)

Both of my books have been widely read by other educators. Consequently, I've been invited to give keynote lectures and workshops, which has led to new opportunities to collaborate with wonderful colleagues across the United States and in other countries. My research and writing have had a profound influence on my teaching at Lesley.

My Research Informs Teaching

My writings on the Interest-Based Model of Reading have benefited my Lesley students by spurring me to create new approaches to teaching and learning—approaches that I use in my Lesley classes. My students and I design compelling hands-on activities that promote excitement, engagement, and deep understanding of texts. These interactive, multisensory activities integrate reading and writing with the arts and the senses, and include seeing, hearing, touching, moving, chanting, drawing, painting, and dancing. These techniques engage students in active reading, writing, and performing of Readers' Theater, rap songs, group poems, debates, discussion, and so forth. I use these activities in conjunction with the marvelous new online forms of literacy; but they differ from the instantaneous communication of online literacies in one significant way: Each activity requires more time for reflection, and often more personal involvement and action, in order to promote deep understanding and reflective comprehension.

POPULAR HANDS-ON ACTIVITIES

Recently, I presented some of the most popular activities described in *Why Jane and John Couldn't Read* and *Inspiring Reading Success* at three special Lesley events: Lesley's Annual Scholarship Days (March 31, 2009, and March 31, 2010) and the Lesley College Honors Symposium (December 3, 2009). Together with students from my English Composition and Struggling Readers and Writers classes, I demonstrated active learning techniques that help students expand vocabulary, deepen reading comprehension, and refine expressive and persuasive writing skills. To these ends, I employed my extensive background as a professional dancer. (I studied choreography and dance with Martha Graham and performed and taught dance in my earlier career.) My dance background helped me incorporate movement, music, and rap into these Lesley University presentations. Attending Lesley students and faculty worked in small groups and used traditional folktales and modern literature as springboards for creating new scripts of their own with new 21st-century endings. Together, faculty and students performed their original scripts, using scarves to enhance movement, create scenery, connote costumes, and indicate characters. These collaborative group activities included Readers' Theater with Dance and Scarves, Original Script Writing, Short Story Writing, the Telephone Book Expressive Reading Technique, the Semantic Impressions Vocabulary Method, Poetry Writing and Poetry Festivals, "I" Poems, Bio-Poems, Rhythm Walks, Dramatic Story Readings, Photography, Video Shows, and Rap Songs. Rap songs, plays, videos, and poems included "The Obama Rap," "He Leads the Nation Despite Discrimination," "He'll Take Our Country Out of Economic Hell," "Private School, It Ain't That Cool," "Shrek and Fiona," "Cleaning Up," "Humpty Dumpty," "Gun Control," "The

Ethical Nature of Photography," and "The MCAS Rap." (The words to "The MCAS Rap" appear at the end of this section.)

"The MCAS Rap" was created by urban students to enhance test taking. Performed with compelling rhythmic movement, this lively song and dance was created as a follow-up activity based on the books we read and the activities we did in my Struggling Readers and Writers class at Lesley. After creating original raps in class, Melanie Gavin, one of my students, applied the activity in her experiential learning classroom at the Neighborhood House Charter School in Dorchester, Massachusetts. Creating their own rap songs about how to become good test takers helped Melanie's inner-city students prepare for the MCAS tests. Writing and performing their own lyrics with their own choreographed movements enabled Melanie's students to comprehend, remember, and internalize the meaning of the text that they themselves had created. This type of interactive, hands-on experiential learning is the hallmark of a Lesley liberal arts education.

PAOLO'S PROJECT

The hallmark of hands-on learning at Lesley was demonstrated in a project by another student of mine, Paolo Morales, through his PowerPoint and video presentation titled "The Ethical Nature of Photography." The project was based on Morales's research paper for my English Composition class, and explored several intriguing questions: (1) Who is the "owner" of a photographic portrait—the photographer or the subject? (2) What moral responsibility, if any, does a portrait photographer have to the individual whose image appears in the photograph? And (3) What are the lines between "truth" and "fiction" in the art of photography?

To investigate these thought-provoking questions, Morales used captivating photographs by world-class photographers such as Sally Mann and Jacob Riis. In addition, he included Lesley students in his photographic presentation. For example, the next photograph shows a Lesley student doing an assignment at Boston's Museum of Fine

Arts. The student is viewing a painting in an exhibit of Impressionist masterpieces that includes a sculpture by Edward Degas, *The Dancer,* which is one of my personal favorites. The Lesley student in Morales's photograph appears to be deeply engaged in an assignment that required her to (1) go to the Museum of Fine Arts in Boston, (2) view and reflect upon great works of art, (3) integrate paintings and sculptures by artistic masters into her own experience, and (4) develop her own unique creative and analytical work based on this hands-on experience. As a result of being physically present and viewing original paintings and sculptures close up, rather than using paltry reproductions, the student experiences a work of art in all its splendor and integrity. She sees for herself the richness and intensity of the colors, the thickness of the paint. She feels the immediacy and awe of being in the presence of an artistic masterpiece. The preparation for this firsthand museum experience—extensive background reading; a professor's expert lectures; and thought-provoking activities in class—makes it even more deeply meaningful.

This type of well-designed, experiential education promotes deep, memorable learning. I am happy to be part of the great Lesley tradition of experiential learning, and I look forward to contributing new ideas to Lesley University in the 21st century.

THE MCAS RAP

Created by Melanie Gavan and the Neighborhood House Charter School students in Dorchester, MA, in conjunction with lectures and hands-on activities in Rosalie Fink's Struggling Readers and Writers Class:

Chorus

We are here today
To rap about a test
Called the MCAS
So you can do your best

Verse

My name is Keishawn and the first thing that you do
   Is to read the directions all the way through
My name is BJ and the next step that you take
   Is to read the title; don't take a break
My name is Tavari and the next thing that you do
   Is to read the italics; that is what you do
My name is Caitlin and the fourth thing that you do
   Is to read the questions; then go back and review

Chorus

We are here today
To rap about a test
Called the MCAS
So you can do your best

Verse

My name is Star and after we review
   You start the story; that is what you do
My name is Christian, and when we find the answer
   We make sure to highlight, to get the right answer
My name is Dominique and I have a suggestion
   After you highlight, read the next question
My name is Marlayeeka and we've shown you the way
   To conquer the MCAS, so have a nice day!

THE OXFORD STREET PLAYERS OF LESLEY UNIVERSITY: THE PLACE WHERE GOD LIVES

The theater, according to Tina Packer, artistic director of Shakespeare & Company and the woman whose Text class forever changed my life, "is the place where God lives" (Lecture, Packer, June 1993). If we read God to be the human spirit, the human voice, then theater is the classroom of huge emotions and complex rhythms, especially as found in Shakespeare. On stage, in rehearsal and performance, the actors express feelings in poetry or prose and in action. The literature classroom is different; it is the place where God is visited and revered, and in the writing/creative writing classroom, the place where God is created. We speak differently, in a different voice, not in the stage voice. We are silent as we write our own text; the page we create speaks for us.

In the spring of 1993 I was promoted to associate professor, accepted into Shakespeare & Company's June Intensive Workshop and Summer Training Institute, and granted a year-long sabbatical. When I returned to Lesley in the fall of 1994, I was no longer only an English professor and the faculty advisor for *Commonthought Magazine*, but a fledgling director and an actor who had returned to the stage after a 19-year absence, and who soon assumed the role of artistic director of the Oxford Street Players (OSP) of what was then Lesley College. The Oxford Street Players had been conceived in 1993 through the efforts of Dr. Stephen Trainor (then the program director of liberal arts in the women's college), Lisa Risley, and myself (Pluto). Shakespeare's *The Merchant of Venice*, directed by Lisa Risley and produced by me, was our first season.

The three months spent at Shakespeare & Company in Lenox, MA, transformed my life and gave Lesley a theater company. June 1993 was spent immersed in Shakespeare. My training included text work, bodywork (Alexander technique, medieval and Renaissance dance, and stage combat), and Linklater Voice work. Back home in Boston, I audited text and movement courses at Emerson College, continued studying voice at the Linklater Studio (with Kristen Linklater herself), and was cast as Fabian in a production of Shakespeare's *Twelfth Night*. The connection I found between voice, breath, and text has informed all my teaching and scholarship.

In January 1994 I returned to Lesley to direct my first play, Shakespeare's middle-class comedy *The Merry Wives of Windsor*. Since 1994, as the artistic director of the Oxford Street Players, I have been involved in the following plays as director or producer, or both:

1993 *Merchant of Venice (producer) [preSShakespeare & Company]*
1994 Merry Wives of Windsor (producer and director)
1995 *Twelfth Night Fever (producer and director)*
1996 *Romeo and Juliet (producer and director)*
1996 *The Comedy of Eros* (cowritten, produced, and directed with Lisa Risley)
1997 *The Two Gentlemen of Verona* (producer and director)
1998 *Comedy of Errors (producer and director)*
1999 *All's Well That Ends Well (producer and director)*
2000 *Thomas of Woodstock (producer and director)*
2001 *The Tempest (producer and director)*
2002 *Dr. Faustus (producer and director)*
2003 *Henry VI, Part I (producer and director)*
2003 *The Laramie Project* (producer, directed by Kevin Carr)
2004 *The Rover* (producer and director)
2004 *The Glass Menagerie* (producer, directed by Kevin Carr)
2005 *The Winter's Tale* (producer and director)
2006 *Blithe Spirit (producer, directed by Kevin Carr)*
2006 *Much Ado About Nothing* (producer and director)\
2007 *The Merry Wives of Windsor, Texas "shore know how to git a man down..."* (producer and director)
2008 *Measure for Measure* (producer and director)
2009 *The Merchant of Venice* (producer and director)

In addition to producing and directing these plays, I developed the Play Production Shakespeare course, which accompanies the Shakespeare productions, and the non-Shakespeare productions course. Both courses are challenging to teach. While focusing on the world and text of the play, we design and build the set, design and sew the costumes, and construct the props. It is theater done from start to finish in 10 weeks. The course has a lab, which consists of set and costume construction for the technical crew, along with Linklater Voice class, movement class, stage combat workshops, dance and music class, and scene rehearsals for the actors.

The spring 2006 production of Shakespeare's *Much Ado About Nothing* had another component: math and science. Sets cannot be built without knowledge of the Pythagorean theorem and cannot stand without following the simple rules of physics. Dr. Jim O'Keefe joined us to teach geometry, and Dr. Linda Grisham instructed us in physics. Dr. David Morimoto gave a lecture on the flora and fauna of Sicily. Theater is the most interdisciplinary of the arts. Both courses and their linked productions are open to students across the university; they may take the course twice for credit and participate in OSP productions their entire Lesley career and beyond. My stage manager of 13 years, Andi Wakefield, was a student in my English Composition course in the fall of 1994, and began working with the OSP in 1995, pulling the curtain for *Twelfth Night Fever. Measure for Measure* was her final production with OSP. In 2009, Ariana Balayan, a first-year graduate student in the Community Arts Program, joined us as stage manager. This became her internship, and she was supervised by Dr. Terry Chance, a recipient of the Paul A. Kaplan Visiting Artist Fellowship.

In addition to Terry Chance, we have had several guest artists over the years. Gianni di Marco of the Boston Ballet was our choreographer for two shows, *Dr. Faustus* and *The Rover.* Armando Maciel of the National Ballet of Portugal joined us as our choreographer in residence for three Shakespeare productions, *The Tempest, The Winter's Tale,* and *Much Ado About Nothing.* Terry Chance first came to us in 2007; the music he composed for *The Merry Wives of Windsor, Texas, shore know how to git a man down...*was a part of his PhD thesis in Fine Arts at Texas Tech University. Dr. Chance is a professional musician and songwriter-composer in his own right, and we were fortunate to have him back in 2008 and 2009 on a grant from the Kaplan Foundation.

In addition to being the artistic director of the OSP, I designed a drama minor and a drama track in the English major. I have developed courses with other theater professionals, including Introduction to Voice and Acting, with designated Linklater Voice teacher Chris Von Baeyer; and Improvisation and Movement, with Jill Mackavey. In my position as artistic director of OSP, I choose the play and hire the Linklater Voice teachers, the choreographers, the stage combat and movement teachers, musical directors, and assistant directors for each production. As producer I am responsible for the budget, and I work with the Development Office, raising funds for the Friends of the Oxford Street Players of Lesley University and overseeing the business interns who sell the program ads and run the box office. My director's role involves 15 hours of rehearsal time a week with the actors. Besides preparing for the rehearsals, I attend the Linklater Voice class, where I assist the voice teacher, and I help choreograph the stage combat and assist with dance rehearsals.

Theater courses examine the world of the play, the life of the playwright, historical context for the play, and relevant theater history. This examination always includes a look at religion, politics, gender, and class in addition to the literary and dramatic devices of the prose and poetry, the dialogue, and the structural elements of acts and scenes. As a class, we do an in-depth analysis of the play script; all the students in the class (and the production) come to the read-through of the entire play, which serves as the first day of the rehearsal process. As the actors read their parts, we stop at the end of each scene to talk about the plot and clear up any surface mysteries (and there is a great deal that is mysterious in Shakespeare, Christopher Marlowe, and Aphra Behn). That is only the beginning; the textual analysis continues throughout the entire 10-week process and, up to the final dress rehearsal, we are uncovering new meanings and how to "play" them. I teach the structure and rhythm of the verse to both the class and the actors (as not all the actors are in the class) and lead them through a visualization exercise called the Elizabethan Worldview to establish the hierarchy of the Elizabethan world, and go over the difference between verse and prose and what that would mean for an actor or character. It is vital for actors to understand the difference between iambic pentameter and prose, and to understand why some characters speak only in verse, or prose, or why characters might use a combination of the two.

The rehearsal process begins with my concept of how the play will "look" and what the play will do, but this concept changes as my relationships evolve with the actors, the technical director, and the stage manager. The play production course is constructivist learning at its best. Empowering my students and engaging in dialogue with them is imperative to my teaching and my scholarship. The play evolves from day one until the final matinee performance; nothing is static. In 2003, as the United States was preparing to attack Iraq, I chose a cameo role in Shakespeare's history play *Henry VI, Part I.* I had worked on a version of that play in 1993 at Shakespeare & Company, and the impending war in Iraq and the bombing campaign in Afghanistan compelled me to revisit the original play. It begins with the funeral of Henry V, but his widow, Catherine of France, and their baby son, Henry VI, are absent. I created a text for Catherine, by borrowing the sonnet from the end of *Henry V.* During the funeral, Catherine and veiled ladies speak the first 12 lines of this sonnet:

> Thus far, with rough and all-unable pen
> Our bending author hath pursu'd the story
> In little room confining mighty men,
> Mangling by starts the full course of their glory.
> Small time, but in the small most greatly lived
> This star of England: Fortune made his sword,
> By which the world's best garden he achieved,
> And of it left his son imperial lord.
> Henry the Sixth, in infant bands crown'd King
> Of France and England, did this king succeed?
> Whose state so many had the managing,
> That they lost France and made his England bleed.

The ladies then listen in horror to the dead king's brothers and uncles, who vow to continue war with France. Taking other liberties with the text, I rewrote the character of Joan of Arc, from Shakespeare's crazy whore, Joan la Pucelle, to the young girl who truly believed in the voices of saints prophesying her destiny as the savior of France. Rewriting Shakespeare is a daunting challenge, but this is what directors do and are allowed to do with the bard. Shakespeare is the universal playwright; his plays are translated and produced all over the world; his insights about family, politics, and love have stood the test of time; his extraordinary poetry and complex prose express the passions of characters who lived before the onset of industrialization and psychoanalysis. They *can* speak their feelings, and they attempt to live their desires. Whether as an actor or director, the theater provides a place to examine the world in the shadow of one's private life. I have witnessed the positive change in my students through the text and the Linklater Voice work.

In 2001, President McKenna, in her 15th year at Lesley, joined us as the goddess Juno in *The Tempest*, our 10th anniversary production. Writing a larger part for Juno (in iambic pentameter) was another opportunity to rework Shakespeare.

In my Shakespeare productions, I incorporate the authorship question into my vision of the play. I am an Oxfordian, and I am in good company with Sir Derek Jacobi, Mark Rylance, and Kenneth Branaugh. I don't accept William Shakesper of Stratford upon Avon as William Shakespeare the author of the plays, but believe, on account of circumstantial evidence surrounding his life and work, that Edward de Vere, the 17th Earl of Oxford, is the author of the play and poems. Richard Whalen's 1994 book *Shakespeare—Who Was He?* is a required text in my class, and serves as an introduction to the authorship question. Whalen presents the case both for William Shakespeare, otherwise known as the Stratford Man, and for Edward de Vere. Students have a myriad of responses to this; for some it is painful to go past the idea of the middle-class genius. Shakespeare looks something like us, whereas an eccentric aristocrat is problematic, perhaps even impossible, to identify with. Beginning the course with the Elizabethan world picture and examining the hierarchy of this world allows the students to enter the authorship question. It's eye opening to my students that wherever they fall on the question is not important to me, but that they know this scholarly problem exists and that research and writing are both powerful and dangerous. The search for the truth is not easy, and perhaps in some cases, the truth may never be found.

In theater the search for the truth remains an elusive goal. My students grow by living in the moment and working together to create a world alive with rich language, memorable characters, and intriguing plots. The years I have spent producing, directing, and teaching have been rewarding. I carry each script around like an old friend, and am proud of my students' accomplishments. Several of my students have gone on to theater careers in Boston and New York; others have continued the Shakespeare tradition on middle school and high school stages; and still others have attended graduate school to study theater and theater in education.

CONCLUSION

Many Lesley students are deeply inspired by their liberal arts professors. Consequently, many pursue careers in fields that are related to what their professors teach. Responding to Lesley's unique teaching approaches, students become fired up and are motivated to seize opportunities that are offered in their liberal arts classes. As a result, Lesley students develop deep knowledge, experience passionate involvement, and achieve intellectual and emotional transformations that can last a lifetime and make a difference in the world.

REFERENCES

DiConti, V. D. (2004). Experiential learning in a knowledge-based economy: Is it time to re-examine the liberal arts? *The Journal of General Education, 53*(3 4), 167 183.

Fink, R. (2006). *Why Jane and John couldn't read-and how they learned: A new look at striving readers.* Newark, DE: The International Reading Association.

Fink, R. (August 12, 2008). "Motivation to read in an age of high-stakes testing."

Massachusetts Reading First Conference, Sturbridge, MA. The Massachusetts

Department of Elementary and Secondary Education. PowerPoint Slide Presentation available at: http://www.doe.mass.edu/literacy/presentations/0808fink

Fink, R., & Samuels, S. J. (Eds.). (2008). *Inspiring reading success: Interest and motivation in an age of high-stakes Testing.* Newark, DE: The International Reading Association.

Fink, R. P. (2002). Successful careers: The secrets of adults with dyslexia. *Career Planning and Adult Development Journal, 18*(1), 118 135.

Fink, R. P. (1995,1996). Successful dyslexics: A constructivist study of passionate interest reading. *The Journal of Adolescent and Adult Literacy, 39,* 268 280.

Fink, R. P. (1998). Literacy development in successful men and women with dyslexia. *The Annals of Dyslexia, 48,* 311 346.

No Child Left Behind Act of 2001, Pub.1, No. 107-110, 115 Stat. 1425 (2002).

Schneider, G., & Shoenberg, R. (n.d.). *Contemporary understandings of liberal education.* Washington, DC: Association of American Colleges and Universities.

Whalen, R. F. (1994). *Shakespeare-who was he? The Oxford challenge to the bard of Avon.* Westport: CT: Praeger.

CHAPTER SEVEN

The Birth of a Profession: Lesley University's Division of Expressive Therapies

MITCHELL KOSSAK, PhD, LMHC, REAT

The year was 1974. The Vietnam War was winding down, and the Soviet war in Afghanistan was about to become major news. Richard Nixon had refused to surrender 500 tapes and documents that had been subpoenaed by the Senate Watergate Committee, and he was about to be impeached. From the counterculture of the 1960s, including the antiwar movement, civil rights, the rise of feminism, and the assassinations of three major figures, came major trends in the 1970s. Among these were advances in civil rights, increased influence of the Women's Movement, a heightened concern for the environment, and increased space exploration. Many of the "radical" ideas of the 1960s gained wider acceptance in the new decade, and were mainstreamed into American life and culture. Amid war, social realignment, and presidential impeachment proceedings, American culture and education flourished. The events of the times were reflected in and became the inspiration for much of the music, literature, entertainment, and even fashion of the decade (Frum, 2000).

The radical and experimental ideals that emerged from the counterculture of the 1960s also led to the humanistic and open education movements in higher education (Hein, 1975). The terms *human education* and *open education* were used as early as 1972. Both movements stressed the ideals that were coming out of the social constructs of the time, as well as what was specifically emerging in humanistic psychology; namely, the importance of looking at the whole person, including the relational, the social, and the acceptance of affect as important contributors to growth and learning. Both movements stressed dialogue between student and teacher and an equal emphasis on affect. One of the strongest emphases from these philosophical stances was on the liberal arts, including a holistic or whole-person approach to education that took into account "cognition, feeling, creativity and social interaction—a reaction to the dominance of scientific or behaviorist approaches to education that had held sway since the 19th century" (Hein, 1975, p. 29).

The writers and theoreticians associated with humanistic education came out of what is known as the third force of development in the field of psychology, which took off from the pioneering work of Carl Jung, who emphasized understanding the psyche through exploring the worlds of dreams, art, mythology, religion, and philosophy. Jung was the first in the world of psychology who emphasized that art could be used to alleviate or contain feelings of trauma, fear, or anxiety and to repair, restore, and heal (McNiff, 1998). Others in the world of psychology who influenced this new humanistic movement were Abraham Maslow, Carl Rogers, Fritz Perls, and Rollo May. Interestingly, these theorists did not reject what behaviorism had to offer but rather saw the need for a more integrative approach. In psychology, humanists also believed that therapy needed to go beyond just utilizing a cognitive approach to include the body and more action-oriented approaches. The humanistic movement included emphasis on healthy, self-actualized models as opposed to traditional Freudian emphasis on illness or disease. The humanistic model drew from such pioneers in childhood development as Jean Piaget and Erik Erikson, emphasizing the importance of understanding developmental processes through observation of individuals in their environment and through their personal interactions. These principles had far-reaching influence in other realms of education.

Paralleling the views of philosophy and psychology, John Dewey's Art as Experience (1934) and Suzanne Langer's *The Principles of Art*

(1950) were both groundbreaking works in relation to education and specifically in relation to arts education. Dewey's emphasis on the importance of experiencing art through process "from its physical manifestations in the 'expressive object' to the process in its entirety, a process whose fundamental element is no longer the material 'work of art' but rather the development of an 'experience'" (p. 336) began to take hold as an important philosophical agenda in arts-based and liberal arts education. Likewise, Langer's emphasis on "nondiscursive symbolic form" (1950, p. 515) related to all forms of art, and showed them to be:

> [a]ll equally creative, equally important and original, equally intellectual, emotional, and moral, yet each independent, and ultimately self-sufficient. Every art-work is a perceptual form, addressed to some phase of direct perception: sight, hearing, or their combination, or to that less-known organ of direct intuitions, imagination, whereby we perceive separate events, each under its own Gestalt, in the fluid welter of experience. (p. 516)

Another influential figure in the world of arts-based education was the psychologist Rudolph Arnheim (1954), who maintained that a person's knowledge of the world is rooted in objective sensory experience. It is also important to note the critical influence of J. L. Moreno, pioneer of psychodrama, sociometry, and group psychotherapy. A trained psychiatrist, Moreno was directly influenced by the work of his predecessors Darwin, Marx, and Freud. He introduced the idea of spontaneous theater, emphasized creativity over behaviorism, and believed in the principles of love and mutual sharing as powerful and indispensable working principles in group life. On meeting Freud he said:

> Well, Dr. Freud, I start where you leave off. You meet people in the artificial setting of your office. I meet them on the street and in their homes, in their natural surroundings. You

analyze their dreams, I give them the courage to dream again. (Moreno, 1985, p. 12)

ROOTS AND BEGINNINGS

The overflowing energies in social, cultural, political, and creative endeavors that began in the 1960s and continued into the 1970s had their influence at Lesley College, leading to the establishment of the Institute for the Arts and Human Development in the graduate school in early 1974. The newly formed institute was the inspiration of Shaun McNiff, who prior to this had been an artist and pioneering arts therapist using therapeutic techniques at Danvers State Hospital. McNiff's groundbreaking use of space and art with the patients at Danvers State is well documented in his book *Art as Medicine* (1992). Influenced by the work of Langer and having studied directly with Arnheim, McNiff began to think outside the box of conventional therapeutic arts training and began instituting ideas related to full, whole expression. He also began literally to go outside the box, or the confines of the institutional mental health facility, by taking the patients he worked with at Danvers State Hospital to the Addison Gallery of American Art at Phillips Academy in Andover, MA. With the support of Christopher Cook, the director of the Addison Gallery, McNiff established what was just beginning to be thought of as *outsider art* (Cardinal, 1972), a term used to describe artists who are not trained in traditional art schools and who often are living with extreme mental states.

McNiff himself was influenced by the social and political landscape of the 1960s and 1970s. He graduated from Fordham College in 1968, where Bobby Kennedy was to be the graduation speaker before he was assassinated, just two months after the assassination of Dr. Martin Luther King. McNiff recalled in a recent interview: "It was a time of tremendous change and re-visioning of institutions, and at Lesley progressive ideas were flourishing."[16]

In 1973, McNiff took these ideas of outsider art, full expression,

16 All quotes not attributed to a reference are from personal interviews conducted in 2009.

and the intelligence of the creative imagination to Lesley College and began to teach the first art therapy course in what was then an experimental January semester. This course led to other courses focused on art therapy and learning disabilities in the new Special Education graduate program led by Jill Hamilton. These new program offerings were a great success, and it quickly became clear that there was a growing interest in these innovative kinds of interdisciplinary learning experiences.

At the time, McNiff was doing research with Rudolph Arnheim at Harvard University on art and visual perception. In 1973, McNiff was organizing an exhibit at the School of the Museum of Fine Arts in Boston that was well received by *Boston Globe* critic Robert Taylor. The dean of the Museum School, Bill Bagnall, saw what McNiff was doing in the world of art and at the Addison Gallery of Art and at Danvers State Hospital, and invited him to start a program at the Museum School. McNiff ultimately decided to remain at Lesley, where he saw more potential to integrate the arts in education and in therapy. He said:

> What we did could not have happened, in my opinion, at any other institution in the United States. Progressive education was flourishing at Lesley through the leadership of Cynthia Cole, who was directing the Open Education Program, which integrated the arts with core academic areas. Progressive education is all about integration and the creative process— putting things in new relations to each other, something we could not do in such a comprehensive way at the Museum School. This atmosphere permeated Lesley and the special education program that Jill Hamilton led.

THE INSTITUTE FOR THE ARTS AND HUMAN DEVELOPMENT

The early successes in 1973 led to the establishment of the Institute for the Arts and Human Development, later simply called the Arts Institute. The newly developed institute began to initiate programs devoted to integrated arts and whole expression, combining cutting-edge ideas of creativity and psychology that were emerging from these two evolving fields. Further, the new institute developed two education tracks, one that was established to explore the arts in the therapeutic context, and a second track that focused more on integrating the arts in education, special education, and cultural institutions. While the two tracks were separate, it must be noted that the liberal and creative atmosphere of the time lent itself to following an interdisciplinary approach by allowing students to take courses from each core focus. In both tracks students were not just encouraged but required to take courses in all art forms, thus emphasizing the ideas of whole expression. The ideas of how visual art can influence movement, or how studies in movement can influence music or drama (Langer, 1950), were introduced in the context of learning, teaching, and therapy in schools and in mental health institutions (McNiff & McNiff, 1976).

FIRST FACULTY

The first person invited to teach in this new program was Norma Canner. Paolo Knill recalls having met McNiff and Canner at a symposium at Harvard University sponsored by Project Zero, which was founded at the Harvard Graduate School of Education in 1967 by the philosopher Nelson Goodman to study and improve education in the arts (Gardner, 1989). McNiff had heard about Canner from his first wife, Karen Gallas, who was a graduate student in what was at the time the Open Education Program at Lesley and suggested they meet. Canner, a pioneer in the field of dance movement therapy, was also known for her early and significant contributions working with children and youth with disabilities. In the 1960s, Canner established a pilot program for the Massachusetts Department of Mental Health in movement and dance for preschool children, which resulted in the emergence of 14 statewide centers where preschool teachers and aides received training in the dance modality. This program became a model for what we now know as early intervention (Marcow Speiser, 1990). Canner brought with her a history and reputation for creative interventions, and was just the kind of innovative thinker and activist that McNiff was looking for.

Canner was teaching in the Tufts University Experimental College when she and McNiff met, and found mutual connections to learning through the arts. McNiff invited Canner to become the first core faculty member in the Arts Institute. In a recent interview Canner said of this time:

> I had been working at Tufts when Shaun came along with this idea, and it was very exciting to be able to leave a very traditional place to go with a whole faculty who was creating a new program, so it was a very rare experience and I'm very lucky to have had it. We just thought it was fun, and it was exciting to have that support to experiment and have a place to do that kind of work, because you knew when you said the expressive arts therapies or dance therapy, really, especially dance, people didn't know what you were talking about. So it was just fun to have a place where there was so much excitement about the program. It was wonderful. So it was a beginning and we looked forward to building it.

Canner also brought with her a background in theater, having been an actress in New York City for many years, and what she had learned about improvisation from her time studying with Barbara Mettler, an innovator in improvisational dance as a means of liberating and cultivating the natural creative movement resources (Canner, 1975). When Canner started to teach at Lesley, she was already established as an innovator of creative and successful programs using music and movement with chronic schizophrenics, children with multiple sclerosis, and others experiencing a wide range of disabling conditions.

Following the appointment of Canner, McNiff invited other innovative thinkers from Tuft's experimental school to teach in the newly formed Institute for the Arts and Human Development. These early "first" faculty included Paolo Knill, Mariagnese Cattaneo, and Elizabeth McKim, who were all experts in their own arts-based field of study as well as experts in integrating the arts and child development.

Paolo Knill, a physicist, was trained in the sciences as well as music and theater. Coming from the European tradition of interdisciplinary or integrated approaches to education, he was looking for an institutional home where he could integrate his interests in science and the arts. In 1959, he was invited to the Massachusetts Institute of Technology as an aerodynamics research fellow. He also worked half-time at MIT in the Department of Musicology studying ancient music. In a recent interview he stated that this early work in multiple disciplines directly influenced his later thinking in interdisciplinary arts-based theory and practice. Knill was also very influenced by the polyaesthetics work of Wolfgang Roscher (1991), who had written about multiperceptual consciousness and the idea of integrating arts and sciences in education. Knill recalled that "The intermodal way of education started with Roscher-community art and education. Salzburg University had an institute, and also Hans Helmut Decker-Vogt had an institute for "intermodial arts" in Hamburg, Germany, and I worked clinically from these models, intermedia and polyaesthetics, where each mode is in each art." Knill came to Lesley and began teaching music therapy and music improvisation for special education teachers, and began to deepen and develop his theoretical and intermodal philosophies and practice.

Another early first faculty was Mariagnese Cattaneo, who also came from the European tradition of education. Her first degree was from a music conservatory, where she became interested in music education. She became a kindergarten teacher using all of the arts. "I was interested in how to allow children to increase their listening skills. I used Piaget as a theoretical model, with an emphasis on learning through the senses. I used music, movement, storytelling, and sound." Cattaneo stressed that when she first began to teach at Lesley, there was a lot of experimental work taking place that mirrored the social and political landscape.

It was the time of open education—one classroom. It connected with that time in education. It wasn't something

175

separate in the arts and education and radical therapy. New things were happening, and how do we frame what we were doing? I framed it in Piaget pedagogy in special education.

Cattaneo also talked about changes that were happening in the world of art: "It was in conjunction with modern music, contemporary music in Europe, and it was the time of the living theater; there were also dance groups and so many groups influencing the work we were doing at Lesley."

Cattaneo recalled that this was also the time of the Vietnam War, and the arts were used for social change in the classroom and in the streets. She recalled a lot of informal discussion among the faculty that led to implementation in the classroom, and that there was no separation between those involved in education and those involved in therapy. Everyone took classes together: "As much as the teacher brought it in and created the environment, there was not the separation between student and teacher. We learned from each other."

In addition to the above-mentioned faculty, there was Elizabeth McKim, who had also come from the experimental college at Tufts. McKim was an established poet whose roots came out of the oral tradition of song, story, and chant. She brought an understanding of words and rhythm, sound and performance arts. Iris Fanger and John Langstaff were also early first faculty. Fanger was an early innovator in improvisational drama, having studied with Viola Spolin. She eventually became the coordinator of the Integrated Arts in Education master's program at Lesley. Langstaff and his wife, Nancy, were experts in the area of arts integration, and were the founders of Revels, the nonprofit performing arts company that produced *The Christmas Revels,* an annual winter solstice celebration that was started in Cambridge, MA, and is now in 12 cities across the country.

THE EARLY PROGRAM

In 1973, through the suggestion of William Goldman, MD, the Massachusetts commissioner of mental health, McNiff used the term *expressive therapies* for the new master's program he proposed. The emerging field uniquely focused on integrating all of the arts in therapy. The program was set up with a cohort model, or what were called "core groups," which consisted of students studying in a particular modality such as dance therapy, art therapy, psychodrama, or expressive arts therapy. Students could choose a specific core group that held concentrations within the larger program. They could also choose a specific modality, but there was a requirement that they had to take courses from other core modalities. As McNiff conveyed:

> These were all means of furthering arts integration. This was at the core. Some of us, led by Paolo, studied arts integration by exploring ways of working with all of the arts together in a session, and others chose to simply work with different arts modalities in response to particular situations. We strove to achieve integration through individuals experiencing their own processes of synthesizing experiences rather than through a prescribed curriculum.

Another idea instituted early on was that faculty would often learn and teach together. Knill recalled:

> Part of the commitment was to take each other's classes. It's the only way to learn intermodal because we each have our specialty. It was always the case that there was a specialty group-intermodal, dance, art, and psychodrama came later, first with Joe Powers and then later with Peter Rowan.

There were also teams of psychiatrists and clinicians working with artists as faculty. McNiff was on the advisory board of the Massachusetts commissioner of mental health, and got a grant to do multidisciplinary training with clinical psychologists, social workers, and expressive arts therapists involving the Greater Lawrence Mental Health Center, St. Anne's Home in Methuen, and the Addison Gallery of American Art. In the beginning, the master's program recruited a number of traditionally trained clinicians to teach. These included psychiatrist Douglas Buchanan, who taught psychotherapy and group therapy courses together with Richard Goldwater, MD, Joan Klagsbrun, and Dick Geist, a clinical psychologist from Children's Hospital. Psychiatrist and calypso musician Shep Ginandes was also part of the early programming. Ginandes ran an arts-based therapeutic center for adolescents called the School We Have (1973). This innovative school established a site at Lesley and was housed at 35 Mellen St. Students from the newly formed Expressive Therapies Program would work directly with the clients at this program, and often classes were held right at the school. As Knill said, "The whole spirit here was teaching, and we had our own facility to do teaching and research." A theoretical basis for an integrated arts approach in a therapeutic context was being developed from the experimental work that was being experienced. Knill stated:

> Shaun and I thought the theory of any art therapy and expressive arts needs to examine [the question] What is an indigenous theory of expressive arts? It helped right away having artists teaching the theory—developed by artists and specialists in the field. So we studied all the arts therapies and looked at, Do they have a way to talk about the arts? How is aesthetics talked about and incorporated?

Knill brought his perspectives from Europe in science and phenomenology, and McNiff brought his from the world of art, depth psychology, and his experiences working in the field of mental health. As McNiff (2009) recently wrote, "we were two wings of one flight" (p. 1). McNiff went on to say:

> Norma Canner was our collective muse. I trusted her judgment. She was a spiritual core of the program, helping us hold all the tension you have in an experimental community. She was a master in dance and taught us about improvisational sound and movement. The other principal figure in growing

our community was Paolo Knill. He was the one who helped me shape my ideas concerning expressive arts therapy and art-based psychological inquiry. I may have introduced him to the arts and psychotherapy, but he quickly became my most sensitive partner and developed a significant body of work on his own which has been internationally recognized. We were "two wings of one flight."

In a recent interview with one of the early "first students," many of the memories conveyed by the early first faculty and founder were echoed. Vivien Marcow Speiser came to Lesley in 1975. She grew up in South Africa and immigrated to Israel in 1970. In 1973, after the Yom Kippur War, she volunteered in a rehabilitation center with soldiers and began to see the damaging effects of the war. This was a very difficult time for Israel, and Marcow Speiser witnessed the effects of trauma firsthand. She had a BA in psychology and had studied dance for many years. In 1974 she moved to Boston, where she first heard about dance therapy, and began looking for programs. "It was a new thing. I was very entranced in being a dancer and combining it with psychology, and in 1975 I came into the program," she said. She was part of the first core group for dance therapy students. She recalled:

In my core group there were three people. I never heard of Norma before but I wanted to study in the area of psychology and dance. The main buzz at the time was Shaun and Norma. There were no other faculty around then. Shaun was the instrumental figure. There was always a sense of integrated arts and experimentation. It felt like we were on the cutting edge of a phenomenon.

Another first student was Laury Rappaport, who had come to Lesley in 1977 after completing a self-designed degree in art therapy at SUNY Buffalo. Rappaport was looking for a graduate program in which she could further her understanding of this new field. After working for two years at a residential school for adolescents using art and video, Rappaport began to look for programs and found that Lesley was the only program that used all of the arts. She remembers that there were no other programs that even talked about interdisciplinary arts. She recalls McNiff conducting the interview for entering the program and emphasizing the importance of doing a group interview in order to see how people interact, because this was such an important part of the work being done in the classes and out in the field. In 1977 Rappaport entered the program and participated in the opening "colloquium," a four-day retreat held at the Addison Gallery:

> It was an incredible environment. Norma was so electric. She had such an ability to bring people together and you felt a part of it. She would make contact with each person and there was a sense of being a part of something and being welcomed.

In these early days all faculty were part of cocreating the program. Rappaport recalls that McNiff's vision was to bring to the colloquium individuals who were immersed in a creative process. In addition to the poet Elizabeth McKim, he included avant-garde artist Don Burgy, who brought a ritualistic arts perspective, and Gloucester poet laureate Vincent Ferrini and historical novelist Truman Nelson. McNiff stressed the importance of arts and how artists have always deeply engaged themselves in the psyche, recalling: "Therefore I brought them into the program; they became mentors to us all."

According to Rappaport, there was so much about preserving the artist identity, which was part of the overall vision:

> The powerful thing about being there was the interrelated connections. Each one came with a mastery of their own art form, and they each loved being with each other. And you could see how Norma's movement would affect Paolo's music and Paolo's music would influence Elizabeth's poetry and Norma's dance and everybody would be so interrelated. And that was what it was like. There was this fullness.

McNiff invited Harvard psychiatrist and Pulitzer Prize winner Robert Coles, who at the time was studying the creative process and how art heals children. He also brought in social psychiatrist Maxwell Jones from the therapeutic community movement. Again McNiff recalled:

> We had these world-renowned figures who were constantly moving in and out of our community. In a course for the entire community, called Personal and Societal Perspectives on the Arts and Therapy, Truman Nelson invited leading figures from the Civil Rights Movement like Conrad Lynn, the distinguished civil rights lawyer and defense counsel for the Harlem Six. It was quite a time.

Another important figure McNiff engaged in the early programming was the archetypal psychologist James Hillman. According to McNiff, Hillman and Arnheim "attuned me to the universal qualities of the artistic experience." Hillman's archetypal Jungian perspective was extremely appealing and had a significant impact on McNiff and on the field of expressive arts therapy.

Rappaport also recalls having clinical training with McNiff, where the whole group would go to Danvers State Hospital.

> We would sign out the patients and we would divide them up and drive them through this wooded area—people who have never been out of the hospital—and we went to the Addison Gallery. We would do all of the arts (Chris Cook and Shaun designed this). So there were different arts going on in each room. And you could see the transformation in these patients just from the environment and we brought the spirit that was at the colloquium. After returning the patients we would go for supervision with Shaun and talk about what happened, sharing what happened and looking at videos (each session was videotaped).

In the second year of training, Rappaport worked in Lawrence in a day treatment center with some of the same patients who were at The School We Have. At the Lawrence site there was a full-time expressive therapist, Jessica Ronalds, and another clinician, Shelly Cushner, who was also a graduate of the program. So the site became an extension of the rich environment. Rappaport summed up her experience: "We learned a lot about groups. Those of us that went through it—it became a deep knowing; there was a depth to the experience."

Marcow Speiser also remembers the psychologists who were integrated into the program, such as Patrick Valianti and Joan Klagsbrun, who was her supervisor and thesis adviser. She remembers that in her second year, Canner took all of the dance therapy students to the Perkins School for the Blind, in Watertown, MA. This tradition was rich for the students in the Lesley program and for the students at Perkins, and was documented in the film A Time to Dance (1998). The tradition of taking students to Perkins is still in effect today. In what Marcow Speiser called "the second wave of influences" she recalled that faculty such as Penny Lewis and Ilene Serlin, both dance therapists and psychologists, taught psychology courses and influenced the "second generation of students."

Rappaport wanted to honor another early first faculty, Peter Rowan, now deceased, who came from the world of social work and the developing field of psychodrama. Rappaport said that Rowan brought a more traditional or mainstream sense to the program from his days as a social worker, while being a brilliant clinician with large groups. He also had his own psychodrama institute in Central Square, where he had "open" sessions that were attended by students and that were open to the general public.

INTERNATIONAL AND COLLABORATIVE PROGRAMS

In 1978 Marcow Speiser, after completing her degree at Lesley and working as a therapist, decided to return to Israel. She was immediately hired as an expressive therapist in a treatment center for the municipality in Tel Aviv. She began to teach expressive therapy classes and to supervise other clinicians. There was a lot of interest, and the classes filled quickly. "In 1978," she said, "I contacted Shaun to talk about starting a program in Israel. Shaun was interested in expanding. So without any formality we began to offer courses." McNiff began to work together with Marcow Speiser, to formalize the program on an institutional level, and established the Arts Institute Project in Israel (AIPI). Marcow Speiser soon brought McNiff, Canner, Knill, and McKim to Israel to teach classes.

Students would train in Israel during their traditional academic year and then travel to the Cambridge campus during the summer to take classes. Marcow Speiser would come to the Cambridge campus to teach at the four-day colloquium, and the Israeli students would make up one of the core groups. In 1983 Marcow Speiser returned full-time to the Cambridge campus to run the dance therapy core group. The Lesley Israel program continued to flourish under the leadership of Baruch Zadick and later Tali Mor, and then Dalia Ben Shoshan and Sam Schwartz. Marcow Speiser kept her connections to the Israel program as the assistant dean of the graduate school from 1984 to 1987. During that time she also ran the summer schools, and afterward she served as director of International and Collaborative Programs. In 1996 the Israeli government changed the law so that affiliate programs were no longer recognized. It was at this point that the program in Israel became a full extension of Lesley University.

Paralleling this process, in the 1980s Knill developed affiliations with programs in Switzerland, Canada, and various institutions in the United States. In 1980, in cooperation with Hans Helmut Decker-Vogt in Germany, Knill arranged a Lesley affiliation with the latter's Institut für Medien und Ausdruckstherapie. Later, this organization in both Germany and Switzerland was called the Lesley Institut für Medien und Ausdruckstherapie (the Lesley Institute for Media and Expressive Therapy, or LIMA), and it become a Lesley affiliate program. In 1985 LIMA changed its name to ISIS, the International School for Interdisciplinary Studies. In 1980 another Lesley graduate, Phillip

Speiser, founded the Scandinaviska Institutet for Uttrykande Konst (Scandinavian Institute for Expressive Arts) in Gothenburg, Sweden, and this program became affiliated with Lesley University in 1981. Speiser coordinated the first annual Nordic Conference on Expressive Arts in 1982. In the first 10 years the Cambridge on-campus program had students from more than 40 countries, from every sector of the world, and the program in Israel had graduated many more.

REACTION AND DIVISION

Marcow Speiser, Rappaport, Canner, Cattaneo, Knill, and McNiff all recall the richness and excitement of these early years; each also remembers when the tides began to change. Knill stated that the necessity to form divisions took over from this experimental time of integration. "Like a reaction—historically it began to swing back. And then we couldn't take courses from the other division and it took away the power and took away any creativity of creating new fields." Cattaneo thought that times changed and the needs of students changed as they began asking for more theory. "The challenge was that sites had a hard time with our students. Students knew how to express, but what do we do after that?" Rappaport thought that this was a prevalent feeling and that by focusing more on a mainstream conception of what it means to be clinical, students would be taken more seriously.

McNiff, following a Jungian perspective, called these feelings of psychological inferiority the shadow side of the discipline, which generated what the art therapist Pat Allen described as a "clinification syndrome" (1992). McNiff believes that the shadow, and the conflicts that arise from it, are always present in all arts practices and in all organizations. As Jung himself said, if we don't understand this aspect of shadow, we will have big problems. And so the belief that art heals through its often primal and expressive nature began to create tensions between those who wanted a more traditional clinical approach and those who wanted a more indigenous arts-based approach.

With the perceived need for greater recognition in the world of traditional clinical practice, changes in the program began to occur. These changes were taking place throughout the field. Developmentally it was not just at Lesley; the whole field was changing. Marcow Speiser remembered:

> Things went wrong along the way. I think when the great splitting happened it was 1985–1986. I was a part of it with licensure, when I cochaired the Massachusetts Coalition of Creative Arts Therapists to bring in licensure. And licensure coincided with expressive therapies being combined with the division of Counseling Psychology.

These changes included more classes taught by clinical psychologists and social workers while an-arts based focus was retained. McNiff remembers this difficult time:

> We were very committed to disciplined clinical practice with the arts, and we discovered over the years that it was the rare psychiatrist or psychologist who could achieve integration or transcend the boundaries of disciplines. Some simply stayed in their perceived "superior" role and reinforced the splits. There were faculty members like psychologist Helene Scarlett who were successful in honoring and respecting the crossover between art and psychology.

Because there was this difficulty understanding the creative process and its place in clinical practice, Knill started teaching the diagnostics courses in the mid-1970s. He used the Diagnostic and Statistical Manual of Mental Disorders (DSM) as the core reading material and interpreted it through the arts. Knill recalls:

> It came almost out of a crisis—like when students took psychopathology with a psychiatrist. We saw that psychology is not necessarily a phenomenological approach. It was a

contradiction of the continuity principle approach of research where an object has to be studied from that object point of view, like physics has to look at forces from forces. So I began to teach psychopathology looking at the DSM IV phenomenologically. This was my first crisis intervention.

Marcow Speiser also remembers the difficulties that emerged within the division:

Everybody had their own motivations and agendas at the time, with very strong personalities. There was a feminist agenda as well as personal agendas. We lost our original vision and focus being true to creativity and in our approach that was embedded in art.

Efforts were made to patch up differences, but the splits were too big. Despite these efforts to find common ground, the program was about to change even more. With the passage of mental health counseling licensure in 1993, all of the specializations within the Expressive Therapies Division underwent significant restructuring, with the curriculum moving from a 48-credit master's degree to include a 60-credit master's degree option that fulfilled requirements toward licensure in mental health counseling in the Commonwealth of Massachusetts. Knill decided to leave Lesley in 1994, and in 1995 McNiff himself decided to leave. McNiff reminisced:

I fully supported the licensure initiative that started when I was the dean. The split that developed later was painful. The departure of Paolo and my close colleague Margot Fuchs greased the wheels of change. It was my baby, my home, my soul place. It was not easy to separate myself. I had to leave in order to let go, to live with it in a new way, to keep creating and advancing the work without what I perceived to be misleading separations between art and psychology—everything we did at Lesley from the start and in my writings integrates the two, but there are many kinds of psychology and the kind I support has always challenged conventional assumptions. I was provost and dean of Endicott College for seven years and traveled to other arts therapy programs throughout the United States that were adopting our art-based practices and ideas. It was good for the work and good for my career. And these tensions, I learned, are eternal and good. Our original vision prospered internationally, and art-based methods, no longer identified with one place, were adopted throughout the arts therapy community. It is quite an irony.

It is interesting to note that McNiff returned to his roots at Lesley University in 2002 as the first University Professor, and Knill, Canner, and Cattaneo all have received the honor of professor emeritus.

PRESENT AND FUTURE

Despite the move toward licensure and greater specialization and regulation within the tracks, the Expressive Therapies Division has remained committed to training expressive arts therapists who are grounded not only in their specific modality but also in an interdisciplinary approach. Every student, no matter which specialization he belongs to, is still introduced to the integrated arts perspective within the program, in addition to a solid grounding in his specialized discipline. Students are introduced to the integrated arts approach through courses in which they are exposed to each of the other arts therapy modalities. Over the past 15 years, there have been four specialization tracks within the Expressive Therapies Division in Cambridge: art therapy, music therapy, dance therapy, and expressive therapies. The latest significant change to take place within the program was the addition of a PhD in expressive therapies (2000) and an undergraduate BS degree in expressive arts therapy (Estrella, 2008).

The strength of this program, and of other programs and institutes that sprang up all over the world, led in the early 1990s to the establishment of the International Expressive Arts Therapy Association (IEATA). The IEATA was formed to support artists, educators, consultants, and therapists who use multimodal expressive arts processes for transformation of the individual and the community, by providing a global forum for dialogue, professional practice, and work; the aim is to increase recognition and use of expressive arts as powerful tools for psychological, physical, and spiritual wellness. The seeds that were placed in fertile ground in 1973 have been dispersed throughout the world. Recently, an international conference sponsored by Lesley University and the Israeli Association of Creative and Expressive Therapies celebrated three decades of expressive arts therapy in Israel. The conference focused on creative solutions to conflict and featured McNiff and Knill as keynote speakers. Lesley University in Cambridge also hosted the eighth biannual IEATA conference in August 2009, which brought the work that has spread far and wide back to its roots.

Today, the Division of Expressive Therapies at Lesley University is in a unique position. As a pioneer in the use of all of the arts in psychotherapy, Lesley University is now known throughout the world as a leader in this specialization. As new master's programs develop throughout the country and the world with a specific focus in expressive arts therapy, and as theoreticians outside Lesley articulate new approaches to expressive arts therapy, the division has maintained its prominence as the premier place to study and train in expressive arts therapy. As Knill stated so eloquently:

> Even though we touched all things in the way—obstacles, these were overcome. The thing we do is still powerful. Even looking at new ways of looking at health, there is still the resilience. I just trained U.N. commissioners from 23 non-Western countries in using the arts to address crisis. So we show that resilience is tied to the arts, and the arts in therapy still come through.

Arts-based learning traditions started here in 1973, and continue to thrive in a new century, in clinics, community centers, government agencies, and institutions around the world. The Lesley program continues to graduate students who are actively engaged in scholarly research and clinicians who are part of the mental health landscape, making a difference in people's lives every day. The tradition begun by Shaun McNiff has been carried on throughout the past 35 years by many. The Expressive Therapies Division has continued to grow and change with the times under the leadership of Cattaneo, Rowan, and most recently Julia Byers. It is my hope and mission as the current division director of Expressive Therapies at Lesley University to continue the tradition of applying arts-based learning to investigation, curiosity, risk taking, exploration, and experimentation with the unknown (Piaget, 1926), in order to find imaginative solutions to dilemmas and difficulties and to embrace healthier ways of living. This tradition, which stands on the foundations laid by such important interdisciplinary thinkers as Dewey, Langer, Piaget, Jung, Winnicott, Arnheim, Gardner, and others who have contributed to our understanding of creative embodied intelligence, can only continue to grow and make a difference. As McNiff has written: "If we stay closely attuned to the processes of creative expression, it will suggest new frontiers of understanding" (1988, p. 47). The understanding that the arts have always served to help individuals overcome adversity and tune into a deeper engagement with life has been the life force of this new profession, and its vitality will sustain it into the future.

REFERENCES

Allen, P. 1992. Artist-in-residence: An alternative to "clinification" for art therapists. Art Therapy: Journal of the American Art Therapy Association, 9(1), 22 29.

Arnheim, R. (1954). Art and visual perception: A psychology of the creative eye. Berkeley, CA: University of California Press.

Canner, N. (1975) And a time to dance. Boston, MA: Plays, Inc.

Cardinal, R. (1972). Outsider art: Spontaneous alternatives. London, England: Thames and Hudson.

Estrella, K. (2008). Expressive therapies and mental health counseling specialization: Program review. Cambridge, MA: Lesley University.

Frum, D. (2000). How we got here: The '70s. New York, NY: Basic Books.

Gardner, H., & Perkins, D. N. (1989). Art, mind, and education: Research from Project Zero. Urbana, IL: University of Illinois Press.

Ginandes, S. (1973). How troubled, fed-up adolescents get together with creative adults at The School We Have. New York, NY: Delacorte Press.

Hein, G. (1975). Humanistic and open education: Comparison and contrast. Journal of Education. 157(3), 27 39.

Keegan, P., & Speiser, V. (1990). An interview with Norma Canner. *American Journal of Dance Therapy, 12*(2), 13 23.

Langer, S. (1950). The principles of art. The Hudson Review, II(4), 515 534.

McNiff, S. (1988). Fundamentals of Art Therapy. Springfield, IL: Charles C. Thomas.

McNiff, S. (2009). Integrating the arts in therapy: History, theory, and practice. Springfield, IL: Charles C. Thomas.

McNiff, S. (1998). Jung on active imagination. Art Therapy: Journal of the American Art Therapy Association, 15(4), 13 23.

McNiff, S., & McNiff, K. G. (1976). Art therapy in the classroom. Art Teacher, 6(2), 10 12.

Moreno, J. L. (1985). The autobiography of J. L. Moreno, M.D. (Abridged), Cambridge, MA: Archives, Harvard University.

Piaget, J. (1926). The language and thought of the child (3rd ed.). London, England: Routledge.

Rogers, C. (1969). Freedom to learn. Columbus, OH: Merrill Publishing.

Roscher, W. (1991). Polyaisthesis: Multiperceptual consciousness and the idea of integrating arts and sciences in education. Wien, Austria: Verband der wissenschaftlicher Gesellschafter Osterreichs.

PART III: 1980–1998

Introduction

JOSEPH B. MOORE

Enrollment in higher education continued to grow through the 1980s and 1990s. Enrollment growth was fed by increasing numbers of high school graduates (the first wave of children of the baby boomers), by state and district efforts to have more high school graduates move on to college, and by the ever increasing number of adult learners enrolling in both traditional and nontraditional institutions of higher education in response to the declining number of middle-class jobs that didn't require some college education.

A number of trends converged and are reflected in the three essays of this section. First, the 1980s brought out the first of IBM's personal computers and the first Apple Macintosh computer with a mouse. The digital age was about to become accessible to those who didn't have access to mainframe computers. While the first personal computers were stand-alone machines able to manipulate numbers and letters, there was a growing sense that these machines could transform teaching and learning. This form of digital technology, pre-Internet, just 30 years ago, required extensive investment in computer labs, hardware, software, and staffing. Lesley's Technology in Education Program, described here by Blakeslee, Carter, Gannon, Roberts, Thormann, and Yoder, became one of the "national" programs at Lesley serving K-12 teachers across the country. Ironically, it was not just the personal computer that allowed this to happen, but (as the authors point out) the Reagan administration's deregulation of the airlines industry. Faculty could now afford to fly to all parts of the country to teach teachers.

A second trend had to do with children who were disabled. The implementation of Public Law 94-142 (the Education for All Handicapped Children Act), adopted by Congress in 1975, took years to implement and in some ways is still being modified to find best practices to serve students with various, particular disabilities. This limited success may be due as much to funding and to the ever evolving research around particular disabilities as it is the political will to serve these students. In just six years following passage of PL94-142, Lesley University initiated the Threshold Program, under the leadership of faculty member Arlyn Roffman, to serve young adults with disabilities who had the potential to live independently but for whom there were few postsecondary programs to provide assistance. Roffman, Osten, and Noveck describe Threshold from its beginnings in the early eighties to its comprehensive offerings 30 years later.

Third, adults were returning to college in unprecedented numbers well before policy makers became aware of the trend. As the economy shifted from manufacturing and agriculture to services, the income gap began to widen. The deregulatory emphasis of the Reagan administration (1980–1988) also contributed to this gap as the rich got richer, the poor got poorer, and the middle class began to evaporate. Adults returned to college to earn degrees in hopes that they could gain employment in the moderate or high-income side of the service sector (finance, technology, education), as opposed to the explosive growth of jobs in the low-income side of that sector (home health aides, retail, fast food production, security services). The current focus on education as a pure economic investment with standardized tests to measure the ROI (return on investment) gained its momentum during this period, especially with the 1984 report *A Nation at Risk*. Deregulation helped some industries produce short-term gains for their investors, but this period also marked the beginning of a new era of regulation for the nation's schools.

Again, as McKenna describes it, Lesley played a key role in designing educational opportunities for an underserved population, adult learners. The first wave of adult learners were pioneers who enrolled in colleges and universities that most often did not customize programs and services for adults who were working and raising families, and who were active in their communities. By the early 1980s, there were many reports and studies about how to build such programs to serve adults. If the GI Bill opened college and university doors for veterans; if desegregation legislation, the Civil Rights Act of 1964, and Affirmative Action opened those doors to persons of color; and if PL94-142 opened K-12 doors to children with disabilities, then it was the adults themselves who forced open the doors of higher education to meet their educational needs and aspirations. To this day, the federal government, and the organized lobby of higher education, will not modify financial aid policies to better serve adult learners out of fear that this will reduce funding for traditional-age students.

Edith Lesley was a businesswoman. She understood the dynamics of the public marketplace: an increasing demand for kindergarten with district school boards deciding to add kindergarten, and a paucity of programs preparing kindergarten teachers. She built her school as a proprietary institution before handing it over to a board and having it officially registered with the state in 1941 as an educational nonprofit institution.

This capacity to look objectively at society, to understand historical shifts taking place, and to identify needs or gaps in the marketplace is, in many ways, a testimony to the commitment and creativity of Lesley University faculty and administrators throughout Lesley's first century.

CHAPTER EIGHT

Responding to a Revolution

George Blakeslee, EdD
Richard Carter, PhD
Marie Gannon, MEd
Nancy Roberts, EdD
Joan Thormann, PhD
Maureen Yoder, EdD

In the late 1970s a revolution began that changed the world. Computers, previously owned only by large corporations and government agencies, became available through universities. Nancy Roberts first realized the potential of computers in education while doing her doctoral research in Sue Friel's fifth-grade classroom in the Lexington, MA, public schools. She introduced students to a computerized system dynamics ecology model, as a game. The students' goal was to save the world. Nancy took their worksheet information, entered their data on punch cards, and submitted them to the Boston University (BU) mainframe computer for processing. Her young students responded enthusiastically, and Nancy's passion and vision for technology in education were ignited.

EARLY COMPUTERS: POTENTIAL AND GROWTH

In 1975 both Nancy Roberts and Sue Friel joined the faculty of Lesley College. Friel managed to procure two terminals for the undergraduate school's mathematics room, connected by telephone lines to the BU mainframe.

In the summer of 1978 Roberts taught Lesley's first educational computer course. She and her husband had convinced Digital Equipment Corporation (DEC) to donate a PDP 11 to Lesley. The DEC had four terminals and a server, demonstrating the concept of time-sharing. With a class of 12 students, 3 could work at each terminal. The course consisted of an introduction to the BASIC (Basic All-purpose Symbolic Instruction Code) computer language, developed at Dartmouth, and to DYNAMO, the system dynamics simulation language, and Logo, both created at MIT. Jim Slattery, director of the Lesley Library, agreed to pay $2,000 per year for the annual maintenance fee. The computer was housed in a converted closet on the second floor of the library.

MIT donated six electronic mail accounts to Lesley. The accounts were on the MIT network Bitnet, Because It's There Net, a forerunner of the Internet. Marie Gannon, on the Lesley library staff, mastered e-mail and file sharing and taught Roberts and other account owners. E-mail was accomplished through a hookup using the telephone lines, and worked amazingly well. Words emerged letter by letter on the display screen, and connections were dependent on telephone lines.

By the end of the decade computers had become widely available in small and affordable versions known as personal computers. Never before had the average person had access to a tool that, as Apple cofounder Steve Jobs promised, will "harness the power of the computer for the individual." Perceiving the possibilities for education, and the challenge of educating teachers to use computers in their classrooms, the Computers in Education master's degree program at Lesley College was established in 1980.

> Here is the problem: You have a generation of students who, as adults, will need to know how to use computers as surely as they will need to know how to read and write. And you have a generation of teachers, few of whom know how to use a computer and many of whom are wary of computers.

How do you open up those teachers to the educational possibilities of computers? How do you get them to jump the technological generational gap so they can teach their students without passing on any of their own prejudices?

"The first step is to cure them of their fears and prejudices," according to Nancy Roberts, the director of a new program in computers and education at Lesley College in Cambridge, MA. (Coit, 1981, p. 1)

Educators flocked to introductory seminars and left feeling empowered and enthused about using computers in their classrooms. "We give them a taste and hope they come back for more," said Richard Carter, then a graduate student at MIT and one of the instructors in the introductory one-day seminars. Those interested in more in-depth study enrolled in the degree program. Karen Gremley, Angie Ferris, and Maureen Yoder were among the first graduates, and all had become members of the program's faculty by 1983.

Ricky Carter teaching with Apple 2E

Photograph courtesy of Nancy Roberts.

In 1981 the faculty assembled a lab of Apple computers on the second floor of the library, then located on the quadrangle. In 1984 the lab and the growing software collection moved to a larger space in the renovated basement of the library, and were overseen by Ricky Carter until 1990. Additional growth, along with a need for office space and a work area for students, resulted in the renovation of the library's fourth floor, where the lab and work area were located until the creation of the Information Commons in 2009.

Eileen Barnett, a 1989 Computers in Education graduate, became the educational software coordinator and later the director of the Microcomputer Center. Barnett cultivated relationships with software companies, formulated agreements for site licenses, negotiated donations of software, and initiated a software review center for educators. The center became a thriving resource for faculty, students, alumni, and local teachers. Many became computer specialists in their schools and leaders in their districts. Now, with the availability and power of the Internet, online resources have replaced the software collection.

COLLABORATING ORGANIZATIONS: GATHERINGS OF LIKE MINDS

From the very beginning, people in the Greater Boston area who were interested in educational computing were invited to Lesley College. An informal interest group developed that included people from organizations such as Bolt, Beranek and Newman (BBN), Technical Education Research Centers (TERC), Terrapin, MIT, the Boston Computer Society, and the Lexington Public Schools. The group established the Computers in Education Resource Coalition (CERC), which from 1979 to 1993 published a newsletter and helped Lesley run an annual one-day conference. At the first conference in 1979, Ricky explained a computer math game called Go Fish, an early example of using a computer to provide a visual representation, or model, of a mathematical idea. The player tried to catch a fish by dropping a line down from a boat. If the depth was wrong, the program replied "too deep" or "too shallow" with a line on the screen that represented the fishing line. Simulating a laboratory, it allowed a learner to try out a hypothesis, receive immediate feedback, and then modify her idea. In 1979 this was revolutionary.

At the second computer conference, in 1980, program faculty provided hands-on sessions with a variety of donated machines, including Apples, Pets, TRS-80s, and Lesley's DEC. The profits from these computer conferences were used to purchase additional Apple computers for the Lesley program.

In addition to the conferences in Cambridge that became available when Lesley launched a national computer and education outreach program in 1980, four-day residential conferences were held in Colorado and Wyoming from 1985 to 1999, bringing together current students and graduates from across the country for an intensive series of workshops and courses.

In 1989 and 1994, Lesley was the sponsoring organization for the National Educational Computer Conference (NECC) in Boston, then the largest gathering of educational technology speakers, participants, and vendors in the country. The 1994 NECC, held at the newly rebuilt Hynes Auditorium, attracted more than 8,000 participants.

The CERC and Lesley collaborations resulted in awards of several National Science Foundation and Department of Education grants, which greatly enhanced Lesley's national reputation.

A PIONEERING MASTER'S DEGREE PROGRAM

In 1980 Sue Friel wrote a proposal to require a two-credit computer literacy course for every undergraduate, one of the first courses of its kind in the country. At the same time, Friel and Roberts, with the help of CERC, developed a 33-credit master's degree program. George Miller, then vice president of Lesley's undergraduate school, and Dick

Wylie, then dean of the graduate school, gave the faculty six months to prove the viability of the program.

The Lesley graduate program and the member organizations of CERC had a common view on the impact computers would make in the schools. Computers "will help human creatures understand better how it is that we learn and think…The introduction of microcomputers into the formal educational environment…means an internal, institutional realignment of the educational culture over the coming years" (Polidori, 1983, p. 4). "Quite possibly, the role of the teacher, particularly as it pertains to the use of advanced technologies in the classroom, may change from repository of all knowledge to that of group leader in charge of mutual learning activities" (p. 6).

The program's content and format reflected the needs and skills of adult learners. Classes were offered in the afternoons or evenings once a week for 15 weeks so that students could attend after work. In the summer, intensive three-week classes were scheduled to coincide with school vacation.

Students demonstrated their newly acquired knowledge by creating projects that were practical and individualized. The first course in the sequence, Computer Literacy for Educators, introduced students to innovative applications such as word processing, spreadsheets, databases, and educational software. Students learned about system dynamics and computer modeling. They used a paper model to understand how a computer worked.

Ricky Carter developed the Programming in Logo class, where students entered commands to move a triangle "turtle" around the screen. Logo incorporated the philosophy of Seymour Papert's (1993) book *Mindstorms* and the concept of teachers experimenting alongside their students, not always knowing what the outcome will be. Students programmed a robot turtle as well as a programmable toy called Big Trac.

Henry Olds, working on an Apple II

Photograph courtesy of MTA Today.

For the software evaluation course, local developers and innovative thinkers, including Tom Snyder, Henry Olds, Bob Tinker, and Art Bardige, were guest speakers. They later became entrepreneurs and owners of successful companies, but generously gave their time, shared their ideas, and listened intently to feedback from Lesley students.

In the Fundamentals of Computer Structures course, students took apart computers and reassembled them. They learned about operating systems and programmed in machine and assembly language with rudimentary commands and simple outcomes. Using wire and diodes, they built a "full adder," modeling the base-two language underlying friendlier user interfaces.

Students learned to program in BASIC and Pascal, skills that were abandoned after a few years when software became more sophisticated and the average teacher no longer needed to write her own programs. Over the years new courses were developed, reflecting the trend to integrate computers into subject areas. Multimedia and digital video became more user-friendly and prompted creative classroom applications. Technology expanded the possibilities for special needs students and for a variety of learning styles. New approaches that were proven to enhance teaching and learning were incorporated into Lesley courses, reflecting the needs of teachers and their students.

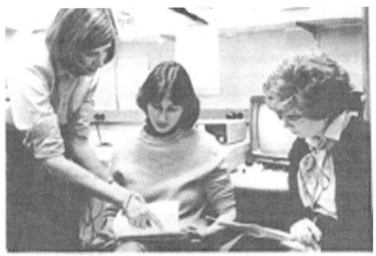

Nancy Roberts with students, 1982

Photograph courtesy of MTA Today.

GOING NATIONAL: AN ERA OF EXPANSION

As mentioned earlier, in 1980 Lesley launched the Computers in Education off-campus outreach program. Dick Wylie, dean of the graduate school, had come to Lesley from the University of Colorado. His Colorado colleague Frank Cordell told him the University of Northern Colorado would not continue to support out-of-state programs, so Dick suggested that Frank offer the programs through Lesley instead. The timing could not have been better. Frank and his wife, Louise, formed Professional Outreach Associates and, for 25 years, they ran the off-campus programs out of Greeley, Colorado. When P.O.A. began to market Lesley's computer program in Colorado, the information meetings drew large numbers of potential students.

Frank and Dick visited Apple Computer's office in Cupertino, California, and asked for a donation of computers for the Lesley labs. Three months later, a Coors truck delivered a load of beer to California and brought back a load of Apples to Colorado. Apple was committed to supporting teachers, and donated several more labs for Lesley student use.

In Cambridge, the National Outreach Division, under the leadership of Dean Mary Huegel, was created to adapt, coordinate, and deliver the program. In many largely rural western states the distances to a college or university were too great for a night course, so the program was developed into an intensive weekend format. The courses provided the conventional 45 "contact hours" typical of three-credit graduate courses, but in a concentrated time frame. Students met for two weekends, a month apart, with sessions on Friday night from 5 p.m. to 10 p.m. and Saturday and Sunday from 8 a.m. to 5 p.m. Cohorts of students, meeting in local school computer labs, could study together and complete the 11-course sequence in 22 months. The intensive weekend format proved attractive to teachers who found weekday night courses difficult to attend.

Michael Goodman was hired as the off-campus national program's first director for states west of the Mississippi. Maureen Yoder was the first program director of the off-campus Regional Outreach Program covering New England. Frank and Louise Cordell hired Tim Greenshields to recruit students. Tim, a graduate of one of the early Colorado cohorts, was an enthusiastic and energetic promoter of the program, and helped increase its size in both rural and urban areas in the western states.

In 1985 George Blakeslee replaced Michael Goodman as program director of national outreach. George was instrumental in assembling an education software collection to support the off-campus courses. It was housed in his office closet until it outgrew this location, and was moved to the computer center in the library.

Under Lesley's newly appointed president, Margaret McKenna, the college engaged in the development of a vision and mission. These specifically cited a commitment to serve "the underserved" and attract students who worked in the "professions that put people first." Both goals directly aligned with the outreach effort and played an important role in the sustained college support that the Technology in Education Program has received since that time.

The "theory into practice" pedagogical philosophy of the School of Education was equally well received. Students were pleased that they could learn something they could use with their classes "on Monday" as well as foundational knowledge to guide long-term use and adaptation of educational technology.

Teacher certification requirements and local salary schedules, both of which rewarded graduate study, were incentives to pursue further education. In addition, students found that the cohort model provided them with a community of learners and an ongoing environment of mutual support. Through its willingness to "bring higher education to the student," Lesley University's off-campus programs grew and prospered.

The off-campus format has expanded to include cohorts of students in 22 states. Core and adjunct faculty have taught in locations as close as Somerville, MA, and as far away as remote islands in Washington State. Two hundred and twenty students (10 cohorts) were pursuing their master's degrees by 1985; 660, by 1990 (30 cohorts); and 880, by 1995 (40 cohorts), peaking at 1,400 in 2000 (65 cohorts), where the number has remained relatively stable. In the 30 years in which the program has been offered, more than 20,000 educators have earned a Technology in Education master's degree from Lesley. As the program grew, so did the faculty, now numbering 12 core members of the division, four national faculty, and 180 adjunct faculty.

Dick Wylie's confidence in the program led to entrepreneurial efforts that included an accelerated approval process for new courses, residential conferences in Colorado, and even a one-week, three-credit Voyage of the Mimi course offered on a 95-foot schooner organized by Angie Ferris. Dr. Wylie recalls his role at Lesley with memories of exciting new initiatives and a collaborative spirit: "Lesley gave me the opportunity to develop an environment where faculty were encouraged to be innovative and creative. I saw my role as helping others achieve their dreams. The faculty showed that an entrepreneurial spirit and quality academics could survive and prosper together."

In the late 1980s significant effort was placed on receiving formal recognition and accreditation for the intensive weekend graduate education model. This was accomplished in 1989, the same time the program was recognized as an exemplary model for in-service technology integration education by the U.S. Department of Education. The program subscribes to a "good practice based on good theory," and emphasizes the effective integration of technology into classroom practice to improve student achievement. Based in the pedagogy of adult learning, the Technology in Education Program provides students both with skills and with immediate benefit.

ADJUNCT FACULTY: ESSENTIAL INGREDIENTS TO SUCCESS

Concurrently with the creation, development, and growth of the Computers in Education off-campus programs, the airline industry was being deregulated. This created the modern "hub and feeder" system that brought air travel to many regions of the country. It became progressively easier to fly faculty to and from cohort sites in the space of a weekend. Early morning "commuter flights" would bring faculty to airline hubs where they could readily make connections to even the most remote Lesley site. With the rise of the commuter airlines, almost every city in the United States soon had access to regularly scheduled flight service.

Faculty from Cambridge, and adjunct faculty from around the country, flew out to urban and rural off-campus sites. Dick Wylie, who became the president of Endicott College in 1987, reminisced: "While student interest and demand was high for the master's program, an unexpected benefit came from the graduates who became our disciples. They became the catalyst for computers in education across the country, and they became our teachers of teachers. They formed a powerful Lesley College network."

To protect the integrity of the program, Lesley Technology in Education faculty trains its own adjunct faculty members. The faculty developed procedures that have since been adopted by other Lesley programs. At the outset they recruited students who had completed the Lesley technology master's degree, since there were no similar degree programs at that time. Those who were interested in graduate teaching in the program chose a course, applied to be a teaching assistant (TA), and, if selected, went through the course again as a TA. If the TA experience was successful, the former student could then teach the course. In later years, with other technology in education graduate programs coming into existence, it became possible to recruit prospective adjunct faculty more widely. Initially the program recruited at local, state, and national educational technology conferences.

In 2000, with the advent of the National Programs office and the creation of additional off-campus degree programs, Ellen Jackson was hired to direct a central office for adjunct faculty recruitment and to conduct regular faculty training workshops. Over the years the program has held many adjunct faculty meetings to review and update courses. These meetings assure that every faculty member covers approximately the same material without overlapping the content of other courses. Adjunct faculty, almost all classroom teachers, brought the real world of education to the program. Some even developed new courses for the program, such as the robotics and telecommunications classes.

STAYING AHEAD:
TEACHING ON THE CUTTING EDGE

Also contributing to the success of the outreach effort in the late 1980s and early 1990s were significant developments in technology, travel, and socioeconomics. The microcomputer, originally considered a hobbyist's toy, became a respected business tool with the advent of the IBM PC, Microsoft Corporation, and VisiCalc's spreadsheet program.

Apple Computer responded with the creation of the Macintosh computer and the graphical user interface. The open architecture of the PC sparked the development of "PC clones," and Microsoft created the Windows operating system. This back and forth "platform war" has driven technology development ever since and has resulted in tremendous advances in desktop computing power and capability. The Technology in Education Program has benefited from the growth of interest in technology, tapping into a strong cultural movement to improve teaching and learning with new tools and techniques.

In 1986, George Willett and Len Scrogan developed Lesley's first telecommunications class. When Willett, Scrogan, and Yoder taught those first few years, they loaned 300-baud modems to students and used local bulletin board systems. When on the road, they became system operators of temporary bulletin boards, set up in students' homes. Classes were run with one phone line, often accessed by a 100-foot modular jack cable connected to a school nurse's office, or by an alligator clip device attached to the nearest pay phone, or by using an acoustic coupler. In spite of the rudimentary resources and without the power of the Internet, Lesley students still formed collaborations with teachers and their classes around the world, an empowering concept never before realized.

Sometimes the Technology in Education Program cultivated a new technology that did not become widely accepted but that provided students with a creative challenge and experience. In 1987 Marie Gannon and Maureen Yoder taught two different weekend courses in videodisc production. Students designed, storyboarded, and videotaped segments that were later sent away to be "pressed" onto a 12-inch videodisc and programmed, with BASIC, to be interactive. The fleeting popularity of videodiscs was a precursor to easily burned and interactive compact disks (CD-ROMs).

Through these forward-thinking innovators, the program has continued to provide educationally sound courses that keep our students up-to-date on the latest technology tools and resources, and it has continued to help teachers integrate these tools and resources into their curricula in thoughtful and effective ways.

GOING VIRTUAL: EXPANDING TO ONLINE

George Blakeslee developed the first Technology in Education online course in 1995. In 1996, with the support of a Sloan Foundation grant, he developed a second, more technical online course. In the fall of 1997 the fully online version of the degree program was launched under the direction of Maureen Yoder. Core and adjunct faculty began to transform their courses into fully online formats. Online support tools were in their infancy, and faculty created their own class websites with web page authoring tools, linking them to a free discussion tool called NetThread.

To launch the online program, Yoder passed out information at conferences and sent flyers to 300 international schools. The first 15 students began in September of 1997. They were a self-selected group of pioneers who chose the online program on account of its convenience and flexibility. The asynchronous nature of the assignments, and the ability for students to go through the program at their own pace, continue to be attractive advantages of taking classes online. All online students participate in a "virtual graduation." They listen to "Pomp and Circumstance"; choose a virtual cap, gown, and hood; view video greetings from their online instructors; and watch the president grant them their diplomas. They post messages such as:

> I really enjoyed the asynchronous format that allowed me the flexibility to complete the coursework on my time schedule. With teaching, coaching, and starting my family, it was a big responsibility, but with self-discipline, hard work, and understanding instructors, I was able to get through it.

Another noted, "The best part was that even though I was in an online program I never felt isolated from my classmates." Hundreds of students from every state and 37 foreign countries have graduated from the fully online program. The program continues to attract students who otherwise could not complete a master's degree because of distance, personal responsibilities, or scheduling constraints.

More and more Lesley weekend courses and blended classes are incorporating substantial online elements as the technology improves and students appreciate the benefits of online learning. In addition to the master's program, newly updated off-campus Certificate of Advanced Graduate Studies (CAGS) and Education Specialist (EdS) programs started in the fall of 2004, with several online courses. In 2006, a blended program was introduced, consisting of shortened intensive weekend hours along with online coursework.

CHANGING LIVES: IMPROVING LEARNING REFLECTIONS ON THE IMPACT OF THE TECHNOLOGY IN EDUCATION PROGRAM

From the vantage point of the 21st century, clearly the Technology in Education Program has consistently fulfilled the mission of the university. Wherever it has been offered, it has had a profoundly positive impact. This can most readily be seen in the reflections of those who have been affected.

To assess the Technology in Education Program, the authors interviewed many of the people who were involved in the early years. Their remarks fall into four categories: impact on teaching philosophy; collaboration, research, and development; impact on education policy; and implementing the vision.

IMPACT ON TEACHING PHILOSOPHY

In the days when Nancy Roberts was gathering support for the Computers in Education Program, June Fox was dean of the Graduate School of Education. She recalls Roberts coming to her with the idea of offering a computer course:

> I went to Dick Wylie, dean of the graduate school at the time. Dick went back and forth with me and finally said if it

will not cost the school any money and if the course brings in three times Nancy's salary, she could do it. Dick found a closet off the library's second floor to use as a classroom. The wiring was completed to connect the PDP 11, donated by DEC. Students loved the course.

We used our own graduates to grow the program, though some of our first graduates taught computers in education courses at surrounding colleges, becoming our competition. With the rapid growth of the Computers in Education Program and the start of the off-campus programs in Colorado, however, Lesley became an institution with a national reputation.

REFLECTIONS FROM EARLY GRADUATES

The impact of the program on those who graduated in the 1980s was unmistakable. Many graduates organized technology initiatives in their districts, rising to newly created leadership positions or making innovative changes in their classrooms.

A poignant reflection on the impact on her career came from one of our first graduates, Jane Manzelli (CAGS):

> As a grade 6 teacher in 1979, I realized computers offered new ways for children to learn. I remember programming a turtle on the screen, and a robot on the floor, and understood the potential to visualize math concepts for my students. Every Friday, I borrowed a computer from Henry Olds at EDC. I pulled into the school parking lot early and my entire class was waiting for me! My principal witnessed the learning going on and used PTO funds to buy an Apple II for the school, which cost $2000! At faculty meetings, I would demonstrate Lemonade Stand, Oregon Trail, and Print Shop. We were the mavericks, the risk takers, and the pioneers in our school systems.
>
> The impact of having graduated with a CAGS in Computers in Education was enormous. In 1984 I became the computer

education coordinator for Brookline Public Schools. I've consulted with Brookline's sister school in Nagoya, Japan, been a board member of the Boston Computer Society and an Apple Distinguished Educator, and became a principal in the technology-rich Morse Pond School in Falmouth.

Another early student, Phyllis Kalowski (CAGS, 1985), reported:

For me, professionally and personally, the courses at Lesley inspired me to stretch beyond the limitations of a classroom teacher. My world expanded. I designed and published software for elementary students, contributed articles to computer magazines for teachers, and presented workshops to school systems and conferences.

Additionally, a student from our first class who stayed on for many years as a faculty member, Angie Ferris (CAGS, 1984), explained:

Because I was both a student and faculty, I had both perspectives. The early days were very exciting times. I was involved in something that had never been done before. It was the first program in the country, so it attracted students from all over, many of whom went back to their hometowns and led their schools in the computers and education initiative.

Finally, a Lesley graduate from the undergraduate college in the 1950s, Molly Watt, who also taught in the graduate programs, shared her memories of learning with Logo:

I believe Lesley College and I offered the first graduate course in Logo in the world, in the Hamilton Wenham School district. When Lesley began offering Logo courses on campus, Ricky Carter invited my husband, Dan Watt, or myself, to give guest lectures. We were part of a growing Logo teachers learning community, sharing insights and process freely.

By the eighties, when I taught in Golden, CO, in Lesley's Computers in Education Program, I had devised procedure plays. Any Logo procedure could be considered a script. Painter hats for the procedure name, carpenter aprons with pockets for the input, and we were ready to understand recursion!

COLLABORATION, RESEARCH, AND DEVELOPMENT

The impact of collaborating on grants, both for Lesley and its early associates, comes from three people representing three of the organizations with which Lesley worked—BBN, TERC, and Enablearning, Inc.

First is Wallace Feurzeig, principal scientist at BBN Technologies:

A major thrust of the TIE program has been the development and use of advanced computer technology as an integral component of teacher preparation programs. Lesley realized early that instructional technology would have an increasingly important role in supporting inquiry and project-based learning in mathematics and science education. From the 1980s on, Lesley education faculty pioneered the classroom use of new instructional software. Some of that effort came through close collaboration with colleagues from the Cambridge research firm BBN. Key Lesley faculty, including Nancy Roberts, Richard Carter, William Barowy, and Frank Davis, worked with Wallace Feurzeig, John Richards, Beverly Hunter, and other BBN Education Department staff on several innovative research and instruction projects centered on educational computing.

One major NSF supported-project, Power Tools for Algebra Problem Solving, investigated the use of educational software for teaching algebraic concepts such as variables, equations, and functions to sixth-grade students. Another NSF project,

Setting a Research and Planning Agenda for Computer Modeling in the Precollege Curriculum, brought together educators and educational software developers from several universities and research institutions to address the issues involved in bringing computer modeling into precollege teaching.

This second grant produced the book *Modeling and Simulation in Science and Mathematics Education*, edited by Wallace Feurzeig and Nancy Roberts.

The second reflection comes from Robert Tinker, founder of Technical Education Research Centers:

At the time the Lesley Technology in Education Program began, I was leading the struggling TERC organization, a nonprofit in Harvard Square that was committed to improving math and science education. We were interested in electronic instrumentation for science education in general, and in lab interfaces specifically. We realized that there was great potential to be gained by connecting electronic sensors to computers and using the computers for real-time data acquisition and display. Adeline Naiman shepherded these kits from dreams to products. Adeline later became a member of Lesley's board of trustees. TERC staff and Adeline often presented talks and workshops at Lesley College's annual technology conferences. I saw my first Macintosh in the 1984 meeting and was struck by the possibilities inherent in its graphical interface.

I knew of Jay Forrester's System Dynamics group at MIT's Sloan School and had read their literature that contained the intuitive drawings they made of systems of "stocks" and "flows." I realized that with the Macintosh, a student could design a system and then the software could crank out the solution using simple numeric methods. This could be revolutionary. Nancy Roberts had recently earned a doctorate for her work in applying system dynamics to education. We recruited Jay

Forrester and Mary Budd Rowe and submitted a proposal to the NSF to explore the educational potential of this idea. In 1985 NSF awarded us the grant for what became known as the "modeling" project.

The basic ideas of probes and models that we developed at TERC and Lesley in the 1980s will turn out to be among the most important contributions of technology to science education.

The third reflection is from Art Bardige, president of Enablearning, Inc.:

One of Lesley University's great strengths is its outreach not just to schools but also to the educational business community. Just the opposite of the ivory tower institutions that too often talk only to each other, Lesley has made it a practice over my 30 years of experience in educational software to reach out to the developers and publishers of educational materials and software. It has offered us much needed guidance, support, and community. We, in the business side of education, all too often are isolated from the academic and teaching side. Lesley has hosted events that bring us together and give us a chance to interact with faculty and students. We have presented our creations in classes and got them critiqued. We have been able to get help on research and on grants. And we have been able to link our enterprises with interested faculty members who help us get them right.

This kind of cooperation and interaction has made a major difference in our ability to create great educational products. So on this centennial anniversary, I want to applaud Lesley University for its great contribution to education and to educational technology through collaboration with industry. I want to thank all of my friends at this farsighted institution of truly higher learning for their help and guidance. I feel very fortunate that my educational software companies have been housed in Cambridge and can work with Lesley.

IMPACT ON EDUCATION POLICY

The third category of reflections on the Technology in Education Program considers its impact on education. Beth Lowd eloquently spoke of this as she described her association with Lesley:

> My motivation for taking courses in the Technology in Education Program was to learn how to use computers in the classroom. I was moving from teaching middle school English to being a "computer specialist" for the Lexington Public Schools, and I needed to know much more than the little BASIC programming I had picked up on my own. Lesley helped me develop a philosophy and ways to help teachers learn. As computers and software changed and matured, Lesley's program helped us all make sense of the changes and see how they could impact learning.

Beth Lowd, computer education specialist for the Lexington schools, helps students discover the finer points of programming a battery powered truck.

Beth Loud, helping students program a Big Trac

Photograph courtesy of MTA Today.

I saw Lesley as a community of learners. The early conferences really helped those of us in the schools to connect with thinkers, academics, researchers, and software developers. Lesley brought in the experts from so many other worlds to share what they knew. Much of what I learned at Lesley I was able to bring directly back to my teachers. I felt supported by the faculty and other students—we helped each other.

My particular niche was at BEST—Business and Education for Schools and Technology—the informal lobbying coalition that Bob Pearlman and I founded to educate the state legislature about the need to fund technology in the schools. The many relationships I developed at Lesley, Lexington, MassCUE (Massachusetts Computer Using Educators), and MCET (Massachusetts Corporation for Educational Telecommunications) served me well. We all helped to pass the Education Technology Bond Bill that funded the original wiring of the Schools for Internet in 1996.

Adeline Naiman also commented on the impact of the TIE Program on education policy:

In 1968, the American Association for the Advancement of Science (AAAS) had its annual meeting in Boston, and I took my 10-year-old along one day. I was then editor of the Elementary Science Study at the Education Development Center (EDC). Seymour Papert and Marvin Minsky, with whom I had done some work at MIT, brought four terminals connected to the MIT PDP-8 mainframe and invited visitors to try them.

My son had a ball, and I had a kind of revelation of the empowerment computers could now bring to everyone. In 1975, I joined the corporation and later the board of Lesley College, and took part in its computer conferences that began in 1978. I became friends with Sue Friel, Nancy Roberts, and Beth Lowd, who shared my vision. In 1979 I became managing director of TERC, where Bob Tinker was pioneering the use of early personal computers in science education. I influenced his bringing his science probes to younger students, and when

215

Apple, Texas Instruments (TI), and IBM brought out the first commercial individual computers, the world exploded.

When TERC moved to Massachusetts Avenue in the early eighties, the interchange between TERC and Lesley became more frequent. Tinker worked on his probeware, and I joined HRM Software to direct publication of this and other curriculum tools for classroom computer use. Lesley became a center for teachers to learn to use computers in the classroom and took on distance learning, establishing branches around the country.

And Dan Watt shared his memories of Lesley, TIE, and Logo:

For me, the beginnings of Lesley's Computers in Education Program coincided with my own professional beginnings as an advocate for appropriate uses of computers in schools. My connection to Lesley College began in the late 1970s when Nancy Roberts and Sue Friel called a series of meetings for people interested in educational computing, to advise the college on how to make use of a PDP-11 minicomputer donated by the Digital Equipment Corporation. It quickly became clear that the folks who came to those meetings—representing Lesley, MIT, BBN, TERC, and several public school systems—felt a strong need to continue meeting as an interest group.

Adeline Naiman with a temperature probe

Photograph courtesy of Lois Russell

We started having monthly meetings on Saturdays, breaking up into interest groups. I was in the "computers and human values" group with Andee Rubin, Tim Barclay, Lynn Nadeau, and others. We focused on two main issues: equal access to technology and making sure that students and teachers kept control of the computers, rather than being controlled by them.

We decided to hold a conference at Lesley about educational uses of computers—the first ever in the Boston area. Then there was the annual Lesley Educational Computer Conference, which was another marvelous opportunity to share projects in progress and talk with other developers, teachers, administrators, and Lesley faculty and students. It was an event to which I always looked forward with pleasure.

John Richards, one of the very first supporters of the Lesley graduate program for Computers in Education, also has strong memories of the early days:

In the late 1970s and early 1980s, the Apple II, the TRS-80, and the Atari dominated the personal computer market. Macs and PCs weren't invented yet, and society was unaware of the changes that were about to happen. Schools were told that technology was the answer, but we didn't even know the question, and teachers had no place to turn for answers. At that moment in time Nancy Roberts created the Lesley graduate program for Computers in Education to provoke questions and to provide answers. The program led to a research and teaching community that persists to this day. More important, it provided a critical mass of people working to understand the practical impact of computers in teaching and learning that complemented the more esoteric research being conducted by some of its better-known neighbors.

My own contribution was to create and coteach a couple of courses that would become staples of the program. Lesley was a truly collaborative environment. When you created a new course, the rest of the faculty sat around the room taking notes, preparing to improve it and then teach it themselves.

National recognition of the program was established when, in 1989, Nancy Roberts and Susan Friel cochaired the National Educational Computer Conference in Boston. Lesley sponsored it and I served as program chair. The conference was the largest NECC ever held, and was a testament to the closeness of the community.

Len Scrogan, a longtime adjunct faculty teaching in our off-campus programs, reflected on the impact of the program on the country and on himself:

> The Lesley Technology in Education Program has reached thousands of educators across the country, clearly contributing to the technology revolution in schools more than any other single institution. Due to my longevity, I have seen dozens of Lesley graduates reach leadership pinnacles in their respective careers. I have seen the transformation of many hundreds of teachers into district and state coordinators, principals, assistant superintendents for technology, and leading-edge consultants. It's astonishing. In the early years, the graduate students were clearly proudest of the national recognition afforded to Lesley University's outreach program by the U.S. Office of Technology Assessment. Lesley was recognized as the leading outreach program in technology in the country. I saw so many students swell in pride as they considered their own part and parcel of this historical effort.

EdnaMay Duffy, a professor in the program, reported on the impact of the course she teaches, ECOMP 6101, Technology: Impact on Society and Schools. When I joined the Graduate School of Education I discovered that teachers, armed with technology skills, could be investigators using their classroom as a laboratory. ECOMP 6101, the capstone course, focuses on change through research, and includes grant writing as one of its assignments, an assignment that integrates research with the knowledge and skills acquired throughout the entire program. Over the years, Lesley ECOMP 6101 students have been awarded monies for technologies and change-making curricula. This funding represents the impact that one course has made on schools all over the United States. If multiplied by the number of these courses taught over the years, a real sense of the significant impact the Technology in Education Program has made can be realized.

Implementing the Vision

The fourth category of reflections focuses on implementing the newly emerging educational technology vision. Two of the early program graduates who went on to work at Lesley, Ron Koehler as an adjunct faculty and Jeff Pankin as director of the Computer Laboratory, contribute to this section. Tom Plati speaks for our western Massachusetts collaborators, and faculty member Bill Barowy recounts the ability of the program to inspire and guide district-level system impact.

Ron Koehler remembered beginning his Lesley experience in the second class of students entering the Computers in Education Program.

> "Computer literacy" seems a quaint concept in today's world of connected students, but curriculum integration is another matter. At Lesley, curriculum integration was always about using technology tools to promote the skills that matter: using information, problem solving, collaborating, and creating—the skills that have become increasingly important and are today listed among what is called "21st-century skills."
>
> When I began teaching in the TIE Program in 1984, the only online piece of the curriculum was an e-mail demonstration we did in a course called Computers in the Schools. Today, second graders in my school district work on cooperative learning projects with seven-year olds in the U.K. and India.

School technology was not ready for the future in those days, but Lesley was. By emphasizing technology's role in promoting the skills that matter, the TIE Program was shaping educators who could prepare students for the global society long before anyone used that term.

Tom Plati, now director of curriculum, assessment, and technology for the Lexington, MA, public schools, recalled:

> The Lesley University environment in the 1980s, propelled by its visionary educators, was the single largest force in helping us first understand the power of technology in education in our region. As math and science director in Shrewsbury, MA, in the early 1980s, I was fascinated by the introduction of the new microcomputers, and searched for different strategies for utilizing this new technology, learning them by taking courses at Lesley. Ricky Carter taught Logo I, Logo II, and the Software Evaluation class and became an important mentor and coach to me and to others. To inspire us, Ricky brought in the who's who of technology at the time: Tom Snyder, Art Bardige, and Seymour Papert. New instructors provided excitement in other areas: Maureen Brown Yoder in multimedia and Angie Ferris and Karen Gartland in technology curriculum development through the Voyage of the Mimi. Wow! And how could any of us early adopters ever forget the "must" technology conference we just had to attend each year. It wasn't the MassCue Conference or even NECC. It was the Lesley Computer Conference, held on a warm spring May day, that always provided us with rich sustenance in so many educational areas.

Jeff Pankin, an early graduate of the program and now a senior IT consultant at MIT, was the first director of the computer lab and reported on what it was like at the beginning of the Computers in Education Program in the early 1980s:

My vision of the future is one in which schools become more humane places to learn and work. I came out of the open school movement and then latched onto technology. To me technology held the promise of freeing teachers from mounds of paperwork and students from boring, tedious lessons. Technology also meant teachers would be better equipped to serve each child, with technology tracking progress and supporting teachers' pedagogic decisions. Schools would become more fun and turn out more sophisticated thinkers. I think we all shared some vision of schools being better.

Voyage of the Mimi

Image courtesy of Bank Street College.

Bill Barowy, faculty member and academic advisor to the Raymond, WA, cohort, illustrated the system impact that the Technology in Education Program has had on one rural Washington State community:

> Our 1998-2000 Technology in Education cohort from Raymond and South Bend Washington knows wholeheartedly what it means to belong to a community. In 1998 I became the cohort's advisor and later traveled to Raymond to teach a class. I observed the social conditions that follow when a 19th-century boomtown depletes its natural resources of shellfish and trees and the economy goes bust. The teachers felt challenged but much needed. The students were consistently performing one year behind grade level. When the local hotel burned, many migrant families were displaced, and the high school gymnasium housed them for many weeks. Teachers gathered clothes from the community, and the school fed its new inhabitants.

Cindy Jouper, who was a Lesley student, Lesley's lab coordinator, and a teacher turned teacher-trainer, assembled the computer lab every Lesley weekend and put the computers back in the classrooms during the intervening time to maximize their effectiveness with the children. The community obtained this equipment and a modicum of training by winning a Technology Literacy Challenge Fund (TLCF) grant for $400,000. Linda Brummell recalled how the whole community pulled together to complete the proposal swiftly. Sandy Weller, another Lesley student, oversaw the completion of all the tasks. Jouper conducted the training for the year-long grant, leaving the school without its resident expert in technology. The staff searched for master's programs that would further their abilities, and discovered Lesley. Brummell became the site coordinator.

Brummell, Vivian, and other Lesley students wrote additional proposals and won subsequent Gates grants, which brought more resources and training. The TIE cohort model had significant effects on the educational practices of the entire school—a "critical mass" for change.

CONCLUSION: AN ESSENTIAL THREAD

Throughout the history of the program, both faculty and students have developed valuable connections and collaborations. Faculty have published many books and articles on a variety of topics, and presented papers nationally and internationally. It was the faculty's practice to work together on these publications. In various combinations, Bill Barowy, George Blakeslee, Ricky Carter, Angie Ferris, Margery Staman Miller, Nancy Roberts, and Maureen Yoder wrote several books collaboratively.

For the educators in our classes, many assignments have empowered them to document their newly acquired knowledge, to raise funds for important initiatives, and to create materials to enhance their teaching and benefit their students and colleagues.

George Blakeslee, EdnaMay Duffy, and others teaching the Technology: Impact on Society and the Schools course require students to write a grant. Many of these have been funded, resulting in hundreds of thousands of dollars' worth of equipment, professional development, and innovative ideas implemented in classrooms. Stephan Cohen, Bill Arrigoni, and other faculty who teach the Website Design and HTML: Web Publishing for Educators class have motivated students to create Web pages for their districts, their schools, and themselves. Jo-Anne Hart, in her class Technology and Social Studies, involved students in a Growing Voters project, promoting a national effort to register voters for the 2004 and 2008 presidential elections.

Students have also published articles with the support and encouragement of faculty members. Since 1999 Joan Thormann, in her class 21st-Century Teaching: Supporting All Learners on the Ability Spectrum, requires students to write an article for publication that focuses on some aspect of technology use in special education. To date 10 articles have been published in a variety of journals. Mary Seegers, one of the published students, wrote, "I am now in awe at the thought of how our efforts have combined to potentially result in someone somewhere—someone whom we will never know or see—receiving some type of assistive technology software or hardware device that will significantly change their life."

Judi Mathis-Johnson, another core faculty member, summarized the impact the program has on students:

> Our philosophy has been to provide real applications in the current classroom, and we continue to do that today. We change teachers, classrooms, schools, and curricula from the moment students take that first weekend class. We don't wait until students emerge with a degree to take leadership roles; we set them up with the philosophy and tools to begin that role immediately, so they can take on an even greater role later on.

Over the years, the master's program has been continually updated as hardware and software capabilities have changed and innovative new approaches to using technology in classrooms have emerged. Internet-based resources, advanced communications capabilities, and virtual worlds offer exciting new possibilities in the years to come, along with technologies and applications about which we can only dream.

A spirit of educational entrepreneurship has characterized the Lesley Technology in Education Program from the very beginning. As Sue Friel said, "Everything we did was lots of fun, was very creative, and everyone at Lesley supported us." That spirit has spread outward from Cambridge and now exerts positive educational change in communities in 22 states and in graduates' classrooms around the world. The Technology in Education Program clearly illustrates the huge benefits accruing from faculty and community collaboration with administration that allows and supports entrepreneurship. As one of our recent graduates said, "The Lesley program was life changing. It made me a better teacher, and I can't wait to use what I've learned."

REFERENCES

Coit, L. (1981). Teachers, computer, prejudice, and Lesley College, *Christian Science Monitor, 16.*

Papert, S. (1993). *Mindstorms: Children, computers, and powerful ideas.* (2nd ed.). New York, NY: Basic Books.

Polidori, J. (1983). Face to face, *MTA Today,* March 31, 1983, pp. 4 8.

CHAPTER NINE

Threshold Then and Now: Lesley's Transition Program for Young Adults with Disabilities

ARLYN ROFFMAN, PhD, LMHC
FRANCES OSTEN, MEd
CAROLE NOVECK, MS

In 1981, at a time when there were few options after high school for young adults with disabilities, Lesley boldly showed initiative and supported the development of Threshold, an innovative transition program that 29 years later would still be proudly preparing students with significant special needs for work, community integration, and lifelong learning.

SOCIAL CONTEXT

Transition was a newly emerging term in the early 1980s. Chapter 766, the Massachusetts law guaranteeing a free and appropriate public education (FAPE) for students with special needs, had been passed just a few years before in 1974, followed even more recently by its federal equivalent, Public Law 94-142, the Education for All Handicapped Children Act. Despite the great step forward in special education represented by these pieces of legislation, their impact was initially limited largely to elementary and middle schools or to programs for children with varying levels of retardation (Grossman, 1983). The ongoing needs of older youth with disabilities went virtually unaddressed for several more years until educators and policy makers finally began to recognize that most disabling conditions persist into adolescence and that many are never outgrown at all. Only then did they acknowledge the associated lifelong challenges and mandate that long-term goals extending beyond the high school years be addressed in the Individualized Education Programs (IEPs) of secondary-school special education students with both severe and moderate disabilities (Sitlington & Frank, 1990). A major turning point occurred in 1984, when Madeline Wills, assistant secretary for the U.S. Office of Special Education and Rehabilitative Services (OSERS), wrote her seminal "Bridges" paper (Wills, 1984) and propelled the transition movement into federal policy. Although Wills, like her predecessors, described transition in narrow, job-related terms as "an outcome-oriented process encompassing a broad array of services and experiences that lead to employment" (p.1), when she added that "success in social, personal, leisure, and other adult roles enhances opportunities both to obtain employment *and enjoy its benefits*" (emphasis added) (p.1), she paved the way for a broader discussion of transition. Picking up on this new line of thinking, Halpern (1985) wrote that "living successfully in one's community should be the primary target of transitional services" (p.480), a perspective that opened the door to a more holistic approach toward transition, and that validated the thinking behind the Threshold model, then several years old.

Despite the federal mandate from OSERS, few public schools adopted the comprehensive approach that would foster development of the full range of skills needed for entry into the adult world. The dearth of services seemed all too apparent when Halpern (1985) conducted a survey of the entire population of teachers and administrators in Oregon along with a stratified random sample of parents about transition practices in that state's schools. The study's 90% response rate, which led the authors to believe the results could be generalized, suggested that although 9 out of 10 high schools offered instruction to pupils with disabilities, fewer than 50% of those students "actually received instruction in such important areas as vocational preparation, functional academics, home living skills, and community living skills" (p .483). At least half of the Oregon teachers cited a need for more vocational preparation and community living instruction. These results suggest there was a need that was not being met, despite the federal government's directive for transition programming.

Even those programs that did exist in the 1980s tended to be limited in scope, focusing largely on development of vocational skills. As a result, high school graduates with LD and other special needs who had not had access to any independent living training were significantly delayed in their ability to achieve independence and tended to live at home with their parents longer than their peers without LD (Haring, Lovett, & Smith, 1990). Moreover, even with vocational training, few were able to earn anything more than minimum wage (Edgar, 1987) or to successfully support their move from school to community. Thus, the prospects for life beyond high school for students with special needs were severely limited; good programming was clearly needed.

THE LESLEY CONTEXT

Threshold was launched in the fall of 1982, during a period when the graduate school was highly entrepreneurial and particularly welcoming of creative innovation. A phone call from an eager parent of a would-be student in the fall of 1981 mobilized then Assistant Professor Dr. Arlyn Roffman to apply for funding to disseminate the model of the Para-Educator Program at New York University (NYU), a vocational training program targeted to young adults with severe LD, to other colleges around the country. As a member of the graduate school faculty, Roffman approached Dean Richard Wylie for support of her plan to make the bold move to significantly expand upon the NYU model and create the first *comprehensive* campus-based postsecondary transition program in the nation.

Initial funding provided by the Para-Educator Foundation and the Foundation for Children with Learning Disabilities (now the National Center for Learning Disabilities) supported Threshold through the first two years, to the point when it would be fully populated and financially self-sustaining. The target was emotionally stable young adults aged 18 to 26 with severe learning disabilities and low to average cognitive functioning whose test scores on standardized tests of intelligence ranged from 75 to 90 and whose basic skills were at least at fourth-grade level. This population of students had up to this point been sorely underserved; too highly functioning for sheltered workshops but too challenged by the academic demands of typical college degree programs, they had historically "fallen through the cracks" and had had little opportunity to reach their full potential. The program aimed to serve those who met the criteria just specified and who had both the desire to live an independent life and the drive to work hard to achieve their goals.

Basing this nondegree program at a college was an innovation in itself. At the time of Threshold's inception, when higher education was increasingly being viewed as the normative path for high school graduates in America, few youth with severe special needs dared dream that they could step forward with their peers into postsecondary life. By basing Threshold on a university campus, participating students would have the opportunity to have the *normalized experience* (Wolfensberger, 1972) of attending college while building the practical skills needed for working and living independently. They would take their courses in campus classrooms, eat in the college's dining facility, have access to the library and gym, and be able to participate in many campus clubs and social functions.

MODEL: WHAT THE PROGRAM WOULD LOOK LIKE

The Threshold model was designed to prepare its students to become independent, responsible, productive working citizens. Its holistic approach would help students prepare for all aspects of adult life through a comprehensive program that included vocational education, preparation for independent living, social skills training and other psychosocial supports, and development of leisure-time interests and skills.

VOCATIONAL TRAINING

Through coursework and 15 to 18 hours of supervised fieldwork each week, students would prepare for paraprofessional positions in one of two majors, early childhood or human services. The first year would be devoted to career exploration, allowing students to study and experience the two majors for a semester each. In the second year, students would concentrate solely on the major that best fit their interests and abilities. The vocational portion of the program would focus on general job readiness and on skills that were specific to the need of the vocational majors. Thus, students would learn prevocational skills, such as how to search for employment (e.g., preparing a resume, interviewing) and job-specific skills related to child or elderly care. In addition to an on-site supervisor, each student would be assigned a Threshold vocational advisor who would meet with the student on campus, visit the field placement for observations, and consult with the on-site supervisor about student progress.

INDEPENDENT LIVING

The independent living component of the program would prepare students for community life. A series of courses would focus on such practicalities as money management (e.g., banking and budgeting); apartment living skills (e.g., meal planning and preparation, cleaning); sexuality; and daily living (e.g., personal hygiene and medical self-care).

PSYCHOSOCIAL SUPPORTS
AND COURSEWORK

Psychological support would be offered both formally, through weekly therapeutic small-group meetings with a licensed psychologist, and informally, through mentoring by faculty and staff. Training in social skills would be provided through a weekly course, and its lessons would be reinforced ecologically throughout the program, in classes, in the residence halls, and at the field placements.

LEISURE-TIME SKILLS

Students would be assisted in planning satisfying and productive use of their leisure time. Electives in writing, drama, and fine arts would promote development of their creativity, and support would be offered by mentors and by residence staff as students independently managed their free hours.

IMPLEMENTATION: HOW THE MODEL WAS PUT INTO EFFECT

In late winter of 1981 a flyer was mailed to Boston-area high schools announcing the opening of Threshold and welcoming applications. Since campus housing was not made immediately available to Threshold, the first applicants anticipated being commuters. Thirty applications were submitted for the 18 openings in the pioneer cohort, reflecting a clear demand for the innovative transition programming. The campus opened a 10-bed residence hall for women; the men lived in private apartments near campus. The next year, with the admission of a second cohort of 18, the number of beds increased significantly, and establishment of a small men's dorm made it possible for male students also to experience residential life.

TRANSITION SUPPORT

During Threshold's second year in operation, it became apparent that although students had acquired many important work and community skills during their two years on campus, they would benefit from additional support as they made the adjustment from their campus-based program to mainstream community life. A $100,000 grant from the Jessie B. Cox Charitable Trust backed the development of the Transition Year Program, which would provide postgraduate assistance and skills reinforcement as graduates moved into the community and embarked upon their independent adult lives. During the transition year, students would benefit from the services of an independent living advisor, who would help them find apartments in the Cambridge area and who would visit them for 100 hours over the course of their first 12 months beyond graduation to help them apply the skills learned during the two-year program. A vocational advisor would guide them through the job-search process and support both them and their employer as they adjusted to their first paid position. Further, a weekly seminar would bring them back to campus for additional coursework related to real-world issues and skills.

The Transition Year Program quickly became the option of choice for 75% of Threshold graduates. Thus, for most students, Threshold became a three-year experience. At one point there was serious consideration of lengthening the program to incorporate a third year for all, but it was determined that this would make the program prohibitively expensive for some and would not fit the needs of the few who, after two years, were still not quite ready for community life. To address the needs of this small group of graduates, a Bridge Year was developed. This intensive, individualized program was designed to be a half-step toward independence; students would still live in Threshold residence halls but would work more hours in internships and receive additional training to help them achieve readiness for the transition year.

CAMPUS LIFE

Threshold became a largely residential program. Although the goal was always to integrate students to the fullest degree possible on campus, the particular special needs of the Threshold population necessitated more residential supports than were available in mainstream Lesley housing. Thus, from the program's first years, Threshold students have been housed in separate Lesley residence halls, allowing them to benefit from additionally trained residence staff and supplemental structure to support the development of their independent living skills and their social growth.

Despite the separate dorms, Threshold resident students have been well included in campus life, eating in Lesley's dining halls, enjoying full access to the university library and fitness facilities, participating in the Lesley College student governance, Unity Choir, theater productions, and other mainstream clubs, and playing weekend basketball games along with Lesley undergraduates and Threshold alumni at a neighborhood elementary school. They have also benefited from a comprehensive schedule of Threshold-specific programming, the highlight being the semiformal dance, attended by scores of current students and by alumni who return year after year.

The Evolution of the Model

Over the past three decades, Threshold has evolved to meet the changing needs of its students and to respond to changing times. Its dedicated faculty and administration, most of whom have worked at the program for more than 15 years, provide a long-term perspective that has enabled them to be particularly sensitive to evolving patterns of student needs. In response to workplace and technological changes that have had the potential to impact students and graduates, they have implemented a variety of modifications to the program.

Vocational Training

Among those changes have been a number of alterations to the original vocational offerings at Threshold, including several modifications of the majors.

The initial goal for graduates majoring in early childhood was qualification for jobs as aides in nursery schools and day-care settings, but it soon became clear that a significant percentage were capable of assuming a higher level of responsibility in child care, many as teachers. For a time, those who were interested in becoming fully qualified as early childhood teachers had to turn to other institutions to earn the necessary credits; however, by the early 1990s, six college credits in either major could be earned right at Threshold, and the program's early childhood curriculum and practicum experiences officially fulfilled the Massachusetts requirements for early childhood teacher qualification. Since that time, although not all students majoring in early childhood have been ready to assume a position as a teacher upon graduation, licensure qualifies them to grow into that role.

The career exploration year was altered within the first decade. The original concept of structured exposure to two vocational fields was sound and effective; often, students who had applied to Threshold expecting to major in one area discovered through their own observations as well as their supervisors' that the alternate major would be a better match for their interests and talents. The challenge was that every year there were students for whom neither early childhood education nor human services was an appropriate career match. Although not well suited for such heavily people-oriented fields, these individuals had the potential to thrive in other career paths. Responding to the vocational needs of this subset of students, the vocational portion of the program was expanded to include a clerical services major, which offered hands-on training in office skills. Subsequently, when interest in human services studies declined over the years, that major was dropped, and clerical services joined early childhood education as the second vocational option for the career exploration year.

Ever alert to changes in the work world, Threshold faculty continued to modify the new major so that it would be responsive to current job demands and work availability. Office environments were themselves evolving, as new computer technologies were revolutionizing the workplace. When the clerical services major was first designed, entry-level business positions, such as mailroom clerks and file clerks, were plentiful, but these jobs became a relative rarity as computer use grew more prevalent. As a result, the major was renamed business support services, and was expanded to provide training for other jobs in addition to office work, in such diverse business-based positions as retail sales and stocking, university or hospital food service delivery, and patient transport or escort services in health-care settings.

There have been unanticipated benefits from adding the new major to the program. First, there was a notable effect on the applicant pool, with a marked increase in applications from qualified males, whose numbers grew from 20% to 50% by the program's third decade. This change could perhaps be attributable to gender stereotypes about the early childhood and human services fields, which are too often viewed as "women's work"; for those subscribing to this line of thinking, the addition of the business support services major may have provided a more gender-neutral vocational option, making Threshold more attractive to both men and women. A second continuing benefit of adding this major is that the training it provides in keyboarding, word processing, e-mail, and responsible use of the Internet has improved the communication skills of all students, regardless of their career track, with invaluable additional applicability in their day-to-day lives.

INDEPENDENT LIVING

Program staff have developed and refined an orientation to help new students adjust to their enlarging world, which includes the Threshold and Lesley communities, the Cambridge and Harvard Square neighborhoods, and the Greater Boston environs. Orientation has been designed to help students ease into the level of independence offered within the program, and topics have ranged from an introduction to the work world to lessons on being safe in an urban environment, and from instruction on how to use Boston's public transit to hands-on workshops on using laundromats.

A series of practical courses developed to prepare students for community living has been refined over the years to address emerging issues. For example, Sexuality, a course that always covered such topics as reproduction and decision making, was adapted by the mid-

235

1980s to include the topic of HIV AIDS. A course in computer safety was added by the early 2000s to help students navigate the Internet responsibly.

The Medical World course, designed to help students manage their own health care, began to address obesity and nutrition in greater depth when those topics emerged as increasingly prevalent issues.

Apartment Living, the course designed to teach how to live independently, has changed over time as well. As they have since the program began, students continue to learn about leases and paying bills, cooking and grocery shopping, living safely and cooperatively with roommates, and using the resources available within their urban community; however, when a two-week dorm-based apartment experience that had been established early in the program as a lab for independent living ultimately proved less than optimal, it was replaced by a weekly Food Lab. This workshop provides second-year students more weekly hands-on experience in the kitchen and the opportunity to focus intensively on meal planning and preparation, cleanup, and kitchen safety. Through sharing family recipes, students have also been encouraged to explore their culture and identity. For example, several students connected to their culture by exploring its culinary arts:

> Aadrike was able to connect with her Indian heritage by researching recipes for meals she had enjoyed when she visited restaurants serving Indian cuisine. She developed an association with a Lesley College student from a similar background and they worked together to make samosas and lassis. They adapted the recipes and shopped together to find authentic ingredients. Another student provided Lithuanian selections and described why and how the ingredients reflected that culture. A Peruvian recipe was important to a third student and helped him identify and describe his background.

The Personal Finance course, too, changed over time. The need for explicit instruction and assistance in money management has been evident from the program's inception. It was clear early on that students would benefit from support as they learned the many facets of managing checking and savings accounts and the principles of sound budgeting (Roffman, 2000). Originally a requirement only for first-year students, this course was extended to four semesters to provide second-year students an opportunity to continue focusing on money management and consumer skills throughout the program. Recognizing that awareness of the news of the world further prepares individuals for community life, Threshold added a weekly Current Events class within the program's first few years. Designed to help students understand and keep abreast of major local, national, and world events, this course provides a forum for discussing timely issues. It is a particular point of pride that Threshold students have registered to vote and have participated in major elections since the early 1980s.

PSYCHOSOCIAL SUPPORTS
AND COURSEWORK

Young adults benefit from encouragement when embarking on new endeavors. This is especially true of Threshold students, whose disabilities frequently make the steps toward adulthood seem particularly formidable (Roffman, 2007). The psychological and social scaffolding provided within the program takes a variety of forms.

A Social Skills course helps students focus on increasing their interpersonal effectiveness with others by developing their social perception and general assertiveness. This course, too, has been refined with the times by adding emerging topics, such as cell phone etiquette, social networking, and the benefits and dangers involved in developing Internet relationships.

The Pathways to Health course was added in Threshold's third decade to help students learn about stress, including its causes, symptoms, and strategies for management. In this class students are helped to distinguish between the elements of their lives over which they do and do not have control and to develop an Individualized Stress

Management Profile, which focuses on identifying stress-reduction techniques to use as they contend with the issues they identify.

From the beginning, Threshold has been committed to helping students build on their strengths and work around their areas of challenge. Many students arrive all too aware of what they *cannot* do and are not attuned to their individual "islands of competence" (Brooks, 2001), their unique set of strengths, skills, and positive attributes. To foster the awareness of their "islands," a course titled Understanding Strengths and Challenges was added in the late 1980s. Designed to promote self-awareness and self-understanding, the course helps students learn the definitions, characteristics, types, and known causes of various disabilities. They identify their own learning styles and areas of difficulty and how these contribute to specific problems in their day-to-day lives. They then develop an Individualized Learning Profile that summarizes their strengths and weaknesses and lists strategies for capitalizing on the former and compensating for the latter. This information is shared with faculty, who are subsequently able to help each student employ her individualized list of strategies in all aspects of the program and to develop new tactics as needed. The Learning Profile is revisited and updated before students graduate, and students are coached to use it as a reference tool as they transition into work and community life (Yuan, 1994). In addition, students learn about their rights and responsibilities under the Americans with Disabilities Act (ADA), which stipulates that individuals with disabilities must self-disclose and self-advocate in order to access needed accommodations. To prepare them for this responsibility, the final exam for Understanding Learning Challenges requires students to explain their learning problems to others and to demonstrate their ability to effectively use self-advocacy skills to request the accommodations they need in order to perform optimally on the job or in classroom settings. A study by Roffman, Herzog, & Wershba-Gerson (1994) validated the efficacy of this course and the carryover of self-understanding and self-advocacy into graduates' work and community lives.

Personal Growth is a weekly group led by a licensed psychologist to help students better understand themselves. Participants have an opportunity to speak candidly about issues of concern to them, to set and work on personal goals, and to discuss the responsibilities and challenges of young adulthood. As might be expected, issues raised by students—always addressed with sensitivity—have changed with the times. Originally conducted as an open-ended group called Talk Session, this course has become more structured in recent years to focus on particularly pertinent areas relevant to personal growth. In addition to the classroom exercises that students experience in this course, meetings with program mentors and individual conferences with faculty all have the psychosocial benefit of encouraging students to identify, develop, and share their skills and interests. Matthew's story demonstrates the transition from isolation to confidence and inclusion:

> Matthew resisted the Threshold experience when he first arrived in the 1980s. He purposely separated himself from his peers during his first semester, did not take his work seriously, and refused to acknowledge either his learning disability or his severe hearing loss. Although he attended his classes, it was not until he was placed in a human services setting, working with individuals with more extreme special needs, that he found himself and realized that among his own "islands of competence" was an ability to offer this population understanding, empathy, and patience. Gradually, he accepted his own learning challenges, stopped fighting his need for a hearing aid, and took full advantage of Threshold's offerings. After graduation he was hired as a counselor by a program for individuals with severe special needs and continues to thrive on the job, even being named Employee of the Year in 1996. Married to another Threshold graduate, with whom he has two children, he now recognizes that he has *many* "islands" and has confidence that along with his limitations he has great strengths.

LEISURE-TIME SKILLS

Most students arrive at Threshold longing for friends. Although some in each cohort reported having enjoyed a satisfying social life during their high school years, most did not share this positive experience. Some had managed to establish friendships in high school only to be isolated at home; others had been marginalized at school and had suffered from pervasive and chronic loneliness throughout their childhood and teen years. Thus, development of social relationships has always ranked high on the priority lists of students and the program faculty and administration. Residence staff members have worked along with faculty to facilitate students' participation in planned activities, to assist them in shaping unstructured leisure hours, and to help them weather the interpersonal challenges of dorm and program life.

The classes designed to foster development of leisure-time pursuits have varied since the program first opened. At one point there was a course in dance, another in sewing. For the past two decades, students have had three options: Creative Writing, which produces a magazine each semester, with selections of work from all class members; Fine Arts, which offers an art show at a local gallery each year that showcases students' paintings, photography, and sculpture; and Theater Project, which produces a dramatic performance for the Threshold community during the fall and spring semesters.

Threshold has always encouraged its students to be active and fit. Physical education courses have evolved over the years along with the expansion of Lesley's PE facilities; a Saturday bowling league was popular for a time; and a weekend basketball game at the neighborhood school currently attracts students, alumni, and even, on a fairly regular basis, President Moore! Those with interest in sports on campus have been encouraged to join teams, which became more feasible when the door to involvement in intercollegiate sports opened in 2009. Until then, NCAA rules had prevented students in nondegree programs from competing on college athletic teams, and the only option for Threshold students seeking a team experience had been intramurals. One gifted athlete spoke up and changed all that:

When David, a particularly talented Threshold tennis player, expressed interest in training and competing with the Lesley College team, the university contested the exclusion policy, the rule was waived, and the student was able to join the team in intercollegiate matches. David became a highly ranked and respected captain of the team.

Integration into other aspects of Lesley College extracurricular life has flowed from good fits between the abilities and interests of Threshold students and the activities themselves. Music and dance are pursuits of choice for a number of Threshold students:

Dan and Sally were soloists in a year-end performance of the Lesley chorus, and for a time several other Threshold students worked tirelessly with the Lesley University dance team. These experiences helped Threshold students bond with their peers on campus, and, equally important, served to educate Lesley College students about the very real potential of young adults with disabilities.

Students have additionally been encouraged to take advantage of the many available cultural, dining, and shopping opportunities within their reach in the Greater Boston area. Formal and informal activities have included visiting area museums, shopping in local malls, attending concerts, watching games in neighborhood sports bars, and attending live sporting events.

EVALUATION OF THE EFFICACY OF THE THRESHOLD PROGRAM: OUTCOME DATA

For nearly three decades—over the life of Threshold—there has been a continued commitment to formally documenting program outcomes, and much has been learned about the program's alumni. An initial study of the first four cohorts of graduates from 1984 to 1987 (Posthill & Roffman, 1991) was followed by a study of outcomes for the first 12 cohorts (henceforth referred to as "the early group") through 1995 (Reisman & Yuan, 1996), and in 2006 an additional study (Yuan, 2006) investigated how students in the subsequent 10 years of the program, from 1996 to 2005 ("the later group"), had fared. More recent research (Osten, 2009) was conducted to gather further information about the early group as they approached and reached middle age. An in-depth look at employment of Threshold graduates from the employers' perspective was conducted in 1996 (Osten & Noveck).

The studies all sought to take a comprehensive look at graduates' lives, investigating their progress in each of the four major domains of the program: vocational, independent living, psychosocial adjustment, and use of leisure time. Beyond vocational status, the studies explored their living patterns, independent living skills, personal growth, and use of support mechanisms, along with their level of satisfaction in various arenas of their lives,

Respondents in all of the follow-up studies had attended the core two-year Threshold Program, and nearly 75% had also attended the program's Transition Year Program. Comparing data across time, there is impressive consistency in what the numbers convey about the histories of adults who have graduated from Lesley's Threshold Program. The bottom line is that the group as a whole has fared well. As will be seen through the remainder of this chapter, despite ongoing challenges, there have been many triumphs and successes.

PROFILE OF ALUMNI

Threshold alumni are a diverse group. Consistent with the admissions criteria established when Threshold was founded, intelligence test scores have remained within the low to average range over the years. The mean Full Scale IQ of the earlier cohort was 81 (range = 65 109), mean Verbal Score was 85 (range = 63 114), mean Performance Score 78 (range =62 122). The scores of the later group were remarkably similar. Standardized achievement test scores have consistently averaged fifth to sixth grade in reading and fourth to fifth grade in math.

In addition to their learning disabilities, most Threshold students face physical challenges, including vision problems, seizure disorders, mobility limitations, and hearing impairments. Many have also been diagnosed with attention deficit hyperactivity disorder (ADHD), Asperger's syndrome, or psychological conditions, such as mood disorders—or with a combination of these problems. The older graduates reported a significant increase in diagnoses of psychological conditions over time (almost double), particularly depression and bipolar disorder, and, as might be expected with aging, a similar jump in chronic medical conditions, particularly obesity or diabetes, or both. An increase in diagnoses of Asperger's syndrome and bipolar disorder among applicants and graduates in recent years is undoubtedly reflective of emerging awareness of these disorders among clinicians.

Despite the significant challenges they face, many Threshold students have demonstrated remarkable strengths, including character traits that have allowed them to persevere over the years and, in many cases, to succeed beyond the expectations envisioned when Threshold was founded. One student who was accepted from the wait list despite particularly low test scores is a case in point:

> Jennifer demonstrated an "emotional intelligence" not captured by standardized test scores. From the day she entered the program, she displayed a unique understanding of children's needs and an extraordinary ability to foster their growth and development. She continued to grow throughout her training at Threshold and has been successfully employed as a teacher of young children for nearly 20 years.

Living Patterns

Across studies, although approximately 25% of alumni returned to their hometowns following graduation, the 75% participating in the Transition Year resided in apartments in Greater Cambridge for at least the duration of the program, and tended to remain in the Boston area for a long while. In fact, at least 60% of respondents still lived in the area 10 years after graduation. Like graduates of other local colleges and universities, Threshold alumni have found many reasons to remain in the Boston area; however, the decision to stay in the city has been especially compelling for this population, as doing so has afforded them the opportunity to enter a well-established, ever growing social community comprised of earlier Threshold graduates—an important source of friends, roommates, and life partners. Further, Boston's extensive and accessible public transit system has been freeing for the many who lack a driver's license or a car. Another draw has been the opportunity for many graduates to continue in the positions they secured during the Transition Year.

Across studies, almost 45% of graduates reported having lived independently for at least a 10-year period after graduation. At the time of each of the research investigations, only 10% to 20% were living with parents; however, this does not tell the entire story, as 35% to 50% of graduates had lived at home *at some point* after graduation, depending on the cohort. For one third of the earlier group this was a temporary situation of less than one year due to ill health, apartment transitions, or transitions between jobs. An equal number of graduates had lived with parents for one to three years, and another third had lived in their parents' home more or less permanently, citing difficulty finding affordable housing, unemployment, lack of a roommate, need of family support, desire to be involved with family, or simply a wish to live at home.

Participation in the Transition Year after graduation seems to have increased the likelihood of living outside the family home. Transition graduates lived independently of their parents 85% of the time in the first 10 years after graduation, while those who had only completed the two-year program lived independently of their parents just 50% of the time.

In their first years after graduation, those who lived in apartments or condos tended to do so with roommates, but the 2008 study showed that as the group matured, only 17% lived with a roommate (most often with another Threshold graduate). One third lived alone, and 40% lived with a spouse or a child, or both.

RELATIONSHIP STATUS

Across studies, in the first 10 years after graduation, less than 10% of graduates were married and less than 1% had children; over time, that picture changed for the early group. By 2008, 37% were married (4% were divorced) or in a civil union. Among those who had married, 50% had wed another Threshold graduate, and 11% had one or more children.

A 2007 qualitative study by Yuan investigated the effect of a learning disability on the marriages of 10 couples comprised of two Threshold graduates. Although there were instances of remarkable independence among some, it became clear that it is far from easy for most who become parents. One couple has two children with hints of learning challenges of their own. The parents remember their own struggles and are fearful of their children being teased at school, as they were. "We knew there was a chance [that our children would have LD]. It's not like we're going to love our children any different. It's just going to be a challenge" (Yuan, in press).

A number of graduates live in multigenerational homes with their parents and their own children. Other support models are in place as well: One child with special needs is being raised by a graduate's parents; two graduates, including one with newborn twins, are living with their children and a parent; a third couple (both Threshold alumni) have reached out for significant help to raise their son, who has autism. Some have persevered with little support:

Lisa, who had a child immediately after graduating from Threshold, raised her daughter as a single parent while working as a day-care teacher. She eventually took additional coursework and became a day-care director. Now her daughter is now completing college.

INDEPENDENT LIVING

Developing independent living skills has been a central goal of Threshold. Graduates in each of the Threshold outcome studies were asked to evaluate their own functioning across a range of skill sets, and there was remarkable consistency in their self-assessments.

Money management. In the area of money management, more than two thirds reported spending within their means (limiting themselves to the money they had available). Nearly that many reported balancing their checkbook regularly, and three fourths reported regularly paying bills on time (85% in 1996).

Health care. Graduates consistently reported that they had been conscientious about routine medical and dental checkups over time. Nearly 90% percent reported seeing a doctor and going to the dentist at least once a year. (NB: these high percentages may reflect the need for monitoring of health issues described earlier in this chapter.)

As with the general population, ongoing attention to exercise and diet has proven more problematic. About two thirds of graduates reported exercising regularly, and just over half reported watching their diet and weight. While it is encouraging that the trend is toward greater participation in physical activity, it is disturbing that 10% also report living with obesity or diabetes—or both—or with pre-diabetes.

Psychosocial development. Seventy-five percent of graduates reported that they attempt to resolve problems with the use of good social skills. Within their work lives, approximately 90% reported getting along with their clients, co-workers, and supervisor, and said they manage to keep personal problems to themselves at work. Responses from the employer study suggest that Threshold graduates are equal to other employees in terms of their ability to get along with co-workers and supervisors.

Leisure time. As stated earlier, for many alumni, childhood was fraught with isolation or social missteps, and in many instances admission to Threshold marked the first opportunity to develop meaningful friendships. Thus, it was gratifying that in each of the studies, when alumni were asked to name how they were most likely to spend their free time, being with friends consistently topped the list.

When asked *with whom* they tended to socialize, graduates mentioned family members, followed by other Threshold alumni, a spouse or partner or children, co-workers, people met through acquaintances, and people met through an organization or through a religious or social group. Favored leisure activities included going to clubs, restaurants, and movies; watching TV; engaging in physical exercise or hobbies; and using the computer and the Internet.

Sixty to seventy percent of graduates were satisfied with their social life; however, when asked what would improve their current life situation, significant numbers expressed a longing for increased social opportunities, more chances to develop friendships, a life partner, or more opportunities for dating.

It was notable that satisfaction was highest among alumni who have remained in the Boston area. They reported more social activity than those who moved back home to other areas; 76% (versus 68% of the total sample) reported initiating and planning social activity once a month, and 70% (versus 58% of the total sample) reported socializing at least once a week. Many Threshold graduates maintain their connection to Lesley, repeatedly returning to campus to take part in social activities, to participate on panels on Family and Friends weekend, and to join in on alumni events. Their involvement speaks to their integration into the life of the university as a whole:

On September 17, 2009, two alumni who had graduated in the 1990s took the day off from work to march alongside hundreds of Lesley faculty and students as proud representatives of the Threshold community to the Centennial Academic Convocation at Sanders Theater, commemorating the university's 100th anniversary.

It is notable that a greater percentage of this Boston-based group has married or has a committed relationship with a long-term partner.

Those living with parents have been less socially engaged. Although 60%—a number comparable to the larger sample—reported initiating and planning social activities at least once a month, only 40% reported socializing weekly. Fewer than half reported being satisfied with their social life, compared to 60% of the entire sample.

Alumni living away from Boston, who lack the same access to other Threshold graduates, have had to extend their reach to form friendships. They socialize more than their Boston peers with co-workers, neighbors, and people met through organizations and through religious or social groups.

EMPLOYMENT

Threshold's vocational training has enabled graduates to exceed the expectations of the program and of families. Indeed, the employment record of Threshold graduates has been consistently impressive. Over the years, 80% or more alumni have been employed at any given time, which compares favorably with their peers who have no disabilities, and which stands in contrast to the employment rate of 35- to 45-year-olds who do have disabilities, which according to some sources may be as low as 35% (Bureau of Labor Statistics, 2008).

The follow-up studies suggest that where a graduate resides has an impact on employment. Those living in the Boston area were significantly more likely to be working (91% in 1996, 94% in 2008) than those living in other areas (73% in 1996, 77% in 2008). Those living with parents were less likely to be working (60% versus 77% of the entire cohort in 2008).

The various studies suggest that participation in the third-year program has a positive impact on employment. Eighty-four to eighty-seven percent of those who completed the Transition Year were employed at the time of the various studies, versus 74% to 76% of those who had not continued beyond graduation.

More than two thirds of respondents who were working were employed full-time. Another 24% were working at least 30 hours per week, which is significant when taking into consideration the large percentage of Threshold graduates who are employed in early childhood positions, where the work day is frequently shorter than 8 hours. Approximately 15% reported being employed in more than one job.

Job stability. The data suggest that Threshold graduates make stable employees. In the 2008 study, more than half of the sample reported never having been unemployed in the past 10 years, and nearly 75% reported having held a job for more than 5 years at some point in their working life.

The various studies investigated job changes. Forty-nine percent of the early group admitted to having lost a job at some point in their career; about half of this group reported that the job was cut, but others cited a bad job match, where they were unable to do the necessary tasks.

In 2008, 61% of the early cohort reported having left a job voluntarily. Approximately 30% had resigned to take a better position, but other reasons cited included an excessively long commute, insufficient salary, unkind behavior of other workers, and interpersonal tension with their supervisor. Twelve years earlier, members of this group had seemed to be struggling to find their niche; in addition to the preceding reasons for leaving a job, they had cited the position's having been too difficult, having lacked adequate supervision, or having not liked the line of work.

In 2008, 42% of those graduates who were not working cited health reasons. About 20% reported they were caring for children or explained they could not work because of restrictions related to their receipt of Social Security Disability Insurance.

Where they work. Threshold graduates have served in early childhood positions ranging from aides to lead teachers; one remarkable graduate worked her way up through the ranks to become the director of her day-care center. Alumni who majored in business services have worked in a wide variety of roles—in hotels as receptionist, bellman, or front-desk associate; in offices as file clerk, assistant office manager, or office manager; in retail as stock person or sales associate; and in supermarkets as bagger, cashier, or front-end manager. In health settings they have worked in escort or transport jobs and as food service or gift shop personnel; in group homes they have been activity assistants or program managers.

The few graduates who have achieved a level of competence and confidence in their field that has enabled them to act in a supervisory capacity have become powerful role models for second-year students doing their field placement:

> At least two alumni working as teachers in preschools or day-care centers have supervised Threshold interns, teaching them to prepare curriculum projects and providing a high level of guidance, direction, and reinforcement from the unique perspective of individuals who themselves had attended the program.
>
> Peter, a young alumnus, was so successful working on his job in a business setting that his supervisor asked him to find another Threshold graduate with similar skills to fill an open position. In this case, the graduate served as both a recruiter and a supervisor.

Salary and benefits. Although most graduates are not employed in jobs where they are getting ahead financially, 41% of the early cohort reported supporting themselves solely on their income. Alumni typically earn more than minimum wage (mean wage was $11.89 per hour), and the hourly earnings have risen steadily over the years, ranging from $5 an hour up to $20 an hour.

Across all the studies, 50% to 60% reported working in positions that have provided benefits, including health insurance, paid vacation, and sick days, and, in smaller numbers, dental insurance, tuition reimbursement, and pension plans.

Job performance. Graduates tend to feel good about their job performance. In both 1996 and 2008, 80% to 95% of the early cohort stated they were in positions where they were able to perform well, and more than 85% of all respondents reported they were dependable, had the ability to get along with clients and co-workers, had the skills to perform the tasks required, completed tasks quickly enough, followed directions, remembered what to do, and got along with their supervisor. Seventy-eight percent felt they consistently initiated performing job tasks without being told.

In the 1996 study that investigated employment of graduates from the perspective of employers (Osten & Noveck, 1996), work supervisors confirmed that Threshold alumni bring many strengths to the job. When asked to compare them with other employees in terms of job performance, employers rated Threshold alumni as equal to or better than their nondisabled co-workers in attendance, punctuality, appropriate dress and hygiene, dedication to the job, attitude toward co-workers, and co-workers' attitude toward them. Threshold-trained workers scored *nearly* at the level of their peers in their ability to communicate their needs, accept supervision, and keep personal problems from interfering with work. However, relative to their co-workers without disabilities, Threshold alumni were observed to experience more difficulties learning and completing new tasks in a timely manner and demonstrating executive functioning skills (e.g., prioritizing tasks, generalizing learning, solving problems, and making decisions).

When asked about accommodations that are made for Threshold graduates, employers listed modifications of the job description, time adjustments, and altering staffing patterns to meet the needs of both the employee and the worksite. Seventy-seven percent of employers indicated they would hire their graduate again, a heartening response indeed since, despite the passage of the Americans with Disabilities Act (ADA) in 1990, employers throughout the United States have too often continued to be reluctant to hire individuals with disabilities.

Disclosure. As noted earlier, in their Understanding Learning Challenges course, Threshold students learn that in order to benefit from the civil right protections afforded under the provisions of the ADA, an "otherwise qualified" employee must disclose his or her disability and ask for what he or she needs in order to perform "the essential functions of the job"(ADA, 1990). Though many of the early group attended the program prior to the passage of this landmark law, a full 83% reported that they had disclosed their learning disability at work. Fifty-one percent had done so on their application or during the interview process. In about 10% of the cases, the employer knew the graduate had attended Threshold and, thus, disclosure was unnecessary. An additional 10% disclosed upon accepting the position or before beginning to work. Fifty-four percent of graduates had advocated for their own needs at work, identifying and requesting accommodations that would enable them to optimally perform their job. Of those who did not disclose, 58% felt they could do the work without identifying their learning disability, 16% feared disclosure would cost them their job, and others either felt unsure of how to disclose or didn't want to be thought of as less than capable.

There appears to be a strong correlation between disclosure and job success for Threshold alumni. The employer research (Osten & Noveck, 1996) indicates that graduates who self-disclosed during hiring or soon thereafter were rated by employers as equal to or better than their nondisclosing peers on a list of criteria, with the exception of dress and hygiene and ability to follow through on assignments. Despite research that warns of the dangers of self-disclosure of one's LD during the hiring process (Gerber, 2006), 79% of Threshold alumni who disclosed near the time of hire received raises or promotions, or both, compared to 25% of those whose disabilities were discovered over time.

Being proactive about their needs and disclosing their LD up front led to more accommodations. Thirty-nine percent of those who disclosed received some change in their job description to accommodate their learning disability, compared with only 26% of their nondisclosing peers. Twenty-eight percent received the increased supervision they needed, compared with 11% who did not disclose. Of those who disclosed, 19% were given increased responsibility, compared to 6% of those not disclosing.

CONTINUING EDUCATION

Many Threshold alumni continue their education after graduation. More than half of the early cohort reported having taken at least one college-level class, although not necessarily for credit, in the years after completing their Threshold experience. Beyond the aforementioned further education sought by some graduates to become teacher qualified, others have chosen to pursue either Child Development Associate (CDA) training or an associate's degree to supplement the credits earned at Threshold and meet the teacher qualifications of the National Association of Education of Young Children and of the Commonwealth of Massachusetts. Although it was not an anticipated path for alumni when the program was conceptualized, and to date it remains an unusual achievement, several graduates have received bachelor's degrees:

> One woman returned to Lesley more than 15 years after graduating from Threshold to pursue her bachelor's degree, which she completed in January 2010. Another Threshold graduate, Cathy, received a BA from Cambridge College in 2008. A handful of other Threshold alumni have gone on to graduate from degree programs in colleges across the United States.

SUPPORTS THAT GRADUATES USE

The achievements of Threshold graduates have not been accomplished in a vacuum; many sources of support have helped alumni along their way. Like their peers in the general population who often live with parents or receive some financial help as they begin their adult lives (*New York Times*, 1988, 2009), the largest source of ongoing support for Threshold graduates is family. Relatives have at various times and to varying degrees provided shelter, subsidized coverage of medical needs, helped bridge periods between jobs, provided legal advice, assisted with taxes, helped graduates move from one residence to another, or contributed toward a car or a home. But the most continuous focus of assistance from Threshold families has come in the form of emotional support. Three quarters of the families of the cohorts studied reported that they provide encouragement, often during critical moments of decision making. Smaller numbers continue to help by arranging for support services, assisting in their graduate's search for a job or apartment, or helping with home maintenance or repair.

The latest study of the early cohort suggests that as graduates mature, they tend to widen their support networks beyond their parents. Many reported independently managing needs that had formerly been met by others. Parents often report that their greatest worry is the long-term well-being of their adult children after parents are no longer alive to provide assistance and support; thus, it is heartening that 95% of the parents in the studies expressed confidence that their graduate had someone other than themselves to whom they could go for advice or help, including siblings, their spouse, friends, therapists, rehabilitation professionals, and even Threshold faculty.

CONCLUSION

Research suggests that Threshold alumni are thriving as productive citizens and enjoying a satisfying quality of life. Ninety-one percent of graduates who have participated in several follow-up studies have expressed satisfaction with their lives (nearly half being "very satisfied") and, equally telling, 87% of their parents have reported being either somewhat or very satisfied with their graduate's overall level of independence.

Nonetheless, despite evidence that Threshold students graduate with a strong set of skills, they face many challenges as they live their lives—like all adults. Many seek continuing support from the program even years after graduation when they face employment challenges, experience changes in their living situation, find themselves in precarious financial situations, or need further emotional support. In the past, faculty were able to individually provide this assistance or refer graduates to appropriate resources; however, this service has become too unwieldy as the numbers of graduates has grown. Thus, since the early 1990s, faculty and administration have proposed development of a Threshold Life Resource Center to address the ongoing needs of alumni and their parents.

Threshold students often arrive with physical disabilities along with their learning issues. Since the program has long been housed in buildings that are inaccessible for individuals with mobility issues, the university is seeking funds to fulfill Threshold's dream of building office and dormitory space that every student and faculty member is able to access.

It is costly to provide the intensive services required by the young adults with multiple disabilities who are served by Threshold, and raising funds for increased scholarship support is a continuing priority. The goal is to ensure that Threshold programming is within the financial reach of all qualified students while still maintaining its high level of service, including its 1:3 staff-student ratio. Although the Threshold scholarship fund, federal grants and loans, and support from such agencies as the Department of Vocational Rehabilitation have been available to ease the burden, the need for financial aid has never been greater.

Twenty-nine years after accepting its first cohort, Threshold continues to make every effort to respond to the changing needs of the students and community. For example, with the current shift in U.S. demographics and the subsequent anticipated increase in need for services for senior citizens, reintroduction of the human services major as a vocational training option is being considered. The early childhood major may soon be expanded in order to comply with the increasing number of government-mandated requirements in that field. Further, technology is being integrated to a greater extent in all aspects of the Threshold experience, with assistive technology increasingly being implemented to enhance print access and to facilitate students' ability to communicate.

Two years after Lesley's centennial anniversary, Threshold is flourishing. From the mailing of the first admissions flyer in 1981, Threshold's applicant pool has been robust, and the admissions process has been competitive. Applicants have hailed from 25 U.S. states and from countries around the globe, from Colombia to Saudi Arabia to Mexico to England. More than 565 graduates are demonstrating the skills to manage the responsibilities of adulthood; are leading far more independent lives than they were when they first entered the program; and are offering proof that transition programming can and does help individuals with disabilities to meet their potential.

REFERENCES

Brooks, R. (2001). *Raising Resilient Children.* Chicago, IL: Contemporary Books, 138 140.

Bureau of Labor Statistics. (2008). Retrieved on April 4, 2009, from http://bls.gov/cps/cpsdisability.htm.2008, p.4

Edgar, E. (1987). Secondary programs in special education: Are many of them justifiable? *Exceptional Children, 53,* 555 561.

Gerber, P. (2006). Acceptable loss versus potential gain in self-disclosing in adults with learning disabilities, *Thalamus: Journal of the International Academy for Research on Learning Disabilities, 24,* 49 54.

Grossman, H. (1983). *Classification in mental retardation.* Washington, DC: American Association on Mental Deficiency.

Halpern, A. (1985). Transition: A look at the foundations. *Exceptional Children, 51,* 479 486.

Haring, K., Lovett, D., & Smith, D. (1990). A follow-up study of recent special education graduates of learning disabilities programs. *Journal of Learning Disabilities, 23,* 108-113.

Kutner, Lawrence. (1988). Parent & Child. July 14, 1988. Retrieved March 22, 2009 from www.nytimes,com/1988/o7/14/garden/parent-child, 1 3

Osten, F. (2009). Where life has taken them: A longitudinal outcome study of Threshold graduates. Unpublished report.

Osten, F., & Noveck, C. (1996). The employment of individuals who disclosed their learning disabilities: The employer's perspective. Unpublished manuscript.

Posthill, S., & Roffman, A. (1991). The impact of a transitional training program for young adults with learning disabilities. *Journal of Learning Disabilities, 24,* 10, 619 629.

Roffman, A. (2000). *Meeting the challenge of learning disabilities in adulthood.* Baltimore, MD: Brookes.

Roffman, A. (2007). *Guiding teens with learning disabilities: Navigating the transition to adulthood.* New York, NY: Random House.

Roffman, A., Herzog, J., & Wershba-Gerson, P. (1994). Helping young adults understand their learning disabilities. *Journal of Learning Disabilities, 27,* 7, 413 419.

Sitlington, P., & Frank A. (1990). Are adolescents with learning disabilities successfully crossing the bridge into adult life? *Learning Disability Quarterly, 13,* 97.

Wadler, J. (2009). Caught in the Safety Net. May 14, 2009. Retrieved from www.Nytimes.com/2009/054/14/garden/14. 1 7

Will, M. (1984). OSERS programming for the transition of youth with disabilities: Bridges from school to working life. Washington, DC: Office of Special Education and Rehabilitative Services.

Wolfensberger, W. (1972). *The principle of normalization in human services.* Toronto, Canada: National Institute on Mental Retardation.

Yuan, F. (1994). Moving toward self-acceptance: A course for students with learning disabilities. *Intervention in School & Clinic, 29*(5) 301.

Yuan, F. T., & Reisman, E. (1996). Transition to adulthood: Outcomes for graduates of a non-degree post-secondary program for young adults with severe learning disabilities. *Learning Disabilities, 10*(3),153 163.

Yuan, F. (In press). Life as a married couple with learning disabilities: Rewards and challenges times two. *Learning Disabilities: A Multidisciplinary Journal.*

CHAPTER TEN

Adult Learning: Theory in Practice

Martha McKenna, EdD

> Lesley's Adult Baccalaureate Program gained a reputation as the place that would nurture an adult who had experience, who had places to go and things to do.

—Barbara Vacarr, Class of 1986

Respect for what adult learners bring to the learning process has long been the foundation of Lesley's constructivist teaching and learning approach in the Adult Baccalaureate Program (ABP). The growth in the 1970s and 1980s of entrepreneurial graduate programs at the university paved the way for the development of a baccalaureate degree completion program for adults seeking preparation for graduate study. Created in 1980 in the graduate school, the Adult Baccalaureate Program was a reflection of its time and place.

The original ABP model was a course-based evening program in which adult learners pursued degrees, primarily in education and human services, through coursework in the graduate school. This early model, called Continuing Career Development for Adults, soon grew to include options for self-designed degree programs pursued on the weekend (Weekend Learning Community) and intensive residency (Adult Degree Option) formats. All three models were student centered: students worked with faculty to design degree programs that met their personal and professional goals. Students and faculty created collaborative learning communities that empowered members to bring their unique knowledge and experiences to the learning process. Students were encouraged to complete their degrees through transferring course credits from previous college-level study and by earning credits for prior learning experiences through a portfolio review process. A critical component of the program was the requirement that students direct their work toward a final thesis or integrative project, constructed to integrate prior knowledge and skills with new learning, which would serve as the foundation for their professional careers.

In April 2010 I met with Barbara Vacarr, director of the PhD in Adult Learning Program and the Learning Community Bachelor Program, to discuss the growth and development of the Adult Baccalaureate Program. What follows are the highlights of our conversation.

ABP's Beginnings

Martha McKenna: When I joined the program in the mid-1980s there were three distinct models of the ABP, each led by a faculty director. I directed the Continuing Career Development for Adults model, which was a degree completion program drawing on coursework in the graduate school that was offered on campus in the evenings and off campus throughout Massachusetts on the weekends in a monthly cohort model. Anita Landa directed the Adult Degree Option, which was an intensive residency model in which faculty and students met twice a year for a 10-day residency. Each residency consisted of intensive instruction to construct students' degree plans, followed by one-on-one study for the next six months through correspondence. The third model, the Weekend Learning Community, was created in 1984 through a U.S. Department of Education Fund for the Improvement of Post-Secondary Education (FIPSE) grant to provide adult students with a unique interdisciplinary, theme-based cohort model that met conveniently on the weekends. Its director was Jill Tarule, who in 1986 brought recognition to the program through her work as part of a research collaborative that published the seminal text *Women's Ways of Knowing* (Belenky, Clinchy, Goldberger, & Tarule, 1986). The work created quite a stir when it was published, for it provided a very different perspective on female development, in stark contrast to William Perry's research at Harvard on male development. Proposing a different paradigm for women's ways of knowing, the authors suggested that women move from a place where they are silent knowers to received knowers, and finally to constructed knowers, when provided the opportunity through education. While building on the work of Carol Gilligan at Harvard and Mary Belenky at Wellesley, *Women's Ways of Knowing* also reflected what we were doing at Lesley in the 1980s. Supporting all three models, Luke Baldwin, who was a graduate of the Harvard doctoral program in adult literacy, was in charge of Prior Learning Assessment (PLA). Steeped in John Dewey's educational philosophy and David Kolb's model of experiential learning, Baldwin brought an understanding of how adults, if able to document their learning outside the formal university setting, are empowered to build a degree and reclaim a sense of knowledge they acquired through their experiences in their work and with their families.

Nineteen eighty-six was a defining year for the ABP. The program was growing significantly on campus and regionally, so we needed a faculty to provide academic advising and oversee all of the coursework in the liberal arts disciplines to support the professional majors drawn from the graduate school. We hired Sharlene Cochrane to oversee history and the humanities; Marjorie Farrell led literature and psychology; Sharon Simone was our scientist; Luke Baldwin was the writing faculty, in addition to coordinating PLA; and I led the arts and humanities. In 1988 we created the position of academic advisor, and Barbara Vacarr, who had just graduated from the program, was hired to oversee this area.

DEFINING CHARACTERISTICS OF THE ABP

MM: The program flourished because of its faculty, its philosophy, its focus on adult pedagogy or andragogy, and its design. The faculty were all products of the 1960s, interdisciplinary scholars who had pursued self-designed doctoral programs at progressive institutions. We had earned our degrees the hard way, with all the pressures of career and family, so we had a clear understanding of what it was like to earn a degree as an adult. While we were not students of adult learning theory, we nonetheless had practiced it in designing interdisciplinary doctoral programs that met our life goals. We all believed in crossing disciplines and in centering the learning in students' personal and professional goals. Fortunately, we had arrived at an institution that allowed us to carry this on with our students.

Recognizing the need to connect theory with practice in adult learning, the faculty created its own learning community, the Collaborative on Adult Research and Practice (CARP), to share reflections and analyses of developmental theory in regard to our teaching practice. Strongly influenced by the writings of John Dewey (1938) and David Kolb (1984), the faculty of CARP published an article for the *Journal of Museum Education,* "Passionate and Purposeful: Adult Learning Communities," which perhaps best captures the philosophy of the program:

> Our understanding of adult development and our experience in successfully educating adult students have led us to understand our work as a three-step process: purposeful engagement in the content of the experience; reflection, evaluation, and analysis (as individuals and as a group); and the application of new learning to concrete situations... Throughout these processes, adults are both passionate and purposeful. And that blend enlivens learning communities and contributes to the building of personal and intellectual support systems. (Baldwin, Cochrane, Counts, Dolamore, McKenna, & Vacarr, 1992)

These processes enabled learners to integrate new learning with past experiences, creating meaning for the present and questions for future study.

Barbara Vacarr: The program made theory explicit. Experience was the ground upon which learners were invited to observe, to reflect, and to generate meaningful and relevant questions to guide their own learning. The objective was for adult learners to conceptualize about the world of ideas or theory in connection to their own experiences and then to actively experiment with theoretical understandings in new situations; always asking, In what new ways or in what new arenas can I now use this knowledge? In this model, students' experiences were truly at the center, and the curriculum shaped itself around the individual, instead of the learner abandoning experiential knowing to accommodate curriculum that remains at an intellectual distance.

As an adult learner who chose to complete my degree in ABP, I was most attracted by the valuing of my lived experience, what I already knew. Lesley, in its adult programs, knew how to balance the tension of learning situated at the center of individual experience and community as the dialogic container for learning.

MM: Another defining characteristic of ABP is our collaborative learning approach both inside and outside the classroom. Collaboration is at the heart of what we do—collaboration between faculty and students, students and students, and faculty and faculty, who are all participating in the learning process. In the late 1980s Lesley participated in a second FIPSE-funded project to document collaborative learning models and share our approach with other adult educators. We believe that collaborating with others in the learning process makes it all the more powerful. For example, in teaching we would often start a class with a faculty member's thoughts or reflections on a reading, and then move to small groups so that students could collaborate in analyzing what they read and capture their insights. When the groups would report back, it was not what the faculty taught the students but what the faculty and students taught one another that marked the learning experience. In the end it was a much richer experience, because everyone was engaged in the dialogue and responsible for the learning. This model was central to both teaching and advising, as faculty and students co-constructed degree plans, designed internships and individually guided studies, and developed theses proposals.

BV: What is central is that people do not learn in isolation; people learn in dialogue, in collaboration with faculty and peers. I think Marjorie Farrell says it best: We're not covering a curriculum; we're helping people to uncover the curriculum. There is an ethos that we're uncovering this together, and while I come to this endeavor with disciplinary knowledge and experience and while I can help others uncover ways of knowing in that discipline, we create an environment in which together we explore and interrogate the terrain. The philosophy is that the curriculum is open for all to explore and discover, and that happens in a shared dialogue where everybody's voice is heard, and the result is the co-construction of knowledge.

MM: Perhaps the most unique aspect of ABP was its location in the graduate school. Adults had the opportunity to study with other adults. Students were able to say to their families and friends, "I'm studying in the graduate school at Lesley."

BV: That meant so much to me. It was the tangible evidence that my experience mattered.

MM: No one asked what degree they were pursuing in the graduate school. Adult baccalaureate students sat in graduate-level courses because they brought experiences that equipped them to be graduate students. We would often say the difference between graduate students and the adult undergraduate students was that graduate students came in theory rich but experience poor. Often they would have just completed undergraduate school and be knowledgeable of critical theory of the disciplines in their field, but they didn't have a lot of experience. The adult baccalaureate students, on the other hand, were often experience rich and theory poor. They would bring rich experiences from the field, but not the benefit of four years of formal education. The adult baccalaureate students had to do the same assignments, carry out the same research, and meet the same requirements, and were graded exactly the same as the graduate students in their courses. If an adult baccalaureate student was not ready for graduate work, she would not move into these courses. But once the students were ready, we encouraged them to pursue graduate courses so that they could be challenged by this advanced work. We eventually built dual-degree programs based on this philosophy. We created bachelor of science and master of arts dual-degree programs for students, like Barbara, who came in well prepared to do graduate work and accelerate their professional training.

STUDENT-CENTERED LEARNING

BV: The student is at the center of his learning, and all learning grows out of the questions and the experiences that the student brings. Student-centered advising dynamically attempts to understand the student, the experience he brings, and what it is that he most wants to know.

MM: The central component of this program has always been strong academic advising, empowering students to be aware of all the options, so that they can construct the best degree plan. Faculty advisors were all trained in adult pedagogy and practice by Deborah Sherman, the assistant dean of the Outreach and Alternative Education Division. She believed that we needed to empower students to be able to become agents of their own learning, helping them integrate personal goals and professional aspirations. Through advising sessions, we created something together that linked personal and professional goals. Students were never told, "You need to do this series of courses because this is the degree"; rather, we would begin advising sessions with "What do you know? What do you want to do? How do you want to do it?" I found myself in a world where I was no longer telling students what they needed to do; rather, I was supporting students in determining what they wanted to do. The faculty had to be trained in this model, so Sharlene, Marjorie,

Sharon, Luke, Barbara, and I were constantly at one another's doors during the first few years, learning from one another how to support students in designing their degrees.

BV: We understood that advising was really teaching and that it was central to the learning experience for all students. We recognized that adults brought in a wealth of experience, and that experience sat at the center of their learning, as opposed to the curriculum sitting at the center of their learning. This was true in all of the models, for there was a place in all of the degree programs where students individualized their study around their experience, their interests, and their aspirations.

MM: Our goal has always been to be able to move adults to finish a degree; to understand where they want to go and help them get there with knowledgeable advisors. From the day the student first arrives, expressing an interest in Lesley, we work with the student to understand what it is he wants to study and how he can accomplish this in a variety of baccalaureate options, whether it's the intensive residency program, courses offered on campus evenings and weekends, joining a cohort of learners in one of our off-campus sites, or online. In addition to sharing with the student the variety of options for pursuing a degree, we also outline the many ways of earning credit to complete the program, including transferring course credits and earning credit through prior learning assessment. Finally, we begin the process of degree planning to meet the student's personal and professional goals. I think we are unique in cocreating with our students self-designed programs that weave prior learning with new learning at the university into an integrated whole, providing them with the foundation for a career or graduate study. The advisor serves as a mentor, in the sense of Daniel Levinson (1978), where the student forms a significant relationship with the faculty member to facilitate his dream.

Lives in Context

MM: Central to the programs was the introductory course Lives in Context, designed and taught by the core faculty, in which students read biographies and autobiographies to examine the choices individuals make in the context of their lives. The work of Jack Mezirow (1991) on transformative adult learning theory, published in the same year in which this course was created, informed our design, for we sought to engage students in critical reflections on their experiences, leading to perspective transformation.

> Perspective transformation is the process of becoming critically aware of how and why our assumptions have come to constrain the way we perceive, understand, and feel about our world; changing these structures of habitual expectations to make possible a more inclusive, discriminating, and integrating perspective; and, finally, making choices or otherwise acting upon these new understandings. (Mezirow, 1991, p. 167)

We read the life stories of famous and not so famous individuals to think about the themes in their lives and the choices they made in the context of their place, class, gender, economic reality, and political and social times that shaped their lives. We read wonderful works, always with the intent to reflect on the subjects' life choices and how they might relate to the students' own lives. As the course's final project, students had to write a chapter of their own autobiography or another's biography, focusing on a period of time in their life to describe, reflect, and interpret major life choices that presented themselves. This provided students with an opportunity to go back and reflect on their lives within the context of the choices available to them.

BV: The development of Lives in Context grew out of faculty discussions in which we reflected on our teaching practice. We were noticing that when adults returned to school, they had a story to tell.

The stories were compelling, and inevitably personal narratives would find their way into all writing, including the kinds of writing, like research that necessitated a more public voice. We recognized that adults needed a place where they could tell their stories, where they could move from a personal to a more public voice. I remember the conversations, in which we discussed adult development and learning theory and how we could use it to construct learning experiences that would support developmental movement from embeddedness in personal story to a stance of reflective observation of experience. So we considered context as the organizing principle to engage people in looking at how our narratives are shaped by the contexts in which we live. In this sense the focus is not just about a person telling her story; it is about a window into understanding how lives are shaped by cultural, political, and geographic contexts and how, in turn, individuals shape those very contexts. In this sense adults were able to see both the impact of these contexts on their own lives and themselves as active agents in shaping the world around them. They were also, often for the first time, cognizant that all knowledge is contextual.

MM: I never ceased to be amazed at the transformation in voice of the students in Lives in Context. While the students often entered seeking "truths" from the faculty experts, they quickly learned that they had much to share, and in so doing developed a greater understanding of their own competence and achievements. The faculty witnessed the students moving from a reliance on authority through recognition that truth is relative, to an understanding that knowledge is constructed. Students gained a more informed and powerful voice. Robert Kegan (1982) defines this movement from an "interpersonal" stance to an "institutional" stance as the central transformation in adult development.

BV: We focused on teaching people how to think, not what to think, and I believe that really defines Lesley's adult learning approach. It is about helping students become critical thinkers, reflecting on experiences and the world in which they live. The understanding is that when learners know how to think more deeply about one or two things, they become lifelong learners, applying this skill and strategy in all subsequent learning. So we worked with students to develop their questions so that they could approach thinking about their lives and work in new ways.

Transforming Students' Lives

MM: Two stories of students whose lives have been changed by this program will always stand out for me. The first is Carol Ann, a friend and neighbor, who did not have the chance to complete her degree at Lesley while a student in the 1960s. Marriage and children prevented her from finishing, so her dream was to complete her degree before her last child finished college. A bright woman, extremely well read, she felt that a part of her was unfinished. I worked with the Admissions Office to create an adult baccalaureate program in American studies (her love was history) in Shrewsbury, and she, along with another neighbor, recruited the group. Carol Ann was diagnosed with cancer during the process of completing her degree, and the cohort of Lesley students became her greatest support in both fighting the cancer and completing her degree. She graduated with a transcript filled with A's and enjoyed her graduation more than anyone I can recall. Carol Ann died two years later from the cancer that ravaged her body, but her mind was liberated through the education that Lesley had provided, an education that was created especially for her!

The second student is one of the leading artists or *santeros* (makers of saints) in New Mexico. While teaching the Traditions and Cultures Institute in Santa Fe, I came to know Marie, and discovered that this talented and accomplished artist did not have an undergraduate degree. She was pursuing coursework at a local community college, for without a degree she was finding it difficult to publish her texts on the art of the *santeros* of New Mexico. I encouraged her to pursue her bachelor's degree with Lesley through our Intensive Residency Option. The program would provide the opportunity for her to complete the requirements of her degree while focusing her research and writing in the field that she loved. The problem for Marie was the high cost of study and travel to Lesley; however, I was able to help her with this by identifying financial aid funds. Marie, in gratitude, gave Lesley one of her priceless works of art. During the course of her studies at Lesley, Marie produced several papers that became published articles, and her thesis is now a published work, *Tortilla Chronicles: Growing Up in Santa Fe* (Cash, 2007). Upon graduation I nominated Marie for a Javits Fellowship for doctoral study at the University of New Mexico, a fellowship that she was in fact offered. Marie's fame as an artist and writer continues to grow, and she credits Lesley with playing a major role in her success. Carol Ann and Marie are just two examples of how the Adult Learning Programs respond to students needs, adding true meaning and value to students' lives.

BV: So often adults came in to the programs, women in particular, who had remarkable experiences. When asked in advising sessions to talk about what they had done in their lives in order to think about how they might earn credit for prior life experience, they responded, "Well, I haven't really done anything." Upon the advisor's further probing, we discovered amazing things. I remember a woman who had worked with Mother Theresa, and when asked about her life experiences she started by saying "Well, I haven't really done anything." So many accomplished adults began their responses with "Well, it's just been my experience..." as though its having been "just something they did" lessened the power of the experience and its impact. It was profound to observe the transformation of experience into owned knowledge as students reflected and wrote about their experiences.

MM: We encourage students to become agents of their own learning, and one example of a student's agency stands out for me. A faculty member teaching an introductory psychology course asked her students to look into what opportunities in Cambridge might be available during the semester to hear lectures of the renowned psychologists in the area. This is a normal occurrence, since learning experiences outside the classroom have always been central to our work. One of the students called the office of Dr. B. F. Skinner at Harvard, and was surprised when he answered the phone. She explained that she was a student in a psychology class at Lesley, and asked Dr. Skinner if he would be lecturing in the area in the fall semester. He was not giving a talk, but he responded that since he appreciated what Lesley was doing for adult learners and we were just across the street from his office, he would be glad to come and talk to the students in her class. So this celebrated behavioral psychologist met with this woman's class for an hour one Friday morning and talked about his latest research on a more humanistic approach to behaviorism. I remember vividly the experience of these students sitting in a circle engaged in a dialogue with B. F. Skinner about behavioral psychology. It was a life-changing experience for us all. It was amazing that all it took was a call from one of our adult baccalaureate students to make it happen, or perhaps, it was only such a call that could have made it happen.

BV: I realize that so much of what's important about the way we work with students is engaged learning, discussion, and peer interaction. Central to what we do is the belief that knowledge and self get constructed in relationship and in dialogue. It is this approach that leads to the kinds of transformation, personal development, and evolution that we've observed in our students. Education at this level is really something that is healing, in the Jungian sense that it creates a wholeness of the parts of us that have not been integrated. The whole educational process is a process of creating wholeness of oneself and of the world.

MM: Examining their life choices leads students, especially women, to accept their choice of family and careers over completion of a degree earlier in their life. Carol Gilligan (1982), in her groundbreaking study *In a Different Voice,* identifies "women's embeddedness in lives of relationship, their orientation to interdependence, their subordination of achievement to care, and their conflicts over competitive success" (p. 171) as characteristics of human development. Applying this theory to their life choices liberates students to honor their past and integrate it in their learning.

BV: For most adults, returning to complete an undergraduate education is an emotional experience around competence and self-esteem. Learning is both an emotional and a cognitive experience. The realization for adults that they've lived on the margins in society without a first degree is a painful experience. Recently, one of our brightest students graduated from LCB. She stood at the degree completion ceremony and, full of pride, she said, "I would like to thank all of those people who over the years when I did not have a degree looked down their noses at me. They were the ones that motivated me to finally do it." I think that we hear this narrative over and over again.

This kind of transformation was documented in a research project that I worked on with Luke Baldwin and Joan Dolamore. We were interested in how our students developed voice during their time in the program. We examined writing at three distinct periods of their degree programs. We read their admissions applications, their prior learning assessment portfolios, and their final projects or theses. We discovered that most adults entered our program with a very personal, subjectivist voice and most left with a more public, procedural voice.

MM: Perhaps the most amazing story of student transformation, Barbara, is yours. It is fitting that I'm sitting with you today to reflect on the program that we both entered in 1986. I was the director of the program and you were coming to finish your degree. I admitted you and was pleased to serve as your advisor. I hired you to be our first academic advisor when you entered the master's degree program in counseling psychology. Upon completion of the doctoral program at Union, we hired you to be a faculty member in ABP. Soon after you would go on to direct the Learning Community Bachelor's (formerly Adult Degree Option) Program in ABP, bringing your skills in interdisciplinary learning and adult pedagogy to bear. When our PhD Task Force discussed the creation of new intensive residency doctoral programs, you took the lead in designing a new PhD program in

CYNTHIA FARR BROWN AND MICHELE FORINASH, EDITORS

Adult Learning. Building on our expertise in adult learning theory and practice, developed over three decades, you are now integrating what we've learned into a doctoral program to share with others. How ironic, even as we speak about our history in adult learning, that you are preparing to move from directing the doctoral program to the next position in your career, the presidency of Goddard College. How fitting that you will lead Goddard, a college that was founded on the principles of adult learning that are practiced here at Lesley. The transformation learning that we described above is illustrated in your personal and professional success.

ABP TODAY

Three decades have passed since the founding of ABP, and while much has changed, the program remains consistent with its origins in constructivist pedagogy and transformative learning. There have been changes in the administration of the program, which is now housed in the Center for the Adult Learner in Lesley College, providing students with access to all of the faculty, curriculum, and resources the undergraduate school offers. Students now pursue coursework in the Graduate School of Arts and Social Sciences, the School of Education, and the Art Institute of Boston through the Lesley Passport Program, which is designed to make the resources of all schools accessible to ABP students. The Lesley online learning environment, myLesley, now avails students in the Adult Bachelor's Residency Program (formerly the Adult Degree Option) greater contact between the residencies and with their faculty and peers through discussion boards and threaded conversations. In addition, online degree programs have been launched in the past two years in business management and psychology, popular programs for today's adult learners.

The underlying philosophy of the programs continues to value and respect what the adult learner brings to the learning process and remains the foundation of all curriculum and instruction. The central role of academic advising, provided by professional and faculty advisers, ensures that students are able to design degrees that meet their personal and professional goals. Through the Prior Learning Assessment process, students have the opportunity to identify the knowledge and skills that they bring with them, and earn academic credit that moves them forward in meeting degree requirements. The faculty, many of whom have taught in ABP for more than two decades, continue to develop scholarship that reflects their growth in adult learning theory and practice. It is these same faculty who now serve in the PhD program in Adult Learning, where they shape the next generation of scholars in the constructivist approach to mentoring adults. The historical position of transformative learning for adults in undergraduate programs at Lesley continues to evolve.

REFERENCES

Baldwin, L., Cochrane, S., Counts, C., Dolamore, J., McKenna, M., & Vacarr, B., (1992). "Passionate and purposeful: Adult learning communities." In *Patterns in Practice: Selections from the Journal of Museum Education.* Washington, DC: Museum Education Roundtable, pp. 162 167.

Belenky, M. F., Clinchy, B. M., Goldberger, N. R., & Tarule, J. M. (1986). *Women's ways of knowing.* New York, NY: Basic Books.

Cash, M. R. (2007). *Tortilla chronicle: Growing up in Santa Fe.* Albuquerque, NM: University of New Mexico Press.

Dewey, J. (1938/1997). *Experience and education.* New York, NY: Macmillan Publishers.

Kegan, R. (1982). *The evolving self.* Cambridge, MA: Harvard University Press.

Kolb, D. (1984). *Experiential learning.* Englewood Cliffs, NJ: Prentice Hall.

Levinson, D. (1978). *The seasons of a man's life.* New York, NY: Alfred A. Knopf.

Mezirow, J. (1991). *Transformative dimensions of adult learning.* San Francisco, CA: Jossey-Bass.

Perry, W. G. (1970). *Forms of intellectual and ethical development in the college years.* New York, NY: Holt, Rinehart and Winston.

PART IV:
1998 TO THE PRESENT

Introduction

JOSEPH B. MOORE

In the early part of the 21st century, we find ourselves more concerned than satisfied with the direction of American higher education. The widening income gap and related disparities in educational opportunity and health care pose significant threats to our social fabric. In our K-12 system, students from the upper quartile in income are eight times more likely to attend college that those in the lowest quartile (Mortenson, 2010). Median family income has declined by 5.4% since the year 2000, while tuition and fees continue to rise steadily in both public and private postsecondary education (Mortenson, 2010). These trends are not sustainable.

Federal and state governments are unlikely to increase financial aid funding for postsecondary education, especially following the prolonged economic collapse of 2008. Colleges and universities increasingly will be left to their own creativity and strategic planning, and the same holds true for students.

At the same time, colleges and universities are under political pressure to improve their graduation rates, and public scrutiny is being brought to bear as well. Congressional hearings in the summer of 2010 highlighted the significant debt burden assumed by students attending for-profit institutions, and noted specifically the dire financial conditions for high-debt students who never complete their degree programs. While these hearings focused on the for-profit sector, this dynamic is increasingly a problem for students in the nonprofit side of higher education, both public and private.

In an era of limited institutional resources, traditional and nontraditional partnerships are about to become more important. These partnerships will be more complex than student internships in various organizations, and will include detailed business plans, revenue and expense sharing, co-branding, digital partnerships, and shared market analysis, as well as new ventures that might redefine faculty and administrative work responsibilities. In addition, as digital technology becomes ever more pervasive, powerful, timely, and affordable, it will change our patterns of work and our assumptions about markets, program delivery, and student engagement.

In the five essays that follow, these and other themes emerge. Nesbit's description of Lesley's independent study master's degree program has its origins in the open education practices of the late 1960s, engaging students with mentors in degree design and the studies to earn that degree. This unique program thrusts the student into the community for a two- to three-year learning experience, supported by mentors within and beyond academia. The assumption is that expertise and experience exist beyond colleges and universities, and that most topics worthy of graduate students are more appropriately studied and experienced in context, not on a campus. The partnership between the student, the university, and individuals in the community makes this approach work.

One of the most significant partnerships in Lesley's history began with the 1998 merger with the Art Institute of Boston (AIB). Fertitta and Lanza provide a detailed account of the conditions that led to this merger, the concerns that the smaller AIB had about becoming a school within Lesley University, and an appraisal of the merger impact thus far. This case study illustrates the benefits to both parties when a partnership works, and makes clear that sustaining a meaningful partnership is not a one-time event, but a continuing challenge to realize benefits and constrain any (unintended) negative effects.

The tension between deep expertise and interdisciplinary study is part of the history of most programs. In their description of the development of Lesley's two MFA programs, Barry, Cramer, and Pocorobba show how a faculty can design programs that are accessible to adult learners but that also establish a standard of quality. These low-residency programs rely on the interaction of artists and experts with the engaged graduate students, and also on the interaction of the students with one another to create a viable learning community. In each program, students develop areas of focus, while the presence of other students with different foci is seen as programmatic strength, not program dilution.

The essay on "community-embedded practice" describes the details necessary to make a meaningful and effective connection between the classroom and the community. Bromfield, Cattaneo, Deane, Miller, and Roffman identify the importance of a field training office, identification of internship sites, clinical (field) supervisors, site supervisors, and faculty. In these partnerships between academic programs and the professional field, each party must live up to the expectations of the other. When we talk about such partnerships, we make them sound obvious, reasonable, and beneficial to all parties. What we often don't describe are the details, the faculty and staff work, and the deep commitment to transformative learning that effective internships require.

The final essay brings us full circle. It is more detailed than the words of Edith Lesley, but it addresses a topic with which she was familiar and to which she was committed: the arts. Diaz and Donovan, building from the tradition of Edith Lesley and many others who preceded them, argue that the arts "offer even more to our students than the aesthetic qualities so recognized and cherished in the arts. They offer a way of thinking that stimulates innovation, curiosity, and new ways of being in the world." Here you can learn how contemporary faculty are driven to make art an experience for all students; to empower all teachers (not just art teachers) to integrate art into their own days and their students'; and to do so in ways that develop critical skills and imagination. It involves partnerships, planning, new delivery models, and addressing complex issues such as student assessment and standardized testing.

In each of these essays, we witness faculty engaged with the world beyond higher education, assessing how to customize learning experiences for students to provide opportunities for deep learning. And we also witness students who are seeking to have an impact on the world through their own pedagogy, their writing, their art, or their daily work in business and nonprofit organizations. These essays are unique because we are able to get behind official curriculum and accreditation reports to see some of the considerations that drive this complex faculty-student relationship.

REFERENCE

Mortenson, T. (2010). *Postsecondary education opportunity.* October 2010, No. 220; and December 2010, No. 222. Oskaloosa, IA. Retrieved from www.postsecondary.org

CHAPTER ELEVEN

Alumni of the Independent Study Degree Program

Marion Nesbit, PhD

Some people just don't take no for an answer. They don't allow naysayers to extinguish the fire in their belly or turn their minds away from an insight that intrigues them. They refuse to be dissuaded from following their gut feelings and intuitions and instead stay focused on their ideals and dreams amid the pushes and pulls of conventional wisdom. Passion drives them; it propels them forward; it keeps them on course.

These people are the adults who have a vision, with clarity that if only one thing—that *x* factor—is put in place, others will be helped somehow. Systems will run more effectively, and the world will be a better place because of the introduction of that something new or value-added way of doing things. Envisioning that possibility, that potential for change for the greater good, creates a stir within that pulls up what Annie Rogers (1993) calls "ordinary courage" (p. 265), connecting heart and mind in action.

Fortunately for this small group of adults, Lesley College provided a welcoming place, a beacon whose light gave hope for achievement. The light source was a small, innovative program housed away from the mainstream, with a diverse group of traditionally trained faculty whose minds flourished in the midst of creative, even offbeat, intersections of ideas.

This chapter is devoted to Lesley's vision and wisdom in promoting generative scholarship through the Independent Study Degree Program (INDS), a unique structure that recognized graduate students as individual catalysts for change. While in some ways the instructional delivery system Americanized the Oxford University mentor-tutor model, INDS pedagogy went outside familiar structures and cloistered walls, encouraging students to go into the world to find the brightest minds, best practices, and highly respected founders and teachers in their fields, regardless of geography. By simultaneously promoting and scaffolding each INDS student's exploration of new ideas and ways of doing things, Lesley invested in the creative capital of learners who crafted plans of graduate study to delve deeply into critical analysis of academic literature, construct new models for ideas and practices, and explore innovative ways to enrich the lives of others.

While the chapter includes a brief historical review and presentation of the program model, the primary focus will be to show how INDS students and alumni influenced the creation of important methods and fields of study and, consequently, helped to shape Lesley's role in developing the context of higher education.

Recognizing the value of linking academic goals with personal and humanitarian significance, this program celebrated adults of the ilk that Paul Ray and Sherry Ruth Anderson discussed in their book, *The Cultural Creatives* (2000), as people who value authenticity; plan with ideals in mind; act on behalf of the weak, marginalized, or exploited; and engage courageously in creating solutions to societal and global problems. While arguably many graduate programs share humanitarian visions, and their students study toward similar aims, the difference here is that the unique, sometimes traditional with an unusual interdisciplinary bent or quirky *n*-of-one students that beat their own drum learned outside the collective, the common syllabus structure, and the "we" advantage of the cohort model. Their idiosyncratic vision differed enough from the mainstream to require different avenues of study.

These students frequently faced a difficult paradox. Studying independently tends to become isolating and can be lonely, separating students from a natural collegiality afforded through class peers' sharing common experiences and meaning of ideas. Not wanting to suffer ostracism, or a sense that they are a square peg in a round hole, even independent students still enjoy and need the company of others. To mitigate anomie, Lesley faculty and staff worked hard to provide a supportive environment with different forms of effective communication. Over the years these ranged from in-person meetings, letters, and phone calls to e-mail and teleconferences.

Faculty embraced the social dimensions of their students' learning experiences and helped students look at their learning holistically. They encouraged advisees to develop the quality of critical thinking required for scholarly work but also the social, emotional, and ethical learning that balances it (Noddings, 2006). Faculty further recognized the importance of helping students practice the types of thinking and reflection that are essential for situating themselves in their fields, to give themselves the grounding they needed to communicate their ideas effectively and to put them into action in a way that the intended audience could take them on.

The INDS program expanded the mentor relationship from one core advisor to a team that included two experts in the fields of study. Students took on the challenge of fulfilling their study plans under the guidance of their team, engaging in thoughtful planning, hard work, and meaningful action. It is fair to say that, judging from alumni responses to surveys, few overestimated the intensity and depth of the INDS study commitment.

INCUBATING GRADUATE DEGREES
FOR LESLEY

Lesley was not and, some would say, still is not easy to find. Back in the 1970s and early 1980s Lesley mostly was known as a small women's college with a nascent graduate education program. If one even knew it existed, a cloistered setting across from Harvard Law School wasn't a likely place to pursue nontraditional graduate study. For those motivated to look further, though, Lesley did provide a small, alternative graduate education program that offered students a new way of teaching based on an open, community-centered, and theme-oriented learning model.

The INDS Program grew out of the open education movement of the late 1960s and early 1970s. This movement broke down walls, figuratively and literally, in public and private K-12 schools. The opening of innovative undergraduate programs, like Hampshire College's, which did away with distribution requirements in favor of innovative portfolio and narrative student evaluations, paved the way for INDS. The connection was also rooted in administrative delegation. Before she became the first director of INDS, Cynthia Cole led Lesley's Open Education master's degree program.

Like the teachers and teachers-to-be who shunned barricades and did not see the value of literal or metaphoric walls in schools, adult learners who sought INDS did so because they wanted to permeate boundaries of disciplines and engage in unconventional learning activities. Though sympathetic to the Vietnam War protests and antiestablishment challenges against institutions and corporate conglomerates in the late 1960s and in the 1970s, these adults were more inclined to follow enlightened humanitarian leaders and to favor working developmentally and relationally, with people rather than profit at the center of their work. Eschewing radical or revolutionary actions for which degrees were inconsequential, they recognized the merits of collaboration for building bridges between factions, to shore up dysfunctional systems, or to come up with a formula for building new ones instead. Turning away from experimental communes and psychedelic culture, they became information "junkies," seeking interesting ways to marry theory and research offerings from different disciplines to form foundations for new theories and new ways of doing things. They believed that earning a graduate degree would give them access to a system in order to change it, and so they sought institutions where they could develop plans of study in pursuit of their own learning goals, thus extending and crossing boundaries of traditional American higher education.

INDS students ranged in age from 22 to 75. Whether beatnik or classic, liberal or conservative, extraordinarily wealthy or pulling themselves up from their bootstraps, these students wanted to meld the intellectual with the personal to accomplish something new and meaningful, and they wanted all that Lesley had to offer them. More bridge builders than rabble-rousers, they sought independence along with the safety of a structure to bounce off of and check in with, for the exhilaration of exploring uncharted territory and the rapprochement in return. They wanted freedom to learn, but with access to libraries, faculty, and institutional resources to support them.

Lesley College's INDS program was such a place. While other successful innovative programs required students' presence in a campus environment for stretches of time—for example, a residential model of learning in community, like Lesley's own Interdisciplinary Studies Program or Goddard College's Low Residency Model in Vermont—INDS chose not to do so. While others used a course-based arrangement—like the University of Oklahoma's Special Interdisciplinary master's degree—the INDS educational model afforded students the opportunity to benefit from the resources of a conventional college with the freedom to study elsewhere.

INDS opened up the learning process to welcome and support uniquely individualized plans of study that were tailored to a particular student's academic focus rather than to specific institutional degree offerings. It accepted a student who did not want certification or licensure (INDS offered neither) but who was attracted to "the Lesley way," and helped that individual stay at Lesley to earn a degree through constructing a viable degree plan. INDS was also a program that occasionally took in students who were dissatisfied or disgruntled by their realization that their original degree program was not personally appropriate, or individuals whose geographies or other life circumstances had changed midstream through a program, and helped them integrate their newfound ideas and goals into more suitable degree plans.

Two of Lesley College's top academic administrators in the program's nascent years, Dean Bill Perry and Vice President Dick Wylie, realized the institutional benefit and potential of the INDS

Program. When the Open Education Program morphed into a more formal education degree program, Perry tapped Cynthia Cole to begin an "official" program for independent study. During the 1970s and 1980s he was joined by others who recognized that the climate was ripe for new program development. Dick Wylie recently recalled his role in mounting exciting collaborative initiatives at Lesley:

> Lesley gave me the opportunity to develop an environment where faculty were encouraged to be innovative and creative. I saw my role as helping others achieve their dreams. The faculty showed that an entrepreneurial spirit and quality academics could survive and prosper together. (Personal communication, April 3, 2009)

This quotation not only captures a model of insightful leadership but also reflects the spirit, process, and academic core of INDS, in which faculty dedicated themselves to helping bright, entrepreneurial students achieve their academic and professional dreams. In short, the INDS Program became a microcosmic exemplar and instigator of Lesley's own growth and development.

THE INDEPENDENT DEGREE STUDY PROCESS

Distinguishing its academic offerings within a scholar-practitioner model that embraces multiple dimensions of learning, Lesley's INDS Program earned its status in a handful of top U.S. independent academic programs through its focus on scholarly mastery, personal integrity, and a carefully honed system of academic checks and balances.

The admissions process required construction of a study plan that demonstrated prospects' capability and the clarity that was requisite for engaging in a substantial two- to three-year course of study. Prospects presented autobiographical statements; degree goals; evidence of preparedness and a proposed schedule of learning activities, resources, and multiple methods of documentation to demonstrate achievement; and a conceptual paragraph that pitched an idea for a culminating master's level, substantial thesis or book or final project. This prospective study plan was used to determine whether an individual had the vision, clarity, background, and access to resources that she would need to muster and engage in an independent learning endeavor. At its best, the study plan review involved observing whether students possessed other essential qualities that were intricately woven into INDS pedagogy: the ability to receive and apply feedback, and to engage in dialogue and stretch into a wider context around ideas; a willingness to embrace diversity; and the ability to work to high standards, including a willingness to write many drafts in order to polish academic work products. From a program perspective, speed was not an issue; some prospects worked over the course of a year to get their study plan into shape. Once complete, those efforts paid off, because that well-worked study plan became the road map for the graduate journey.

THE TEAM STRUCTURE, PROCESS, AND ALUMNI EFFECT

Once admitted to the program and immersed in their individually designed studies, INDS students did not travel alone but with the benefit of a team that was carefully chosen to support and monitor their progression through the study plan. Rather than a hierarchical structure with a power dynamic of faculty as knower and student as receiver of that knowledge, the INDS Program espoused a pedagogical model that assigned each student one dedicated faculty advisor who guided him from inception through completion of his graduate studies. Further, because no one faculty member can be all knowledgeable and resourceful about any given interdisciplinary or novel topic, students selected two additional faculty to join their instructional team. These individuals, called team faculty, typically came from the richly endowed New England region, and they brought expertise in the students' fields, a host of resources, networking potential, and evaluation skills to the INDS process.

Team faculty became indispensable assets in the Lesley College community, and they expanded Lesley's reach and reputation. Though paid only modest honoraria, team faculty signed on to engage with INDS students because they found them creative, thoughtful, deep, energetic, and productive. Sometimes, when the process revved up to its full power and the student's entrepreneurial spirit, vision, mission, and passion built off a team expert's own work, team faculty gained insights, themselves, to venture beyond their current conceptual and professional boundaries.

Meeting with INDS students, team faculty reviewed and evaluated students' graduate study and achievements four times a year: once at the beginning of the program, twice in the middle, and once at the end, before graduation. Two weeks before each meeting, students sent team members documentation packets that contained academic papers and other work products such as DVDs of performances, curriculum plans, and research findings. The meetings focused on ensuring that students were achieving the goals of their study plans and that their mastery was increasing.

At their best, the synergistic dialogues that emerged from these meetings led to a new insight, a different perspective, or a heightened understanding of an idea or practice. Two examples come to mind. Author, philosopher, and classical musician Tom Moore's Imaginal Institute work, rooted in archetypal psychology and Jungian theory, inspired students to extend theoretical applications into the arts and even into astrology, in the case of INDS alumna Jean Lall, a Fulbright scholar who later helped to found and organize the Washington, D.C., Jung Institute Library. Sarah Jackson effectively integrated theory and artistic expression into personally meaningful work. She exhibited her art in several galleries and shows in New York and the Berkshires. The imaginal work that was rooted in Jungian theory inspired her so deeply that she decided to develop her knowledge so she could pass on the gift on to others. To that end, she enrolled in the Jungian analytic training program in New York City and became a Jungian analyst.

Bonnie LaMothe is another team member whose mentorship influenced INDS alumni. As founding director of the New England Montessori Teacher Education Center (NEMTEC), sometimes referred to as the Harvard of Montessori programs, she influenced tens of INDS students over 25 years and was formative in the education of alumni who went on to change dimensions and practices of the Montessori field. For example, as a Montessori teacher and administrator, INDS alumna Erin Galvin Gutierrez expanded the teaching of science by making science instruction more accessible to early childhood teachers who may not have advanced science knowledge. Coming into INDS as a geologist with the U.S. Geological Services in Woods Hole who had discovered an affinity for teaching, she developed a user-friendly early childhood science curriculum titled *Science for Everyday: A Montessori-Based Science Curriculum* (2001), which is congruent with state standards and curriculum frameworks and is now used by non-Montessori teachers as well. Her career path included helping a large urban school system integrate Montessori philosophy into public education.

Many examples of talented team experts in the fields of education, arts, research, and organizational development can be drawn from the more than 1600 faculty who taught during the program's nearly 40-year span. We are grateful to these extraordinary scholars, practitioners, educators, and performer team faculty who served INDS, and thus, Lesley, by expanding Lesley's faculty expertise and contributing generously to students' ideas of mission and alumni professional development.

Some of those team relationships continued to develop after students graduated, and INDS alumni sometimes performed with team mentors or became teaching colleagues. For example, Bonnie LaMothe assisted Montessori students in networking into professional positions, and encouraged them to present at regional and national conferences. Erin Galvin Gutierrez exemplifies this connection, and after graduation was hired as science faculty for the New England

Montessori Teacher Education Center. Recent NEMTEC Montessori alumna Meiko Nevels completed a progressive music curriculum supported by academic rationale, while Kimberly Paquette, an early childhood and yoga teacher who is now a Montessori program director, recently published her guidebook *Lessons to Inspire Peace in the Early Childhood Classroom* (2009). NEMTEC-INDS alumni accomplishments are extensive and, more important, have changed the lives of children through enhancing their early childhood educational and life experiences.

Sometimes team faculty recognize that their students' ideas merit further development, and they encourage students to pursue advanced degrees that will provide the credibility they need to teach in higher education or to be recognized formally in their fields of practice. Because they demonstrated mastery by completing a thesis or scholarly integrative academic project during the final semester of graduate study, INDS students had a written presentation of their ability to include with doctoral applications. Familiar with presenting, discussing, and sometimes defending their work in the four team meetings, students had experience with oral presentation that helped them to stand out in interviews. Ultimately, at the end of their program, students constructed a two-page summary of their work—a synopsis that revealed the breadth and depth of their graduate experiences.

The INDS Program Spawns Lesley Fields and Degree Programs

The INDS Program was a catalyst for Lesley's conversion from Lesley College to Lesley University. INDS students' accomplishments, coupled with the power of the team model, offered an institutional vision for development and expansion of Lesley's offerings. When George Hein—organic chemist by training and educator, museum studies professional, and educational evaluator by profession—directed INDS after Cynthia Cole left to rejoin the Peace Corps, he forged an important additional connection between the INDS Program and the Program Evaluation and Research Group, or PERG, as it came to be known. Under Dick Wylie's leadership, these units were merged into the Division of Advanced Graduate Study and Research, thus recognizing organizationally the work in advanced graduate study that commenced in 1976.

Since its earliest days in the 1970s, from time to time INDS faculty and students moved out administratively to form other programs. For example, after the practitioner-oriented Open Education Program shifted to the Education Division, Cynthia Cole saw faculty colleague Professor Shaun McNiff direct his energies toward founding the Institute for Arts and Human Development, where his vision and leadership became instrumental in creating and building the nascent field of expressive therapies.

INDS alumni also extended the program's effect by creating new programs. Alumna Diana Becker expanded the concept of traveling to locations to learn about the intersections of nature, culture, community, and government by founding in Vermont the Trailside Country School, which specializes in educating through the environment. Later, she cofounded the Audubon Expedition Institute, which for more than 30 years has been helping students gain a better understanding of ecological and environmental issues by participating in field-based programs that feature multidisciplinary and multicultural inquiry.

Nancy Langstaff, another early INDS alumna whose reputation as an educator, musician, and performer earned her a position on Lesley's faculty, was frustrated by the lack of recognition of the arts in schools beyond adjunctive curriculum. Disappointed by the marginalization of arts as "frills," Nancy had a vision of integrating the arts fully into the learning process, and this goal became her mission as an early leader of Lesley's Creative Arts in Learning (CAL) program (affiliated with the previously mentioned Institute for the Arts and Human Development). Seeing a large group of INDS students with common vision and mission, Nancy and her close colleagues united in CAL to embrace active, multidimensional learning by integrating the visual, musical, movement, and dramatic arts directly into curriculum—not just extending learning experiences through the arts, but actually teaching through arts integration.

In the mid-1970s, Professor George Hein, director of INDS, observed that some of the most talented Lesley INDS alumni craved continuation of the individual learning model into advanced study. Consequently, the graduate school received authority to award the Certificate of Advanced Graduate Studies (CAGS) in 1976, and Hein gathered a small group to begin discussing doctoral study in 1978, which was formalized when the Lesley College Board of Trustees approved development of a doctoral degree plan in 1984. The small group of division heads, which included Professors McNiff and Knill, swung into action with the submission of a petition to the Massachusetts Board of Regents for Lesley to grant the PhD degree in the fall of that year. While three doctoral programs were vetted, two were put forward, Educational Studies and Expressive Therapies. Following two years of state and trustee review, during which Hein simultaneously led a public internal planning process, the first Lesley College doctoral program was mounted in Educational Studies.

The doctoral program committee decided to back first the idea of a doctorate that was based directly on the success of the INDS Program model. Bringing Drs. Frank Davis, faculty and PERG research and evaluation expert, and Marion Nesbit, INDS faculty, onto the committee, Hein created an expanded team to formalize plans for a student-oriented, individually designed program that would model the structure and pedagogy of INDS and that would follow Lesley's humanitarian mission. The program adapted INDS core ideas to the doctoral level; entering doctoral students were matched with senior faculty advisors to guide them through the first phase of graduate study and often through completion of their dissertation and conferral of their degree, thus creating a seamless advisement process. A second notable adaptation of the INDS Program was the requirement for students to develop a doctoral study plan, an individual road map of doctoral study that is reviewed by a faculty committee. A third similarity is that the PhD in Educational Studies embodied the idea of connecting Lesley students with outside experts and organizations through collaborative action and opportunities to take two courses at other doctoral institutions. The details of the program were hammered out by a college-wide Advanced Graduate Council, comprised mainly of founding committee members, validating the intention that the program be embraced as belonging to the college as a whole, with shared ownership and responsibility for its success.

Though the Division of Advanced Graduate Study and Research was later disbanded and split among academic divisions, the special INDS, PERG, and doctoral program connections continue today. Lesley University's current director of PERG is Dr. Debra Smith, an alumna of both the INDS and the Educational Studies doctoral programs. Before returning to Lesley as director of PERG, she was instrumental in creating a program at the University of Southern Maine in collaborative inquiry and development that contributed to the professional development of Maine teachers. At PERG, she spearheads grant writing and research and evaluation initiatives on diverse educational, science, and museum topics with a team of research associates. INDS and Lesley College alumna Dr. Donna Buonopane also works for PERG. Dr. Buonopane earned a doctorate in higher education at Boston College and spends most of her time now working out of her DMB Consulting group. Her research shows that principals' leadership practices are influenced both by their knowledge of mathematics and by their instructional leadership style (Buonopane, 2009, para. 3). And, before he left Lesley to assume the presidency of TERC, Frank Davis extended his faculty role and research connection with the Algebra Project by serving as director of the Educational Studies PhD program for 22 years.

Two related institutional developments are important to note. First, the Expressive Therapies doctoral program was mounted successfully with the Graduate School of Arts and Social Sciences, under the leadership of Dr. Julia Byers, EXTH division director, and division colleagues in 2000. Thus, the vision of Lesley's gaining status as a university—which was the goal of George Hein and the committee with whom he worked in the 1970s—was realized. Second, the INDS program became a grandparent. The Educational Studies doctoral program now has three program divisions: Leadership, Adult Learning, and Individualized Studies. Each has a unique model of instructional delivery, with Individualized Studies most closely following the original format rooted in INDS.

Alumni Contributions to Lesley, Education, and Humanity

Successes of INDS alumni are wide-ranging and diverse. While only a few alumni are featured here, it must be said that others equally deserve recognition. Examples that follow were selected to illustrate the reach and impact of the program.

Trailblazing INDS alumni pursued their passion to open up mathematics education to all learners. Having earned his doctorate at MIT and having worked in the private sector, Dr. Ricky Carter currently serves as faculty in Lesley's Technology in Education Program, and works to make learning math relational and enjoyable through creating unique assignments and organizing web and in-person conversations about math experiences. Similarly, INDS alumna Dr. Sue Friel's mission to make math accessible to students and teachers spurred her to complete a doctorate in mathematics education. While serving Lesley as faculty and later as administrator, Friel was instrumental in laying the groundwork for Lesley's development of a center for mathematics education. Now professor of mathematics education at the University of North Carolina at Chapel Hill, she continues to follow her passion. Reckoning with individuals who have math anxiety and insecurities, her mission is "to empower others to make sense of mathematics" (2009, para. 1).

Other INDS alumni have contributed to Lesley as faculty and administrators. The core faculty of Lesley's CAL Program are notable examples. In addition to alumna Nancy Langstaff, three INDS alumnae helped Langstaff and Dr. Vivien Marcow Speiser, CAL's former codirector, build the program's reputation regionally and nationally: Dr. Priscilla (Prilly) Sanville and Dr. Kate Austin, both of whom currently serve as CAL faculty, and Dr. Lee-Ellen Marvin. Sanville coordinates the Community Arts Program and holds specializations in multicultural education and drama as a medium for learning. She is well known for her work on diversity initiatives and was one of the national experts who were invited into Columbine to help that community deal with the terror and painful loss following the school shootings. Austin's talents focus on the value of integration of the arts in learning in early childhood education, and the value of movement in education and life. Like Sanville, she is a proponent of using the arts to address cultural misunderstandings and issues of diversity in the schools and society. The third catalyst was Lee-Ellen Marvin, a well-known storyteller who performed with the New England storytelling community and who, at Dick Wylie's initiation, was instrumental in bringing the New England Storytelling Center to Lesley and in developing CAL's former storytelling specialization. Marvin left to earn her doctorate at the University of Pennsylvania in folklore, and is an avid performer, human service program director, and instructor in upstate New York. Along with other INDS alumni who have taught for CAL over the years, these four remarkable women all shared a common vision and passion to channel the power of the arts into mainstream education in order to enhance students' learning and enrich their lives, and into communities to seek artful expressions, facilitate peaceful resolutions, and build bold initiatives.

INDS alumni have also made an impact as teachers. Dr. Thomas Newcomb recently retired with 35 years of public service after winning numerous teaching awards, including Trumbull County Teacher of the Year, the Class Act Award, and the A+ Teacher Award (twice). His ecological leanings led him to learn and write about the Amish and Mennonites as sustainable communities and, later in the 1990s, he pursued his passion for nature by participating in the reintroduction of gray wolves into Yellowstone National Park.

Teachers of the arts have also benefited from earning their master's degree through the INDS structure. Gary Moore was a successful classical ballet dancer turned teacher when he entered INDS to combine memoir with cross-disciplinary study. Codirector of dance at the Booker T. Washington Magnet High School (AL), Moore received the Disney Teacher of the Year Award and the Star Fellowship Award for his exceptional teaching of dance, choreography, and production. He was recently named the first recipient of the Alabama Power Educator Award for outstanding teachers who make significant contributions in the classroom. Also a writer, Moore has inspired disadvantaged students and other teachers toward disciplined, polished performance and artistic achievement as avenues for succeeding in life.

Another talented INDS alumna and teacher who returned to serve as team member, Katherine Gasper teaches at the Saltonstall Elementary School in Salem, MA. As a teacher in a school that applies multiple intelligence (MI) theory, Gasper's INDS studies, fostered by team member leaders in the MI community, led to an opportunity to teach at Harvard's summer Project Zero Institute for Teachers, and to put her research on the value of applying MI theory to formation of classroom communities into practice. She has also written articles for teacher audiences since graduation.

An alumnus with shared interest who preceded Gasper by 30 years, Dr. Thomas Armstrong is one of the most prolific INDS authors and speakers, with over a million copies of his books[17] in print (in 24 languages) and with 800 keynotes and presentations given across the United States and internationally. Having most recently published *Neurodiversity: Discovering the Extraordinary Gifts of Autism, ADHD, Dyslexia, and Other Brain Differences* (2010), he writes on the importance of linking human development with education, looking in a more humane way at students who have learning differences, and attending to multiple intelligences and ways of knowing, and his work has influenced countless teachers, administrators, and parents over the past three decades. His placement of value on each child and adult learner as uniquely endowed, and the ways in which he intersects different educational theories and creative challenges to

17 Among Dr. Armstrong's other books are *7 (Seven) Kinds Of Smart; In Their Own Way; You're Smarter Than You Think: A Kid's Guide To Multiple Intelligences; The Best Schools: How Human Development Research Should Inform Educational Practice; The Human Odyssey: Navigating the Twelve Stages of Life;* and *Multiple Intelligences in the Classroom.*

educational practice are consonant with the INDS Program's unique orientation to an education that buttresses the talents and interests of each student.

Perhaps best known at Lesley of all INDS education alumni is Edes Gilbert, former corporator and chair of Lesley's board of trustees from 1999 to 2003 and recipient of the Sally Lenhardt Professional Leadership Award.[18] Well known for building the Spence School into a high-quality selective girls' school in New York City, she is president of Resource Group 175, a consulting firm that is rooted in her considerable expertise and experiences in leadership and governance of independent schools. Yet, this is not all that distinguishes her. Possibly her most special contribution, besides her board role, is the gift of her daughter, who followed in her mother's footsteps to become an INDS alumna. Sarah Wilson, prolific author, along with her husband, Brian Kilcommons, on the topic of companion animals (e.g., *Metropets,* published in 2002, and *Good Owners Great Dogs,* in 1999), is an award-winning international speaker, website builder, columnist, and featured TV and print media personality.

INSPIRATIONAL DISSATISFACTION

Perhaps some of the most interesting INDS alumni were spurred by what the perennial optimist William Clement Stone (1962) called "inspirational dissatisfaction." These are the people who are driven by personal knowledge that there is something missing or wrong, that there is "a better way" to do things, and that they have "the answer." Motivated by successive institutional challenges in the 1970s, these INDS students analyzed institutional practices and found holes and disconnections. Rather than going in fighting, they chose to build trusting alliances and to work with those in power to create change. In some cases they did so successfully. INDS alumna Dr. Mary Louise O'Connor comes to mind. ML, as she was known, recognized the void

18 It should be noted that the late Sally Lenhardt, former Lesley dean, was also an INDS alumna.

in her own cancer treatment and found happiness as well as solace in creating art through poetry and painting. Passionately driven to share her experiences with others, she forged an administrative partnership, notably with Susan DeCristofaro, who was then director of patient and family education at the internationally renowned Dana-Farber Cancer Institute, in order to pioneer the idea of using the creative arts as companion therapy in cancer treatment. ML vehemently, though almost always with irresistible grace, dismissed the idea that making art was just a "nice thing" for wealthy women to do outside the hospital; rather, she devoted her final years to creating space for any patient or family member to express withheld emotions and ideas through the arts. Her story is recounted in an article by Nesbit and DeCristofaro (1999).

Another indefatigable alumna is Dr. Vicki Sartorio, who was passionate in her belief that speech-impaired, multiply disabled children should not be overlooked or shuffled to remote corners or basements of school buildings. Observing that children who could not communicate in typical ways with teachers or age peers were set off physically and socially as well as educationally, Sartorio constructed a study plan to search for alternative methods and new technology to assist these children in the learning process. Long before the Internet came into existence, she wrote to companies to learn about new adaptive, instructional products, and she conducted research to identify ways to make these products effective with her own student population. Sartorio's Lesley success was achieved through the students' publication of their thoughts, experiences, and ideas in a school newsletter, created through the use of head pointers, touch or light talkers, and other assistive devices. Her advocacy and initiative, and her students' accomplishments, were mind shifting for previously perplexed and disbelieving educators. Her INDS master's work indicated that children's minds are spinning with ideas behind their own inability to express them. These marginalized children inspired Sartorio and propelled her to extend her work into doctoral studies and, eventually, to become a chief learning resource specialist in her state.

Coming from a different geography, background, and worldview, the Venerable Praghyalok Bhikkhu, known to INDS as Bhante Pannaloka, dedicated his studies to helping children in Nepal not only thrive physically but also continue and complete their education programs. As founding president of the Karunamaya Human Development Foundation, he created and fostered the structure that made it possible for the 30 poorest children in a Nepalese orphanage to continue their education without interruption.

ML O'Connor, Vicki Sartorio, and the Venerable Pannaloka capture the power of the *n*-of-one fired by the nexus of vision, mission, and passion as a force to be valued and emulated.

EMBRACING THE NATURAL WORLD

Learning for INDS alumni went beyond developmental concerns of humans into the natural world. On occasion, an INDS student broke out of the traditional classroom in favor of learning in the field, sometimes quite literally, and preserving natural resources. Long before Howard Gardner (2000) coined the term *naturalistic intelligence,* these students blazed trails in the fields of eco-psychology, created wilderness vision quests, studied the multiple benefits of farming organically in community, taught nature education for pre-K-12 students to supplement clean-handed book learning, and engaged in interdisciplinary study with nature as a focal point. Others similarly interested in the natural world worried about diminishment of global resources. Some, like Maureen Wild, dedicated themselves to building sustainable communities by developing farming cooperatives and green building projects. Alumna Nicki Johnson, whose focus embraced global ethics, human rights, and sustainable development, designed a three-phase recycling program for an area in Bosnia and Herzegovina after she witnessed hunger and homelessness as an outcome of war.

FINDING AND CLARIFYING VOICE

INDS alumni have explored the concept of *voice* in several intriguing ways, including advocacy, professional theater, and higher education. Among many other accomplished peers, four such alumni are Christopher Von Baeyer, Kate Wilson, Lois Roach, and John Feudo.

Christopher Von Baeyer, who was then teaching faculty at Emerson College and who later became a senior consultant with the Ariel Group, brought Kristin Linklater, a member of the faculty at Emerson and cofounder along with Tina Packer of Shakespeare & Company, to Lesley as one of his team members. Linklater inspired Von Baeyer and hundreds after him to free their natural voice and work from the inside out. Von Baeyer was struck by the personal and professional connections that emerged through working with her 1986 book *Freeing the Natural Voice*. The legacy continues with Melissa Baroni, a talented actress who studies voice with Linklater's lead trainer in New York City.

Kate Wilson came to INDS from Shakespeare & Company not only to learn more about speech and dialect for her work in the theater, but also to discover how to make that knowledge more accessible and user-friendly for actors. To that end, Kate moved to New York City to complete her studies, which included an internship under the guidance of Professors Elizabeth Smith and Ralph Zito, drama faculty at the Juilliard School. Wilson's outstanding student work and her performance as an intern led to a progression of roles that culminated in Juilliard's hiring her as core drama faculty in speech and dialect. For her final INDS project, she extended her studies into voice and dialect coaching for stage and film actors, which earned her an outstanding reputation in her profession and helped her achieve the vision that she had generated for her INDS graduate studies.

Well known in the local media and arts community, Lois Roach entered INDS to study the intersection of communication, media, and the arts. Along the way, she studied the history of African American theater, techniques of script writing, and media presentation. Her

CYNTHIA FARR BROWN AND MICHELE FORINASH, EDITORS

awards and accolades are too numerous to mention here, but it should be noted that she won an Emmy for a work she completed while she was director of public affairs for a major Boston TV network. Moreover, she has established herself as a major figure on the Boston arts scene, and recently completed a 16-year role as part-time drama faculty at Wellesley College. In all capacities, she has applied her considerable talents to bring issues, strengths, and possibilities of marginalized populations into the public arena.

Working from a different perspective, Dr. John Feudo has also been involved in promoting meaningful communication through improving voice and speaking abilities. He has achieved success in helping individuals speak publicly through facing their fears and projecting their knowledge and personality in public. Feudo uses his own talents effectively in his newest position as associate vice president of Boston College, where he is in charge of alumni relations. His books on this subject (e.g., *Alumni Relations: A Newcomer's Guide to Success*, published in 2009) have garnered favorable reviews as well as awards. He has made numerous keynote presentations in the United States and abroad and has served as president of the National Council of Alumni Association Executives. He also consults with organizations and coaches other directors of alumni relations.

MUSEUM EDUCATION

In his roles as program faculty, director, and dean of the Division of Advanced Graduate Study and Research Division, Professor George Hein attracted the attention of museum professionals to INDS as a place to pursue graduate study. Some alumni have applied their constructivist knowledge to create museums; Emily Mikolayunas, for example, helped develop the Eric Carle Museum of Picture Book Art in Amherst, MA. Other alumni of museum studies at INDS have contributed to local museum operations, including the Boston Museum of Science, the Boston Children's Museum, the Worcester Art Museum, and the John F. Kennedy Presidential Library and Museum.

Two INDS alumni capture the flavor of these contributions. Catherine Hughes built on her INDS experiences in her book *Museum Theater: Communicating with Visitors Through Drama* (1998). She combined theatrical talents, knowledge of museum constructs, and the Museum of Science vision to connect visitors with museum offerings through drama. She created a collaboration between the museum and Harvard Medical School to script and present a play that deals with addiction and neurobiology; she also brought science history alive through acting in a play based on the life of Ada Byron King, one of the first "computer" programmers. As the founding executive director of the International Museum Theater Alliance, Hughes has consulted with many institutions, and she recently completed her PhD at Ohio State University, where she studied spectator response to museum theater performances.

Sam Rubin explored museum studies from his background as a teacher with a passion for history and love of biography. As an alumnus serving in the role of education coordinator at the J FK Museum, he has cocreated numerous exciting programs that invite teachers to explore notable American figures through biographical explorations and primary research opportunities made available through museums. In various venues, including specific institutes and conferences and more widely through *New Frontiers,* the JFK Museum library's newsletter for educators, Rubin has encouraged educators to schedule excursions for their students that incorporate primary learning experiences that can help them discover their own passion for educational studies and locate inspiration for their lives from historical mentors, particularly those who were raised locally. He brings history alive for teachers and students in ways that go beyond reading and discussing a text.

PROFESSIONAL AND PERSONAL COACHING

As Kate Wilson uses coaching to extend skill and opportunity for actors, three notable INDS alumni—Bonnie Gorbaty, Lauren Mackler, and Dan Shepard—use coaching to help individuals succeed in their careers and lives. Gorbaty applied her INDS studies in the psychology of motivation and achievement and her research with mid-level insurance professionals toward creating a platform of professional enhancement and organizational development based on the intersection of knowledge and personal qualities. She founded Inner Resources, Inc., a company that focuses on building employees' personal strengths and drive toward achievement of personal and corporate success through cultivation of intrinsic motivation. Gorbaty's accomplishments were recognized by others when she was named a top 10 Female Executive Coach in New England.

Lauren Mackler came to INDS by a different route, returning to college as an adult to complete her education. With a string of professional accomplishments that include prominent media exposure, Mackler turned her trailblazing in a different direction, on a mission to help top professionals assess internally what matters most when they find an emptiness after achieving what they thought would bring full satisfaction. In short, she teaches how to find personal satisfaction amid and despite professional accomplishment. Mackler has recently mounted a coaching program to teach others how to help adults take risks and explore avenues that will lead to personal satisfaction. An accomplished motivational speaker and author, she published her most recent book, *Solemate: Master the Art of Aloneness and Transform Your Life,* in 2009. She also has her own satellite radio show on Hay House Network.

As one alumnus, echoing voices of others, said recently, "My experiences at Lesley changed my life." Dan Shepard believes that Lesley's investment in his ideas and personal support provided exactly the incubating environment he needed to flesh out his thoughts and dreams so that he could help others do the same. After launching a major career transition to enroll in INDS, Shepard's risk taking was rewarded: having interned as part of his graduate studies at Essex Partners of Keystone, a top executive career management firm that mentors CEOs, COOs, and others in following their visions, he was tapped to become a partner there, in effect creating mini-INDS programs for his clients. Shepard now engages in meaningful assessment, teaching, and coaching by applying the theory and practice of appreciative inquiry in a way that is true to his own values.

AWARD-WINNING AUTHORS

Faith Adiele is a poet and award-winning author (e.g., Best American Essays listing) and university faculty who has a host of publications ranging from a coauthored account of the travails of being an undergraduate woman of diversity at Harvard to a feature on a PBS special. Her book *Meeting Faith: The Forest Journals of a Black Buddhist Nun* (2005) won the PEN/Beyond Margins Award, among other recognitions.

Another highly regarded INDS author, Barbara de La Cuesta, won the Gival Press Novel Award for *The Spanish Teacher* (2007), a book that explores social politics and human dilemma. De La Cuesta has an impressive record of publication since her Lesley graduation and has received several noteworthy fellowships. Her literary works include *The Gold Mine* (novel in 1989), *Westerly* (nonfiction in 1993), and a long poem, *If There Weren't So Many of Them* (1991).

SO MANY TRAILBLAZERS

Almost all INDS alumni have followed what Robert Frost described as the road "less traveled by," and deserve recognition for their remarkable accomplishments and influence. Regrettably, this chapter's length excludes them in letter, but they certainly are present in spirit. What follows is still an incomplete recognition: Maureen Ricci and Denise Carpenter, for their work helping students through promoting family literacy in the Providence Public Schools; Deborah Addis, for her advocacy on behalf of asbestos cleaning and redress to victims; Lina Abiad, for her work in international early education in the Middle East; and Brenda Stockdale, whose administrative leadership role at the Cancer Institute in Georgia led her to write the book *You Can Beat the Odds: Surprising Factors Behind Chronic Illness*

& Cancer (2009). Kim Archung created an inclusive literacy program at the Paige Academy in Boston and then taught in New York City. Having earned her doctorate, she now serves as professor in and director of the Claflin University (SC) graduate education program that emphasizes teacher leadership; her role affords her opportunities to pursue her INDS interests in methods and practices of successful African American teachers, multicultural education, and urban teacher education. And, in promoting the power of music in peace education, former music teacher Cheryl Melody Baskin has journeyed as composer, performer and recording artist, playwright, educator, and keynote speaker, and has seven CDs for children and adults to her credit. Her accolades include the Parents' Choice Winner Award and, most recently, the 2010 Kidlutions Preferred Products Award. It should be noted that all her children's CDs won Kidlutions awards— coveted because the winner is determined by votes of teachers, parents, and family therapists across the country for products that enhance children's social and emotional development.

Other alumni have used their INDS accomplishments to make a difference in local communities around Lesley. Kathleen Kolman applies her integrative studies incorporating musicianship (eight instruments), vocal performance (recent CD release), Brazilian culture, and educational curriculum development to succeed in teaching a diverse population of pre-K to eighth-grade students at the King Open School in Cambridge. Christopher Ellinger's True Story Theater, headquartered in Arlington, builds on the tenets of Playback Theater to explore issues of conscience and sensitivity through compassionate listening with immediate response through dramatic means and dialogue. Joanne Pressman's transformation of the Lexington Community Nursery School was notably inspired by her studies of the Reggio Emilia approach. Nancy Megha Buttenheim contributes her multidisciplinary talents as a master teacher, leader, and visionary at Kripalu Institute. Award-winning producer Michelle Sweet is well known locally for the quality of classical music at WGBH (NPR) radio. And, the formation of nonprofits like Brio, Sahar Ahmed's foundation established in Winchester to integrate the differently abled in shared community experiences, similarly grew from seeds planted in Lesley INDS graduate study. We applaud the achievements of so many other INDS graduates whom proscriptions of space prevent us from mentioning here.

In Closing

In remarkable ways, graduates of the Independent Study Degree Program have been the harbingers of Lesley University's future. The extraordinary visions and the collective efforts of INDS students and alumni who inspired the development of five divisions of Lesley University's graduate schools, along with its Educational Studies doctoral program, have perhaps been the most visible stimulus in moving Lesley's mission forward over the past 40 years.

Each aspect of Lesley University's current mission statement has been realized in the accomplishments of the hundreds of passionate souls and visionary leaders who graduated from INDS, from its nascent period in the 1960s through today. While contributing their extraordinary talents toward furthering humanitarian goals, INDS alumni connected Lesley's heritage with its future.

REFERENCES

Adiele, F. (2005). *Meeting Faith: The forest journals of a black Buddhist nun.* New York, NY: W. W. Norton.

Armstrong, T. (1999). *7 (Seven) kinds of smart.* New York, NY: Plume/Penguin-Putnam.

Armstrong, T. (2000). *In their own way.* New York, NY: Tarcher/Penguin.

Armstrong, T. (2002). *You're smarter than you think: A kid's guide to multiple intelligences.* Minneapolis, MN: Free Spirit.

Armstrong, T. (2006). *The best schools: How human development research should inform educational practice.* Alexandria, VA: ASCD.

Armstrong, T. (2007). *The human odyssey: Navigating the twelve stages of life.* New York, NY: Sterling.

Armstrong, T. (2009). *Multiple intelligences in the classroom* (3rd ed.). Alexandria, VA: ASCD.

Armstrong, T. (2010). *Neurodiversity: Discovering the extraordinary gifts of autism, ADHD, dyslexia, and other brain differences.* Cambridge, MA: DeCapo-Perseus.

Buonopane, D. M. (2009). Professional web page, DMB Consulting & Associates. Retrieved August 2, 2009, from http://leadershipinmath. com/About/about.htm

De la Cuesta, B. (1989). *The gold mine.* Pittsburgh, PA: Latin America Literary Review Press.

De la Cuesta, B. (1991). *If there weren't so many of them you might say they were beautiful.* Delhi, NY: Birch Brook Press.

De la Cuesta, B. (1993). *Westerly: Finding an integrative focus for a nursing home activity program.* Hollywood, FL: M & H Publishing Co.

De la Cuesta, B. (2007). *The Spanish teacher.* Arlington, VA: Gival Press.

Feudo, J. (2009). *Alumni relations: A newcomer's guide to success* (2nd ed.). New York, NY: CASE.

Friel, S. N. (2009). Faculty web page, The University of North Carolina at Chapel Hill. Retrieved August 2, 2009, from http://soe. unc.edu/fac_research/profile/friel.php

Galvin-Gutierrez, E. (2001). *Science for everyday: A Montessori based science curriculum.* London. England: Nienhuis.

Gardner, H. (2000). *Intelligence reframed: Multiple intelligences for the 21st century.* New York, NY: Perseus.

Hughes, C. (1998). *Museum theater: Communicating with visitors through drama.* Portsmouth, NH: Heinemann Press.

Kilcommons, B., & Wilson, S. E. (1999). *Good owners great dogs.* New York, NY: Grand Central Publishing.

Kilcommons, B., & Wilson, S. E. (2002). *Metrodog.* New York, NY: Grand Central Publishing.

Linklater, K. (1986). *Freeing the natural voice.* Hollywood, CA: Drama Publishers.

Mackler, L. (2009). *Solemate: Master the art of aloneness and transform your life.* Carlsbad, CA: Hay House.

Nesbit, M., & DeCristofaro, S. (2007). Creative arts as companion therapy in cancer treatment: A patient partnership. *Journal of Pedagogy, Pluralism, and Practice,12*, 1 13.

Noddings, N. (2006). *Critical lessons: What our schools should teach.* Cambridge, England: Cambridge University Press.

Paquette, K. (2009). *Pathways to Peace: Lessons to inspire peace in the early childhood classroom.* Retrieved from http://www.Iuniverse.com

Ray, P. H., & Anderson, S. R. (2000). *The cultural creatives: How 50 million people are changing the world.* New York: Harmony Books.

Rogers, A. G. (1993). Voice, play, and a practice of ordinary courage in girls' and women's lives. *Harvard Educational Review, 63,* 265 229.

Stockdale, B. M. (2009) *You can beat the odds: Surprising factors behind chronic illness & cancer-the 6 week breakthrough program for optimal immunity.* Boulder, CO: Sentient Publications.

Stone, W. C. (1962). *The success system that never fails.* Englewood Cliffs, NJ: Prentice-Hall.

Some INDS students took advantage of the local Cambridge option of taking four courses on campus and then completing two thirds of their program outside conventional course structures, while others completed the program in its entirety studying in other places, locally or internationally, where the level of sophistication in the chosen area was at the pinnacle of the profession or on location with a particular mentor considered a leader in the particular field.

CHAPTER TWELVE

Synergies, Collaborations, and Transformations

ANGELO FERTITTA, MFA
JOHN LANZA, MFA

Photograph courtesy of The Lesley University Archives.

In 1998, Lesley began to blossom in a different fashion. Instead of putting out new shoots from within, the college looked out across the landscape, seeking partners. The first hybridization was with the Art

Institute of Boston, a college whose roots went back almost as far as Lesley University's. And, just how did that come about?

> "Look, Mother," said Benjamin B. "Look at the house across the street."
> His mother looked at it.
> "It is different from our house," said Benjamin B.
> "Yes," said Mother. "It is different from our house."
> "Hurry and get up," said Mother. "This is going to be a different kind of day."
> (Evans, 1955)[19]

What did that house across the Charles River look like? In AIB, Lesley saw a high-energy community of artists who were immersed in the process of exploration and discovery. Students worked alongside their creations, which were manifested along the hallways for all to see. It was a college where students were bouncing off the walls, creating work that was, well, bouncing off the walls. The story of the Art Institute of Boston began in 1912, with the School of Practical Art, one of the first private, nonaffiliated art schools. The founder, Roy Davidson, was a pioneer in the field of commercial art education. Instead of continuing the practice where artists worked through a long apprenticeship, Davidson founded a school where students could train within a reasonably short time, empowered to become professional artists in the field (Pacy, 2007). At the time, the *Boston Herald* stated, "This seems to be a school for students of moderate means who wish to make art a business and it has the indorsement [sic] of some of the largest buyers of commercial art in the city" (Davidson, 1918–1919).

The monthly fee of $15 and full tuition of $110 seem moderate indeed today. It is instructive to look at the school's mission then—a response to the needs of those times, different from what one would find today. In the school's brochure just after World War I, Davidson advertised, "The School of Practical Art, as its name implies, is devoted to the teaching of only such drawing as has a commercial

19 Admittedly, this children's story is about Benjamin, not about Lesley, but artistic license is invoked.

value and fills a long felt want among art students with a living to make" (Davidson, 2007).

Photograph courtesy of The Lesley University Archives.

Clearly, earning a living was *the* priority of the times. While this need is mindfully relevant today, we have evolved as a culture, and institutions of higher education have grown to embrace a larger responsibility.

Davidson remained at the helm until 1940, when Harold Pollock became director. In 1945 Pollock became president, a role he held until 1962. In 1967, during the term of William Willis, Sr., the school became a nonprofit institution and was renamed the Art Institute of Boston. In that time, AIB expanded its pedagogical scope, adding programs in fine arts, photography, and liberal arts.

When President Willis, Sr., stepped down in 1977, his son, William Willis, Jr., known as Tuck, succeeded him. During the seventies and early eighties AIB was accredited by the National Association of Trade Schools. Under Tuck's guidance, the school sought and received accreditation from the National Association of Schools of Art and Design, and in 1988, it received the authority to grant the bachelor of fine arts degree from the state of Massachusetts. AIB had become a strong, professional art college.

AIB had made significant progress during the eighties in becoming a competitive college of art; however, as an independent institution, it struggled with enrollment and finances. In 1990, when Tuck resigned, AIB undertook a search for a new president with strong fiduciary skills, and a year later, Stan Trecker was chosen to be the new leader. Under his leadership, enrollment stabilized and began to grow—the college flourished. With balanced budgets and healthy enrollment, AIB had moved into a position where seeking a partner was a viable option.

During the 1996–1997 academic year, the Art Institute of Boston completed a self-study and received an accreditation visit by the New England Association of Schools and Colleges (NEASC). The result of the application for accreditation by NEASC was that AIB was given "Candidacy Status" with two areas of concern. The first and foremost was its financial status. From 1991 through the time of the NEASC visit, AIB managed to maintain solvency; however, this was partially the result of low profit margins, which limited the institute's ability to pay competitive salaries or to improve infrastructure. The second area of concern centered on the quality and quantity of books in the library. The charge, therefore, was to remedy both these concerns within the ensuing five years.

As the AIB board of trustees and key members of the administration led by President Trecker pondered scenarios that could have a positive impact on the institution, it became clear that partnering with another institution of higher education would be the most effective solution to achieve regional accreditation, maintain academic integrity, and secure the financial future of AIB. Thus, during the last half of 1997 and the first few months of 1998, members of the board of trustees approached several institutions, including Lesley College.

In addition to the pragmatic aims cited by NEASC, AIB considered other factors as relevant to its future, including housing for students, technology, liberal arts, increased financial aid, and better benefit packages for employees. When considering the option of an affiliation, the following five concerns were deemed paramount: (1) maintaining its name, (2) retaining its identity as a professional art college, (3) maintaining its urban location, (4) supporting AIB programs and faculty, and (5) initiating an immediate investment in AIB. In view of these considerations, the AIB constituency decided that Lesley College was the most suitable institution with which to create this partnership; and, by the end of 1998, the merger was completed and approved by all appropriate bodies.

For Lesley, the merger meant that the arts could become central—a core element instead of just an area of service. Lesley had a strong and diverse arts-related and arts-supportive culture, but little in the way of an actual art program. It knew it wanted more. With the addition of all of AIB's resources, faculty, and lively student body, the arts could become one of the pillars of the college. This meant that instead of building a substantial art program from the ground up, Lesley would gain a full-fledged, fully operational art college. It would be able to expand its liberal arts offerings to reach a larger undergraduate student body. "The merger also reinforce[d] Lesley's commitment to maintain its long-term viability through its profile as a responsive, entrepreneurial, multi-faceted institution" (Fertitta, 1999, p. 2). Lesley College, with its already extant schools, wished to move toward becoming a university. Joining with AIB became an important step toward that goal.

The similarities in the two schools' mission statements, including a professional orientation to educational programs and a commitment to community service, provided for Lesley the philosophical link desired in the partnership. Beyond pedagogical affinities, Lesley discovered synergetic connections in a shared social consciousness in the mission statements of the two institutions:

> The Mission of The Art Institute of Boston is to provide a comprehensive art education that develops in its students the aesthetic awareness, the perceptual and conceptual abilities, and the humanistic perspective necessary for a career in the visual arts. (AIB Faculty Handbook)

> ...A distinctive and fundamental aspect of education at Lesley College is the conviction that people matter, and that the professionals who respond to their needs provide a unique service to society. (Lesley Faculty Handbook)

The two colleges were alike in their humanistic and student-centered ways. The merger has served to bring together strengths, ideals, and resources to achieve the goal of better service to all students. More important, it has brought Lesley University to a clearer awareness of itself and its possibilities. The merger's synergies and collaborations affected transformations at all levels—pragmatically, pedagogically, and philosophically—creating something that had not existed before.

Pragmatically

With the mutual goals of ensuring their futures and serving their students, Lesley University and the Art Institute of Boston entered into an agreement to merge. With almost no redundancies in the academic programs and with strengths that dovetailed, the institutions fit together well. In synergy, they shared important aims and perspectives: quality of academic programs, small class sizes, student-centered programs, individual attention, field-based learning, faculty practitioners, and professional orientation. In collaboration, the merger allowed for a sensible and symbiotic allocation of resources and distribution of responsibility by disciplines. Lesley assumed responsibility for all liberal arts courses, while AIB managed all art studio and art history courses. The collaboration resulted in numerous benefits and broadened the number of cocurricular activities available to AIB students, including theater, clubs, and athletics. Quite simply, AIB students have gained an expanded sense of student life, which continues to grow and develop.

For Lesley, the merger has enhanced offerings in the studio arts. All the cultural and aesthetic elements of the AIB Program—art exhibitions, gallery events and openings, and artist lectures—have become available to the entire university body. The growing list of activities has expanded and deepened the realm of offerings for both personal and curricular enrichment. The arts have become as important as other aspects that define a more creative and diverse Lesley University. Both Lesley and AIB offer strong academic programs, share a commitment to quality learning in a student-centered environment, and follow thoughtful processes for the allocation of resources to support these strengths and commitments.

This collaboration between institutions weaves a fabric of support, so that Lesley is able to continue its emphasis on teacher education, human services, management, and the arts, and so that AIB can continue to focus on developing students' artistic ability and expression alongside their professional and marketable skills. While continuously evaluating and updating its BFA degree programs in design, illustration, fine arts, and photography, and in the animation and art history programs that have been added since the merger, AIB has been able to remain true to its mission.

The merger of AIB and Lesley has brought about transformations and improvements in administration and governance. AIB, the fourth school at Lesley University, now operates within Lesley's governance structure. The dean of the college leads AIB and engages in all aspects of academic planning at the university. As with all the schools within Lesley University, AIB department chairs drive the curriculum and the academics, under the leadership of the senior associate dean of Academic Affairs and with the help of its faculty-based Curriculum Committee. Across the university, AIB helps to shape matters of academic policy by participating in various committees, most notably as part of the newly formed Academic Advisory Committee. The faculty and the administration joined with the provost to create a council, which now facilitates cross-university communication by bringing together faculty and school representatives, deans, and the provost to a roundtable discussion.

Administrative functions have grown more centralized. The University Office of Student Administrative Services provides registration, financial aid, and bursar services to all students. The Office of Student Life and Academic Development oversees residence life, student activities, student government, career resources, academic support services, disability services, and athletics. University Technology furnishes the umbrella for all administrative and academic technology. Sherrill Library coordinates all library services, and, the Office of Enrollment Management supervises admissions for the University.

The expansion of work groups in each administrative area has resulted in a larger pool of expertise to deal with issues and a broader group of colleagues with whom to work and learn. Turnover of positions at both institutions has provided new employment opportunities, resulting in expanded and upgraded career opportunities. AIB's core faculty has been able to join in the Faculty Assembly, which gives voice to the faculty under the university's governance structure. Faculty who are members of the assembly serve on all the university academic committees, such as the Committee on Rank and Promotion, Faculty Affairs and Academic Policies, and Faculty Life and Development. An AIB faculty member was recently elected to serve as chair of the Lesley University Faculty Assembly. AIB faculty have become full members of the Lesley community, peers with their Cambridge colleagues. New structures integrate both the larger and smaller administrative and faculty units of both institutions into a more comprehensive framework, effectively creating one whole, new institution, to the enrichment of all.

Because of the enduring emphasis on professional focus, the faculty at AIB, like the faculty at Lesley University, comprises practitioners in their fields, who teach and bring the benefit of their expertise to their programs. This faculty of working professionals has engaged in cross-teaching opportunities and collaborations that serve the students at all four of Lesley's schools. These collaborations include development of new courses, new minors, and new programs. An array of faculty development programs, workshops, coffee hours, and training sessions provide forums for the faculty, university-wide, to engage in programmatic and pedagogical discourse. The university practice of relying on adjunct or part-time faculty to teach in the academic programs continues the custom prevalent at AIB and at art colleges throughout the country. This use of adjuncts, who are practicing professionals in the fields in which they teach, honors an ongoing commitment to offer programs that combine theory and practice.

The integration of the two institutions expanded the diversity of faculty expertise and experience; created opportunities for faculty to teach different populations at different levels in the various university settings; and provided access for AIB teachers to faculty benefits, such as sabbatical leave programs, faculty development funds, and the grant-writing assistance that is available to the university's core faculty. These offerings take many forms, including travel and grant-funding opportunities, support for academic projects, and learning opportunities in a variety of areas. To date, most core AIB faculty have been granted sabbaticals, which have assisted them in their professional development. Their growth and achievements continue to enrich the university.

In regard to library services, the merger afforded AIB a tenfold increase in title access, as well as access to online and full-text databases, interlibrary loan agreements, and affiliations. Additional services that have come to fruition since the merger are online art collections such as ARTstor.org; and, reciprocally, the university's overall library collection has been enhanced by the acquisition of the AIB art-book and slide collection. Again, this collaboration and distribution of resources has created a subtle but profound transformation—enabling a flourishing expansion and dedication of the art library, to the betterment of the entire university.

The Art Institute of Boston Library supports students' academic and visual research needs. The AIB Library greatly benefited from the merger with Lesley University and its larger library department. Students and faculty have expanded access to both print and online resources. The focused art collection, specializing in the fields of fine art, art history, illustration, design, and photography, has grown to more than 10,000 volumes. Through membership in the Fenway Libraries Online network, direct borrowing privileges are extended to nearby colleges, including three art libraries. Many more academic disciplines are supported by the Lesley University Libraries' main collection, which features a growing eBook collection. The past 10 years have marked extraordinary changes in electronic publishing and searching. The AIB Library collections were automated to allow for searching materials online. Electronic database subscriptions provide online access to hundreds of full-text art journals and nearly one million high-quality art images. These changes have made it possible for students to complete research assignments from any location. (D. Verhoff, personal communication, November 23, 2009)

All student services have been centralized on the main campus under the leadership of the dean of Student Life and Academic Development. Some services are provided on-site at AIB, where representatives schedule time each week at designated offices. Counseling services are available at AIB several days a week. Of course, all student services for AIB students are also accessible on the main Cambridge campus. The Career Resource Center and the Center for Academic Achievement have added a vital dimension to the services available to AIB students. Since the merger, the staff in the Career Resource Center has included an art specialist who has an understanding of the various art fields and who is, therefore, very sympathetic to the needs of art students and graduates.

The physical improvements are easiest to spot. With responsibilities coordinated, initiatives could be focused where needed, in improved studio spaces, in state-of-the-art professional technologies, and in library expansion. The AIB facilities in Boston, at 700 Beacon Street and 601 Newbury Street, have been improved since the merger. In fact, renovations were among the first benefits to materialize. The 700 Beacon Street building houses studios, classrooms, a gallery, a library, a student lounge, photography and technology labs, and faculty and administrative offices. The facilities at 601 Newbury Street include animation studios and labs, art studios, individual senior studio spaces, a technology lab, student gallery, and offices. The division of responsibility between Lesley and AIB has advanced many projects and initiatives. AIB has been able to address its physical plant better. Students use expanded and state-of-the-art animation labs, computing and digital technologies, and photographic facilities. All AIB equipment and materials used to support teaching and learning are maintained in sync with Lesley's cycles of equipment and facility maintenance, renewal, and replacement. This technological support alone is an incalculable benefit to the entire community.

All of Lesley's Cambridge facilities, including the library, auditoriums, dining facilities, and classroom spaces, are available for use by AIB faculty and students. University Hall (formerly the Porter Exchange building) has undergone a wonderful metamorphosis. With its art and dance studios, classrooms, modern science labs, multiphase auditorium, lavish new home for the School of Education, eateries, bookstore, administrative and commercial spaces, and a new, professional art gallery, we realize a new presence and begin to look to future possibilities. With new development, the university's vision becomes clearer, and the next goal emerges.

During the past five years, great progress has been made toward providing new facilities for AIB in Cambridge. In the last two years, the two institutions have chosen a site, hired an architectural firm, and processed designs, and they are now seeking approval from the neighborhood and the city of Cambridge. The dialogue has been comprehensive, inclusive, and responsive. Stan Trecker has resumed his position as dean of AIB, with a primary goal of realizing this landmark venture—the creation of a Cambridge-based arts community and facility, with Lesley and AIB as its cornerstones.

Sociologically, the merger brought together two undergraduate college populations—AIB and the Women's College (now Lesley College). One was coed; one was not. The presence of men in Lesley's liberal arts courses created a coed institution, expanding its vision, its mission, and its reach.

Having sought out partners with similar and supportive missions, Lesley was able to answer very challenging questions about its own purposes. Some programs needed to be reevaluated, and other programs were waiting out there with open arms. With its own image sharpened, Lesley was able to make strong, informed choices about its affiliations.

PEDAGOGICALLY

The merger has created opportunities to expand and develop new programs for students at both schools. "AIB students can now enroll in minors in a variety of disciplines such as creative writing, history, environmental science, management, and psychology" (J. Stanwood, personal communication, April 9, 2009). New programs at the university that trace their inception to the merger include an MEd in art education; two MFA programs, one in creative writing and the other in visual arts; two BFA programs, one in animation and the other in art history; a dual-degree program with a BFA and an MEd in art education; and a BA in art history. Soon, students will have "the opportunity to earn a BFA/MA in expressive therapies" (J. Stanwood, personal communication, April 9, 2009). The addition of a studio arts curriculum to Lesley's offerings strengthened the basis for developing the PhD Program in Expressive Therapies. The PhD program was approved by the Massachusetts Board of Higher Education in 1986, and played an important role in Lesley's becoming a university.

The merger also provided more diversity for students in course selection, methods of learning, and student activities. As a result, students can more easily change direction and pursue another course of study within the same institution. More fundamentally, the breadth and richness of combined offerings allow students to come into their own. For example, the illustration program and the animation program that grew from it have benefited pragmatically from the university's investment in technology and other resources, and they are pedagogically enriched through access to programs such as creative writing. Artistic voices are now developed in narration so that visual and verbal communication reinforce each other.

One of the most important changes at the university was the development of a General Education Program that serves all undergraduates. The GenEd Program had its genesis in a very early collaboration of the faculty across the university. At the advice of the Academic Program Planning (APP) group initiated by the provost, the faculty met on a regular basis for two years, in a process that was supported by funding from the Davis Foundation. The results included collaborations on course development between faculty from different schools; the beginnings of a sense of unity across the schools' faculties; and the realization that major programs like general education needed to be reevaluated in light of the blending of the two undergraduate populations.

Following the APP effort, a formal working committee began to focus specifically on general education. This task was led by the dean of Lesley College, and included members of the AIB faculty and the Lesley College faculty. By the fall of 2005, a new GenEd Program was available to both undergraduate populations. Having reviewed the benefits of the program since its inauguration, the university is moving to augment the breadth and depth of its GenEd offerings.

The work of the past few years has yielded significantly broader educational opportunities in the liberal arts, social sciences, math, and sciences for undergraduate students. The ongoing review of the General Education Program ensures that enhancements to the curriculum have expanded the diversity of offerings and pedagogies while meeting the needs of each school's professional programs. As an outgrowth of this expansion, larger core and adjunct faculties are able to better support the university's range of academic programs and pedagogies.

Enhancements in programs and faculty life have also led, increasingly, to collaboration among faculty members on curriculum and on professional development. Administrative structures have likewise benefited from the different perspectives of the schools within the university. The art library that formerly served as the library for AIB has been able to focus exclusively on the visual arts, greatly enhancing resources for curriculum development and professional activity in arts-based and arts-related programs across the university.

On the individual level, many students travel abroad to study. Lesley maintains affiliations with programs in Italy, France, Holland, Ireland, and Japan. Locally, there is any number of bus trips, museum trips, conferences, panels, and lectures to take advantage of. We are part of a growing culture that draws visiting artists and lecturers into all areas of our university community. Conversely, the required internships for all majors send all AIB students out into the professional community. We expand our exposure and our vision.

Programmatically, one of the first places identified as an opportunity for collaboration was between GSASS and AIB in the area of teacher education. Lesley University is renowned for its programs in teacher education, but until AIB merged with Lesley, it was not feasible to have a teacher education program that focused on the visual arts. With faculty from both schools working together, a new program for a master of education in art education was developed, and was presented to accreditors for approval. The program was implemented and has been successfully graduating art teachers for several years. The existence of this master's program opened the door to a new dual-degree program for students receiving the bachelor of fine arts degree. Students now are able to do preliminary work toward the MEd in art education during their undergraduate years and, therefore, are able to shorten the duration of their master's degree work significantly.

Almost simultaneously, work began on master of fine arts degrees in visual arts and in creative writing. Work on these new initiatives began at the college level; AIB forged the foundation for the MFA in Visual Arts, and GSASS laid the groundwork for the MFA in Creative

Writing. In the later stages of development, there was significant collaboration between the work groups from each school. The synergy between these programs lay in their both being low residency by nature, which allowed the programs to run concurrently and share resources, including visiting artists and faculty.

The MFA in Visual Arts grew out of a proposal made in 1993, an idea that languished until the merger, when it piqued the interest of Lesley's president and provost. As the program's original director recalled:

> My original proposal was for a six-week summer program in painting, but discussion in committee generated a broader curriculum in visual arts in general and semiannual 10-day residencies—both of which deepened my vision that the program encourage independence and pluralism of viewpoints. (A. Apesos, personal communication, April 15, 2009)

Repeatedly, we encounter passion and support for a variety of personal and sociological perspectives, a shared value in the life of our university.

At AIB, the MFA scene is a lively one indeed. Transforming the classroom and gallery facilities during intersession breaks, artists infuse every inch of space into kiosks of wildly diverse and challenging artwork. These artists are developing their unique voices. Participants in the MFA in Visual Arts Program grapple with the ever evolving art scene, responding to such issues as globalization and world citizenship. What is the reality? What are the politics? What is the resulting pedagogy (Barry, 2007)? Art, for the past two decades, has blurred national boundaries in much the same way as have other aspects of society and the economy. Artists have been exhibiting in a global art world. The effect of this has been to infuse art with a new political and social consciousness, as well as broadening the landscape of what art is, how it is made, and for whom it is made. With the artists debating a "return to craft" versus a "de-skilling of art" (Steck,

2009), giving meaning to the term *master* is seminal. Many of the MFA faculty teach locally at other institutions, and they provide an influx of ideas and ways to connect with the changing and evolving art scene.

Although there seem to be considerable overlaps between studio art programs offered at AIB and an art therapy program, a salient philosophical difference hinders tying them together neatly. The programs differ in intent; one envisions art professionally, and the other, therapeutically. The studio arts programs are production oriented, and focus on the individual who is making the work. The art therapy programs are based in counseling and use art making as a therapeutic tool. Efforts are under way to open a more direct pathway for students in BFA programs to meet some of the requirements of the master's degree in Art Therapy or Expressive Therapies. This would further meld undergraduate programs in studio art at AIB with graduate programs at GSASS. It is in the philosophical interactions that we uncover the richest dialogue.

Philosophically

The initial rationale for engaging in the process of merger— better service to students and new program opportunities to support Lesley's profile as a multifaceted institution—continues to shape many developments at the university. The Lesley-AIB merger has lived up to its promises of enrolling more aware students in both institutions and providing them with a fuller and more diverse educational experience. Both graduate and undergraduate students have enjoyed the richness of the combined cultures and of the educational programs that have evolved during these explosive 10 years. The mission of the university has been substantially bolstered by the combined efforts that have resulted from our partnership. We are free to examine more deeply what binds us together.

The compatibility between Lesley and AIB in regard to their missions and values has allowed the potential that was perceived at the time of the merger to flower. Lesley has helped AIB turn its vision outward to the nonprofit sector and community-based organizations. Since the merger, AIB has been examining the world of visual arts with an expanded sense of community service and connection.

Lesley's citizens have been broadened by the addition of a strong, professional arts culture. Students are at first surprised, then beguiled, by how art can be a fundamental force, a means, or a goal. Art is more than just the product. It is about the journey and the discovery. "The goal is always nebulous. We keep pushing, trying, falling down, and pulling ourselves up again... Art is a game—a joyous game. Play is important. We strive—we never arrive." (Lanza, 2008, p. 63)

Art education is profound, and it deals with reality. It is not about making pretty things or about elevating the masses. Depending on the arena, art's aims can be very different indeed. Philosophical differences in the cultures and expectations of the communities within the university have been used to engage in discussions about the meaning of those differences, leading to clearer understandings and to better education. Early on, the university brought together its faculty from the two undergraduate schools to explore and deepen the "foundation experience." Ideally, the foundation moment never stops: the basics are always relevant, and what is relevant becomes basic. Artists, as learners, are neotenous by nature: curious children in the world. So, if artists are constantly responding and growing, what are they responding to? How do we help our students to stay curious, to grow, and to speak about our world? How do we kindle the spark?

At Lesley, because of its students' wide range of vocational diversity in approaching the study of art, the mixture plays out experientially. To illustrate, one can say that too many students today are focused inward. A typical art student might come to class bringing the idea that art depends totally on talent. This is similar to the notion of ranking people by IQ. Curiously, Alfred Binet designed the IQ test to identify students who were not profiting from Paris schools and who had need of different educational programs to help them (Dweck, 2006). He believed that there were major differences in people's backgrounds and in the ways they learn. Binet did not profess that an individual's intelligence was fixed and unchangeable. Ironically, a sector of the public is wedded to the doctrine that "smarts" are either there or not there, an idea that totally undermines potential and growth. People who believe in a fixed mindset spend a lot of their time trying to prove their already existent abilities. They arrive with the assumption that they must already be artists. Afraid of taking risks and fearing failure, they learn through imitation and repetition (Wertschek, 2007). They seek praise and aspire, merely, to hone their craft, resisting new learning experiences. Unfortunately, society perpetuates the myth of artists being specially endowed creatures who hibernate in garrets. Something more, something different, is needed.

In response to our changing world, the first year in college must engage learners on many levels—addressing sensibilities in ethics and world citizenship, practicalities in art and design skills and working skills, and competencies in visual and verbal language, research, and moving an idea (Keathley, 2007). While skill *is* important, so is the communication of ideas and feelings. Reflection and maturity provide evidence that talent is not the only factor by far. Education must deal with the whole person and the whole picture:

> As the field of visual production has expanded, so too has our approach to educating young artists. It is no longer sufficient to focus on teaching our students a prescribed set of technical skills or aesthetic sensibilities. Today, our goal is to provide aspiring artists with the capacity to think beyond the perceived boundaries of any one discipline, and to approach the process of making art as both an intellectual and an expressive pursuit. As educators, we must train practitioners who are creative, resourceful, and responsive—responsive to both the outside world and their own values. (Grossman & Steck, 2007)

Working with a richer mix of students has ignited an examination of what it means to be a student in the arts and in the world. The university has embarked on a journey of exploration and experimentation to discover what questions need to be asked and answered.

AIB and Lesley have entered into a more capacious environment. In bringing together their varied student populations, they have created a forum where students can respectfully observe one another's needs and sensibilities. Given the scope of our creative programs, we have a potential for philosophical growth that we are only beginning to envision. Perhaps this is one of the more significant transformations that emerged from our collaborations—creating a world of possibility where we can openly examine the passions, desires, and mindsets that people bring with them to the arts.

Now, when we stir in students whose majors are not in the studio arts, an interesting dialogue starts to emerge. If one has had very little experience in making art before coming to an art school, then it is sensible to approach a class as an atrium of possibilities. With nothing to prove, a student can engage in the same art-making pursuits with an open mind or growth mindset (Dweck, 2006). Not only does this create a wonderfully provocative mixture, but it creates a delightfully unexpected and expanded potential for achievement as well. The combination of adventure and ability is a strong tonic for all of our programs. Such a paradigm fosters multiple connections across disciplines, societies, and cultures. Emotive and synaptic associations embrace. What happens when the tent is expansive enough to include visual artists, philosophers, teachers, therapists, writers, actors, dancers, and maybe musicians? The music of composer Modest Mussorgsky painted *Pictures at an Exhibition*, and art can sing, art can move, art can tell a story. Art reflects the world, and art is in Lesley.

Throughout this adventure, we have found synergies; we have collaborated; we have transformed ourselves. Our university world has grown larger and richer. We have become more inquisitive. Together, we have created something new and different.

REFERENCES

Barry, J. (2007a). Liminal zones/coursing flows. In S. Yard (Ed.), *A dynamic equilibrium: In pursuit of public terrain.* San Diego, CA: Installation Gallery.

Barry, J. (2007b). The space that art makes. In S. Yard (Ed.), *A dynamic equilibrium: In pursuit of public terrain.* San Diego, CA: Installation Gallery.

Davidson, R. A. (2007). The School of Practical Art Catalogue, 1918 1919. Course Catalogs Art Institute of Boston, Cambridge: The Lesley University Archives. Lesley University, Cambridge, MA.

Dweck, C. S. (2006). *Mindset.* New York, NY: Random House.

Evans, E. K. (1955). *Something different.* Boston, MA: D. C. Heath & Company.

Fertitta, A. (February 24, 1999). Report on substantive change. Report to NASAD submitted by The Art Institute of Boston. Boston, MA: The Art Institute of Boston.

Grossman, A., & Steck, S. (February 2007). *Designing a foundation program for the 21st century.* Panel Presentation at the College Art Association, New York, NY.

Keathley, G., & Towers, J. (October 2007). Repositioning core curricula in foundation. *Rethinking the Core* (pp. 25-27). Parsons the New School for Design. AICAD Symposium. New York, NY: Pratt Institute.

Lanza, J. (2008). *Figures in environments: Course manual.* Boston, MA: The Art Institute of Boston.

Lesley College Mission Statement. (2009). *Lesley faculty handbook.* Cambridge, MA: Lesley College.

Mission. (1997 1998). *The Art Institute of Boston faculty handbook.* Boston: The Art Institute of Boston.

Pacy, A. (April 15, 2007). Historical note from finding aid. The School of Practical Art Catalogue, 1918 1919. Course Catalogs, Art Institute of Boston. Cambridge, MA: The Lesley University Archives. Lesley University, Cambridge, MA.

Steck, S. (March 31, 2009). *The de-skilling of art.* Presentation at the Art Institute of Boston. Boston, MA.

Wertschek, J. (October 25 27, 2007). Teaching to the student. *Rethinking the core.* EmilyCarr Institute of Art & Design, Vancouver. AICAD Symposium. New York, NY: Pratt Institute.

CHAPTER THIRTEEN

The Master of Fine Arts at Lesley University

JUDITH BARRY, MFA
STEVEN CRAMER, MFA
JANET POCOROBBA, MFA

Lesley University houses two master of fine arts programs—the Low-Residency MFA Program in Creative Writing and the Low-Residency MFA Program in the Visual Arts. The Visual Arts Program inaugurated its first residency in the winter of 2003, and the Creative Writing Program welcomed its first entering class a few months later, in the summer. These two programs are like siblings: in most ways they behave differently, but they share a family name and bear some resemblances.

Creative writing and visual arts programs follow the studio arts model of teaching and learning. The assumption that underpins both is that a fresh mode of artistic mastery is its own justification. Both programs, then, focus on teaching students how to turn demonstrable promise into settled—or perhaps more realistically and usefully, *un*settled—accomplishment.

Both programs also share a viewpoint regarding, for lack of a better term, the "social utility" of the visual and verbal arts. In his celebrated elegy "In Memory of W. B. Yeats," W. H. Auden (1979) famously wrote that "poetry makes nothing happen" (p. 82). Taken out of context, this mordant claim—an artist consigning to inconsequence the very art he practices—seems a kind of self-abnegating nihilism. But Auden makes the further assertion, not so much counter as complementary, that "[poetry] survives/In the valley of its saying…[a] way of happening, a mouth" (p. 82). Auden's full articulation praises the true artist's tough-minded and disabused idealism about his or her art. This open-eyed self-reliance both programs seek to instill in their students.

This chapter tells the story of how two distinct "ways of happening" happened. Judith Barry wrote "The MFA in Fine or Visual Arts" and "The MFA at AIB"; the remainder of the chapter was written by Steven Cramer and Janet Pocorobba.

THE MFA IN FINE OR VISUAL ARTS

What constitutes a great MFA program in fine or visual arts is continuously evolving, and it is up to each MFA program to respond to how the artists and students in the program understand their MFA education and to aid them in making the best use of their MFA degrees.

Hence, each semester in the MFA program at AIB, we explore a variety of issues having to do with this question, both as a faculty and in an informal way with our student advisees. The question of the evolving MFA circulates around several issues that have to do with our mission statement:

- What is art? As art becomes more transdisciplinary and more global in its reach, how are the definitions changing that circulate around notions of art? For instance, can new forms of art practice now be seen, as some advocate, as a form of research and development for the culture at large? If so, then should we ensure that our students receive grounding in research methodologies?
- Can art be taught, and if so, how? Further, what do our artists need from an MFA program, and how can we best provide it?
- What is the place of a skill set or craft skills within a postindustrial, postmodern, and global art world?
- How can we give our artists access to useful strategies for making productive lives out of creative impulses?

- What does an MFA degree mean in today's art world and beyond? What privileges will an MFA confer on the holder of this degree?

I will put these questions into perspective through the lens of my own history. I began showing my work in the international art world when I was still a student in the late 1970s. In those days the first question in the preceding list was the one most debated by MFA students. In the late 1970s, an MFA education was much less expensive, and as it was well before the mid-1980s art world boom, every art student knew that being an artist was a lifestyle choice infrequently associated with stardom, glamour, or money. The dialogue that circulated then concerned issues of how something might take on the status of being called art as well as simultaneously the questions of both if and then how art might be taught. Was being an artist something that you could actually learn in school? As a young artist I learned as much from my peers as I did from my teachers. I think that is still true today.

John Baldassari, then teaching at California Arts in Los Angeles and building on the legacy of Black Mountain College, used to say that he didn't think art could in fact be taught, but that he as a teacher could make a place where art could happen. He also said that if he had seen art that he had liked, he wouldn't have felt the necessity to make his own. Hence his famous quip, "I will not make any more boring art." Baldassari and artist Michael Asher were at the forefront of the "poststudio practice" debate that came to be associated with the rise of postmodernism in art, but the debate has a much longer history within the realm of alternative art practices, beginning with Dada at the beginning of the 20th century and continuing up through various mostly European art movements, finally taking hold in the United States in the late 1950s with *Happenings* and other forms of art that eschewed painting, sculpture, and other traditional forms.

This craft debate, most recently referred to as "skilling and de-skilling" in John Roberts's (2007) useful book of the same title is still very much with us. However, it continuously evolves in relation to the social circumstances of each brief epoch. At stake is the philosophical question, which must be continuously addressed by every artist, What does it mean to be an artist, today, right now? How artists ask and then answer this question affects the work that they will make as well as the kind of art world they will inhabit. In our MFA program we strive to be transdisciplinary, with a strong recognition that the skills sets artists need evolve in relation to their artistic practices and may even be outside the realm of what is currently considered art. Hence, we encourage our artists to learn the skill sets they need with the recognition that this is an ongoing process. Further, we encourage our artists to use the art-making strategies they have acquired over the course of their lives creatively within all their endeavors, as we recognize that the model of art practice, as a way of thinking, does have value in today's economic climate. All of this determines what our artists need to learn during their MFA education as well what they need to learn in the art worlds they will inhabit locally, nationally, and internationally.

The second and third questions in the list that follows represent more recent issues that arguably began to circulate in the mid-1980s as the art world was booming.

- How can we give our artists access to useful strategies for making productive lives out of creative impulses?
- What does an MFA degree mean in today's art world and beyond? What privileges will an MFA confer on the holder of this degree?

After the boom in the art market in the 1980s, art making as a career suddenly seemed like a viable aspiration, and there was exponential growth in the number of MFA programs offering the MFA in fine or visual arts. Increasingly, to be considered for a full-time, tenured-track college-level teaching job in art departments, the MFA, as the terminal degree in the field, was required. While an MFA is an enabling tool for competing for a teaching job, the main reason most artists seek an MFA degree is that they want to take their work to the next level. The focus and intensity of an MFA program allows them to do this while they are earning an advanced degree.

Additionally, art making in one form or another, including and alongside the MFA, can now be seen as an alternative to working in corporate culture. For a brief moment, in 2004, the MFA was considered by some MBA programs and, touted as such, as "the new MBA." This phenomenon is perhaps best described under the rubric of "the rise of corporate creative," for while the *Harvard Business Review* took these claims very seriously, there is very little mention of the MFA as the new MBA among MFA programs in fine or visual art. But perhaps this moment is now to be short-lived, as some U.S. institutions have begun to offer studio-based PhD programs as a way to recognize artists as well as train them to bring social science research methodologies into their art practices. This would be one way of legitimating what artists perhaps already perform as the research and design of the culture at large. While this studio-based doctorate is still in its infancy in the United States, current thinking about the status of an MFA is somewhat embroiled in the debate about how this new model of art education will transform the landscape of the "art world."

THE MFA AT AIB

The master of fine arts program in Visual Arts at the Art Institute of Boston at Lesley University is dedicated to encouraging the creation of an artistic practice that sustains growth and exploration not only while the student is enrolled in the MFA program, but over a lifetime of creative work. As a low-residency MFA program, it proposes a fundamentally different model of education than the traditional MFA residency program. While students in AIB-Lesley's MFA program are full-time, they perform their semester's work in their home communities, often far from Boston and other large metropolitan areas. Our program encourages students to build on their experience in their home communities as it prepares them to enter the art world; however, they choose to define that world as they integrate their MFA experience into the fabric of their daily lives. During the two-year 60-credit program, they attend five 10-day residencies, work with nationally or internationally known mentors, and formulate their own positions about how to best participate in the contemporary art worlds.[20] Hence, the disconnection that is often felt by recently graduated MFA students as they leave school and struggle to define themselves out of school is mitigated by our very different approach to the MFA process at AIB-Lesley.

The low-residency model at AIB-Lesley was proposed by Tony Apesos in his first year as chair of AIB's Fine Arts Department in 1993. As he stated:

> I presented to then Dean Bob Simon a proposal for a low-residency MFA program. After my own experiences in getting my master's and from my knowledge of other artists' experiences, I believed that there was a need for an approach to graduate art education that valued the vision and aesthetic of each individual student, and I realized that AIB had the facilities for such a program. (A. Apesos, personal communication, April 15, 2009)

While there was interest in 1993, this type of program did not receive serious consideration until after the AIB and Lesley merger, when Dean Stan Trecker reintroduced it in 2001. It was of particular interest then, as Lesley has a great deal of experience both with low-residency models and with alternative forms of graduate education. In January of 2003, Tony Apesos, as director of the program, and faculty members Shelia Gallagher, Jane Marshing, and Tim Norris welcomed the first 12 students into the program. I began my position full-time in March 2005.

Since I have been at AIB-Lesley the program has grown to its maximum size of 72 full-time students, and has now graduated 127 students. The faculty has also grown to between 14 and 16 members, depending on enrollment, and is a mix of nationally and internationally known artists. Each semester I organize an Art Talks series to coincide with the residency and invite internationally

---

20 I use the plural here as there are many art worlds now, not just one. Judith Barry

known artists and curators to come to AIB-Lesley to lecture and to work with our graduate students. Recent notable visitors include Xu Bing, Marilyn Minter, Andreas Fogarasi, Ellen Harvey, Dan Graham, Barbara London, Adam McEwen, Dike Blair, Rebecca Morris, Barry Schwabsky, Jacqueline Humphries, and Cory Arcangel, among many others.

The Art Institute of Boston MFA program is transdisciplinary and pluralistic: all approaches to visual art are considered valid fields of exploration, including some that would not usually be considered art. Artists working in any visual medium may participate in the program, including painting, photography, sculpture, installation, video, new media, graphic design, animation, and bookmaking. Artists are free to explore new ways of combining these mediums into new forms and methods for producing art.

The flexibility of our program makes this range of inquiry possible, and the nature of contemporary art and society makes it imperative. In a community where diverse ideas, artistic visions, and technical knowledge are embraced, cross-fertilization is inevitable. For example, students who enter the program with a background in photography may explore the use of drawing or painting in conjunction with their photographic images, or painters may wish to utilize computer technologies to enhance their image making. Perhaps more important, our interdisciplinary, pluralistic community of artists is a place where assumptions can be challenged, revised, or strengthened. Our MFA students push the boundaries of their art-making practices and deepen their artistic vision.

All students develop an individualized plan for studio and academic work in consultation with their faculty advisor during each residency. They accomplish this plan during the six months of their semester's work in their home community, before returning to the next 10-day intensive residency. This self-defined curriculum lets our students relate their academic work directly to their own interests, including bringing in material from nonart fields. Most important, they accomplish these goals within the context of their lives. For the second year in a row, as I write this, a student artist in our MFA program has been awarded a Joan Mitchell Scholarship Award. This is quite an accomplishment for a program that was so recently launched.

As a way to illustrate the breadth of the program, here are a few profiles of our recent alums.

PATRICK LOEHR MFA, 2009

"My AIB education has given me a model for how I will pursue my artistic practice from now on." Loehr enrolled at AIB on the advice of a friend and alum of the program. A self-described, "self-taught artist" who has written and illustrated two popular children's books, he found the formal art education that he was seeking in AIB's MFA program. "Being at AIB was the best educational experience that I've ever had, and it was integral in getting hired at my new job." From self-taught artist to chair of the Department of Art and New Media Design at the Community College of Aurora, Patrick Loehr has come a long way.

"I try to deal with my students in the same respectful and open way that my AIB professors worked with me," said Loehr. He cites the programs ("…impressive faculty made up of outstanding artists and scholars") as a major benefit of studying at AIB. "When I walk into my classes now, I think about the excitement and knowledge that my professors brought, and it inspires me to bring the same to my students," he said.

ANNE BAUMGARTNER MFA, 2010

A student travels across the country to find her ideal arts community.

For Anne Baumgartner, being at a school with "amazing people, rigorous standards—and in a great city for the arts" was entirely worth the trip to Boston from her home in Seattle. Baumgartner came to AIB determined to get all that she could out of her studies, and it has paid off. "Being at AIB has given me an opportunity to immerse in my studio work. I've been challenged and pushed in all ways from both faculty and peers," she said.

Baumgartner saw her vision and work expand when pushed to consider new perspectives in group discussions. The program's strong emphasis on critique and mentoring created a space where each voice became a valuable asset for growth. "The residency atmosphere is intense, with nonstop honest input and feedback. The combined voices of my advisors, studio mentors, and classmates have brought big changes in my work. I've never worked harder."

JANE RAINWATER MFA, 2007

"I ask questions with my art that will challenge people's thinking." Jane Rainwater's art gets attention. "Curators at galleries where I show my installations tell me that it draws in more people than they have had before." The installation that draws people in? It's her AIB thesis project, *The Golden Pawnshop,* a collection of objects gilded in gold on display in the façade of a pawnshop. Jane has shown the work, which she says is ever evolving, in multiple shows since graduating from AIB. "It's a display of the dark side of beauty. We think gold is perfect and valuable, but once it's in a pawnshop, all of the sentimental value is gone."

The art world has certainly noticed the value of Rainwater's work. A 2009 recipient of the Radius Artist Award from the Aldrich Museum of Contemporary Art, Rainwater said, "I never would have done the work I'm doing if I hadn't gone to graduate school. AIB's interdisciplinary approach and outstanding faculty opened me up to reach new places in my art."

These short profiles, three very different stories, demonstrate the range of our MFA students. Recently, two more of our students received the prestigious Joan Mitchell Scholarship Award. These $20,000 grants are given to graduating artists to aid them in their transition from grad school into the art world. Competiton for the award is very intense, and our students successfully competed with top students from residency MFA programs in the United States. While there is not enough room in this chapter to write about each of our 127 alums, all of their stories are testaments to how a flexible structure for delivering an MFA can achieve remarkable results.

THE LOW-RESIDENCY MFA PROGRAM IN CREATIVE WRITING

Before the birth and maturity of the Internet, you could count on one hand the number of low-residency MFA programs in creative writing in the United States. In 2001, when the proposal for such a program at Lesley University received accreditation from the New England Association of Schools and Colleges, roughly 15 analogous programs existed. In 2003, when Lesley's MFA in Creative Writing welcomed its first entering class of 22 students, there were about 20 MFA creative writing programs that used the low-residency model. It would take all fingers on at least eight hands to count the number of these programs today in the United States, Canada, and England.

Clearly, to survive, let alone thrive, in such a competitive field, a program needs not just some distinguishing features, but a distinctive ethos. Lesley's program has both. First among these features is, of course, the distinction of its faculty: passionate writers and teachers who produce their own stunning work in five genres: fiction, nonfiction, poetry, writing for stage and screen, and writing for young people. Second, Lesley's program is the only one of its kind situated in, not just near, a major American literary city (some would argue that Boston is the major American literary city). Third, Lesley's program presupposes, and makes concrete in its curriculum, the notion that all writers are "interdisciplinarians"; that is, by nature and by habit, they need consistently to look up from the page in order to infuse that page with the writer's most essential technique: life experience.

The program's ethos, while less easily quantified, is no less specific. To borrow from Seamus Heaney's (2002) brilliant essay, in any rigorous creative writing program, "a fair and honest estimate of the student's gifts—good or bad—has to be communicated, but the communication must be done with respect and a care for the emotional tissues" (pp. 76-77). Good writers know they must not settle for anything but their best, but they also need the spirit to put one word in front of the other, for a lifetime. Every faculty member who teaches in Lesley's program understands this exasperating but life- and art-sustaining paradox. In the residencies and distance-learning semesters, the Lesley program focuses on the individual student's developing gifts, particular craft challenges, and aesthetic aspirations. All the faculty mentors provide useful critique that is artistically rigorous, and often painful for the student to hear, but never personally ruthless. What may be initially painful to hear gets metabolized, as it were, by the self-reliant apprentice artist, building and toning the aesthetic muscles. And that's how the aspiring artist grows and the work gets strong. As one of our faculty members recently wrote in an e-mail to a very gifted but somewhat defensive student, "Criticism means I care."

So, obviously, careful, challenging feedback from distinguished writers and dedicated teachers is crucial to any aspiring writer's growth. But what else feeds an apprentice's writing? No less obviously, to the writer who wants to engage in art, not just self-expression, a diet of challenging yet nourishing reading is crucial. At Lesley, students engage in creative reading as well as creative writing (art breeds art), and they are encouraged—no, required—to read on the edges of their seats. As the poet Marvin Bell (1991) has written, "The writer is looking for what he or she can use…The writer goes slowly, and doubles back" (p. 221).

Less obviously, however, something individual and often eccentric also feeds a writer's work or, as is often the case with the graduate student, that writer's aspirations to work in a literary field after graduation. The Lesley program's interdisciplinary component honors just how widely that "something" can vary. Whether it's a publishing internship, learning how to conduct insightful author interviews, reviewing books, teaching workshops, researching subjects relevant to a student's work-in-progress, or simply getting one's hands into clay, our students enhance their ongoing writing, or their aspirations for future writing careers, through this unique component.

Lesley's program now has well over 100 alumni and approximately 100 continuing students. Tom Kealey's The Creative Writing MFA Handbook (2005) named the Lesley program "among the more distinguished low-residency programs" (p. 53). What specific work went into creating the program, and what decisions shaped its trajectory?

HISTORY OF THE PROGRAM

Developed by Lesley University's provost and the Graduate School of Arts and Social Sciences (GSASS), Lesley's master of fine arts in creative writing envisioned four genres of concentration; fiction, nonfiction, poetry, and writing for young people, as well as an interdisciplinary component. The Massachusetts Board of Education approved the school's proposal in late 2001. Administrative changes in the university—resulting in the decision to house the program in the GSASS Division of Interdisciplinary Inquiry—and a prolonged search for a program director delayed implementation for just over a year. In January 2003, the newly hired program director, Steven Cramer, began to flesh out the following programmatic concepts:

- the low-residency delivery system involving one-on-one mentoring via semester-long distance learning
- specific curriculum for two annual residencies that would form the basis of the distance-learning semesters
- a structure and faculty to support and develop the program's unique interdisciplinary studies (IS) component

In addition to these curricular elements, between January and the first residency in August 2003, the program director hired 15 distinguished writers as teaching faculty and, along with the assistant director for Student Services, Jana Van der Veer, wrote promotional materials, including brochures; advertising copy; and a viable website in order to attract qualified applicants to take a chance on an untried program.

The program faculty reviewed applications for an inaugural August 2003 residency and fall 2003 semester while developing a coherent, seminar-based residency curriculum and a distance-learning structure. Twenty-two students enrolled for the August residency: nine days of workshops, seminars, individual study-plan conferences, and panels; and presentation by faculty and two visiting writers— Robert Pinsky and Maurice Sendak.

The program grew with each residency and semester and, in January 2005, graduated 19 of those original 22 students. For the January 2009 residency and spring 2009 semester, we had an entering class of 22, and a total of 95 students and 31 faculty. For the June fall 2009 residency and semester, the program welcomed an entering class of 31 students, chosen from among 130 applicants.

CURRENT CONTEXT

While the fundamentals of the program have remained constant, many spontaneous discoveries and changes have developed along the way. Currently, there are two nine-day residencies, one in early January and one in late June. The residency curriculum has developed both in complexity and rigor. Crucially, the MFA writing faculty has grown into a diverse, distinguished, and unusually international group of passionate teacher-practitioners.

In July 2006, Janet Pocorobba, half-time assistant coordinator, was hired as core faculty with administrative duties to take on all aspects of the IS component. In January 2008, the MFA program added a fifth writing genre, writing for stage and screen (WSS). One and a half years into the new track, 14 students enrolled in the fall 2009 semester. We have incorporated films and staged readings into our evening faculty events, and have held panels on fiction-to-film adaptation and WSS publication. In 2009, three further residency innovations were developed: the Interdisciplinary Fair; the writer's toolbox sessions; and Your First Foot Forward, an innovative publishing event.

PURPOSE AND GOALS

A master of fine arts in creative writing is recognized by the Association of Writers and Writing Programs (AWP) as the terminal degree for the creative writing practitioner and teacher. The Lesley MFA program in creative writing prepares students to become active literary professionals through a rigorous course that emphasizes:

- The development of craft skills in the student's chosen writing genre
- Students' capacity to think and write critically about their chosen literary genre
- Experiential knowledge in working as a public writer: teaching, publishing, reviewing, etc.
- Expansion of students' abilities as writers through an interdisciplinary component that encourages experimentation and innovation

DESCRIPTION OF PROGRAM STRUCTURE

In a program designed for intensive residencies, one-on-one mentoring, and a wide range of interdisciplinary studies projects, conventional course-based syllabi cannot adequately support the learning model. Rather, three key components constitute the MFA program's academic structure, requirements, and policies: (1) the MFA Low-Residency Program in Creative Writing Handbook; (2) the individualized study-plan contracts students prepare with their MFA writing faculty mentors and IS advisors; and (3) the residency seminar descriptions and required readings.

Therefore, rather than relying on the classroom, the program is better described as a learning community, consisting of a balance between community-oriented residencies twice a year and six-month distance-learning semesters. At residencies, students have the support and instruction of faculty, both formally and informally, as well as fruitful interactions with fellow students in other genres, graduating students, and program staff. Thus, the distance-learning semester of one-on-one mentoring is regularly "refueled" by the experience of the intensive group work of the residencies.

Residencies

The residency curriculum includes seminars for first-, second-, third-, and fourth-semester cohorts; genre seminars reserved for all students working in a given writing concentration; elective seminars; graduating student seminars; faculty readings and events; presentations by visiting faculty; and intensive writing workshops. Workshops meet in large and small group formats over the course of the same nine days.

Before arriving on campus, students are paired with faculty mentors who lead the workshop discussions of the students' writing and meet in conference to create individualized, nine-credit study plans for the distance-learning semester. These study plans tailor creative writing submissions to the student's particular aspirations and challenges; incorporate rigorous reading lists of books to support and accelerate the student's artistic growth; and require a series of craft annotations (short critical papers) that emphasize literary analysis from a writer's perspective. Students' three-credit interdisciplinary study projects, each of which also requires a detailed study-plan contract, cover a wide range of projects, from internships to independent research.

In the fourth semester, students earn 12 credits focusing on their creative writing, creative thesis, and preparation of their graduating seminar. Following the fourth semester, graduating MFA candidates return for a portion of a fifth residency. During this residency, as a final requirement for graduation, MFA candidates present the graduating student seminar they prepared. This presentation, a noncredit graduating requirement, is monitored by an MFA writing faculty member. Immediately after the seminar, the MFA writing faculty monitor evaluates the presentation in a brief conversation with the student.

Residency Curriculum

Whereas many low-residency programs rely on an ad hoc mixture of large group faculty lectures, team-taught writing workshops, and visiting presentations, the Lesley program has opted for a system of small group meetings that are logistically complex but pedagogically rich.

Residency seminars. Lesley's program uses a system of tiered seminars in the first semester through the fourth, which offer students increasingly sophisticated techniques for mastering the writer's craft. First-semester seminars emphasize first principles of the writer's toolbox. Second-semester seminars focus on revision and more complex ways of thinking about the writer's craft. In their third residencies, students encounter yet more subtle techniques and approaches, and begin to prepare for their thesis semester. Fourth-semester students move to more speculative and more practical topics, preparing for a semester in which they concentrate on their thesis and their graduating seminar.

In all residencies, the craft curriculum incorporates a multi-genre approach. For example, the course the Art of Juxtaposition investigates its subject via poems, a novel excerpt, a section from a play, and a picture book. Genre-specific seminars allow poets to explore their art with other poets, fiction writers with fiction writers, and so on. In this way, the residencies provide both cross-fertilization among the five genres and appropriate focus within a single concentration. The residency structure of seminars also recognizes the qualitative difference between a student's first and second year, both in the first- and second-year genre seminars and in meetings with program staff and third- and fourth-semester students to discuss the graduating requirements and procedures for completing the creative thesis and graduating seminar.

Workshops. The writing workshops are the hub of the residency experience. In large group workshops overseen by at least two faculty members, students receive workshop criticism from their peers and from their assigned faculty mentor, but also have the opportunity to see how other faculty members teach workshop. Small group workshops (the MFA faculty mentor and his or her distance-learning students only) take place later in the residency, and tend to provide discussion of students' more inchoate works in progress.

Faculty readings and visiting writers. Evening readings by MFA writing faculty and visiting writers form a vital part of the MFA program's curriculum. Faculty often read from early drafts of works in progress, literary performance itself becoming a teaching strategy. Typically, two visiting writers are invited to each residency, and the program works to ensure that, over the long term, all five genres benefit equally from the fresh input of visiting faculty. Visitors are especially accomplished and celebrated writers in their field. In the years since Pinsky and Sendak joined our first residency, our visitors have included writers such as M. T. Anderson, Andre Dubus III, Louise Glück, Vivian Gornick, Robie H. Harris, Marie Howe, Lois Lowry, Sue Miller, and Tom Perrotta.

Two special residency events. In the June 2009 residency, we inaugurated a series of 50-minute writer's toolbox" sessions over lunch and dessert in which we invited program alumni to teach some of their skills as a writer-in-the-world in such sessions as "Queries and Hooks," "How to Start a Lit Mag," "Conferences and Residencies," "Websites and Blogging," "Freelancing Tips," and "Creating Community," among others. There were eight back-to-back sessions that students chose as electives. Each session, experiential and skill-based, gave alumni the unique opportunity to mentor current MFA students and pass on what they have learned, what they wish they had known as students, and what it's like out there in the "real" writing world.

These sessions culminated in a new event with editors and agents called "Your First Foot Forward," in which students had a chance to read a brief passage aloud to an editor or agent in the room. The agent or editor responded to the student's work from a professional viewpoint: Would I read more? Do I want to know what happens? What grabbed me or didn't? Listeners in the room also benefited from the feedback. The event impressively achieved its goal, which was to create a forum for students to participate in the publishing process in a more hands-on way than merely attending a talk or panel.

THE DISTANCE-LEARNING SEMESTER

Course of study. To codify the distance-learning work students do for the Creative Writing and the Craft and Reflection courses, faculty and students collaborate on detailed study plans that are developed during the residency and submitted to the program office. Students entering their fourth semester complete a separate thesis study plan. During the distance-learning semester, students make four submissions of creative writing and craft annotations to their faculty mentor, along with a detailed cover letter that reflects on their artistic progress.

Interdisciplinary studies. Interdisciplinary projects include interviewing well-known authors (the results of which often find publication; four or five having appeared in the AWP Writers Chronicle, courtesy of the students' talent and persistence); teaching in public or private schools; designing writing workshops for special populations; taking courses or designing independent work in women's studies, psychology, editing, theater, and art history; and taking studio art courses at the Art Institute of Boston. More and more, our students are finding teaching assistantships at Lesley, or are using their skills in the colleges and schools where they teach.

As the IS component has grown or expanded, new kinds of classes are being offered that focus on ever more subtle and specific writing tools and techniques. The Art of the English Sentence, a hands-on elective seminar on diction and syntax, has been wildly popular. Two more seminars that focus on storytelling and how to develop the writer's powers of observation, imagination, curiosity, and the subconscious have been added. Further, a more in-depth publishing track promises to grow out of the interdisciplinary studies component.

At the June 2009 residency, we held our first Interdisciplinary Fair, in which students, faculty, and staff showcased their work in other genres, forms, and fields. During one afternoon of the residency, poster sessions, talks, presentations, and performances filled the Stebbins classroom building and all participants had a fresh chance to find out "What IS possible!" as one student said. Booths exhibited paintings, prints, photographs, a knitting project, and a handmade book. Talks and presentations included poetry and play readings, a mini writing lesson, yoga poses, a slide show, and a musical demonstration. The event spoke eloquently to how the unique interdisciplinary component of the Lesley MFA Creative Writing Program has come to be one of its most defining features.

WHERE WE ARE AND WHO WE'RE BECOMING

Ultimately, any program proves itself by the talent of the faculty and students it attracts, and by the work that they do. Awards and honors earned by the MFA writing faculty would take up a few pages, but it's worth including some of the most prestigious: the Commonwealth Prize for Poetry; numerous Guggenheim Fellowships and National Endowment for the Arts Fellowships; Canada's Governor General's Award for Literature; the Elliott Norton Award; the Whiting Award; the Koret Foundation Jewish Book Prize; the Lamda Literary Award; the Printz Honor Book Award; the *Los Angeles Times* Book Prize; Booklist Editor's Choice Award; Parent's Choice Media Award; finalist citations for the National Book Award, the National Book Critics Circle Award, Hollywood's Next Success, and Disney ABC's Screenwriting Fellowship; and citations as "notable," "best," and bestselling books by the American Library Association, the *New York Times*, and the *Washington Post*.

But at Lesley, distinguished writers must be distinguished teachers, and the program they teach for is only as good as the learning environment it creates. Here, it's the program's students who should have their say:

- "The individual conferences with my faculty pinpointed exactly what I needed to work on."
- "The multi-genre and interdisciplinary design is what I love about Lesley's MFA program.
- "The effect the residencies have on my motivation is immeasurable. I don't ever want to leave when I am there, and when I come home I feel so charged to do my best work."
- "The workshops are extremely informative. The collective approach—all of our voices contributing—is a dynamic I find very engaging."
- "Meeting with fellow students, listening to inspiring and thoughtful talks, going to readings, and talking with faculty make the week so fulfilling for me."

Finally, it is the achievements of a program's alumni that best testify to its success. After six years, graduates of the MFA Program in Creative Writing have begun to make their mark in the literary world. Six have published books, and many more have published work in magazines such as the *Gettysburg Review,* the *Harvard Review, the Massachusetts Review,* the *North American Review,* the *Seneca Review,* and *Slate.* Lesley graduates have received major honors, such as a St. Botolph Club Emerging Artist Grant in Literature; a creative nonfiction prize sponsored by Columbia: A Journal of Literature and Art; and a "notable" essay citation in Best American Essays 2007. Others have started small-press or other publishing ventures, and many are now teaching creative writing.

The University's Mission and the Program's Mission

As articulated in its mission statement, "Lesley University is committed to active learning, scholarly research, critical inquiry, and diverse forms of artistic practice through close mentoring relationships among students, faculty, and practitioners in the field. Lesley prepares graduates with the knowledge, skill, understanding, and ethical judgment to be catalysts who shape a more just, humane, and sustainable world." How does this mission square with the axiom that the true artist's first responsibility must always be to the materials of his or her art?

Lesley University's merger with the Art Institute of Boston, with its own MFA Program in the Visual Arts, and the parallel development of the MFA Program in Creative Writing, raise in new ways this vexed question of the role the artist plays in the larger culture. What William Carlos Williams (1967) famously wrote about poetry applies to all art: "it is difficult/to get the news from poems/yet men die miserably every day/for lack/of what is found there" (pp. 161-162). This qualified "two cheers for art" testifies that creativity can only indirectly shape a more humane world. Less famously, in a reading he gave at Harvard in 1951, Williams also said: "if it ain't a pleasure, it ain't a poem." It's the miraculous paradox of serious, even tragic, art that its audience enjoys it, even considers it "fun." Should a university teach and offer advanced degrees in the making of something that's fun? Yes, and three cheers for that.

IN CONCLUSION

Lesley's two MFA programs differ greatly in practice, embracing those differences while endorsing a common premise: the purpose of artists and writers is simply (simply!) to make art and literature. Whether those works "make anything happen" is for others to determine. But, of course, art and writing that are true will register a change in the world. Without the self-renewing labor and pleasure that produces new art and literature, a culture loses fundamental ways it sees and says. It is rendered deaf, mute, and blind.

REFERENCES

Auden, W. H. (1979). In memory of W. B. Yeats. In E. Mendelson (Ed.). *Selected poems.* New York, NY: Random House, 1979.

Bell, M. (1991). The technique of rereading. In J. McCorkle (Ed.). *Conversant essays: Contemporary poets on poetry.* Wayne, MI: Wayne State University Press.

Heaney, S. (2002). *Finder keepers: Selected prose, 1971 2001.* New York, NY: Farrar, Straus & Giroux.

Kealey, T. (2005). *The creative writing MFA handbook: A guide for prospective graduate students.* London, England: Continuum International Publishing Group.

Roberts, J. (2007). *The intangibilities of form: Skill and deskilling in art after the readymade.* London, England, and New York, NY: Verso.

Williams, W. C. (1967). *Pictures from Brueghel and other poems.* New York, NY: New Directions Press.

Williams, W. C. (1951/1978). *The poet's voice: Poets reading aloud and commenting upon their works.* Reading at Harvard College, December 4, 1951: The President and Fellows of Harvard College. Cambridge, MA.

CHAPTER FOURTEEN

Community-Embedded Practice:
Lesley University's Approach to Professional
Preparation

Marcia Bromfield, PhD
Mariagnese Cattaneo, PhD, LMHC, ATR-BC
Harriet Deane, MBA, MEd
Margery Staman Miller, EdD
Eleanor Roffman, EdD

INTRODUCTION

Throughout Lesley's history, the dominant pedagogical approach has been one that weaves together theory and practice. The Lesley University mission statement (2008) declares that "Lesley prepares graduates with the knowledge, skill, understanding, and ethical judgment to be catalysts who shape a more just, humane, and sustainable world." Community involvement is at the core of the Lesley mission, which goes on to explain that learning is a collective endeavor and that working collaboratively and with integrity can bring forth constructive change in communities. This chapter provides examples of such community collaborations from two schools—the Graduate School of Arts and Social Sciences (GSASS) and the School of Education (SOE). The initiatives described here emanate from the Field Training and Field Placement Offices of the two schools. The first part of the chapter describes ways in which the Field Training Office of Counseling Psychology and Expressive Therapies in GSASS works and collaborates with the larger community. The second part describes a unique, long-standing partnership between the SOE at Lesley and the Cambridge Public Schools to create the Summer Compass Program, which meets the needs of both constituencies by providing an inclusive summer school for Cambridge children and an urban practicum placement for Lesley students.

THE FIELD TRAINING OFFICE OF THE DIVISIONS OF COUNSELING PSYCHOLOGY AND EXPRESSIVE THERAPIES IN GSASS

HISTORY

Since the inception of the Counseling Psychology and Expressive Therapies Programs in the mid-1970s, the field training experience has been an essential component of the clinical training of students. In the early years, each program had separate field training guidelines and support services for its students. While Counseling Psychology had a field training office, the core faculty of the Expressive Therapies Division, with the support staff, oversaw the clinical training of its advisees. This included finding and maintaining sites and supervising the students' clinical work and progress. In 1994, the Expressive Therapies and Counseling Psychology Programs merged their offices to create one Field Training Office. Within this office, Expressive Therapies and Counseling Psychology work collectively and collaboratively with the larger metropolitan area that encompasses Boston, Cambridge, and neighboring communities.

Purpose and Task

Both Counseling Psychology and Expressive Therapies students do internships in clinical and school settings. The populations they serve are culturally and linguistically diverse; this is key to our philosophy of learning by doing. The clients have varied diagnoses and needs. At the internship sites, students are expected to collaborate with a team and to work within a larger system. Our sites range from early childhood centers to geriatric facilities. Frequently, Counseling Psychology and Expressive Therapies students are at the same sites, sharing their different approaches to healing.

The most important task of the directors and the other staff in the Field Training Office is to meet the needs of students as they take on this vital aspect of their clinical education. It is in their clinical work that students integrate what they have learned in their classes into clinical practice with their own clients. During the students' first orientation, they are apprised of the role of the Field Training Office, and of the expectations they need to meet as students and as clinicians in training. We address not only the organizational issues, but also the concerns of students as they enter internship. We hold meetings that embrace the feelings students have on the threshold of this important experience, and that provide information about the materials and processes with which they will engage.

Organization of the Field Training Office

Not only does one Field Training Office build a bridge between the Counseling Psychology and Expressive Therapies Divisions, it also encourages collaboration between the divisions and with the constituencies they serve. The Field Training Office provides both divisions with training seminars and conferences that address the needs and interests of graduate students, clinical instructors, and site supervisors. Our seminars and trainings originated from multiple motivations. The first and earliest was the belief that we need to give back to the supervisors and organizations that take on the most important task of training our students. Second, we are invested in supporting the site supervisors as they work with our students by providing them with supervisory tools and enrichment. Third, we are indebted to our clinical faculty, who are committed to providing attentive and highly qualified monitoring of our students' progress as they navigate through their clinical education. Our professional development seminars for clinical faculty serve the purpose of addressing pedagogical needs, as well as providing support for the faculty. We recognize the isolation that adjunct faculty can feel, and our seminars address this concern. We have also collaborated within Lesley and outside Lesley to develop conferences that address the needs of clinical organizations that support our work as well as the pedagogical needs of those who teach and supervise our students. Both divisions have different gate-keeping functions that monitor the students' progress throughout their clinical training. We believe that our responsibility is to our students and the clients they serve.

The collaborative nature of the Field Training Office provides students with a central place where they can formulate their options for field training, address regulatory issues, and receive support in establishing their internship placements. Counseling Psychology and Expressive Therapies have a large number of internship sites, listed on a database that can be easily accessed by the students. This list is maintained and constantly updated by the administrative staff. The contact with students throughout their clinical training is most important. Each semester, an extensive evaluation process is carried out to monitor the students' progress in their clinical internships. At the end of the year, students are asked to evaluate their placements so that future interns can access their assessment of the clinical training. Our several assessment processes are further reinforced and strengthened by the attention we direct to both the clinical faculty and site supervisors.

The Field Training Office also provides oversight and supervision of the faculty who teach the required courses that accompany the internship: Clinical Practice and Supervision (Counseling Psychology) and Clinical Skills, Application, and Supervision (Expressive Therapies). Additionally, the Field Training Office provides training opportunities for site supervisors so they can enhance their supervisory skills, obtain continuing education (CE) credits for their professional development, and receive support for their clinical supervision and professional growth.

In carrying out its responsibility for quality control of the clinical training of students, the Field Training Office ensures that site supervisors and clinical instructors have the required qualifications for their assigned roles. This office is responsible for providing internship sites that include clinical experiences and training that aligns with licensure regulations and with the guidelines of various creative arts therapy associations. Our standards for sites, as well as requirements for site supervisors, incorporate what we believe to be the core of a valid clinical experience. Students receive consistent ongoing supervision, engage in in-service education, and are members of seminars that meet their clinical educational needs. They have opportunities at their sites and in their classrooms to address their developing identities as mental health professionals. We consistently hear from sites that our students are well prepared for clinical work and that we are responsive to their needs.

CLINICAL INSTRUCTORS

Supervision is a constantly evolving process. We recognize the centrality and importance of quality supervision for clinical mental health counselors, school counselors, and expressive therapists. All of our supervisors meet state regulations that require that they have at least five years of postmaster's clinical experience and an approved license. Students have an on-site supervisor and a clinical instructor who teaches the course that accompanies the internship. The clinical faculty makes a site visit in the fall semester, and in the spring the site visit takes place on campus. Students in school placements have three site visits. The fall visit provides an opportunity for faculty to assess the clinical site, meet the site supervisor, and hold a three-way meeting with the supervisor and the student. The purpose of this meeting is to evaluate the student's entry into the site, assess her adjustment to the experience, and identify any issues that need to be addressed. Our clinical faculty, many of whom have been affiliated with us for many years, provide the students with support, feedback, clinical interventions, and techniques. They also understand the nature of the clinical sites. They are practicing clinicians within the students' areas of specialty. Because they are practitioners, they are able to resonate with the students' concerns and understand the anxieties of beginning professionals. Our clinical faculty does not teach other courses to students while they are in internships or in their classes. We believe that the special nature of this relationship needs to be preserved. Our clinical faculty includes school counselors, expressive therapists, and mental health clinicians whose major focus is clinical work. The clinical seminars are opportunities for them to integrate theory and application. While many of our core faculty engage in clinical work, this is secondary to teaching. For our clinical faculty it is the opposite. Clinical work is their major focus; therefore, their expertise is current, their understanding of health care is based on experience, and their awareness of systemic issues comes from their ongoing experience. They are also cognizant of the culture of the clinical world and the developmental processes in which the students engage as they progress through our programs. In the evaluations of the instructors, those who receive the highest and strongest commendations from the students are those who are powerful role models, who share their knowledge in ways that students find accessible, and who are sensitive to and supportive of the students' experiences.

Site supervisors come on campus for the spring visit, and have the opportunity to confer with clinical instructors, directors, and staff in an all-day meeting. Meetings are scheduled to accommodate all participants, and supervisors often have an opportunity to network with other site supervisors and enjoy a breakfast or lunchtime meal. If there are any student or supervisory issues that require the involvement of the directors, this meeting addresses them. Typical issues include personality conflicts, conflicts in philosophy and expectations, and students not meeting the needs of the sites in which they are placed. Though students excel academically and appear to be prepared for field training, they may not be ready, and as a team, we are called upon to support, nurture, and challenge them in their areas of weaknesses. At this site visit we may develop a plan of action, create or redefine goals, and clarify expectations.

The Field Training Office also provides ongoing professional development for clinical instructors who teach and supervise our students in weekly supervision seminars that are part of our curriculum. Twice a semester, the directors of the Field Training Office meet with all clinical instructors. Some of the topics the Counseling Psychology Division has addressed are the use of taping as a pedagogical tool, supervision as a developmental process, an existential approach to supervision, violence in school settings and assessing risk, students' self-disclosures, transforming students into professionals, and discipline-based approaches to supervision. This is important because it reflects the realities of clinical work.

Our meetings are forums for clinical faculty to share pedagogical approaches and to receive peer feedback and support. The collegiality of these meetings provides a meaningful vehicle for the clinical faculty to connect with one another and fosters communication so faculty can call upon one another during the semester. While the Field Training Office makes the initial connection and is available for support and consultations, it is the clinical instructor who has a more direct relationship with the site supervisors. Our clinical faculty know that the directors are there for them, and our educational and professional meetings strengthen the clinical faculty's ability to respond to the students and site supervisors.

SITE SUPERVISORS

One of the ways in which we nurture the relationship with site supervisors is to provide four annual seminars on issues that arise within their role as supervisors. Seminars have centered on multicultural themes in supervision; ethical concerns; addressing students whose work is "on the edge"; a developmental perspective on supervision; discipline-based techniques in supervision; and important concerns about the supervisory process and relationship. Guidelines for presenters recommend inclusion of an experiential component in the workshop. These experiential aspects of the training support supervisors, as evidenced by sharing with others in small groups, doing role-plays, evaluating case studies, and being able to share concerns about the highly responsible role they play in our students' education. We demonstrate our support for the sites that accept responsibility for this aspect of our students' education, and our gratitude to the sites, by conducting workshops and granting CE units for supervisors' participation in seminars and meetings. It is our way of giving back to the community and being part of strengthening the mental health and guidance services that are offered. Many supervisors call each year to make sure that students are applying to their sites. They share with us their appreciation of our staff and our preparation and organization of the sessions, issues that are significant during the training experience.

OTHER CONTINUING EDUCATION OPPORTUNITIES

In 2006, GSASS funded a semester-long seminar titled "The Significance of Clinical Supervision in Counselor Education," in which site supervisors met with faculty to explore clinical issues that addressed the nature of supervision, specific approaches, and pedagogical and multicultural concerns. The seminar provided readings that were discussed, as well as experiential exercises that addressed the selected topics. A grant from the graduate school allowed us to provide a stipend for supervisors' participation. Topics included multicultural issues (Butler, 2003; Estrella, 2001), collaborative supervision (Cantwell & Holmes, 1995), and cultural identity (Ortiz, 2000).

CONNECTION WITH LARGER COMMUNITY

Maintaining a connection between the division, students, clinical instructors, and site supervisors is essential for providing the best clinical training for our students and encouraging them to be participants in the larger community of school-based and mental health counselors and expressive therapists. In addition to ongoing professional development for site and clinical instructors, we regularly organize conferences for the larger mental health community.

In 2005, the Field Training Office sponsored a conference titled "Just Supervision," which addressed the integration of social justice issues into the supervisory and clinical relationship. The Field Training Office provided workshops, forums, and case studies of social justice issues that arise within clinical settings and schools. Clinicians from community agencies were invited to conduct workshops on the ways in which their agencies address social issues that are integral to their clients' lives, including poverty, racism, homelessness, and community violence. We addressed the role of the clinician as activist. Together, members of the clinical and educational communities reflected on how they address issues of fairness, social problems, and community responses.

In 2008, a second conference was organized, titled "Inspiration and Leadership: Conversation with Community Activists, Mental Health Professionals, and Clinical Educators." This conference addressed the experiences of those who work with victims, survivors, and perpetrators of violence. One goal was to encourage an authentic dialogue among community activists, clinicians, and counselor-educators, focusing on individuals who were invested in restorative justice and the integration of social activism and mental health practice. The participants explored ways to bridge and transcend the traditional boundaries of their respective positions, and came away with a better understanding of how to collaborate on mutual concerns. By engaging in active dialogue, activists, clinicians, and educators shared diverse perspectives, successes, and challenges. Participants left with an expanded awareness of how all groups could collaborate in the best interest of the health of our communities. It was wonderful to see participants from so many diverse agencies and community-based organizations meeting together. We succeeded in bringing together clinical, community, and educational activists.

Too often at traditional conferences, participants gather, share their concerns, and leave, with no way to bring about real change. The 2008 conference sparked a continuation of its theme of restorative justice and authentic dialogue. In the spring of 2009, several participants convened to continue the dialogue in a "peace-making circle." Students and teachers from two Boston high schools, as well as two of the conference facilitators, gathered to discuss the role of peace-making circles in addressing the suspensions, detentions, expulsions, and interpersonal conflicts that students experience in school settings. The high school students discussed their experiences with peace-making circles and led the Lesley students in the circle activity.

CHALLENGES

We have often responded to external challenges. Over the years, changes in public policies have affected the clinical experiences of our interns. For example, Proposition 2 1/2, passed by the Massachusetts legislature, restricted funding for schools when a property tax cap of 2 1/2 % was established. This limitation had a negative impact on many school programs in which expressive therapists and counselors previously had training opportunities. It meant that the Field Training Office had to try harder to find quality sites for students.

The Field Training Office supported the development and passage of the bill that licensed mental health professionals. Members of the Field Training Office lobbied and encouraged elected officials and educated members of the mental health professional community to support this change. Although the effort professionalized and compensated students with master's degrees in Counseling Psychology and Expressive Therapies, many sites were required to update their training, and the Field Training Office was required to revamp the curriculum. Making the programs license ready required many shifts and changes in the placement process for students, beginning with the screening sites that determined their eligibility for placement. Many sites that had been favorites of our students and faculty had to make changes or face exclusion from our lists of approved sites. In particular, the Field Training Office worked closely with storefront operations, shelters, drop-in centers, and other sites that represented our commitment to training for social change, helping them adapt to the newly instituted professional expectations and regulations.

We work closely with the Massachusetts Chapter of the American Mental Health Counselors Association, which provides advocacy and professional support. The directors of the Field Training Office also participate in the Massachusetts and Rhode Island Association of Counselor Educators and Supervisors, advocating for new policies and legislative action.

The directors of the Field Training Office are heartened by its contributions to quality clinical education, and look forward to meeting the challenges that lie ahead. While the office oversees the provision of clinical sites and the development of clinical faculty and supervisors, we are also dedicated to its role as a presence in the community that is changing the boundaries between the academy and the larger world.

THE LESLEY-CAMBRIDGE SUMMER COMPASS PROGRAM

HISTORY OF COMPASS

Just as Lesley University's Counseling Psychology and Expressive Therapies Divisions have strong connections to the community, collaborative community partnerships are integral to all programs in the School of Education. One unique and long-standing collaboration will be described in this section. For more than 30 years, the Lesley University School of Education and the ethnically and socioeconomically diverse Cambridge Public Schools have partnered in running a summer school program. Summer Compass aims to enhance the academic achievement of children; support the preparation of new teachers; and provide professional development opportunities for veteran educators. The university and the Cambridge school system have accommodated each other's programmatic needs in order to sustain this collaboration.

Compass provides a six-week academic summer enrichment program for 120 to 200 Cambridge schoolchildren in pre-K through grade 6, and satisfies some or all of the requirements for a practicum in the university's graduate and Adult Learning divisions. Aligned with Lesley's mission, it creates an inclusive school environment; reinforces and extends academic skills; and trains Lesley student teachers in a setting where specialists and general educators develop and implement programs for a diverse group of students.

The Compass Program has evolved over the years to meet the needs of the partners and to reflect changes in teaching practices, in the structural organization of education programs at Lesley University, and in the sociopolitical context of education nationally. According to Arlyn Roffman (personal communication, April 7, 2009), a longtime faculty member and Lesley alumna, Compass began with the dream of Jill Hamilton, founder of the Special Education Program at Lesley. She and other faculty wanted to create a school where faculty and students could practice what they were teaching and learning, and where children who were identified as having special needs could benefit from an exciting program. In 1975, the school's inaugural year, it was housed at 14 Wendell St., in the Compass Building, home to the Special Education Department. Even the name "Compass" reflected the vision of the program and the Special Education Department, as "a central point of a wide-swinging arc of services" providing a sense of direction to help families navigate special education mandates (Hamilton, 1975, p. 10). Murals were painted on the walls, classrooms were designed to be appealing to children, and approximately 100 children ages 4 to 12 from 18 Cambridge Public Schools (Hamilton, 1975) were welcomed into the summer program, where they were taught individually and in small groups. This was a critical time in special education. In 1972 Massachusetts had passed Chapter 766, the Massachusetts Special Education Law; in 1975, prior to the summer school's first season, the federal government had passed PL 94-142, the Education of All Handicapped Children Act. For the first time in history, all children with special needs were entitled to a free and appropriate public education in the least restrictive setting, and Lesley was on the cutting edge!

Over the next two years, the program grew to include more than 100 children and 30 graduate student teachers, and in 1976 it moved to the Lesley School for Children. Field trips, music, art, physical education, swimming, and art therapy were incorporated into the program, and graduate students in counseling provided individual counseling to the children (*The Current,* 1976). According to Jerry Schultz (personal communication, May 3, 2009), a former Lesley faculty member who was an early Compass director, the program had an open door policy, accepting children with a wide range of special needs. At the time, children with special needs were generally served in separate pullout programs, and Compass followed this model.

By 1978 the program had moved to the Peabody School in Cambridge. A number of the children had been excluded many times from many places, but the philosophy of the Compass Program was, If not here, where? Schultz remembers the incredible dedication of the staff and student teachers: "Everybody felt like they were part of a mission," he said; "there was a commitment to making something special happen for each one of the kids in the program." Each child had the equivalent of an Individualized Education Program (IEP) for the summer. A great deal of time was spent getting each student ready to go back to school in the fall. All the children received packets that identified their strengths, with the intention that the packets would be shared with the children's classroom teachers.

In 1982, as the efficacy of segregated programs was being questioned, and mainstreaming, or integration, was gaining recognition as the more effective, more democratic approach to serving all children, Compass changed with the times. Massachusetts had developed a teaching certificate in Teacher of Young Children with Special Needs

(TYC), an integrated license for teaching children with and without special needs. Nancy Carlsson-Paige and Mary Snow, faculty at Lesley and codirectors of the program, along with Lynn Stuart, director of primary education in Cambridge, developed a new model for the summer program.

This creative and progressive model was based on mainstreaming and integration, project-based learning, integrating the arts, use of the outdoors, and a whole-language approach to literacy. Now the program began to serve children with and without special needs in integrated classrooms, and again it grew, enrolling approximately 150 children from pre-K through grade 8. One mentor-teacher had oversight of two classrooms, with three student teachers in each class. Nancy Carlsson-Paige described the goal (personal communication, April 8, 2009) as providing a "terrific program that had academic value." Don Holdaway, who brought the whole-language approach to early literacy from New Zealand to Cambridge, was working with both Cambridge and Lesley, and his ideas permeated the partnership.

The Compass Program had evolved from a segregated special education summer school into a mainstreamed program, but it was still seen as an appropriate student teaching setting for special educators only. With the move toward inclusion in schools, however, the roles of educators were beginning to shift. Specialists who in the past had removed children from the classroom to provide services began increasingly to enter the regular classroom. This change required teachers to work together in collaborative models: a major departure from the autonomous, isolated classroom of the past. As children with special needs were being integrated into regular classrooms, their teachers were being integrated as well. We realized the importance of integrating children in the Compass model, but we were slower to integrate our student teachers. It became evident that as models and roles change in the schools, so must the ways in which we train preservice teachers. In fact, perhaps the best way to facilitate the inclusion of children is to train prospective teachers to see an inclusive environment as a natural, positive way to teach. The practicum experience should take place in an environment in which general and special education teachers have the opportunity to serve children collaboratively in classrooms that belong to all.

In 1981 Lesley had merged the two separate divisions of education and special education into the Division of Education and Special Education. For many years the Special Education Division had collaborated with Cambridge on the special education practicum in Summer Compass, while the Education Division had worked with another local school system on the general education practicum. When the two divisions merged, it seemed appropriate that the summer practicum should become an inclusive model of training for general and special educators. As is often the case, integrating two cultures took more than articulating a common philosophy. Offering an inclusive practicum would be another step toward a more serious commitment in the relationship between the Education and Special Education Divisions.

The final catalyst for change was the elimination of a summer school by the district where the general education practicum had been held. Since the general and special education faculties were working more collaboratively, we recognized that we already had a setting in place that could meet the needs of our general education student teachers in a way that fit comfortably with our current departmental ideology and the growing national trend toward inclusion. In 1985, Summer Compass became an inclusive school setting, serving children from general education and special education programs, with student teachers from both general education and special education teaching together.

The most recent phase of Summer Compass has been the inclusion of interns from the Specialist Teacher of Reading Program. These interns act as literacy consultants for the school as a whole, delivering direct services to the children in classrooms and in one-on-one tutorials, collaborating with classroom teams around a myriad of general curriculum and literacy topics, and leading in-service presentations on the language arts.

This phase of the program began in 2000 at the time of the No Child Left Behind Act, which emphasized addressing the needs of failing children and failing schools and identifying research-based practices that would bolster students' ability to read. Changing demographics throughout the country, and the particular needs of a culturally and linguistically diverse school-aged population, were equally compelling reasons to consider the literacy needs of children in Summer Compass. The convergence of these areas of need and the role that literacy plays are seen in the topics chosen for the *Compass Chronicle,* a newsletter produced by the reading interns the first year. The newsletter covered effective strategies for supporting students' comprehension and ways to identify and use reading materials for a multicultural population.

Compass Now

Since Compass provides a summer school experience for Cambridge Public School children, as well as student teaching placements for Lesley, it fulfills important needs for both institutions. Each contributes resources to the program; the Cambridge school system provides classroom space; transportation; and the students, a library aide, an integration specialist, custodians, and a nurse's aide. When possible, Cambridge also provides a Reading Recovery teacher. Eight to 12 participants in the Mayor's Kids program, a summer employment opportunity for high school students, assist in the school and classrooms. Lesley provides the director (who must be a Cambridge Public Schools employee), a curriculum coordinator, an administrative assistant, mentor-teachers, a technology teacher, supervisors, and student teachers. Lesley also supplies classroom materials and support for field trips. Cambridge students pay a nominal fee to attend the program, and scholarships are available.

During the school year, a committee that comprises administrators, faculty, and staff from the university and the Cambridge Public Schools plans and supports the program. The planning committee works closely with the school system's executive director of Student Achievement and Curriculum and with the Family Resource Center.

To ensure citywide representation, the student population is selected by the Cambridge School Department. Approximately 120 to 200 children from the Cambridge school system, grades pre-K to 6, attend the program. About 30% of these children have Individualized Education Programs (IEPs). Primary areas of need include difficult behavior, language and learning disabilities, and physical challenges. Compass students reflect the cultural and linguistic diversity of Cambridge, with significant numbers from Haitian, African American, Portuguese, and Asian households. The average class size is 20 to 25 students. Each classroom team consists of a mentor-teacher and at least two student teachers whenever possible, one in general education and one in special education. A student teacher from the Consulting Teacher of Reading Program is part of each classroom team as well.

The practicum is designed to train graduate students for initial licensure as teacher of Special Needs pre-K-8 and 5-12, Early Childhood, Elementary or Reading Specialist. Lesley University supervisors are on-site several days a week. Weekly three-hour on-site seminars are held for student teachers to reflect on their teaching and discuss issues related to licensure and the Compass Program. Classroom teams meet for an hour after school, four days a week, to plan curriculum and to discuss educational strategies for individual students.

A unique aspect of Summer Compass is that it is newly created each summer. The program rotates among Cambridge elementary schools. After a week of intensive planning and set-up, Compass turns into a real school with a sense of community; teams of teachers; children learning and playing together in an educationally integrated environment; and classrooms and halls crammed with projects, books, and materials.

Since each summer is a new beginning, teams of student teachers and mentor-teachers work as an autonomous group to build a school culture in which collegiality, teamwork, and collaboration are the norm. Support staff include an integration specialist, a curriculum coordinator, a technology teacher, and reading interns. Student teachers learn in a diverse classroom. They are encouraged to reflect on their own teaching in team meetings in practicum seminars, and in daily collaborative planning sessions. While student teachers engage in seminars with university supervisors, mentor-teachers meet once a week with the Compass director and curriculum coordinator to discuss programmatic and mentoring issues.

Each summer, the classrooms choose a theme, and an interdisciplinary, developmentally appropriate curriculum is designed around this theme. Recent examples include Taking Care of the Earth, Each Other and Ourselves; Me on the Map; and Cities and Towns. The curriculum emphasizes hands-on, activity-based learning in the areas of language arts, mathematics, science, social studies, and the arts. Other program components include technology lab, theme-related field trips, swimming, and library. Student teachers in the reading program serve as language arts consultants to the classrooms and work on whole-school activities, such as a newspaper. Breakfast and lunch are provided. Parents and families are involved in the program through activities such as potluck dinners and breakfasts.

The Compass Reading Program has evolved since its inception in 2000, and now has five components: classroom support, assessment, tutoring, in-service presentations, and classroom inquiry. These efforts contribute to children's reading competence and enthusiasm, and they expand teachers' repertoire of literacy strategies and literacy resources.

At the beginning of Summer Compass, every child's reading is assessed as a prelude to forming in-classroom groupings and assigning one-on-one tutors. In order to support the children and the mentor and student teachers at different grade levels, reading interns are assigned to classrooms for the entire six weeks. In their role as reading specialists, they help with theme development and reading incentive programs, and they model literacy strategies.

One English language learner who would be entering fifth grade in the fall benefited measurably from one-on-one tutoring. The student was found to be performing approximately a year below expectation in oral reading fluency and comprehension in narrative and expository text. Her written expression was also in need of improvement. Age-appropriate and engaging literature and poetry were selected to match her instructional reading level, and served as the basis for a series of activities designed to improve reading fluency, comprehension, and written expression. Repeated out-loud reading of poetry served as one effective strategy, and much emphasis was placed on reading and writing about nonfiction text, taking notes, and outlining. By the end of Summer Compass, the student was more proficient in talking about and elaborating on themes and ideas in literature. She had moved from question-and-short-answer format to a more mature conversational format, and her written responses had improved as well.

In their capacity as tutors, reading interns work with two children, one from their assigned class and one from another grade level. Children identified as the neediest on the preassessment receive at least three hours of tutoring a week in sessions that focus on word identification, comprehension, the development of vocabulary skills and strategies, the application of skill in reading varied texts, and the connection of reading and writing. Manipulatives, games, and varied texts are used throughout the sessions. At the end of the six weeks, each child who was tutored receives a final report. These reports highlight the instructional areas of focus, the materials used, and the gains made in the academic and affective domains. In the fall the reports are sent to the principals of the schools that the tutored children attend. Recent data comparing a sample of end-of-year reading scores to fall reading scores on a reading test given districtwide shows that 67% of the children in Summer Compass who received tutoring or services in the classroom stayed steady or made progress. A recent meta analysis of studies on the achievement gap shows that children in the elementary grades often slip as much as three months in a given summer (Allington & McGill-Franzan, 2003).

The reading staff at Summer Compass give valuable in-service presentations to student teachers and mentors on topics determined by student needs, identified in the classroom and in tutorials. By highlighting various strategies, approaches, and types of materials, the reading interns ensure a more pervasive effect across the school to meet the needs of many students. The design of these in-service presentations has varied from year to year. There have been grade-level sessions designed for pre-K to K ("What Is Emergent Literacy?"), grades 1 to 3 ("Designing and Using Literacy Centers"), and grades 4 to 6 ("Comprehension Assessment and Instruction"), and a series of developmentally appropriate workshops on a single topic such as strategies for effective reading of nonfiction. Most recently, interns and mentor-teachers have been able to attend a series of mini-sessions presented in a carousel format on topics such as designing reading and writing lessons to enhance vocabulary development; using Readers' Theater to enhance fluency and comprehension; creating and using author studies for students with different reading-level proficiencies; and teaching features of nonfiction text as a means to enhance comprehension.

The reading interns are also engaged in carrying out an inquiry project. Again, their identification of student needs, their attention to matching strategies and approaches to those needs, and their reflection on action make strong literacy teaching and addressing student needs visible. For example, in 2007 the reading interns chose one question to look across age and skill levels: "Can motivational book talks for nonfiction selections increase the frequency with which students self-select nonfiction for independent or shared reading activities?" Another year, two guiding questions were chosen. Interns working with tutored students in the upper grades asked, "Are there some best strategies for teaching upper-grade ELL students vocabulary?"; those working with students in the lower grades asked, "Will a multisensory approach help a child with a short attention span attend to sound-symbol relationships when learning to read?"

BENEFITS OF THE COMPASS PROGRAM

Summer Compass has thrived over the years because all of its constituencies benefit from the program. Cambridge Public School students and their parents, high school students from the Mayor's Kids program, Lesley graduate students, mentor-teachers, and program administrators all gain in a true learning community. The program's strength rests on the collaboration between Lesley University and the Cambridge Public Schools and the commitment of both partners to the program's value for its students. Summer Compass also provides an opportunity for Lesley to contribute to the school system in the city in which it is located and to give back to the community.

Students. First and foremost, the program supports Cambridge Public School students by providing an affordable summer experience that offers an enriched academic program through an interdisciplinary, thematic approach. The program reinforces reading, writing, and mathematics skills in small group and classroom settings and offers one-on-one reading tutorials for a group of students who would not ordinarily have access to this level of academic support during the summer. Throughout the six-week program, students work with a technology specialist and a library assistant on developing curriculum projects and on enhancing their information-age skills. Students have opportunities to participate in field trips that support the thematic curriculum and that extend their academic experience. These combined experiences work to prevent "summer learning loss," to maintain academic skills throughout the summer, and to produce gains in literacy skills for students in tutorials. The full-day program provides a safe and enriching summer experience for many students who otherwise would not have access to educational opportunities during the long summer recess. The students make new friends with students from a variety of Cambridge schools and become part of a new learning community for the summer.

The Summer Compass Program provides opportunities for summer to be a "learning season" rather than a time for learning loss (Miller, 2007). For many students the summer break equals as much as a three-month loss each year in the elementary grades. This loss leads to big setbacks in reading and to long-term achievement deficits that may never be closed (Allington & McGill-Franzen, 2003; Cooper, 2003). Programs like Compass—which are voluntary, with enrichment and academic components and literacy and math embedded in thematic work, and which emphasize problem solving, collaboration, and cooperation— seem to be the most effective summer models (Miller, 2007).

Another component of Compass that benefits older children is the Mayor's Kids program, sponsored by the city of Cambridge to provide summer employment for teenagers. Every summer, Compass hires 8 to 12 high school students from Mayor's Kids as assistants in the program. The students from Mayor's Kids help with breakfast and lunch, serve as mentors to the Cambridge students, and assist in the classrooms and on the playground. They are supervised by a staff member and receive feedback from the mentor-teachers. Some of the high school students have a special interest in education and will pursue teaching as a profession. They all learn valuable lessons about the responsibilities of working in a highly interactive environment, and they benefit from paid summer employment.

Parents. Parents of the students in Summer Compass are pleased to have a full-day, affordable summer program for their children that provides academic and enrichment activities in a supportive environment. According to surveys distributed to families at the end of the program each year, parents are delighted to see their children immersed in math, literacy, and science activities during the summer months, as well as taking field trips, having access to technology, and enjoying themselves in a social environment. They appreciate the hands-on, active learning approach and the recreational swimming program. Comments include the following: "This was the best for our son! He remained positive and spoke highly about his experiences daily. It was great fun for us as parents, since his first year at kindergarten was difficult."

"Our daughter has loved every day of Compass. Her love of reading grew at Compass, and her confidence in writing also grew." Parents also appreciated opportunities for involvement in the program and enjoyed attending class breakfasts and the school's potluck dinner. Each summer, an afterschool program is housed in the same building as the Compass Program, making it possible for parents who work 9 to 5 to keep their children in one setting all day.

Graduate students and interns. Lesley graduate students benefit by having the option of a summer placement in an urban environment and an inclusive setting. Many of the graduate students cannot leave paid employment during the school year to fulfill their licensure requirements, and the summer practicum makes it possible for them to enroll in the licensure program. The program also provides graduate students with the opportunity to work with a culturally and linguistically diverse population of children.

Professional development workshops during the set-up week, and the weekly student teaching seminar, are tailored to the needs of the graduate students working in diverse classrooms. Faculty from the university offer their expertise on topics such as strategies for working with English language learners, culturally responsive teaching, and strategies for building a learning community. The student teachers have the full experience of setting up the classroom environment, creating structures for helping their students build a cohesive classroom community, and designing curricula and teaching materials.

Additional benefits for graduate students are the learning community and teaming experience that the program creates. Teams of student teachers and mentor-teachers work together to design their classroom environment, create curricula, and assess student work. Classroom teams consist of a mentor-teacher, two graduate students seeking initial licensure (whenever possible a general education student teacher is paired with a special education student teacher), and a reading intern. Planning time with the team is built into the daily schedule. Support staff—an integration specialist, a technology teacher, and the reading interns—work with the teams in planning for the classroom and for individual students. For example, the integration specialist helps the student teachers design behavioral and learning interventions for specific students. The reading interns, who are part of the classroom team and consultants in the area of literacy, model literacy strategies and support theme development with suggestions for literature-based reading and writing activities.

Graduate student teachers in the Compass Program not only learn current teaching methodologies, but are also encouraged to reflect on their own teaching in team meetings, practicum seminars, and daily collaborative planning. They see lessons modeled by mentor-teachers, reading interns, and the technology specialist, and experience a variety of teaching styles. One graduate student commented, "I like the team teaching setting because you get to see your mentor-teacher and other teachers in action, which is helpful. I see different teaching styles modeled and get to question and discuss teaching practices that the whole team is observing together."

The Compass Program reflects the current realities of many schools in which teachers no longer work in isolation in their classroom. The graduate students in Compass experience different teachers working with the same group of students, gain experience conferring with school specialists in a consulting model, and learn valuable lessons about collaboration and teamwork. Beginning on day one of the set-up week, teaching teams in Compass design the classroom environment, create curricula around a chosen theme, and coteach in the classroom, working together on these common goals. Teams meet daily, plan together, and at the end of the day evaluate their students' responses to the plans. Team members quickly learn how to listen to one another's ideas, present their points of view in order to be heard by their team members, collaborate in developing lessons, critique an idea in a respectful manner, and give and receive feedback. They learn when to compromise, how to view a situation from a different perspective, and how to deal with conflicts that may arise. They have practice coteaching lessons and orchestrating the role of each team member.

Mentor-teachers and administrators. Mentor-teachers in the program are veteran teachers with five or more years of teaching experience. They have an opportunity to assume new roles as teacher leaders in their work with the student teachers and to develop their mentoring and coaching skills. Mentor-teachers meet weekly with the staff developer to discuss their mentoring roles as well as strategies for teaming and curriculum planning. They work with the university supervisors to give feedback to the graduate students. When asked to discuss their own professional development over the course of the summer, mentor-teachers have commented on the opportunity to work with such a richly diverse ethnic population of students in an inclusion model, the opportunity to explore running a classroom free of district oversight and directives, and the collaborative aspect of the program. Having to articulate their teaching practices for their team of student teachers makes them more reflective practitioners. Several have commented that they learned from their student teachers, many of whom were trying out strategies and curricular ideas that had been recently demonstrated in their Lesley University methods courses.

The program directors are often Cambridge teachers who have an interest in administration. Most of the former directors of the program have moved into administrative positions in Cambridge and other systems. The Compass Program has helped to round out their administrative experience in an urban setting and has given them experience in overseeing a school that is newly created each summer—an experience that new administrators do not usually have. Compass staff developers have grown professionally as well, and many have moved into curriculum support positions in school systems and the state department.

Other benefits of the school-university collaboration. In addition to benefiting the constituencies directly involved in the program, Compass has met other programmatic needs of the university and the city school system. In 2004, at the request of the Cambridge School Department, a language-based classroom was piloted for three students who needed summer services. The students participated in a self-contained language-based program in the morning and were integrated into the full Compass Program in the afternoon. From 1992 to 1995, the university and Cambridge needed a summer program to provide extended learning experiences to 40 students in the Say Yes to Education Program. Say Yes combined resources with Summer Compass and supplemented the program, providing a guidance counselor and counseling interns, an author-in-residence, a storyteller, and additional funding for supplies and materials.

Summer Compass gives all participants the opportunity to learn during summer recess. For the children, it provides academic enrichment experiences that help them to maintain or make gains in academic skills, rather than losing ground during the summer. For the preservice teachers, mentors, and administrators it provides an opportunity for growth and development that helps them move toward the next step on the professional continuum. Finally, the collaboration enhances the relationship between Lesley University and the Cambridge community.

In Conclusion

This chapter took shape as a collaboration between Lesley University's Graduate School of Arts and Social Sciences and the School of Education. The training models designed for our students in their respective fields embody our shared vision as educators and leaders who value the importance of process and a commitment to community building. Both narratives demonstrate the ways in which the faculty and staff have responded to needs for change within their fields and communities in responsible and creative ways.

The chronicle of the Field Training Office of the Divisions of Counseling Psychology and Expressive Therapies speaks to internal collaboration and external collegiality with members of the area's educational and clinical communities. The Field Training Office is dedicated to active development of quality sites and educational and professional development opportunities for site supervisors and campus faculty. The Field Training Office exemplifies the commitment to community needs, to the professionals who serve the needs of students, and, most important, to the lives of the people with whom our students work.

The Lesley-Cambridge Summer Compass Program is a case example of a collaboratively run program that benefits both the local school system and the university. The process has been one in which the Cambridge Public Schools and Lesley University have worked together to develop a program that enriches the lives of schoolchildren in Cambridge. Further, this case example illustrates the teamwork and collaboration needed to successfully address the educational needs of multiple constituencies.

The values inherent in the priorities of both of these professional training models address key elements of Lesley University's mission, namely, the creation of transformative learning opportunities and a belief in the power of collaboration to increase the well-being of our communities.

REFERENCES

Allington, R. L., & McGill-Franzan, A. (2003). Use students' summer-setback months to raise minority achievement. The Educations Digest, 69(3), 19 24.

Butler, S. K. (2003). Multicultural sensitivity and competence in the clinical supervision of school counselors and school psychologists: a context for providing competent services in a multicultural society. *The Clinical Supervisor.* 22(1), 125 141.

Cantwell, P., & Holmes, S. (1995). Cumulative process: a collaborative approach to systemic supervision. *Journal of Systemic Therapies, 14*(2), 35 46.

Compass program delights children. (Fall 1976). The Current, 5.

Cooper, H. (2003). Summer learning loss: The problem and some solutions (EDO-PS-03-5). Champaign, IL: ERIC Clearinghouse on Elementary and Early Childhood Education.

Estrella, K. (2001). Multicultural Approaches to Music Therapy Supervision. In

M. Forinash (Ed.). *Music therapy supervision.* Gilsum, NH: Barcelona Publishers.

Hamilton, J. (Winter 1975). Especially for special education. The Current, Lesley College, Winter, *10.*

Lesley University Mission Statement. (2008, December 17). Lesley University. Retrieved June 1, 2009, from http://www.lesley.edu/about/mission.html

Miller, B. M. (June 2007). The learning season: The untapped power of summer to advance student achievement. The Nellie Mae Education Foundation. Retrieved August 25, 2008, from http://www.nmefdn.org/Research/index.aspx

Ortiz, A. (2000). Expressing cultural identity in the learning community: Opportunities and challenges. *New directions for teaching and learning. 82,* 67 79.

CHAPTER FIFTEEN

At the Crossroads of Arts, Teaching, and Inquiry

GENE DIAZ, PHD

LISA DONOVAN, PHD

The arts have shaped teaching, learning, and inquiry in the many programs offered by the Creative Arts in Learning Division since the early 1970s. In these programs, graduate students learn to integrate the arts in all aspects of their teaching and learning, and to enrich the field of education through arts-based inquiry. On campus and in programs around the nation and the world, division faculty have offered an innovative approach to teaching and learning to teachers, community-based artists, and other educators, inspiring them to engage their students in learning in and through the arts.

The division has offered master's degree programs, post-master's programs, and certificates, partnerships, conferences, research, and collaborative endeavors through the years. These have been supported by and have benefited from the depth of dedication of the faculty and staff to the concept of arts education for all children. In this chapter we explore the bases for these many endeavors, along with efforts to include the arts as part of educational reform for children in the United States.

Although Abbs (1987) suggests that in teaching there is "no room for charisma, only contracts. No room for radical questions, only ranked percentages. No room for aesthetics, only certificates," (p. 60) the faculty in Lesley's Creative Arts in Learning Division strive to change this condition. As artists they explore their worlds through expressive media; as scholars they ask critical questions of the academy; and as teachers they inspire their students to take risks and imagine the world a more just, humane, and equitable place.

Many teachers go with the flow, not questioning, only assessing and measuring, meeting benchmarks and objectives, with little time to engage in the meaning of teaching or the meaning of life. However, the teachers who study in Creative Arts in Learning Programs know a different way, and they know from their everyday lives in classrooms what needs to change to make learning more accessible and more enjoyable for their students.

In Creative Arts in Learning we teach to encourage change, a change that we believe will offer our students, and their students in turn, a quality of life enriched by aesthetic experiences through the arts. Those who teach in these programs would understand that when John Dewey (1934) suggested it is not enough to insist on the necessity of experience in education and that we need to attend to the quality of those experiences, he meant that an experience with aesthetic qualities is most worth teaching.

While the Creative Arts in Learning Programs were created originally for classroom teachers who were not art specialists, they currently provide in-depth training for what the Arts Education Partnership (2007) terms "the arts teaching workforce," those who teach the arts to the children in this country. This includes generalist classroom teachers as well as arts specialists, teaching artists, community practitioners, and faculty in institutions of higher education. The teaching in arts integration that takes place in this corner of Lesley meets a need that has been recognized across the nation. This was noted by the working group of arts educators who crafted *Working Partnerships* (Arts Education Partnership, 2007).

> If arts education for all children is to be transformed by a highly qualified arts teaching work force, higher education must take a leadership role in the professional development of classroom teachers, art specialists, teaching artists and

instructors in arts and cultural institutions to ensure that those who teach the arts have the highest possible artistic skills and pedagogical abilities. (p. 10)

The motivation to help create an arts teaching workforce with the best possible skills and abilities comes from a belief that the arts represent some of the highest achievements of our culture and society. Throughout the history of the United States, artistic accomplishments have represented our most enduring characteristics. From the poetry of Emily Dickinson and Audre Lorde to the music of the Deep South and the Shakers and John Cage, from the paintings of the Hudson River school to the sculptures of Henry Moore, and from the bare feet of Isadora Duncan to the challenging story of loss in Bill T. Jones's *Still/Here*, (1994) we have demonstrated our capacities to imagine and create. Yet the arts offer even more to our students than the aesthetic qualities so recognized and cherished. They offer a way of thinking that stimulates innovation, curiosity, and new ways of being in the world. Again, from *Working Partnerships* (AEP, 2007):

Our society increasingly makes its living off innovation and discovery, and the arts provide forms of inquiry that engage our minds, our senses, and our creative and inventive capacities. They provide a language of possibility for futures yet to be imagined, and insights that are only gained through aesthetic experiences. (p. 10)

As we explore the various ways in which we offer this language of possibility to our students at Lesley, it is important to recall that this division and these programs began with an idea born of collaboration and collegiality. In 1974 the program now known as Integrated Teaching through the Arts began offering a master's degree program called Creative Arts in Learning (bearing the same name as the division). This program was initially offered in Massachusetts, then off campus in an intensive weekend model in Colorado in 1981; and in 2009, it reached students in 23 states and in Israel. From this one program the division grew to offer eight programs in 2009, six of which lead to Massachusetts teacher licensure, three at the initial level and three at the professional level. The licensure programs include initial and professional licensure in early childhood education and elementary education in collaboration with the School of Education. In 2002, following a merger with the Art Institute of Boston (AIB), the division collaborated with AIB in creating initial and professional licensure programs in visual art education. Requests from graduates of the master's program led to an off-campus Certificate of Advanced Graduate Studies (CAGS), which enrolled students in 2005. A new program in community arts emerged in 2008, based on the former individually designed master's program.

This growth in programming derived from significant changes in the needs of teachers in Massachusetts and across the country. With the withdrawal of resources from art programs, and diminishing numbers of arts specialists in classrooms, teachers have needed to become more creative in their approaches to making the arts available to their students. At the same time, increasing demands for accountability, brought about through federal and state legislation, have pushed teachers away from their professional knowledge and toward test-driven teaching (Meier & Wood, 2004). Those who have been students in Lesley's national programs have called them transformative in their personal and professional lives. Professional development for teachers that requires creativity, imagination, and risk taking offers them renewal and substantive growth. With arts as the basis for their own learning, teachers have enrolled in increasing numbers, and in 2003 more than 2,000 students participated in arts-integrated professional development at Lesley.

The rise in student numbers created a need for more faculty and staff, and for deeper and more versatile faculty scholarship. The program has attracted an accomplished group of 150 practicing artists who serve as adjunct faculty across the country, along with 14 core faculty on campus in 2007. Through artistic and inquiry-based scholarship, the faculty have explored the world, so to speak, as they engage in research and artistic production that brings them into contact with changing norms and practices in the United States. The goal of any university, in addition to engaging students with the history of the world, is to generate new knowledge and create new scholars, and the faculty in this division have clearly met that goal. In addition to the programs of study that lead to graduate certificates and degrees, division faculty have engaged in the difficult work of advocating for, and advising on, policy in arts education, creating community connections between artists and teachers, and designing new national and regional initiatives in arts-integrated education and inquiry.

WHY ARTS INTEGRATION?

Arts integration makes a difference in education. Students are able to engage with content in many ways and to express their understanding in forms that bring their voices and ideas into the mix. The translation process that occurs in the creative endeavor ensures that students take ownership of learning and respond in their own ways. At the same time, learning in, through, and with the arts allows students to pick up clues about who they are along the way. As cellist Pablo Casals observed,

> What we teach children in school is 2 + 2 = 4 and Paris is the capital of France. What we should be teaching them is what they are. We should be saying "Do you know what you are? You are a marvel. You are unique." (As cited in Rothstein, Wilder & Jacobsen, 2007, p. 11)

Mary Clare Powell, division director from 2003 to 2005, noted that:

> It is not stretching too far to claim that having experienced yourself as a creator in the arts, you will be a better teacher in a classroom. The arts help teachers become multilingual, because the arts are many languages. You can say things in music that you cannot translate into words; when you dance

a concept, it is not the same as when you speak about it. The visual arts are their own particular language, not a shortcut for words. (1997, p. 450)

The current educational landscape has indicated a need for education that prepares students to solve the complex issues that face our world—education that uses more right brain thinking. This is a call for innovation and creativity as tools for the 21st century. Daniel Pink, author of *A Whole New Mind* (2006), says that "The future belongs to a very different kind of person with a very different kind of mind…artists, inventors, designers, storytellers, caregivers, consolers, big picture thinkers" (p. 1).

Arts integration can develop the kinds of skills that prepare students for their lives in the 21st century. The arts, by their nature, develop skills that business leaders indicate are crucial to our current and future workforce—collaboration, discovery through trial and error, improvisation, risk taking, problem solving, divergent thinking, and the ability to sit with ambiguity. We are preparing students for jobs and a way of life that we cannot fully envision.

Besides the need for more creative, flexible thinking, there is an achievement gap that must be addressed. In today's landscape of high-stakes testing, students are being taught with one-size-fits-all methods and are receiving assessments that ignore the complexities of the contexts students bring to learning.

As Governor Deval Patrick said in the report *Ready for 21st Century Success* (2008), "The Batch Processing approach to education no longer works in an economy in which the skills needed for college and a job that will support a family of four are virtually identical" (p. 11).

Now more than ever, it's clear that integrating the arts across the curriculum can help spur innovation in education and allow more children to succeed. The arts can level the playing field and allow students to start from where they are, learning in ways that are engaging, interdisciplinary, and relevant. In the current push for standardized testing, learning is measured with increasingly limited methods.

WHAT IS THE IMPACT OF ARTS INTEGRATION?

When teachers use the arts as a strategy for inquiry, exploration, and making meaning, they witness the power of the arts to transform their practice, their classroom, and their school. Integrating the arts across the curriculum bolsters creativity and imagination in teachers and students and creates transformative learning moments.

In 2008, the Creative Arts in Learning Division was awarded a Ford Foundation Grant to study the impact of Lesley's Integrated Teaching through the Arts (ITA) master's degree program on classroom teachers. Research from this study reveals that CAL's professional development offerings for teachers are improving effectiveness of teaching and learning and positively impacting how teachers feel about their role. Teachers report that the program provides important strategies for them to differentiate instruction. They share compelling examples of students who have had limited success with traditional pedagogical strategies but who thrive when the arts enter the classroom.

One teacher in the study noted:

> While working in an elementary school classroom, I always called upon the information I received in the CAL Program. I found that teaching with, through, and about the arts enabled my students to express their learning while keeping them absorbed in the subject matter we were covering. With teaching in an educationally and socially diverse classroom, the need to use creativity becomes even more important. For example, while teaching patterns in math I recognized that a few of my more "physical" learners were having trouble expressing their learning on paper. In order to assess their learning, I had to figure out ways for them to express whether they understood the concepts being taught. So, I created various work stations that dealt with the multiple intelligences. One of the stations

381

was to show patterns using dance, cheers, or gymnastics. My kinesthetic learners flocked to this table and choreographed a dance demonstrating repetition, sequence, adding, and subtracting. Not only did this exercise demonstrate that they understood the concepts, but they enjoyed themselves in the process and the rest of the class got to see these concepts applied creatively. It was a win-win for everyone! (Survey response, 2009)

THE COHORT MODEL

In CAL's off-campus program, the cohort model has served to create a nexus for teachers who become a strong professional learning community. This structure has provided teachers with much-needed support and with a network that often becomes as significant as the learning that occurs in the coursework.

In addition to Integrated Teaching through the Arts, CAL offers a program that focuses on leadership and on arts-based action research. The Educational Specialist Program is offered in Georgia and focuses on teachers as artists, researchers, scholars, and leaders. This program provides teachers with skills to conduct arts-based action research projects that examine urgent questions in their classroom. For example:

- Kimberly Bell of Marietta considered the following research question: How does the integration of the arts improve student achievement and attitudes in the social studies classroom?
- Lisa Rees Misiewicz of Marietta asked, What outcomes are possible when poetry and collage are incorporated as writing process components aimed specifically at exploring the personal experiences and attitudes of college-level developmental writing students as they investigate the intersections of language, power and culture?
- Betsy Parker of Lilburn asked, How does using the art of

storytelling create an environment that supports community building and honors cultural diversity?

Teachers' voices gain power and resonance as they explore new interventions in their classrooms. These strategies, often arts-based, explore important questions in education and uncover answers that move teachers into a position of leadership and voice.

These two national programs (Integrated Teaching through the Arts and the Educational Specialist Certificate of Advance Graduate Studies) have given us a wider perspective on education and the field of arts education, and a clear sense of the amazing expertise, passion, and creativity that teachers possess despite the challenges they face.

BEYOND THE PROGRAMS

Faculty in the Creative Arts in Learning Division continue to identify ways to promote arts education and arts integration beyond the master's degree programs and the certification offerings. This effort grows out of their own research and professional development and engagement in community-based work. Moving beyond course-based offerings, they have developed initiatives that include partnerships with schools and other organizations, regional and national working groups and conferences for teachers and cultural arts leaders, research collaborations, advisory board policy contributions, and innovative offerings for artists who collaborate with schools and teachers. In this section we share some of these initiatives.

In 1999 the Massachusetts Alliance for Arts Education (MAAE) was searching for a partner to further its agenda of advocacy for the arts in schools across the Commonwealth. It proposed an alliance with Lesley that could support its efforts in advocacy, an alliance that was fostered by then dean of the graduate school Martha McKenna and CAL division director Gene Diaz. Diaz joined MAAE at the same time as Meredith Eppel, the executive director of the National Arts and Learning Collaborative (NALC), and they became partners in a new endeavor to bring together regional school leaders who supported the arts. They recognized that the support and leadership of senior school administrators such as superintendents and principals were essential to the success of any arts education initiatives. Thus the Leading with the Arts conference was born, and several subsequent collaborations linked the efforts and resources of MAAE, NALC, and Lesley. The two-day conference took place at Lesley; esteemed educational philosopher Maxine Greene and Geoffrey Canada, social activist and educator, were keynote speakers.

In 2002 CAL faculty member and graduate school dean Martha McKenna was invited to join the Arts Education Partnership (AEP), a national organization that was formed when the U.S. Department of Education and the National Endowment for the Arts came together to shape a group that could actively and effectively foster arts in education across the country. Comprised of the Chief State School Officers (CSSO) and the heads of the state cultural arts, as well as philanthropic organizations, the AEP held three national forums per year, during which Dr. McKenna would have direct access to groups engaged in arts and education partnerships in their various forms. In 2005 she was invited to chair a working group that would inquire into the nature of the participation of higher education in arts education partnerships. Dr. McKenna brought together a national working group that helped shape the AEP publication *Working Partnerships* (AEP, 2007). The group shared its guidelines and the profiles of nine model partnerships at various national education conferences. One of the nine model partnerships was another collaboration that brought together NALC and Lesley's Creative Arts in Learning faculty in a project that took place in the Boston Public Schools (BPS).

The collaboration involved Lesley, BPS, and two private schools, Walnut Hill and Brimmer and May. The professional development program that was created for classroom teachers, specialists, and administrators allowed them to develop skills to integrate the arts in ways that resembled the experience of the Arts and Literacy Mentorship Program (ALMP), in which independent high schools with strong arts programs partnered with BPS. Students from two independent schools, under the direction of their arts faculty, brought arts activities to students in two BPS elementary schools. This partnership grew to include extensive teacher professional development in skills for integrating the arts into the curriculum and engaging students in learning while addressing school improvement plans and state and national arts education standards.

When Lisa Donovan joined the division in 2003, she took on the leadership role in Lesley's involvement with the Charles Sumner Elementary School, along with Robert Shreefter, reflecting the division's commitment to community partnerships. Over several years, this professional development[21] sparked a decision by the Sumner School to become fully arts-integrated. Faculty in the Creative Arts in Learning Division have been actively supporting strategic planning processes and continuing professional development on the way to this goal.

Members of CAL participated in the partnership by offering graduate credit-bearing courses specially designed to support elementary school teachers in developing their own artistic abilities along with appropriate curriculum for their classrooms. The elementary school teachers who participated were encouraged to share their curricula with other teachers in their school, leading their peers in program-related professional development activities and bringing the arts to an even broader group of students. Lesley faculty have supported the ALMP by facilitating conversations between participating high school students on the complexities of being mentor-teachers in urban, economically disadvantaged schools.

An outcome of the partnership work and national and regional collaborations was a regional Massachusetts Arts Education Partnership (MAEP) conference that took place in the spring of 2007 and again in 2008 at Lesley. Bringing together national and regional leaders to discuss arts education in New England, the conference drew on the expertise of local artists and educators and offered workshops on creative collaborations across the region. This conference drew several

21 Supported by the National Endowment for the Arts and Edvestors.

of the members of artists groups who work in residencies around the region, and thus connected yet another offering sponsored by Lesley in collaboration with the state leaders in the arts in the New England states, New England Consortium of Artist Educator Professionals (NECAP).

In 2007, a group of educators launched an initiative to serve the professional development needs of teacher-artists across New England. The new institute, called Cultivating the Field, emerged from discussions among David Marshall, education manager of the Massachusetts Cultural Council; Lisa Donovan, director of Creative Arts in Learning; national faculty member Sandi Levy; and core faculty Louise Pascale, in collaboration with other members of NECAP. They envisioned the institute as a step in the direction of creating a certificate or degree program that would meet the unique needs and interests of teacher-artists, and that would serve to develop the field of artists who teach. As originally articulated, the institute's goals included the following:

- Annualize the institute and follow-up seminars.
- Enlist artists over time to help determine the content and direction of the institute.
- Create a certificate process to give artists new to the field a place for sequential learning.
- Develop a multicultural professional network of teaching artists to share issues and opportunities.
- Disseminate the information emerging from the professional development sessions to other teaching artists, teachers, arts administrators, and educators.

The annual institute quickly exceeded its early expectations, going more deeply into key issues than traditional professional development systems have extended. In May 2008, in collaboration with NECAP and Jacob's Pillow Dance Festival, CAL convened a think tank titled the Artist's Role in Assessment: Student Learning Assessment as a Collaboration between Artist and Educators. Participants included students, teachers, teacher-artists, principals, superintendents, and representatives of higher education and state education institutions. They aspired to challenge personal perceptions, understand the work of different constituencies, and expand possibilities for teacher-artists. Out of their work came a clear need to develop records of student learning with an emphasis on meeting the needs of all those who evaluate student learning.

In 2009 the focus of the institute shifted to documentation of learning and program evaluation and featured a partnership between six state cultural council members of NECAP, Jacob's Pillow Dance Festival, the Art Institute of Boston, and Very Special Arts (VSA). This work brings CAL faculty into schools and communities on a regular basis, ensuring that they continue to grapple with the most current and significant issues in the field. These conversations then inform the work undertaken in the programs.

ARTS AND INQUIRY

As academics and artists we are always exploring new questions and creative processes. The nature of our work requires this. By combining our creative artistic processes with the methodological questioning that is a foundation of educational research, we have found ourselves within a growing community of educational researchers who conduct what is frequently termed arts-based research. As arts-based educational researchers, or artist-teacher-scholars, we explore the world of teaching and learning by including artistic processes or products as part of a rigorous research practice that leads to new knowledge about schools, students, and the field of education. Based on a generous understanding of qualitative research methods because of the qualitative and aesthetic characteristics of the arts, we develop and implement research that engages the senses and requires innovative and imaginative methods for knowledge construction. In this section we explore the connections between our arts-integrated teaching and our arts-based inquiry, from the series of publications developed in partnership with publisher Peter Lang in 1998 to the 2008–2010 Ford Foundation research on the impact of the professional development master's degree on teaching and learning in schools across the nation.

WRITING FOR, AND WITH, OUR STUDENTS

As faculty in the innovative interdisciplinary field of integrated arts in education, we have long been engaged in a struggle to find adequate and appropriate literature for our students. Since we have developed our teaching methods for delivery modes that were unique to Creative Arts in Learning, we realized that the literature we needed had to emerge from, and be based in, our own teaching practices. Thus, in 1999, educational researcher and Creative Arts in Learning professor Elijah Mirochnik initiated a partnership between Lesley and the academic publisher Peter Lang, with the support and guidance of then GSASS dean Martha McKenna. Mirochnik (who also served as series editor) and Professor Emerita Deborah Sherman edited *Passion and Pedagogy* (2002), the first volume of the eight-volume Lesley University Series in Arts and Education; four additional volumes were coedited by Lesley faculty in subsequent years. All of these books were produced with Lesley students in mind; several of the titles, such as *Teaching for Aesthetic Experience* (Diaz & McKenna, 2004)—which was addressed to students in curriculum theory classes—were written for specific Creative Arts in Learning courses. And in each volume of the series the coupling of the arts and education, or the arts and therapy, brings forth the struggle of interdisciplinary or cross-disciplinary teaching and learning. As we integrate the arts and education we encounter elements in each field that don't sit nicely together, but frequently quarrel like unruly children fighting over a cherished toy.

An inherent conundrum or puzzle creates an incongruity between the fields of education and the arts. This same kind of conundrum or incongruity exists between qualitative research and arts-based qualitative research. The puzzle stems from the nature of an organized body of knowledge such as research methods or educational practices, both of which have evolved to demand more formulaic and less heuristic approaches to the application of established methods than do artistic practices, artistic formalism notwithstanding. Education has at its core a study of norms, and the teaching, learning, and enacting of them. The practice of education in the United States in the 21st century demands accountability (of teacher practice and student learning), measurement (days in attendance, scores on tests and exams), and adherence to established norms (in dress, language, lining up, sitting at desks, etc.). Creative actions in classrooms often take the form of what we might understand as "acting out." Creative norm making results in visits to school counselors and the principal's office. Consider the first graders who use their fruit juice to make a puddle in the play yard for their tiny paper boats.

Students in creative arts in Cambridge and across the nation encounter this conundrum throughout their study, and their reflections on the resolutions of it shape their writing, their class discussions, and their course assignments. The transformations that they speak of at graduation celebrations allude to the ways that they have found to bring the arts and education together not just in their classrooms but in their personal lives as well. Their words then have helped us as faculty keep this program vibrant and reflective of the changing needs of teachers over the years. One of those needs was a course in research methods for teachers in Oregon in order for them to meet specific requirements for licensure for the state. We adapted a previously developed course in arts-based research for the program in Oregon, which allowed us to bring our work as arts-based researchers into our teaching practices in the program. *Dancing the Data* (Bagley & Cancienne, 2002), an edited volume in the Lesley-Lang series on arts-based educational research, included chapters by several Creative Arts in Learning faculty, and became a text for this and other research courses in the program.

Another of those changing needs, a need for professional development in arts integration beyond the master's degree, led us to the development of an off-campus delivery for the post-master's

Certificate of Advance Graduate Studies, or CAGS. The CAGS program, with a strong focus on leadership, meets the requirements of the state of Georgia for the graduates to become educational specialists. And again, as in the interdisciplinary nature of integrated arts in teaching, an interdisciplinary arts in research offers specific challenges for faculty and students alike.

In the same ways in which education consists of norm-following practices and actions, for the most part, research consists of following norms and established practices as well. We follow research practices that adhere to established and structured organizational methods for the generation of new knowledge. We follow formal procedures and practices for research design, data collection, and analysis, and incorporate standard components for publishing and presenting our work. These practices come to us today from the now honored traditions originating in anthropology, modified in sociology, and adapted into education. We don't invent these procedures and processes each time we want to conduct a qualitative research project. We follow those that have been established, those that are recognized, and those that are canonized.

Just as an integration of the arts and artistic practices and processes can find a way into the art of teaching, so too can it find its way into the rigorous process of educational research. What is it then that we must respect in established practices when we attempt to create artistic and aesthetic methods in research? With which parts of the research process can we be creatively free to innovate? What parts of the established research practices must we not tamper with or change? These are questions that all of us as artistic and aesthetic researchers have struggled with at some point or another. And the answers have come from each of us somewhat differently.

What does this say then about the actual practice of qualitative research methods in action research in education? Judith Fox and Thomas Geichman (2001), an educational researcher and a visual artist from the shores of Lake Michigan in Chicago, in their article on forming research questions with strategies and perspectives of contemporary visual artists, came up with a set of suggestions from the arts that can inform research practices in general. Writing on the reasons for creating their article, they suggest that we as teachers and as researchers are limited or bounded in our current ideas and actions. We are hemmed in by established practices and seldom venture out to the edges of our boundaries. They write,

> My particular interest...is in the boundary conditions of we who teach and do research, and what we can do not only to bring others to the same edges of understanding that leave us perplexed, but to extend beyond us. Strategies and perspectives of contemporary art may help educators who both teach and do research approach educational understandings in new and disorienting ways. The use of contemporary arts in educational research can further develop our intent as educational researcher to bring neophytes beyond the edges of our understandings. (p. 35)

Although Fox and Geichman were writing about forming educational research questions, their nine suggestions apply to all aspects of the research processes in education. While their strategies and perspectives come from the work of contemporary visual artists, we can use examples for popular art more familiar to most teachers.

INCLUDING THE ARTS IN RESEARCH

Because we insist on the artistic and the aesthetic as part of critical research, the action research we propose is qualitative in nature. Many qualities of the arts resist measurement. Artistic processes are inherently original, authentic, and innovative, thus not availing themselves readily to operationalizing as variables. Artistic processes require—more, they demand—imagination and creative risk taking.

Action research is an established practice in education, with many proponents and many valuable resources already dedicated to its theory and practice (Dick, 2004; Mertler, 2006; Schmuck, 2006).

Action research processes include formalized reflection on teaching practices, a systematic collection of data, accompanied by a plan to change that practice based in a rigorous analysis of that data. In our formulation of the research courses we have drawn upon this collective knowledge to help shape.

Critical action research, too, has generated discussion, especially among educators. Critical action research, according to Kincheloe (2004),

- Is political, ethical, and affective, and rejects measurement and testing as the *only* methods of knowing student progress.
- Requires teacher-researchers to be reflective and conscious of their own values and beliefs and those of the dominant culture.
- Attempts to undo or unveil distorted ideological interpretations of education practices.
- Must reveal aspects of educational or societal norms and structures that are contrary to teachers' values and beliefs.
- Is guided by an awareness of good teaching practice and ways that teacher-researchers can identify actions that can overcome societal obstacles to good teaching.

Arts-based education research requires an aesthetic approach to this process of critical inquiry. From the beginning of the research process to the final sharing of the results of a study, the characteristics of art should be considered as part of the endeavor. These characteristics include, but are not limited to, creative innovation, risk taking, imagination, authenticity, and careful, well-crafted artistic production and performance (Slattery, 2002).

Researchers and artists both construct meaning through discovery, managing curiosity with established processes within their fields. These processes involve "seeking to know the world in new ways, from different perspectives, with added depth of detail and fresh insight" (Diaz, 2002, p. 55). We, as researchers and artists, bring aesthetic possibilities to our meaning-making efforts, possibilities of deep, affective learning where "our spirits commune, where we can hear with shared delight the noises of the soul in play" (hooks, 1994). Arts-based educational research moves beyond research *about* the arts, to research *as* art, research as artistic and aesthetic processes.

Our students move beyond using the arts as decorative features for educational research as they search for what Fox and Geichman call disorientating perspectives, where they focus around the edges of what they understand rather than at the center (2001). Authentic curiosity about educational practices, and about policies, and theories, from an artistic perspective, can then lead to rich and varied questions, especially about critical perspectives in teaching and learning. And the questions that we continue to ask are the ones about teaching and learning and their relationship to the arts.

WHAT HAVE THEY LEARNED?

What do students actually learn in a program with national scope and innovative methods based in the arts? This question has been asked in various ways and addressed through different formats over the years. Mary Clare Powell engaged in a qualitative research project based on survey responses and phone interviews with students in several cohorts from around the country. While the study was not comprehensive, the data from her interviews revealed striking examples of transformation among many of the students. Captured in her set of data poems, *I know why the choking rooster sings*, Powell's (2004) research prompted her own development as poetic researcher while it demonstrated the need for further study about the impact of the program on its students.

In summary, the process of artistic inquiry informs the teaching within all programs in the division, and creates opportunities for students and faculty to develop new knowledge and practices in the field of arts integration. One of the core values of the university—inquiry—illuminates this work in which faculty and students collaboratively search for improved methods for integrating the arts into the curriculum in K-12 classrooms.

THE PATH FORWARD

The division's trajectory emerges from the seeds of past work through the dedicated creativity of faculty and staff. This work forms several strands that shape upcoming directions, including the creation and fostering of international links and global connections; reaching into the surrounding community in new ways; deepening our practice of arts-based research; and creating documentation that reveals the layers of learning and highlights voices that are often not heard.

INTERNATIONAL CONNECTIONS

The CAL faculty has been developing significant international work. This work has fostered global connections and expands our teaching to encompass a larger context for understanding how what is happening in the world influences our work on an individual level. This work is exemplified by the following key projects that faculty are currently engaged in:

- Shabaash Kemeh's community-based work in Ghana using drama to educate the community and create dialogue about AIDS.
- Louise Pascale's creation and distribution of thousands of Afghan songbooks sharing traditional songs across cultural groups. This work, which has been guided by the Afghan ambassador and his wife, and has touched the lives of thousands of Afghan children, has garnered national and international accolades, has been celebrated at the National Museum in Washington, and has received support from *National Geographic*.
- Karen Frostig's exhibition of a series of memory panels, "Erinnerung aus dem Exil/Exiled Memories," is permanently installed at the University of Vienna's Juridicum. The exhibition generated an international conference, which in turn became the launching platform for new curriculum regarding "Displaced

Law" and the Holocaust. Using her grandparents' letters as primary source documents, the project commemorates their lives and sponsors new dialogue about the Holocaust, 70 years after the Anschluss.

- Vivian Poey's photographic research and documentation on the Cuban Diaspora launched a blog that generates dialogue and connection.
- Gene Diaz' sabbatical research in Colombia looks at the power of the arts to understand and create peace in the Desearte Paz project. In this initiative, government, cultural arts, and academic organizations worked in parallel to focus on fostering a culture of peace through the implementation of community- and school-based arts programs within a pedagogical model called a "pedagogy of a culture of peace."
- Young Song and Lisa Donovan's cross-cultural exploration connecting sixth graders in Korea and Massachusetts through the use of Voicethreads to share poems about students' lives.
- Danielle Georges' support of the Haitian community during the crisis in Haiti, through her poetry. Her "Poem for the Poorest Country in the Western Hemisphere" was shared by Bill Moyers on his PBS special (http://www.pbs.org/moyers/journal/01222010/watch3.html).

COLLABORATIVE TEACHING AND LEARNING MODELS

CAL faculty actively pursue ways to take teaching to new levels. Much work has been put into collaborative teaching models that allow for multicultural teams to model the process of bringing together multiple voices investigating themes within diversity. Core faculty Prilly Sanville, Aziza Bey, Kate Austin, Mary Clare Powell, and national faculty Berta Berriz and Terry Jenoure have been actively engaged in this important work.

Two courses have been developed to model culturally responsive teaching and are taught with bicultural teams: An Arts Approach to Multicultural Education and the Collaborative Symposium: The Power of the Arts in Community and Education. The curriculum examines voices that have been silenced or omitted as well as the biases of teachers and leaders in this work.

DOCUMENTATION OF MISSING VOICES

Making teaching and learning visible and supporting the university's drive to create a culture of evidence has become a key focus for faculty in the division. This includes understanding how documentation can reveal layers and focus attention. Several faculty have made substantial commitments to developing documentation that shares the depth, breadth, and layers of arts-based work. Lisa Donovan and Kristina Lamour Sansone's research, conducted at the Charles Sumner Elementary School, developed processes for looking at student work through a design process that creates documentation that can be seen across multiple lenses. Aziza Bey documented the contributions of Arthur Magee, an African American designer whose work shaped by the fashion industry yet had not been acknowledged prior to her careful documentation. The Metropolitan Museum of Art honored Magee's work in the summer of 2009, and he is now listed in the *Who's Who of Fashion*. Kate Austin's film project *Arts Approaches to Re-imaging Cultural History* highlights three women of color, all artist-educators, reflecting on their lives and their teaching. The project pulls together themes of integrated arts with multicultural education and critical pedagogy and holds up a vision of self-reflective teachers engaging with learners to re-image history. These examples demonstrate the commitment of CAL faculty to continue to make the impact of the arts visible. Future work will harness the power of technology to share the work through layering of image, text, video, and sound.

EXPANDING CONNECTIONS IN THE COMMUNITY

Faculty in the CAL division realize the significance of being part of a larger community. New collaborations with community organizations are being developed to create stronger relationships with arts organizations and schools. Faculty are committed to fostering connections in the community to keep a sense of what is current and to continue to develop their knowledge base. Relationships such as the ongoing partnership with the Sumner School in Roslindale and participation in the Boston Public Schools' Arts Expansion Project share the wealth of expertise our faculty have and provide opportunities for us to stay current and connected with the field.

This commitment is further demonstrated in the new Community Arts master's program that was developed and launched in May 2009 by Prilly Sanville, Kerrie Bellisario, and Sam Smiley. This program continues to grow and will build a large database of community agencies that are interested in providing internship possibilities for our students.

ARTS AS AN APPROACH TO INQUIRY

As noted above, arts as an approach to inquiry is central to the work of Creative Arts in Learning. In the last few years faculty have developed strong experiences in arts-based research, a growing area in qualitative research methods. CAL is emerging as a leader in this quickly growing arena. Arts-based action research has been central to the development of our Educational Specialist Program offered in Georgia. In this program, teachers are trained to explore the potential of the arts as a methodology for research, to collect data, analyze data, and disseminate findings. Students on campus have the opportunity to take an Arts-Based Research course. These students are studying to be art specialists, teachers, and community-based artists. They are likely to be the future leaders in the field. Building skills to investigate and decipher the depth and layers of the work through systematic inquiry will serve to deepen and extend the case for the central role of the arts in education.

INFLUENCE OF POLICY

The division has been actively participating in policy development in the field of arts education and in teacher education. Policy work includes a focus on national conversations about creativity and innovation. Division faculty have been active in a number of initiatives that advance policy in support of the arts in education. For example, a faculty panel discussion of Governor Deval Patrick's report *Ready for 21st Century Success* (2008) prompted recommendations to develop a readiness school in the future. Keeping track of policy developments and conversations in the field is critical to considering implications for teacher education. This kind of response to movement in the field will keep our conversations, research, and academic offerings current.

Lesley was host to the Arts Education Partnership meeting in the fall of 2009 in Cambridge, titled "Charting a Course for the Arts and 21st-Century Learning." The division continues to convene leaders in the field to create a space for dialogue and envisioning the future. Reaching out to potential national partners such as the Kennedy Center, Americans for the Arts, and the Arts Extension Service at the University of Massachusetts in Amherst allows the division to identify opportunities to combine our expertise and strength with key organizations in the field.

Continuing relationships with collaborators such as Jacob's Pillow Dance Festival to create laboratory investigations in embodied learning, and with VSA Massachusetts to pilot an online course in the arts and universal design for learning, allow us to develop collective knowledge that will benefit the field while building on the unique strengths of each organization.

These initiatives will allow the division to maintain and grow a national reputation as a leader in arts and education, to create programs that provide excellence in scholarship, and to teach our students to forge meaningful links, learning opportunities, and partnerships in a range of communities. This work will build and expand the important intersection between arts education and teacher education. Staying connected to community, documenting the work, and investigating new pathways for learning offer unlimited possibilities for Lesley to lead the movement toward a more fully arts-integrated curriculum for students across the nation.

CONCLUSION

From the beginning of the initiative at Lesley to bring the arts and education together, the effort has been a collaborative one based in the mission of the university. As members of Creative Arts in Learning who reach out to students in geographically remote areas, we also reach out to those who are isolated and marginalized within urban populations because of their beliefs about the value of aesthetics in learning. We have collaborated with each other to reach those who struggle as first-generation college students, and those who have to make extra efforts to value their different abilities; their linguistic, ethnic, or religious origins; or their sexual orientation. The integration of the arts into the curriculum offers a way to democratize teacher education as it seeks to make artistic experiences available to all children.

As faculty we are learners who explore the unknown. We are curious about the world around us, the world outside the borders of this country, and the worlds within the communities that surround us. As we teach, we inquire. And we teach our students to do the same, to develop a thirst for understanding new perspectives, for creating new knowledge, and for imagining new possibilities for their students through the arts. As we teach, we create. As dancers and singers, painters and printers, actors and poets, we create work that sparkles throughout all that we do in our teaching, our research, or the service we offer the university and community.

Educators advocate for change through growth and learning. As faculty and members of the university community, we advocate for sustained leadership in the field of arts integration. As members of the professional communities of arts and education, we advocate for more coherent and stronger policies in support of the arts in education. By creating community connections between artists and teachers, and designing new national and regional initiatives in arts-integrated education and inquiry, we enact and embody the changes that we believe will lead to an integration of the arts and aesthetics into learning for all children.

REFERENCES

Abbs, P. (Ed.). (1987). *Living powers: The arts in education.* Philadelphia, PA: Falmer Press.

Arts Education Partnership. (2007). *Working partnerships: The role of higher education in arts education partnerships.* Washington, DC.

Bagley, C., & Cancienne, M. B. (2002). *Dancing the data.* New York, NY: Peter Lang.

Bill T. Jones and Arnie Zane Dance Company (1994) *Still/Here.* Retrieved from http://www.fmgondemand.com/play/BillTJ

Burnaford, G., Aprill, A., & Weiss, C. (2001). *Renaissance in the classroom: Arts integration and meaningful learning.* Hillsdale, NJ: Lawrence Erlbaum Associates.

Dennis, S. M., Diaz, G., & McKenna, M. B. (2006). *The curriculum guide: Make way for ducklings for narrator and orchestra.* Boston, MA: Boston Landmarks Orchestra.

Denzin, N. S., & Lincoln, Y. L. (1994). *Handbook of qualitative inquiry.* Thousand Oaks, CA: Sage.

Dewey, J. (1934, 1980). *Art as experience.* New York, NY: G. P. Putnam's Sons.

Diaz, G., Donovan, L., & Pascale, L. (2006). *Integrated teaching through the arts.* UNESCO World Conference on Arts in Education. Lisbon, Portugal.

Diaz, G. (2006). Creating Connections, Shaping Culture: Artist

Teachers in Urban Contexts. In J. Kincheloe, P. Anderson, K. Rose, D. Griffith, & K. Hayes (Eds.). *Urban Education: An Encyclopedia*. Westport, CT: Greenwood Publishing Group.

Diaz, G., & McKenna, M. B. (Eds.). (2004). *Teaching for aesthetic experience: The art of learning*. New York, NY: Peter Lang.

Diaz, G. (2002). Artistic Inquiry: On lighthouse hill. In M. B. Cancienne & C. Bagley (Eds.). *Dancing the data*. New York, NY: Peter Lang.

Dick, B. (2004). Action research: Themes and trends. *Action Research*, 2(4), 425 444. Thousand Oaks, CA: Sage.

Eisner, E. (1998). "Does experience in the arts boost academic achievement?" *Arts Education*, January, 7 15.

Fox, G. T., & Geichman, J. (2001). Creating research questions from strategies and perspectives of contemporary art. *Curriculum Inquiry*, Spring 2001, Vol. 31, No. 1, p. 33.

Freire, P. (1970, 1993). *Pedagogy of the oppressed*. New York, NY: Continuum Publishing Company.

Goldberg, M. (2001). *Arts and learning: An integrated approach to teaching and learning in multicultural and multilingual settings*. New York, NY: Longman.

Greene, M. (1995). Texts and margins, in R. W. Neperud (Ed.), *Context, content and community in art education*. New York, NY: Teachers College Press.

hooks, b. (1994). *Teaching to transgress: Education as the practice of freedom*. New York, NY: Routledge.

Kincheloe, J. L. (2004). (2nd ed.). *Teachers as researchers: Qualitative inquiry as a path to empowerment*. New York, NY: Routledge Falmer.

Meier, D., & Wood, G. (Eds.) (2004). *Many children left behind: How the No Child Left Behind Act is damaging our children and our schools*. Boston, MA: Beacon Press.

Mertler, C. A. (2006). *Action research: Teachers as researchers in the classroom*. Thousand Oaks, CA: Sage.

Mirochnik, E., & Sherman, D. (2002). *Passion and pedagogy: Relations, creation and transformation in teaching*. New York, NY: Peter Lang.

Moyers, B. (Producer). (January 22, 2010). Bill Moyers on the crisis in Haiti. (Audio podcast.). Retrieved from http://www.pbs.orgmoyers/journal/01222010/watch3.html

Patrick, D. (2008). Ready for 21st century success: The new promise of public education. Commonwealth of Massachusetts, Executive Office of Education.

Pink, D. (2006). High concept: High touch. In *A whole new mind: Why right brainers will rule the future.* New York, NY: Berkeley Publishing Group.

Powell, M. C. (1997). The Arts and the Inner Lives of Teachers, Phi Delta Kappan, Bloomington, IN.

Powell, M. C. (Fall 2004). A choking rooster sings. *Journal of Pedagogy, Pluralism, and Practice, 9.* Lesley University, Cambridge, MA.

Robinson K. (2001). *Out of our minds: Learning to be creative.* Chichester, England: Capstone Publishing Limited.

Rothstein, R., Wilder, T., & Jacobsen, R. (May 2007). Educating the whole child. *Educational Leadership, 64*(8). Association for Supervision and Curriculum Development. Alexandria, VA.

Schmuck, R. A. (2006). *Practical action research for change.* Thousand Oaks, CA: Corwin Press.

Slattery, P. (2001). The educational researcher as artist working within. *Qualitative Inquiry,* June 2001, *7*(3), 370.

THE FUTURE

Joseph B. Moore

The essays in this collection provide some insight into what matters most for an educational institution: the expertise, commitment, and energy of its faculty. Through these descriptions of academic program development, we learn how Lesley University faculty strive to maintain a focus on student engagement and student learning, integrate theory and practice, and connect the university with multiple communities beyond our campus.

Each of these programs, requiring insight, analysis, creativity, and resources, was initiated by people who believed passionately in their program's purpose and public benefit. Like Edith Lesley, they saw a need and an opportunity and then collaborated to create something new in response. It is this sense of possibility, this belief in opportunity, and the drive to engage in work that is worthy of our minds and hearts that continues to join all members of this academic community. Perhaps we are most pleased when we learn that our graduates have also created something new—a text, a nonprofit organization, a work of art, a product, a service, or a piece of software-that positively impacts a particular community. We like to think that our engagement with students as mature learners has had something to do with their success.

We are going to need more creativity in the future if higher education is going to serve well our growing, diverse population. As we engage our students, as we encourage them to keep open minds, seek creative alternatives, critique dominant systems, commit to social justice, and aspire to lives of meaning and impact, we must also encourage ourselves within the academy to do the same. Increasingly, higher education is seen by a growing number of our fellow citizens as an unattainable place of privilege. We must develop more significant, scalable, and affordable alternatives to the current model of higher education.

We have much to learn from the faculty who have designed new kinds of programs to meet the needs of new kinds of students, both younger and older. We need to develop better models of universities that are more entrepreneurial and less bureaucratic, and that directly involve the faculty not just in the delivery of programs, but in their design as well.

Our challenges are great. Two out of three American workers over the age of 24 have no college degree. The K-12 education gap is splitting our society along racial, ethnic, and economic lines. Our inner-city schools are more segregated than ever, and teachers at low-performing schools are increasingly seen as the key problem, along with their unions, rather than the impoverished circumstances of their students, their neighborhoods, and the schools themselves.

It is commonplace to think that we can improve student-learning outcomes by allowing some students to choose between their public school and a charter school. We have disconnected schools from their neighborhoods, and now, neighbor from neighbor. We think that programming teachers to train students to do well on standardized tests is the goal of a school day, and, consistent with that perspective, we have often eliminated the most engaging parts of a student's school day—physical education, music, and art, which allow students to move, make sounds, and create.

We think that technology may offer some assistance in teaching and learning. Most schools can't afford sufficient technology for each student, so technology usually reinforces the centrality of the teacher rather than the centrality of the learner. Even as we have made more investments in school technology, student academic performance continues to drop. It may be true that technology is too new and is changing too fast for schools to be able to exploit it in enhancing student learning on a massive scale in poor, underperforming districts.

A university with Lesley's mission and history is obliged to engage these challenges. We must take into account the context of our learners, not just as students at Lesley, but subsequently as alumni with jobs in particular settings. We must be as familiar with those settings as Edith Lesley was with kindergartens through her studies and her experience.

Lesley's programs are now more varied than the kindergarten training of the early 1900s. However, the connection among all these programs is the one that was there in the beginning: dedication to a humanistic education that celebrates culture, equity, opportunity, and justice—and the development of lifelong learners with professional lives who contribute directly to the public good. This mission, as relevant as ever, is what propels Lesley into its second century.

CONTRIBUTORS

Judith Barry, MFA, is an artist and writer whose work crosses a number of disciplines: performance, installation, sculpture, architecture, photography, and new media. Recent publications include *Projections: mise en abyme* (1997), the catalogue for *The Study for the Mirror and Garden in Granada, Spain* (2003), and *Body without Limits, Salamanca, Spain* (2009). Her work is included in such international collections as MoMA, Whitney Museum, Generali Foundation, Pompidou Center, Le Caixa, Goetz collection, and Frac Lorraine, among many others. A survey of her work traveled in Europe in 2010. Her project *Cairo Stories* premiered at the Sharjah Biennial in March 2011.

George Blakeslee, EdD, is a professor in the Technology in Education Graduate Programs in the STEM Division at Lesley University. A graduate of Miami University in Oxford, OH, he completed his master's and doctorate at Boston University. He is the former longtime program director of the off-campus TIE Program. His work focuses on enhancing instruction with digital media, examining the societal impact of technology, fostering effective school change, and applying innovative web-based math instructional tools. He has extensive distance-learning experience, including the provision of intensive weekend graduate instruction at the learners' workplace and of web-based course design and delivery.

Marcia Bromfield, PhD, is a professor and the director of Field Placement and Professional Partnerships in the Graduate School of Education at Lesley University. Her interests comprise university and school partnerships, support for beginning teachers, field placement and supervision, and inclusive environments for individuals with disabilities. She is the author of a number of articles, has presented at many local and national conferences, and has coauthored the book *From Surviving to Thriving: A Guide for Beginning Teachers.* She has served on many boards and committees and is a member of the executive board of the Massachusetts Association of Colleges for Teacher Preparation.

Cynthia Farr Brown, PhD, is vice president of Academic Affairs at the Massachusetts College of Liberal Arts, North Adams, MA. She received her PhD in history from Brandeis University. She worked at Lesley University from 1992 until 2009, starting as a part-time institutional research coordinator and holding successive positions in the School of Education and National Programs, ending as assistant vice president of National Programs. She taught courses in education, writing, and history at Lesley and other area institutions, and she continues to pursue scholarly work in women's history and in the history of education.

Julia Byers, EdD, ATR-BC, LMHC, is the coordinator of Art Therapy graduate studies and is co-coordinator of Certificate in Play Therapy studies. She was director of the Expressive Therapies Division at Lesley University for 12 years. Previously, for 12 years, she was the coordinator of the Art Therapy division at Concordia University in Montreal,. As a university educator for 30 years, she has taught numerous courses in interdisciplinary studies, education, arts therapy, and counseling. She has provided disaster relief support in the Philippines, Israel, Palestine, Turkey, and parts of North America.

Richard Carter, PhD, is an associate professor in Lesley University's Technology in Education Program. His focus is investigating and teaching about the role of technology in mathematics education. He is a software and curriculum developer (e.g., InspireData, Explore Learning), as well as a textbook and professional development author (e.g., Everyday Learning's IMPACT, Teachscape's Seeing Math

Project). He also serves on advisory boards for National Science Foundation projects. He initiated Lesley's online master's program in mathematics education and is running an NSF-funded research project titled "Algebra Immersion Robotics."

Mariagnese Cattaneo, PhD, LMHC, ATR-BC, and Professor Emerita at Lesley University, is the former director of Field Training in the Division of Expressive Therapies in the GSASS. She has presented nationally and internationally and has published numerous articles on art and expressive therapies, clinical training, multicultural issues and competencies, professional standards and ethics, supervision, and the arts in the training of expressive therapies. She is the recipient of the First Art Therapy Educator Award conferred by the American Art Therapy Association. She continues to supervise clinicians and to teach a course on professional standards and ethics as well as other courses in the Division of Expressive Therapies.

Steven Cramer, MFA, is the author of four poetry collections: *The Eye That Desires to Look Upward, The World Book, Dialogue for the Left and Right Hand,* and *Goodbye to the Orchard,* a 2005 Massachusetts Honor Book and winner of the New England Poetry Club's Sheila Motton Award. His work has appeared in numerous journals, including the *Atlantic Monthly,* the *New Republic, Paris Review,* and *Poetry,* and in *The Autumn House Anthology of Contemporary American Poets.* The recipient of a Massachusetts Artists Fellowship and an NEA grant, he directs the MFA program in creative writing at Lesley University.

Harriet Deane, MBA, MEd, is an assistant professor and assistant dean for Academic Services in the Graduate School of Education at Lesley University. Her recent interests include collaborations between families, schools, and communities; partnerships between schools and universities; support for beginning teachers; and academic advisement. She has written articles and coauthored the book *From Surviving to Thriving: A Guide for Beginning Teachers.*

Gene Diaz, PhD, is an associate professor at Lesley University and has been interim associate provost of the university since 2008. She teaches courses in arts-integrated curriculum and qualitative research methods. She presents at national and international conferences and is a member of the editorial boards of the *Journal of Curriculum and Pedagogy,* the *Colombian Applied Linguistics Journal,* and the *International Journal of Education and the Arts.* In 2002, as a Fulbright Scholar, she collaborated with faculty at the Universidad de Antioquia, then returned to Medellin in 2007 to conduct research on *Desearte Paz,* an arts-based network creating a peace pedagogy for the community.

Lisa Donovan, PhD, teaches arts integration, action research, and arts-based literacy courses. She has broad experience working as an arts educator and administrator for Jacob's Pillow Dance Festival, the Berkshire Opera Company, the University of Massachusetts Department of Theater, Boston University's Theater, Visual Arts, and Tanglewood Institutes, and other organizations. She was formerly executive director of the Massachusetts Alliance for Arts Education. She is co-principal investigator of the Integrated Teaching through the Arts Assessment project funded by the Ford Foundation.

Angelo Fertitta, MFA, began teaching at the Art Institute of Boston in the fall of 1969. He has served in a variety of administrative roles, including director of exhibitions, dean of admission, dean of students, and dean of Academic Affairs, and was acting dean of AIB from 2002 to 2003. He received the BFA degree from the University of Colorado in 1966 and the MFA degree from the University of Colorado in 1969. In 2000 he received the Lesley University Impact Award and in 2009, he received the Lesley University Forty Year Service Citation.

Rosalie Fink, EdD, is a professor in the School of Education at Lesley University. She has written books and articles about her Interest-based Model of Reading. Her book *Why Jane and John Couldn't Read— And How They Learned* was an International Reading Association bestseller. Her recent book *Inspiring Reading Success* was chosen as an IRA Book Club Selection. She is a past president of the Massachusetts Association of College and University Reading Educators, and she serves on the editorial board of the *Journal of Adolescent and Adult Literacy.* Her current research centers on innovative ways to integrate literacy learning with instruction in the arts, sciences, and social studies.

Lisa Fiore, PhD, is an associate professor and is the director of Early Childhood Education in the Graduate School of Education at Lesley University. Her recent research interests include inspirations drawn from the Reggio Emilia approach to early childhood education as well as documentation, assessment, and accountability. She is the author of several books and articles, and is a member of the board of directors for Families First Parenting Programs in Cambridge, MA.

Michele Forinash, DA, MT-BC, LMHC, is a professor in and director of the PhD program in the Division of Expressive Therapies at Lesley University. A graduate of Columbus State University in Columbus, GA, she completed her master's and her doctorate at New York University. She is a past president of the American Music Therapy Association and served as chair of the National Coalition of Creative Arts Therapies Associations (NCCATA). She has edited and coedited books and has published numerous articles and chapters on qualitative research, supervision, and feminist issues.

Marie Gannon, MEd, is director of the Kresge Library Media Center at Lesley University. She joined the library in the 1970s, when an already energetic program of education technology was putting video and media making into the hands of teachers and in classrooms, and she supported the earliest efforts with computing. She has developed courses in video and media production, Internet communications, and web authoring, and continues to work closely with faculty and students in integrating media into their work and teaching.

Matthew Hirshberg, PhD, is interested in political psychology and socialization, citizenship education, patriotism, international perceptions, beliefs about poverty, distributive ethics, electoral systems, and broadcast journalism. He taught for 15 years at the University of Canterbury in New Zealand, and is the author of *Perpetuating Patriotic Perceptions.*

Mitchell Kossak, PhD, LMHC, REAT, is the division director for Expressive Therapies at Lesley University. He has worked as an expressive arts therapist since 1983 and has been a licensed clinical counselor since 1994. He has written about and presented his research on attunement, improvisation, and embodied states of consciousness at conferences nationally and internationally. He is executive cochair for the International Expressive Arts Therapy Association and is associate editor of the *Journal of Applied Arts and Health.* He is also a professional jazz musician who has performed for the past 30 years in the Boston area.

John Lanza, MFA, has been a professor of drawing at the Art Institute of Boston for more than 30 years, and is a realist painter who has exhibited in solo and group shows locally and abroad as part of summer residency programs in Trieste, Italy. Graduated cum laude from Amherst College and from Boston University's School for the Arts with an MFA, he studied with Fairfield Porter, James Weeks, and Philip Guston. In addition to awards for his paintings, he has been honored with the Plymouth County Education Association's Distinguished Service Award and with the Conant Award from the Helen Bumpus Gallery.

Mary Beth Lawton, EdD, is an assistant professor of early childhood education and child psychology at Lesley University. Her recent research interests include parent-teacher relationships and parent-child and teacher-child attachment. She presents workshops for early childhood educators, early intervention professionals, and parents on strengthening early attachments.

Vivien Marcow Speiser, PhD, BC-DMT, LMHC, REAT, is a professor and director of international and collaborative projects at Lesley University. She has worked extensively with groups in the Middle East and in South Africa, and her interests include cross-cultural conflict resolution through the arts. She is an expert in the creation and performance of rite-of-passage rituals and in the use of dance and performance in expressive therapies practice.

Ben Mardell, PhD, is an associate professor in early childhood education at Lesley University and is a researcher on the Making Learning Visible Project at Harvard Project Zero. For the past 25 years, he has taught and has conducted research with infants, toddlers, preschoolers, and kindergartners. He is the author of *From Basketball to the Beatles: In Search of Compelling Early Childhood Curriculum* and *Growing Up in Child Care: A Case for Quality Early Education,* and he coauthored *Making Learning Visible: Children as Individual and Group Learners* and *Making Teaching Visible: Documentation of Individual and Group Learning as Professional Development.*

Martha Barry McKenna has served as provost of Lesley University from 2003-2011. She is director of the newly founded Creativity Commons at the University as well as a University Professosr, teaching courses in both the Creative Arts in Learning Program and the Interdisciplinary Studies Program, and has taught courses in aesthetics and art history. A corporator and lecturer at the Worcester Art Museum, she has created lectures, museum guides, and the documentary *For the Benefit of All.* The goal of her work with the museum is to bring greater understanding and appreciation for its fine collection of 19th- and 20th-century art. Access to public art through aesthetic encounters is the goal of her research and teaching.

Shaun McNiff is a painter and is the author of *Trust the Process, Art as Medicine, Art Heals, Art-Based Research,* and many other books, including his most recent, *Integrating the Arts in Therapy: History, Theory, and Practice.* He is internationally recognized in the areas of the arts and healing, creativity enhancement, and arts-based research, and his books have been translated into many languages. He is the recipient of numerous honors and awards for his work, including the Honorary Life Member Award of the American Art Therapy Association. He became the first University Professor at Lesley University in 2002.

Margery Staman Miller, EdD, has published numerous articles and books on content area literacy, comprehension, and the connection between reading and writing, including *Literacy and Learning in the Content Areas: Strategies for Middle and Secondary Teachers.* Her research interests are classroom inquiry, adolescent literacy, and professional development. The core of her commitment and her work has always been preparing students to become reading specialists. As director of Lesley's Language and Literacy Division and of its Reading Program, she established an intensive summer model for training future reading specialists.

Mary Mindess, EdM, is professor of education at Lesley College. For many years she coordinated the Lesley-sponsored New England Kindergarten Conference. As interim director of the Center for Children, Families and Public Policy, she provided leadership for the establishment of the annual Lesley Reggio Emilia Institute. She was a pioneer in online learning, and her online courses have attracted students at Lesley and around the world. She has been an active member of public policy committees and has coauthored books and articles on early childhood education.

Joseph B. Moore became president of Lesley University in July 2007. His professional interests include applications of digital technology that extend educational opportunity to underserved populations and that deepen student learning; the relationship between a university and the communities it serves, especially Pre-K-12 schools; and state and federal policy on higher education, including education finance, financial aid, and policy language. He began his career as a high school English teacher, and has held positions of academic leadership in public higher education in Vermont, Pennsylvania, and New York.

Marion Nesbit, PhD, is a psychologist and interdisciplinarian with subspecializations in law and community psychology and training in the arts. Her 35-year career includes government service, teaching, research, and practice. She recently passed her quarter-century mark as a member of the faculty and an administrator at Lesley, and feels privileged to have served hundreds of remarkable students and to have helped establish Lesley's first doctoral program. One of the many highlights of her career at Lesley was organizing the INDS 20th Anniversary Performathon, a 12-hour production medley celebrating INDS alumni and student talent. She also teaches SOE courses, plays an active leadership role at Lesley, and presents at national and international conferences.

Carole Noveck, MS, is an instructor and coordinator of curriculum for the Bridge Year in Lesley University's Threshold Program, which serves young adults with learning disabilities. A graduate of Douglass College, Rutgers University, she received a master's degree in counseling from Upsala College and did advanced graduate work in family therapy at Lesley University. She focuses on the development of independent living skills. She has presented at many conferences; publishes a yearly cookbook of recipes for students' use; and is completing a manuscript on the significance of food and nutrition education for overall health and well-being.

Frances Osten, MEd, is an instructor in early childhood at the Threshold Program at Lesley University. A graduate of Barnard College, she completed her master's at Eliot Pearson Department of Child Study at Tufts University. She devoted part of her career to teaching and directing preschool and to conducting social science research. During her 25 years as a teacher at Threshold, she has conducted research on employment of individuals with LD and an outcomes study of Threshold graduates, and has presented at numerous conferences on

LD. She is a contributing editor for a disability awareness curriculum for elementary-school-aged children.

Anne Pluto, PhD, is professor of theater and literature and artistic director of the Oxford Street Players of Lesley University, which she cofounded with Lisa Risely in 1991. She is an alumnus of Shakespeare & Company in Lenox, MA, and has studied at the Linklater Studio. A former member of the Small Press Alliance of Boston and editor of *Oak Square Magazine*, she founded *Commonthought—The Magazine of the Arts at Lesley University* in 1987. She has most recently published her work in *Earth's Daughters, The Lyre, Womb Poetry, There—rewriting the landscape* (http://www.therejournal.com/issue2.html), *Blackbox Gallery, Facets, A Literary Magazine, Quadrangle Magazine*, and *88: A Journal of Contemporary Poetry*.

Janet Pocorobba, MFA, is assistant coordinator and faculty in the low-residency MFA program in creative writing at Lesley University, and is a graduate of the program in nonfiction. Her work has appeared in *Harvard Review, The Writer, Kyoto Journal, Indiana Review, The Journal, Provincetown Arts*, and other publications. She is a former editor and feature writer for *Metropolis* magazine in Tokyo, where she lived for five years studying the three-stringed Japanese shamisen. She is currently completing a memoir about this experience.

Nancy Roberts, EdD, is a professor of education at Lesley University, where she has been a faculty member since 1975. In 1979 she founded the Graduate Program in Technology in Education to introduce technology to K-12 schools. Her research has centered on the creation of materials to introduce model building and simulation in the study of complex problems. She has been involved in a dozen NSF and Department of Education grants to improve teacher education through collaboration with urban schools and communities. She has coauthored eight books and many articles. She is currently working on establishing a New Teacher Community to give support to Lesley's most recent graduates.

Arlyn Roffman, PhD, LMHC, earned her BA at Connecticut College, her master's degree in special education at Lesley, and her doctorate in developmental psychology at Boston College. She served as founding director of Lesley's Threshold Program until 1996, when she returned to a faculty role at Lesley. As a professor of special education, she has continued to focus on transition, writing and presenting extensively and training professionals throughout the United States to help youth with disabilities prepare for adulthood. Her book *Guiding Teens with Learning Disabilities: Navigating the Transition from High School to Adulthood* was published in 2007 by Random House.

Eleanor Roffman, EdD, is a professor in Lesley University's Counseling Psychology Division and is director of Field Training, where she oversees site development, student placement, and the professional development of site supervisors and clinical faculty. A member of the faculty at Lesley for more than 30 years, she teaches the Psychology of Culture and Identity: Examining Power, Privilege and Oppression; Feminist Theories and Therapies; and Clinical Skills, among many other courses. Her research centers on feminist pedagogy, clinical training, and international movements for peace and justice. She maintains a clinical practice that focuses on women and members of the GLBTQI communities.

Priscilla H. Sanville, PhD, is associate professor and director of the Arts, Community, and Education Master's in Creative Arts in the School of Education at Lesley University. She is a graduate of the Union Institute, Lesley College, and the University of Denver. Her primary interests are theater and social activism, and she serves on the board of the Cambridge Community Arts Center.

Samuel Schwartz, MPP, is associate director of the Lesley University extension program in Israel, where he has worked since 1998. In this capacity, he oversees five master's degree programs with an enrollment of more than 500 Israeli students. He has managed Lesley's arts-based interventions with a variety of populations, including Ethiopian immigrants and Arab-Jewish dialog groups. As director of and spokesperson for Academic Affairs at the Consulates General of Israel in Boston and Los Angeles in the 1990s, he designed and led numerous conflict-resolution outreach projects in 12 U.S. states. He has published journal articles on conflict transformation, international relations, and cross-cultural community organizations.

Joanne Szamreta, PhD, is a professor at Lesley University who teaches psychology and early childhood education courses in the School of Education and at Lesley College. For the last several years, she has organized the annual Reggio Emilia Institute at Lesley, and she is involved in several collaborations on professional development with Reggio Emilia inspired schools in Greater Boston. Along with Dr. Lisa Fiore, she has led a Lesley delegation to Reggio Emilia, and will do so again. She serves on the board of advocates for Bay Cove Human Services and on the advisory board for Early Education for All.

Joan Thormann, PhD, has been a faculty member at Lesley University since 1989. Before joining the faculty at Lesley, she taught in public and private schools and worked for an educational software company and the Massachusetts Department of Education. She has served on many advisory boards; has presented at more than 50 conferences nationally and internationally; and has more than 22 publications. Since 1991 she has edited a column on technology and special education for *Learning and Leading with Technology.* In 2010 she received the MassCue Pathfinder Award. The focus of her teaching and research is technology and special education, along with teaching and learning online.

Robert Wauhkonen, EdD, is an associate professor of English at Lesley College. He holds a BA in English from the University of Denver, an MA in English from Northeastern University, and an EdD in curriculum and teaching from Boston University. He has taught at Northeastern University and the Art Institute of Boston at Lesley

University, where he served as chair of the Liberal Arts Department for 15 years. Aside from his teaching, he oversees the first-year writing courses at Lesley College. His publications include articles about liberal arts education and study in the humanities. He has given numerous presentations at local and national conferences.

Marueen Yoder, EdD, is a professor at Lesley University. She has 27 years' experience designing and teaching educational technology courses and directing one of the first fully online master's degree programs for educators. She coined the term *electronic constructivism* and has written and presented extensively on emerging technologies and ways to thoughtfully and creatively integrate them into existing curricula. She received her doctorate in educational media and technology from Boston University, her master's degree in computers in education from Lesley University, and her bachelor's degree from George Washington University.

CPSIA information can be obtained at www.ICGtesting.com
Printed in the USA
BVOW072003041012

302245BV00002B/3/P